THE
BUSINESS
INTERRUPTION
BOOK

Coverage, Claims, and Recovery

DANIEL T. TORPEY • DANIEL G. LENTZ • DAVID A. BARRETT

With a Foreword by Daniel Sobczynski

5081 Olympic Boulevard, Erlanger, KY 41018
www.NUCO.com
859.692.2100 • 800.543.0874

The
National
Underwriter
Company
A Unit of Highline Media LLC

This publication is designed to provide accurate and authoritative information in regard to the subject matter covered. It is sold with the understanding that the publisher is not engaged in rendering legal, accounting, or other professional service. If legal advice or other expert assistance is required, the services of a competent professional person should be sought. — from a Declaration of Principles jointly adopted by a Committee of the American Bar Association and a Committee of Publishers and Associations.

International Standard Book Number: 0-87218-714-4
Library of Congress Control Number: 2004103372

Printed in The United States of America

Table of Contents

Foreword

An almost infinite variety of events can lead to business interruption losses. In the extreme, such events severely impair a company's ability to compete. Risk management means taking steps to avoid such unfortunate and unforeseen events and having a strategy for responding to them when they occur. Two things I learned as the Director of Risk Management at Ford Motor Company were that avoiding the unforeseen is difficult—and risk management is not as easy as it looks.

Certainly, business interruption insurance is one of the most important tools in a commercial entity's risk-management arsenal. In theory, recovering from an insurance policy for a business interruption and extra expense loss should be straightforward. As one of the authors notes early in this book, the credo is "Reimburse us for the income we would have earned, but for the insured event."

Business interruption coverages and claims are never that simple in practice. Proving to the satisfaction of an insurer what did not occur but would have occurred but for the interruption can be unexpectedly difficult. Both claimant and insurer need a thorough understanding of business interruption, the coverages and endorsements involved, and the complexities of preparing, filing, and determining claims. In many cases, an extraordinary volume of work must be performed by dedicated specialists, including accountants and lawyers who have particular expertise in handling complex claims, as do the authors of this book.

Anyone who bears responsibility for managing risk for a commercial entity—regardless of its size, location, product, or service—must have tools to understand that entity's risks and exposures. They must develop a strategy for addressing those risks through insurance or some means of minimizing risk. And, if an unfortunate event occurs, they must take the right steps to preserve and maximize the company's insurance assets and otherwise respond to the loss.

Over the years, Ford has had several significant property damage loss claims. When a sizeable loss of property and production was involved, Ford found it most effective to deploy a team of highly skilled insurance practitioners as soon as possible and to have the team pursue a parallel path to recovery. One part of the team focused on mitigating production losses and securing our physical assets to reduce any further damage. The other began communicating with our insurers. At the same time, we found it vital to begin developing, analyzing, and documenting our property and business interruption claim.

I can think of no better group to develop a book on business interruption than the team from Ernst & Young and Latham & Watkins that Ford has asked to help with its own significant claims. Working closely with Ford's Corporate Insurance department, this team not only has provided Ford with an independent view of the company's claims, but they have allowed those with risk management responsibilities to stay focused on other aspects of the job while the claim process moved forward.

The Business Interruption Book: Coverage, Claims, and Recovery is an excellent, thought-provoking resource for anyone with responsibilities in the business insurance arena. For risk managers, insurers, brokers, claims preparers and adjusters, and for the corporate owner either considering endorsements or preparing a claim, this book is a guide to better understanding business interruption insurance, in the purchasing process, in risk assessment, or during the claims and dispute resolution process. When a significant and unexpected event strikes and threatens your company's bottom line, a book like this one is a vital supplement to securing the best claim team possible—allowing you to protect your interests while still focusing on your core business.

Daniel Sobczynski, CPCU, CLU, ChFC, ARM, AIC, AIS
Risk Management and Insurance Consultant
Former Director of Corporate Insurance, Ford Motor Company (Ret.)
July 2004

Editor's Preface

Business interruption insurance is a most complex and difficult subject. It requires an understanding of accounting principles as well as the ability to interpret coverage language that is intricate, yet at times indefinite. And it is called upon when businesses are most vulnerable: after their property has been damaged or destroyed and their operations suspended.

I learned this early on in my insurance career, when my then-boss-and-mentor would caution clients (and me indirectly) about the value of the coverage and the importance to work diligently to establish appropriate values before a loss occurred.

I was fortunate to work for a person like Robert A. Gleason Jr. He was always quick to question whether I had taken the appropriate steps to help our clients understand how the coverage would apply. He wanted to be sure they made informed decisions when setting their limits and selecting from among optional coverages. Those tasks were difficult. Business people who were hard-pressed to take care of their daily duties found it hard to strategically consider what actually would happen should their operations (or a portion of them) be shut down after a property loss. Yet, when the loss was felt, they needed to know that their insurer would be there to help them regain their previous level of business income.

This hasn't changed. Our *FC&S* editors receive questions on business interruption insurance and claims on a regular basis. Subscribers are seeking answers to complex questions that sometimes can be resolved only through prolonged discussion and negotiation. The questions we get are always a challenge because every situation is different, and, as the authors of this book point out, practical information on the subject may be difficult to find.

And so we decided to seek individuals experienced in this area to write a text that would dovetail the importance of the accounting aspects with the coverage intricacies that are inherent in any discussion of this topic. Who better to write the book than Dan Torpey and Dan Lentz, coleaders of Ernst & Young's Insurance Claims team, and Dave Barrett, a partner in the firm of Latham & Watkins? Their learned knowledge, coupled with their practical experience, fulfilled our needs.

In addition to all their technical expertise, the three exhibited wit and humor in developing the claim scenarios that provide practical applications for the material. Most of the graphs and illustrations were designed by Clovis, Inc., which Ernst & Young engaged to help design the graphics for the book. In the end, Clovis took more than a professional interest in shepherding the book to completion. I also acknowledge and thank FM Global, which, through the efforts of Steve Zenofsky, permitted us to reprint its coverage form.

As John Sloan, principal of Sloan Risk Management Services in Wellington, New Zealand, pointed out when he heard the book was being published,

"Many insurance people don't understand the accounting issues involved whilst the accountants don't know the insurance factors. A poor client can be caught in the middle of this sublime ignorance."

We believe this book will help all of us to better understand the complexity of business interruption coverage, claims, and recovery.

Diana B. Reitz
Editor

Preface

People describe the first few days after a business interruption as one big blur, of spending day after stressful day in the affected location with little time for their normal jobs or their families. September 11, 2001, brought this stress to a completely new level. For many companies, it meant devastating loss of life; secondarily it meant their first major property damage and business interruption claims.

Born and raised in New York City, and having worked in downtown Manhattan, I felt shock and emptiness after 9-11. I lost both friends and professional colleagues that day. At the same time my colleagues and I—including Dan Lentz, coauthor of this book—were thrown into a multitude of claims with clients wrestling with property and business interruption losses. We were impressed with how quickly companies managed to get back into business; the media, the hotels, entertainment companies, banks, and the investment community all helped each other.

For many, those events also brought into sharp perspective the complexity of the business interruption claims process.

What to do if your company experiences a business interruption? Are you or a client facing a significant loss—or struggling to develop a detailed claim? This book seeks to capture much of what my colleagues and I have learned about business interruption insurance during our careers in this fascinating field.

Early in my career, as a first-year staff accountant with Matson Driscoll & Damico, I asked Peter Kahn, one of the partners I was working with, "How do I learn more about business interruption claims, the claims process, and about critiquing a claim?" Peter's response was simple. First, he said, was to thoroughly read the policy—in its entirety. Second was to understand the company's business—how it makes its money and operates its production cycles, including where the bottlenecks are. In other words, he said, do your homework on the industry. Third, he said that the more losses I worked on, the more I'd understand each situation. Finally, he advised me to always consult with peers to ensure I'd covered all the bases.

Peter's advice holds true today, and I now share it with my staff and clients—with the hope that everyone on both sides will understand how best to proceed when faced with the situation. Many people who have never been involved with a complex business interruption claim are amazed at the emotions they and others involved in the situation face. I once heard a risk manager of a multinational company sigh, saying "This insurance world of ours would be a lot easier if insureds would actually read the policy and insurers were to review the underwriting of an account." Similar comments are not uncommon, usually earning a chuckle; on occasion they seem entirely appropriate. And, even when insureds have closely read their policies and their insurers understand the business they have underwritten, the most technically proficient and fair of individuals may disagree on claim issues. I hope this book helps each group better understand the other's position, and that is helps to foster a spirit of cooperation during the claim process.

During my tenure with MD&D, our work involved everything from taking inventory at a textile warehouse in Brooklyn after a fire or theft to sifting through years of tax returns and financial statements for a print shop in Manhattan after water from a burst pipe damaged a six-color press. In only a few years, I visited fourteen states and many countries. Some assignments were dramatic. For AIG, I spent weeks in Jamaica after the island was hit by Hurricane Gilbert, auditing property damage, business interruption, and extra expense losses claims from the local brewery, hotels and resorts, a corrugated cardboard manufacturer, and telephone and utility companies. In Puerto Rico, I audited a large fire loss at a manufacturing plant that made lingerie.

After earning my CPA license, I joined Ernst & Young in midtown Manhattan, where I worked on financial statement audits for all types of companies, including one of the world's largest not-for-profit entities. At Ernst & Young, I gained a deep understanding of how companies earn their money and of the importance of exactitude. I learned the value of people and met outstanding professionals, teachers, and mentors. After three years in audit and tax, I decided to return to forensic accounting and insurance claims.

In 1992, I met Les Lowenstein, a former executive and head of claims at then The Factory Mutual and a luminary in the field of property and business interruption insurance. Les had begun to help policyholders after they experienced losses, and he challenged me to see the world through both the eyes of the policyholder and insurance companies, always operating within the framework of the policy. He taught me to go far beyond the gathering of documents to prepare the best, most defensible, most comprehensive claim. In our work we found that many people, including insurance professionals, lacked an understanding of the claims process, a technical knowledge of the policy, or the time to deal with the "overwhelming challenges" of a claim.

Les and I worked for Fortune 500 companies experiencing some of the toughest, most complex of losses. Because a large claim can take several years to resolve, we developed dedicated clients and worked with some of the best and brightest professionals. We made great friends along the way, and I am forever deeply grateful for having had the chance to work with Les. He guided me and has become a great friend.

It was also at Ernst & Young that I met my current colleague, Dan Lentz. Our first introduction to one another was on an extremely complex business interruption claim, where I'd been asked to review the reports of two opposing experts. Dan was representing the insurance company—and while my client was hopeful I could shoot some holes in Dan's report, I actually ended up agreeing with his findings. Further, I was impressed with how sound and reasonable his analysis and conclusions were, as well as with his ability to present the situation succinctly.

Of course, Dan and I ended up as partners in building this practice. We now co-lead the Ernst & Young Insurance Claims consulting practice. We've been called on by policyholders, insurers, reinsurers, and brokers to help evaluate the most complex and largest insurance claims in the marketplace. We've also helped companies with claims involving countless other types of policies. As we expanded our practice, we needed to hire staff and ensure consistency in our work product. We recognized immediately that without a proper training program, our practice would be challenged in its ability to grow. We wanted to develop a course to train young accountants and adjusters about property and business interruption claims.

As readers may already have experienced, reference materials on the unique challenges of the business interruption claims process are scant. Neither Dan nor I could find a sample business interruption claim and calculation to work through. One text we did find helpful was *Business Interruption: Its Theory and Practice* by Robert M Morrison, Alan Miller, and Stephen J. Paris (1986), which does a wonderful job of discussing the structure of the insurance contract and the process of insuring risk while walking through the claims process—including litigation and arbitration. I particularly enjoy Morrison's discussion of the six "P's" (parties, property, perils, productivity, period, profit) and the six "E's" (extent, experience, exclusions, effort, extras, enough). The book also contains some policy forms, an example loss adjustment, many legal case citations, and a good discussion on hindsight and foresight.

A book less well known in the United States is *Riley on Business Interruption Insurance* by David Cloughton (Sweet & Maxwell, London, 1956, 1999), which is probably the leading text on business interruption insurance in the U.K. Cloughton focuses on policy wording and endorsements more than Morrison, but for the non-claims professional the latter is more concise. Cloughton's text is especially valuable for the international claims executive, as it covers policy forms from Europe, Japan, China, Africa, and Australia. Also, Cloughton details policy wording, including narrowly or even undefined areas of insurance coverage, such as residual values, overlap of indemnity periods, sale of business after the incident, and other nuanced situations.

Other key sources we relied on include the "John Liner Letter" and *John Liner Review* from Standard Publishing, the *FC&S Bulletins* available on www.nuco.com, and publications of The International Risk Management Institute (IRMI). Finally, one of the more interesting and entertaining articles from the last ten years was written by two CPAs: Chris Campos of Campos & Stratis and Bill O'Connell of Deloitte & Touche. This article on "Depreciation Debate," published in *Claims Magazine*, does an excellent job of bringing this issue to the forefront of the claims world. I also became the first expert commentator on business interruption for IRMI, which publishes many articles by insurance experts. Not only have I had the opportunity to write many articles for IRMI.com over the years, I have also come to rely on the many other essays published there to continue to expand my own knowledge.

In recent years, I have been tempted to write ever more detailed articles, delving deeper into the many complexities of the business interruption claims process. After 9-11, our practice was deluged with requests for information. Many more articles began to appear in print after those events, among the more formidable and comprehensive of them being a collection of cases and discussions published in *Monthly Mealey's Business Interruption Insurance*.

Dan Lentz had for some years talked about writing a book on business interruption insurance as well. And in 2003, while presenting at Risk and Insurance Management Society (RIMS) conference in Chicago, I was approached by Diana Reitz of the National Underwriter Company, who suggested that we consider writing a definitive book on the subject to fill what her company felt was a gap in the literature. Diana's thought was that since many issues in the process depend on accounting and financial analysis, we could create a premier text on business interruption from the perspective of accountants. The prospective text would be innovative, useful to both insurer and policyholder, with some practical advice so that each could learn from a common theme. At the same time, we both considered that it made sense to have an attorney who specialized in insurance law join us with the work, and there seemed but one choice—Dave Barrett of Latham & Watkins.

Dave Barrett has worked for more than a decade on complex insured commercial losses. I have worked with many lawyers throughout my career, but I find in Dave an attorney who not only knows policies but who also can move the claims process along. Dave focuses on the facts, and on how they apply to the policy, to derive the strongest and most defensible claim. He helps clients pick some of the best experts on a variety of subject matters—experts who communicate well with us, our clients, and the insurance companies. While Dave's work is mostly (if not all) for policyholders, we challenged him to help us write this book from the perspective of both the insurance carrier and policyholder. We are both well pleased with the balance his effort brings to the work.

In this book, we sought always to provide a fair point of view, balancing the interests of insurer and insured—an important balance in today's increasingly risky and litigious environment. Above all, we wanted to bridge the gap between the two sides, giving each insight about the other. To do this we have used claim scenarios with some extreme situations, each designed to drive home a point. Also, we wanted a text that would be equally readable by a claim novice or claim expert, a risk manager or CFO, all the while increasing the knowledge of each stakeholder in the BI claims process.

I must also thank Dan Sobczynski, former Director of Corporate Insurance, Ford Motor Company (Ret.), for taking time to read through our text, contributing the foreword, and providing his perspective on the business interruption recovery process during an interview that is recorded at the back of this book. Dan first hired Les and me for a large Ford claim in Argentina many years ago. Since retiring from Ford, he continues to be both a supporter of ours and someone we turn to for advice. I also appreciate the time that Laurie Champion, current Director of Global Risk Management for the Ford Motor Company, and Dan Ames, manager of the company's Corporate Insurance Department, Global Risk Management, spent with us the last few years. They have shared their insight into how risk managers view the claims process and also took the time to review and offer their counsel on certain sections of the text. I also appreciate the time, effort, and feedback that Steve Truono, Director, Global Risk Management, Avon Products Inc., spent reviewing the text prior to publication.

It is a measure of success that professionals who joined us years ago now help lead Ernst & Young's practices across the U.S. Many also helped develop ideas in this book, and we owe a debt of gratitude to Allen Melton, Jeff Phillips, Chris Brophy, and Ryan Pratt for their significant contributions, as well as to Jason Trahan, Vladimir Korobov, Brad McCloskey, Jessica Base, and all the other Ernst & Young staff who contributed to our efforts. I owe special thanks to Robert Reeves, who was instrumental in helping our practice grow from just the two of us working on a variety of claims to a national practice that has helped the most prestigious Fortune 500 companies with some of the largest claims in the last decade. Robert has been key to the group's growth; always professional, he is a steady comrade. His superior ability to analyze and to render simply and with unarguable logic the most complex issues has been a key force of our team. And all of us owe TJ James—the world's greatest executive assistant—for helping us operate as sane individuals in the wild world of business. The only thing better than TJ's work is her irrepressible laughter.

My thanks also go to our contributing editors, our publisher, clients, and readers. I would also like to thank the people of Clovis, Inc., especially Maggie Hoag, who helped us in the overall formation and editing, and the personal attention of its president, Andrew Baker, whose personal interest and diligence made this a better book. And we also are very grateful to the many people at National Underwriter Company— not least for their patience and certainly for their enthusiasm. Thanks in particular to Diana Reitz, whose patience and persistence guided us to get the best book completed.

My deepest thanks go to my coauthors—and to my family. I am forever grateful to my parents for their gift of faith and guidance and for their insistence that their six children strive to be the best in whatever vocation they chose. These principles I hope to pass on to my children: Sean, Brigit, Brendan and Mary Kate. And I would need more than this space allows to thank my wife, Patti, for her steadfast love and support all these years. Patti has kept our lives in balance during the craziest of times.

Dan Torpey
Dallas, Texas
July 2004

Writing a comprehensive book on business interruption insurance has been a career-long ambition for me, driven partly by my fascination with the complexities and nuances of this oft-misunderstood coverage, and partly by the realization that there was a significant gap in the literature providing guidance in this area. But the magnitude of the task and the success of our practice combined to deny me much time to undertake the project on my own.

I joined Ernst & Whinney in 1983 as a member of our audit practice. Shortly thereafter, I was offered an opportunity to join our consulting practice—at that time a fledgling service among the "Big 8" accounting firms. Not long afterwards I gravitated to insurance claims, and since 1986 I have represented insurance companies and policyholders on surety, fidelity, property, business interruption, political risk, product recall, general liability, environmental, and crime claims, along with many other claims and insurance litigation issues. Along the way, I had the good fortune to work with some of the leading claim advisers in the business, including John Curran, my long-time colleague and mentor. During my many assignments, I have learned from top-notch risk managers and broker representatives. All the while, I hoped that I could leverage my experiences to make meaningful contributions to the understanding of the claims process and the significant issues insurers and policyholders confront.

When the opportunity arose to bring Dan Torpey and some of his team members to Ernst & Young in 2002, I leapt at the chance. Not only did we double the size of our practice, but we brought new dynamism and energy to the group with the infusion of outstanding new professionals. Fortuitously, not long after Dan rejoined Ernst & Young, he met Diana Reitz of National Underwriter. Diana presented us with the proposal Dan details above—the chance to write a definitive text on business interruption insurance. Dan and I discussed the idea—and time and energy that would be involved—and I was all for it! Dusting off a book outline from my initial efforts of years gone by, and working with Dan and Diana, we agreed on a framework and content that we hope readers will find informative, comprehensive, useful, and easy to read. We each agreed that including the perspective of lawyers, claims people, and others in the process would be a key to the utility of the book. I echo Dan's gratitude to the many experts and colleagues, mentors and advisers, editors and writers who have contributed to this significant effort—especially to our coauthor, Dave Barrett.

I am especially thankful to my family and friends for their unflagging support and love over many years of a demanding career, always helping me to balance the priorities of life. My parents taught me enduring faith and the principles of fairness and honesty as the basis for achievement in all walks of life. These values I hope to abide by in all that I do and to instill in my wonderful children, Katherine and Kevin. Most importantly, I thank my dear wife Deanna, for her tremendous support and understanding, her commitment to our family, her friendship, and her love.

Dan Lentz
Washington, D.C.
July 2004

One of the rewards of my practice is the chance to meet so many people working in and around the insurance industry: clients, policyholder and insurer's lawyers, accountants, brokers, underwriters, adjusters, insurance executives, judges, arbitrators, mediators, claims resolution specialists, and experts and consultants in myriad fields. Among them are many of the brightest, most interesting and hardest working people I have ever met. Dan Torpey and Dan Lentz are two of them. They are among the very best in the business, bringing to any claim a base of experience, skill, intellect, and resources virtually unmatched in the industry. I owe them my gratitude for giving me the opportunity to work with them on this project. I also cannot adequately thank Diana Reitz, our editor at National Underwriter, and Andrew Baker, president of the communications firm Clovis, for their immense contributions to this book. Without their skillful drafting, editing, and expertise, this book simply could not have been accomplished.

There are other individuals I would like to thank as well. Dan Sobczynski, the long-time former Director of Corporate Insurance for Ford Motor Company, must know everything there is to know about insurance. I worked with Dan for years when he was at Ford. He was a terrific client—with a formidable intellect and a pragmatic approach to resolving claims. More than that, Dan was a teacher, which is exactly what he has become since leaving Ford, now teaching college-level insurance and in demand as an insurance consultant. Dan contributed generously to this book and was my primary resource for guidance and answers as I drafted portions of it. Dan's contribution is evident not only in editorial comments he provided on early drafts, but in the many extended substantive discussions we had before and during the book's preparation, and the foreword.

John Cadarette is the Managing Director of LECG's Global Insurance Claims Group. John's expertise is helping clients resolve complex claims though strategic business negotiations rather than litigation, and he's been perfecting his craft for more than twenty years. Working alongside him on major claims, I have learned much about how to resolve a disputed insurance claim. His contribution is reflected not only in the valuable comments and editorial suggestions he made to drafts of this book but also in the wisdom he has generously imparted to me over the years.

I received enormous support from colleagues at Latham & Watkins, who made editorial suggestions and written contributions. Mary Rose Alexander, a partner in our Chicago office, has been a co-counsel on numerous major matters with me. Mark Newell, a partner in our Washington, D.C., office, has been the mentor to me that every young lawyer should have. Their contributions are evident in the editorial suggestions they made on earlier drafts and in their profound influence on my development as an insurance coverage lawyer. Aisha Henry, Tom Powell, and Paul Allulis—associates in Latham & Watkins' Washington, D.C., office—also deserve our gratitude for the important substantive contributions they made to this book.

John Dempsey is the founding and managing partner of Dempsey, Myers & Company. Drawing on a wealth of experience in preparing and settling complex insurance claims on behalf of corporate policyholders, John provided insightful substantive and editorial comments on Chapters 3 and 9 that greatly improved both chapters. John also is one of the authors of the chart we included in Chapter 3, comparing key provisions bearing on business interruption coverage in ISO, company form, and broker manuscript policies.

From Lockton Insurance Brokers, Inc., I would like to thank Teena Hostovich, Partner, and Jim Rubel, Senior Vice President. Teena and Jim could not have been more gracious in providing me with access to their impressive knowledge. Their insights helped bring our chapter on manuscript policies to life.

I also would like to acknowledge three individuals at Ford Motor Company: Elaine Mills, Counsel; Laurie Champion, Director, Global Risk Management; and Dan Ames, Manager, Corporate Insurance. I am fortunate to have had the opportunity to work closely with them for years (in Elaine's case, for nearly a decade). In large measure, my contributions to this book were made possible by the experience I gained, and the lessons I learned, while working with these talented and knowledgeable individuals.

A quick note about the book itself: In handling complex insurance claims on behalf of policyholders over the past fifteen years, I've learned that there isn't just one way to resolve a claim. Circumstances should dictate the precise approach. Nevertheless, policyholders, insurers, and claims practitioners can and should consider certain steps and guiding principles when a business interruption claim arises. Likewise, certain principles should inform policyholder and insurer efforts to address risk even before a business interruption occurs. One of the fundamental purposes of this book is to present what my coauthors and I believe are the most important of these guiding principles and concrete steps, so that insurance practitioners can be better equipped to fashion solutions to suit their unique circumstances. Hopefully, this book achieves that lofty goal.

I dedicate this book to my beautiful wife Maria; my wonderful children (Steven, Ryan, Conner, Jack, Robert, and Owen); and my beloved mother (Elisabeth), father (St. John), and siblings (Susan, James, Robert and Anna).

David A. Barrett
Washington, D.C.
July 2004

About the Authors

Daniel T. Torpey, CPA

A Partner at Ernst & Young, Dan Torpey is co-leader of the firm's Insurance Claims team. With eighteen years' experience in forensic accounting, insurance, and reinsurance, Torpey has counseled clients in business interruption and economic loss analysis. He has also helped clients with claims resulting from property damage, product recall, product liability, political risks, employee theft, corporate governance, and D&O issues. An expert commentator on business interruption for the International Risk Management Institute (IRMI.com), Torpey is a CPA and has testified as an expert witness in state and federal court as well as international arbitrations. He earned his BS in Accountancy at St. Johns University in New York.

Daniel G. Lentz, CPA

Dan Lentz is co-leader of Ernst & Young's Insurance Claims team. A partner since 1993, Lentz specializes in claim resolution and insurance-related litigation. He also handles disputes involving agency or broker relationships, regulatory matters, market practice and claims handling issues, receiverships, internal and claim fraud investigations, subrogation, and excess carrier or reinsurer liability. He has prepared or investigated claims under property, business interruption, casualty, and other insurance. Both a CPA and a Certified Fraud Examiner, Lentz has testified numerous times in the past twenty years and has served as independent arbitrator in numerous disputes. He holds a BBA from Roanoke College and an MBA from Loyola College in Baltimore.

David A. Barrett, JD

 A Partner in the Litigation Department at Latham & Watkins, David Barrett focuses on major insurance coverage matters, representing policyholders in a wide variety of third-party liability and first-party property and business interruption claims. In addition, he has represented U.S. and foreign clients in numerous commercial matters, including securities, private contract, government contract, intellectual property, tort, fraud, and subrogation. A member of the bar in California and the District of Columbia, Barrett earned his JD at the University of Texas School of Law.

Contributors

The following members of Ernst & Young's Insurance Claims team contributed significantly to this book:

Allen Melton, JD, CPA

Allen Melton is a Partner at Ernst & Young. Both a CPA and an attorney, he has spent the majority of his career in the commercial insurance industry with an emphasis in business interruption, as well as working in the areas of litigation support and audit. Allen has also provided expert witness testimony at trial.

Jeffrey M. Phillips, PE

Jeff Phillips has over fifteen years of experience in the commercial property insurance industry, including over eight years as an insurance claims adjuster. A Senior Manager at Ernst & Young, Jeff is an engineer and provides strategic advice to companies with complex insurance claims and disputes.

Robert M. Reeves, CPA

A Senior Manager with Ernst & Young, Robert Reeves provides clients with comprehensive financial and strategic advice to resolve complex disputes. He focuses on resolving insurance claims and claim-related disputes, especially in the areas of property, business interruption, fidelity and liability. He also works with insurance and reinsurance companies in arbitration and litigation matters.

Chris Brophy, CPA

Chris Brophy, also a Senior Manager, helps policyholders recover under their property damage and business interruption insurance policies. He has prepared numerous such claims for insureds in the manufacturing, healthcare, financial services, hospitality, retail, transportation, agribusiness, oil and gas, and chemicals industries.

Ryan D. Pratt, CFA

Ryan is a Manager at Ernst & Young and a CFA charterholder whose expertise is managing complex insurance claims and litigation and preparing the quantum of financial and economic damages as a result of business interruption. Ryan has extensive experience in claims management, scenario development, and impact modeling using analytical and statistical tools.

The Stanley Furniture Story

THE TEAM APPROACH TO SUCCESS

By Doug Payne
Chief Financial Officer and Executive Vice President
Stanley Furniture Company

It is not a pleasant experience to see the future transformed in a day—especially when the change results from a significant loss.

Stanley Furniture manufactures wooden furniture in the upper-medium price range for every room in the home. Operating in a competitive market, we rely heavily on our brand's reputation: a dedication to quality and the ability to quickly fill orders. Success in the latter is critical.

In February of 1993, on the eve of going public, a fire interrupted operations at Stanley Furniture's production facility in Stanleytown, Virginia. The initial estimate of the time necessary to rebuild was twelve months—a length of downtime that would challenge us to serve our customers and could have led to a loss in market share.

Fortunately, that loss did not occur. Our management team met immediately after the fire to develop a plan to mitigate our loss and ensure comprehensive financial recovery from our insurance carrier. As with other major financial transactions, we knew that it would take a team of experienced professionals working together for us to achieve our goals. We identified certain executives internally to focus on the claim recovery, while others addressed loss mitigation. Some of us handled both aspects of the project. We sought outside expertise and hired the best insurance consultants and independent claim accountants to work with us throughout this process.

We also established a temporary manufacturing site next to one of our plants, which allowed us to produce and continue to sell key products and greatly mitigate our loss. We estimated and reviewed our business interruption claim monthly so our carrier and adjuster could validate the claim and submit cash advances regularly in order to maintain critical cash flow. Through regular team meetings we met our common goal of resolving differences and limiting the loss. We resolved a claim in excess of $10 million dollars in a fair and reasonable period of time.

Despite an original estimate that it would take a full year to restore full operations, Stanley Furniture rebuilt the Stanleytown facility in less than twelve months.

All of us were challenged by the amount of time we spent dealing with the claim, working it in tandem with our normal duties. But the Stanley family and its advisers pulled together. More than ten years later, our company and its people look back on that incident as proof that business interruption insurance truly can and does work. Having the right insurer and working as a team with that insurer helped us turn around after the fire and have one of our best years ever.

I hope no reader of this book suffers a loss like we did. But accidents happen, and losses do occur. My message is that business interruption and property insurance works. Claims demand that a company's management team collaborate with its carrier to properly manage the claim process. Creating and working with the right team means the difference between success and failure.

Insuring Changing Exposures

The Evolution of Business Interruption Coverage

Regardless of which side of the table you are sitting on, business interruption insurance typically is one of the most misunderstood of coverages.

This is despite the fact that its genealogy dates back more than two centuries, to the late 1700s when court records show that insurance written specifically on income and profits was available.[1] This type of insurance—which indemnified insureds for the loss of rents or profits derived from property or operations—differed from typical property insurance, which even at that time was restricted to paying losses that arose from direct physical damage to the insured property. Legal records show that early standard fire policies would not pay for lost income or profits, with courts differentiating between the direct property loss covered by a fire policy and the subsequent, or consequential, loss of income that could result.[2] Specific insurance on profits and income had to be purchased.

Early forms of this insurance were developed to insure the profits that ship owners counted on through freight shipments or chartering activities. Income from the rental of property also was insured.

Advertisements that appeared in *The National Underwriter* newsweeklies in the early days of the Great Depression illustrate the importance of the coverage at that time. The America Fore Group of Insurance Companies—parent of the former Continental insurance companies—stressed the importance of business interruption insurance as a key element in a complete insurance package of protection for businesses. One of the ads speaks to the ability to include "salaries of essential employees as well as lost profits and those expenses which continue during the suspension of business due to fire, explosion or windstorm."

Those words, though written in 1929, remain true to the importance of the coverage: the need to insure employee salaries, profits, and continuing expenses during a period of suspension. These are the same elements of loss that cost a business its survival today after it has been shut down because of damage from a covered cause of loss.

As Lord Peter Levene, chairman of Lloyd's, stated in an October 2003 speech to a New York Risk and Insurance Management Society (RIMS) meeting:

> Consider, for example, the impact of 9/11. It was not just felt by those businesses and people who were in the Twin Towers. Thousands of businesses were disrupted, some many miles, even thousands of miles away. If one office of an international company is destroyed or has to close, the company's entire operations can grind to a halt. Typical estimates suggest that this cost, the cost of business interruption, accounts for 20-25%—or $10 billion—of the overall 9/11 loss.[3]

From the earliest origins to the extensive business income claims that resulted from the September 11, 2001, attacks on America, insurance on lost income and profits has continued to be seen as critical to the survival of individual businesses.

Different Terminology through the Ages

Although the three basic elements of coverage stated in those ads from 1929—lost profits, salaries of essential employees, and other continuing expenses—remain at the crux of the business interruption insurance coverage grant, there have been many changes in the way coverage is arranged and in the terminology used to describe it.

Originally called *use and occupancy* insurance, the name evolved to *business interruption* insurance in the 1930s—even though use and occupancy forms still could be found. The term *business income insurance* was coined in the 1980s by the Insurance Services Office (ISO), when it introduced its simplified commercial property program.

Regardless of specific name, it is generally accepted that the coverage is part of a broader category of *time element coverage*. It is triggered as a *consequence* of direct physical damage, which gives rise to its being categorized as indirect or consequential coverage.

In lay terms, it is supposed to provide the capital needed to sustain the business while it's shut down and, in some cases, financially support efforts to regain market share after the property is repaired.

Evolution of Coverage Forms

Use and Occupancy Forms

As the original name—use and occupancy insurance—implies, business interruption insurance was designed to provide financial support to businesses when physical damage precluded their owners' ability to *use* or *occupy* their property.

This terminology reinforces the requirement that coverage is triggered not by a loss of business income but, rather, by a suspension of business. In other words, mere loss of revenue after property is damaged is not enough to trigger the coverage—there typically must be an actual suspension of business, i.e., a loss of the ability to *use* or *occupy* the property.

Valued Use and Occupancy Policy

This interpretation was supported early on in a 100-year-old New York case, *Michael v. Prussian Nat. Ins. Co.,* 63 N.E. 810 (1902). The insurance policy in *Michael* was written "on the use and occupancy" of Buffalo Elevating Company property with a limit of $4.77 a day for each working day that the company was prevented from using the elevator and handling grain.

The owner of the grain elevator plant had entered into a pooling arrangement with other elevator properties. The purpose of the pooling arrangement was to establish uniform rates. Members placed all earnings into the common pool, which was distributed to members according to an agreed-upon formula. Each member's share of the pool was not impacted by an inability to use its elevator because of fire damage. Buffalo Elevating, therefore, continued to receive its percentage of the common fund despite that fact that it could not operate after the fire. The insurer, Prussian National, claimed that it was entitled to subrogate against the proceeds paid out by the association during the time of the fire.

The court disagreed, however, stating that the insurance policy in question insured the *business use* of the property and not the loss of earnings and profits. As stated in the court records,

The contract of insurance is quite exceptional in its nature . . .The insurance is neither specifically upon the building, nor upon the machinery which it contains. It is "on the use and occupancy of the property and elevator building, with boiler and engine houses attached."

The peculiar feature of the contract is that it contemplates, as its subject-matter, not the mere material loss of the plant, or any part of it, but the loss to the owner of the ability to use it. . .The policy is in fact a valued one— where the parties intended, and have agreed beforehand, to estimate the value of the subject of the insurance.

Actual Loss Sustained Use and Occupancy Policy

This valued use and occupancy policy may be contrasted with an *actual loss sustained* form that was litigated in the case of *Goetz v. Hartford Fire Insurance Co., et al*, 215 N.W. 440 (Wis. 1927). Hartford and five other insurers appealed a judgment of the circuit court, which directed them to pay equal shares of the expenses incurred by the A.H. Peterson Co. during a business suspension that was caused by a fire. The Peterson Co. was shut down for forty-nine days, during which expenses of over $3,800 continued to be incurred.

The company, however, would have operated at a loss of more than $4,000 during those forty-nine days had it been in operation. In reversing the circuit court ruling, the Wisconsin Supreme Court turned to the wording of the applicable coverage form which, while it was a use and occupancy contract, was written on an actual loss sustained basis. As the supreme court reasoned,

It is not questioned but that at least two separate and distinct elements are recognized in this provision of the contract which may go to make up the "actual loss sustained" to indemnify for which the defendants undertook; namely, one of "net profits," and the other of "fixed charges and expenses." The element of "net profits" drops from this case; the jury having found that none such would have been made during the same period if no such suspension had occurred.

The insured having suspended businesses [because of the fire], it avoided of course such loss of over $4,000, with its consequent [sic] depletion of assets or additional liabilities to that extent.

Since the net loss outweighed the continuing expenses, there was no *actual loss sustained,* and the court reversed the lower court ruling. Interestingly, although the use and occupancy form no longer is used, this 1927 interpretation of the two elements that must be met in an actual loss sustained form remains applicable to many coverage forms used today. It also illustrates the fact that two policies, both entitled *use and occupancy forms,* will be interpreted differently based on the details of the coverage form.

Today, as it was in the early 1900s, it's important to read and understand the details of the coverage form being used.

The "Business Interruption" Forms

Two Item Contribution Form

The next major development in form evolution was the two-item contribution form, which incorporated two insuring agreements: one covering net profits and continuing expenses and the other covering ordinary payroll. The form, which was introduced in the mid-1920s, originally required a 100 percent coinsurance clause, i.e., businesses had to insure 100 percent of their business interruption value or risk a penalty at the time of a claim. The form also required that the second item—ordinary payroll—be insured for the amount anticipated it would need for at least ninety days.

Subsequently, the coinsurance requirement was reduced to 80 percent and coverage for ordinary payroll became optional. The coinsurance requirement applied separately to each of the two elements—businesses had to purchase insurance equal to 80 percent of its annual net profits plus charges and expenses, except ordinary payroll and heat, light, and power. The same coinsurance requirement applied separately to ordinary payroll, and businesses also had to select the number of days that the ordinary payroll would be insured.

The purpose of covering payroll when this form was in vogue and still today is to enable a business to retain employees who might find work elsewhere if they were laid off during a business suspension. It therefore makes sense that the provision for ordinary payroll, Item II in the two-item contribution form, did not guarantee that the business would recover the payroll if retention of the employees were not necessary at the time of the loss in order for the business to resume operations. It was covered on an actual loss sustained basis, with the business collecting only that portion of the ordinary payroll that was needed and actually paid to employees.

In addition, the two items were distinctly separate from one another, and insurance purchased to cover ordinary payroll could not be redirected to the net profit portion of the loss if the insurance fell short in that area.

Difference between Executive and Ordinary Payroll

The differentiation between executive or managerial payroll and ordinary payroll, which was introduced in this form, continues to impact how business interruption insurance is written today. In general, ordinary payroll is comprised of the wages of employees whose services could be suspended in the event of a long-term shutdown without a harmful effect on the business's reopening. They are not considered essential to the business's future success.

Conversely, executive or managerial (at times referred to as extraordinary payroll) payroll is devoted to employees who are essential to the continuation of business. Often they are executives and managers, but they also may include highly specialized employees who are essential to the reopening whose payroll also should be insured. Examples of essential but non-executive employees are nurses in a healthcare setting, master craftsmen in a construction business, and journeyed trades people in a manufacturing setting. Businesses should take care that underwriters understand the types of employees that are essential to the business, and appropriate coverage should be arranged. Typically, the traditional executive payroll is automatically included in the amount to be insured, and ordinary payroll coverage typically may be either insured or excluded.

The current standard ISO business income coverage form continues to permit insured businesses to differentiate between these two types of payroll and insure either both or just the executive salaries. Coverage that is written on an actual loss sustained form still requires that the payroll expenses actually be incurred or the insurance will not fund them.

Gross Earnings Forms

Mercantile and Nonmanufacturing and Manufacturing or Mining

The gross earnings form was developed in the late 1930s in an effort to meet demands for simpler forms. It existed alongside the two-item contribution form for a number of years until the two-item contribution form gradually faded from general use. The gross earnings form was first offered to nonmanufacturing risks, with the manufacturing or mining edition following quickly.

The typical gross earnings form developed by ISO responded to loss that resulted directly from the necessary interruption of business caused by damage to described property from an insured peril (cause of loss). Thus, there had to be direct damage to property described in the policy that was caused by a peril covered by the policy. For example, a shut down and resulting loss of income that resulted from a fire at an insured business typically would trigger the coverage. However, if, for example, flood were excluded on the policy and the damage resulted from flood, neither the direct property damage nor the business interruption loss would be insured.

The difference between the manufacturing and mercantile forms essentially lies in how the "gross earnings" are calculated. "Gross earnings" is defined in the FM Global insurance policy reproduced in the Appendix of this book as:

- for manufacturing operations: the net sales value of production less the cost of all raw stock, materials and supplies used in such production; or

- for mercantile or non-manufacturing operations: the total net sales less cost of merchandise sold, materials and supplies consumed in the operations or services rendered by the Insured. [4]

This discussion of the gross earnings forms is couched in terms of the standard form that was offered by the Insurance Services Office (ISO). That form no longer is available from ISO, but individual insurance companies still may use a gross earnings format. Some forms, like the FM Global property and time element form reproduced in the Appendix of this book, offer a variety of time element coverages, among them gross earnings coverage. Many of the elements of the older forms are similar, or even identical, to the forms that are used today. However, subtle differences may have serious implications on how much coverage is available—or even whether coverage is triggered at all. Therefore, we devote some time to a discussion of the elements in the gross earnings forms.

The definitions reflect the differences in the nature of operations between a manufacturer and a nonmanufacturing operation.

The previously available Insurance Services Office (ISO) business interruption form for manufacturing operations defines "gross earnings" as:

The sum of (a) total net sales value of production, (b) total net sales of merchandise, and (c) other earnings derived from operation of the business. Items that are subtracted from this are (d) raw stock from which production is derived, (e) materials and supplies directly consumed in the manufacturing process or in supplying the service sold, (f) merchandise sold, including packaging materials, and (g) services purchased from outsiders for resale which do not continue under contract.

Most important in this definition are the net sales value of production and the cost of raw stock. The other items are important for businesses that sell merchandise they do not manufacture or provide services in addition to their manufacturing activities. For most manufacturing businesses, the gross earnings form bases the amount of insurance on the sales value of the insured business's production minus the cost of raw stock used in the manufacturing process. A coinsurance percentage of 50, 60, 70, or 80 percent then is applied to arrive at the limits of coverage.

ISO's definition of "gross earnings" in its mercantile gross earnings form, which no longer is used by ISO companies, is:

The sum of (a) total net sales, and (b) other earnings derived from operations of the business, less the cost of: (C) merchandise sold, including packaging material therefore, (d) materials and supplies consumed directly in supplying the service(s) sold by the insured, and (e) service(s) purchased from outsiders (not employees of the insured) for resale which do not continue under contract.

In this definition, net sales are obtained by deducting discounts, returns, bad debts, and prepaid freight (if included in total sales) from total sales. Other earnings, such as commissions or rents from leased departments, are added to that figure before the cost of merchandise sold and materials and supplies used in providing the services or products being sold. For example, a service business such as a restaurant consumes many supplies—food, paper products, cleaning services, etc.—when selling its services. These would be subtracted from the gross earnings calculation because they are not needed when the business is not operating.

Both definitions provide that services purchased from others for resale that do not continue under contract are subtracted from the gross earnings figure. For example, the cost of utilities that no longer are needed during a period of interruption are subtracted unless the business is contractually obligated to continue payments. This reflects the general rule of thumb that costs that will not continue during an interruption should not be insured. Contractual agreements must be reviewed when the gross earning are calculated so that requirements to continue payments during a period of interruption are included in the figure.

Both the manufacturing and nonmanufacturing policy forms may be altered to exclude or limit ordinary payroll. One of the policy endorsements that previously was available excluded ordinary payroll completely and was used by operations that believed they would have access to the necessary employees to restart operations even after a suspension. The other endorsement that was available limited coverage for ordinary payroll to its estimated value for periods of 90, 120, 150, or 180 days.

Importance of Coinsurance

Unlike the two-item contribution form, the gross earnings form covers the entire exposure under one coverage grant. There is no daily, weekly, or monthly limit on the recovery, but the standard gross earning form does include a provision for a coinsurance limitation. In other words, the insured business must carry a specified portion of the annual business interruption value, which is expressed in terms of the annual gross earnings (as defined previously) subject to the coinsurance limitation. Failure to conform to the coinsurance requirement will force the business into a position of sharing in (coinsuring) the loss with the insurance company.

The coinsurance percentage also should reflect the amount of time that the insured business believes would take it to repair or replace its property—the amount of anticipated down time. The current ISO business income work sheet develops a business interruption value that is 100 percent of the estimated exposure for twelve months. A coinsurance percentage of 50 percent, which results in halving that business interruption value developed through the work sheet, infers that the business anticipates no more than a six-month interruption. (The annual estimated gross earnings would be cut in half to reflect an anticipated six-month interruption.)

In addition to the coinsurance requirements, payments are limited by the amount of loss that the insured business actually sustains. They are not valued policy forms.

Another aspect of the gross earnings forms is that loss is covered only for the time required "with the exercise of due diligence and dispatch" to repair, rebuild, or replace the damaged property from which the interruption arises. This is called the *period of indemnity*. For example, if the operation is suspended for three months but the premises could have been restored to operating condition in six weeks with "due diligence and dispatch," the recovery would be limited to six weeks.

An endorsement was available to extend the period of indemnity to allow additional time for the business to reestablish itself and regain customers. This endorsement was entitled the "Period of Indemnity Extension Endorsement." It provides for a period of time after property is repaired or replaced and the business is reopened to regain customers and market share. This often is needed because competing businesses may take customers away while a business is shut down, and the affected business may greatly benefit from supporting business interruption insurance payments during this time.

Earnings Forms

The earnings form (at times referred to as the monthly limitation form) was introduced in the 1950s as a simplified form geared toward the needs of small to mid-sized businesses. The main difference between the earnings and the gross earning forms was that the former did not have a coinsurance requirement but, rather, limited recovery to a specific percentage of the limit for each consecutive thirty days of interruption. It was designed for use with businesses that had no more than a six-month potential period of interruption.

The business could choose a monthly limitation of 33 1/3 percent, which would provide a recovery period of three months; 25 percent, four months recovery; or 16 2/3 percent, six months recovery. The amount of insurance needed was the number of months indicated through the percentage listed times the maximum amount of earnings and continuing expenses that could be lost over a period of one month.

One of the potential drawbacks to this form was that the monthly amount of coverage was not cumulative. So, if a limit of $100,000 was carried with a 25 percent monthly limitation, only $25,000 could be recouped each month. If the interruption lasted only three months, with $40,000 incurred in the first month and $30,000 each in the next two months, the insured business would only be able to collect $75,000 in total, $25,000 less than the limit insured and the amount of the loss. The business would not be able to collect the total amount because the loss was not spread evenly over the four months.

ISO Business Income Form

The current standard form is ISO's CP 00 30, Business Income (and Extra Expense) Coverage Form. It was introduced as part of the simplified property program of the late 1980s to cover the loss of *business income* that is sustained because of the *necessary suspension of business* operations during a *period of restoration*. The suspension must be caused by direct physical loss of or damage to property at the premises described in the policy declarations that is caused by any of the covered causes of loss. *Extra expense* includes necessary expenses that the insured business incurs during the restoration period.

This form is discussed in detail in Chapter 2, and its main characteristics are only introduced in this chapter.

The change in name from business interruption to business income was made to reflect the fact that the insurance covers a loss of income and not merely an interruption of the business. Both a business interruption and a loss of income must be present before coverage is triggered.

Form CP 00 30 includes provisions for extra expense payments, which represent expenses that the insured business incurs in addition to normal operating expenses because of the loss. Alternative form CP 00 32 is virtually identical to it, except there is no coverage provision for extra expense. Conversely, ISO form CP 00 50 covers extra expense only.

When is extra expense coverage important? A computer store is shut down after a fire. In order to retain as many customers as possible, the management takes out large ads in local newspapers and magazines saying that orders will be filled from stock kept at a location not affected by the fire. The company also pays a premium to quickly lease space for a temporary sales floor in order to stave off competing computer stores that likely would try to take its customers away. Both the additional advertising costs and the premium portion of the rental payments may be covered as extra expenses. Taking this situation generally, these extra expenses would be covered on the combined Business Income (and Extra Expense) form CP 00 30 or the Extra Expense form CP 00 50. They would not be paid under the business income form that excludes extra expense, CP 00 32, unless the expenses reduced the total business income loss. This is similar to previous unendorsed business interruption forms, which only paid expenses that were could be shown to reduce the amount of the business interruption loss.

Business income is defined in the form as

a. Net Income (net profit or Loss before income taxes) that would have been earned or incurred; and

b. Continuing normal operating expenses incurred, including payroll.

In addition, coverage may be written to include or exclude "rental value," or it may be limited solely to "rental value." A defined term, rental value in essence means the amount of net profit or loss that the insured would have earned as rent from

tenants occupying the described premises, including the fair rental value of any portion that the named insured occupies in the described premises. Added to this
amount are the continuing normal operating expenses, such as maintenance
expenses, that are associated with rental of the premises, including payroll and
charges that tenants normally would pay that revert to the landlord if the premises
are not habitable.

The current ISO business income coverage forms include a number of auxiliary coverage provisions that are discussed in Chapter 2. In addition, endorsements
are available to customize the coverage to meet specific exposures.

Valued Business Interruption Forms

Valued policies, as introduced previously in the case of *Michael v. Prussian Nat.
Ins. Co.,* are still available and may be useful to insure specific types of exposures.
They typically are written in the London and surplus lines marketplaces and by
domestic insurers that have independently filed coverage forms in some states.

The basic difference between these valued forms and other business interruption and business income forms is that the latter are written on an *actual loss sustained* basis. Claim payments are based on how much the insured business actually loses because of the interruption of operations. On the other hand, *valued* policies feature a preselected agreed amount of coverage that is set per day, week, or
month of down time.

There typically are provisions for a total and a partial suspension of operations,
with the valued amount decreased proportionately to the percentage that business
is decreased. An example of this is a food processor that is shut down for fifty working days after a fire. If its valued policy provides for $5,000 a day in business inter-
ruption payments, the company would be paid $250,000. The coverage usually
would not be available for nonscheduled working days. The amount recovered for
a partial suspension, such as two out of four assembly lines being shut down
because of the fire, is determined by the percentage that production is reduced
because of the loss. In the food processor example, if 50 percent of production is
lost because two assembly lines are suspended because of a covered loss, the business could recoup half of the daily insured amount, or $2,500 per day, during the
fifty days of suspension.

Some valued business interruption forms require that the company that
insures the business's property first pay for the direct property damage before the
business interruption coverage is triggered. These valued forms state that the insurer of direct physical damage coverage must first pay or "admit liability" for a loss to

the insured property before the business interruption claim is validated. The intent of such a provision is to require that the suspension of operations results from a *covered cause of loss* or *insured peril* damaging property that is insured. The valued forms frequently require this because they do not list the insured perils but instead rely on the existence of direct damage coverage by reference to the policies that insure it.

This differs from the current ISO business income coverage form, which merely stipulates that the "suspension" of operations that gives rise to the claim be caused "by direct physical loss of or damage to property at premises which are described in the Declarations and for which a Business Income Limit of Insurance is shown in the Declarations. The loss or damage must be caused by or result from a Covered Cause of Loss," but the damaged property does not have to be insured property.

The valued form—as is seen in the gross earnings and business income coverage forms—includes a *resumption of operations* clause that requires the insured to use other buildings, machinery, personal property, stock, etc., that it owns or controls to get back into business promptly. The insurer is permitted to base payments on the length of time it would have taken to resume operations as quickly as possible, which is a provision that may result in a dispute between the insured and the insurer over exactly what that length of time should have been.

The valued business interruption form typically permits reimbursement for expenses that the insured business incurs to reduce the amount of business interruption loss. The form may require that the insured business secure the insurer's consent and approval before spending money on such extraordinary expenses or risk the possibility that the insurance company will not reimburse them.

Much has been written about the advantages of valued business interruption forms as compared to standard business interruption forms that are written on an actual loss sustained basis, but no categorical statement can be made from an insurance point of view that one is superior to the other. Each has advantages in given situations. To illustrate, a valued form might better serve a new business that has no financial experience on production, turnover, or profits, while the standard form might better be recommended for a business with fluctuations in revenue and expenses.

Valued forms also may be useful for companies—such as biotech research operations—that are often operating at a net loss while conducting research or developing new products. These types of businesses in particular may benefit from a valued form because the typical calculation in the ISO business income form— net profit or loss plus continuing expenses—could result in a negative figure as was illustrated in the previously discussed court case from 1927, *Goetz v. Hartford Fire Insurance Co., et al.*

In *Goetz,* the court ruled that no business interruption payments were due because the company's net loss was more than continuing expenses, so recovery was denied. Companies that are in research and development mode may not be showing a net profit, but they still need to cover necessary continuing expenses while business is suspended. A valued form may be crafted to accurately address this type of situation.

Since the amount of potential recovery is agreed to before a loss occurs, a valued policy also may be easier to apply when handling a claim. Instead of having to calculate the loss of income, profit, or expenses at the time of loss, only the length of the period of recovery must be determined since the valued payments are established when the policy is written. There may be a substantial amount of work involved in setting the valued amount, however, when the policy is underwritten.

Because most businesses do not operate evenly from day to day throughout the year, a business that selects a valued policy form may be in danger of being under-insured or overinsured at specific times of the year. Because of this, the only safe way to provide adequate coverage under a valued form is to issue coverage equal to the *total number of working days times the maximum possible loss for any one day.* This is something that many businesses may be unwilling to do because of the premium that would be developed to cover this maximum possible loss.

The absence of a contribution or coinsurance clause is perhaps one of the greatest advantages of valued business interruption insurance. While it is true that valued coverage is not subject to a coinsurance clause, the fact that the coverage is limited to a fixed daily (or weekly or monthly) amount may also result in insufficient insurance. This essentially makes the insured business a coinsurer unless enough insurance is carried to cover the highest loss exposure for the insured's busiest period.

Optional Coverages

Extra Expense

As noted previously, extra expense coverage is designed to pay additional expenses that a business incurs because of a covered loss. There is no requirement that the expenses offset or reduce the rest of the business interruption loss, but the expenses are time-bounded by the period of restoration and must be used to avoid or minimize a suspension of the business. In considering the previous example of the computer store that is damaged by fire, spending money to advertise alternative sites where equipment is available would avoid a total suspension of business since operations could be continued elsewhere. The same is true of paying a premium to rent and equip sales space quickly—it would minimize the business's suspension of operations.

Both of these activities reduce the period of suspension, but they may not reduce the actual loss of income. When extra expense coverage is provided, the latter reduction is not required.

Rents

Landlords who depend on rental payments, as well as tenants who are benefiting from a favorable lease agreement, face rents exposures in the event that their properties are damaged or destroyed.

Coverage for these types of exposures typically was available in the older business interruption programs and continues to be insurable through the current renditions of coverage. The exposure that landlords face typically falls within the category of *rental value* coverage, which is included within the current definition of *business income* in the ISO coverage format and in many company-developed forms. *Leasehold interest coverage* currently is available from ISO as a separate coverage form (CP 00 60) and may be included within company-developed forms or added by endorsement.

Standardized and Company-Developed Coverage Forms

The ISO forms exist side-by-side with a number of coverage forms developed by individual insurance companies. Some company-developed forms mirror the current ISO wording, but others may pattern their coverage grants and exclusions after the gross earnings or valued business interruption forms. Because of this it is critical for professionals to study the specific language that is offered when the coverage is written before a loss occurs and a claim is filed. Subtle differences may mean the difference between claim payments and claim denials.

It is impossible to represent every coverage version that currently is available in the insurance marketplace. Differences are readily apparent in reviewing the form reproduced in this book's Appendix with those provided through ISO and other insurance carriers. A number of different types of forms are often used to write the coverage, but the manner in which they are crafted differs dramatically one from the other. There is, in fact, a great deal of flexibility on which coverage grants are selected from the FM Global form to provide customized coverage for a business. The ISO forms are relatively broad, and endorsements may be added to them to provide additional choices that are built into the FM Global policy.

The Importance of the Historical Record

The evolution of business interruption coverage is important as more than a mere historical record. It illustrates how, from early on, courts have interpreted certain phrases and clauses as being significant to whether—or not—an insured business can draw on its business interruption insurance. Some of the issues considered by the courts hearing cases hundreds of years ago continue to be of critical importance in the interpretation of coverage today.

Although it is impossible to describe and discuss every nuance of coverage in any book, we concentrate on the wording and issues that typically play the greatest role in a determination of whether coverage is triggered or not. These include:

- The importance of carefully reading the insuring agreement(s), definitions, exclusions, and limitations when selecting coverage to be sure that it is appropriate for a specific business interruption exposure.

- The fact that two elements—a suspension of business and a loss of business earnings—typically must result as a consequence of direct physical damage to property before coverage is triggered.

- The requirement that the physical damage to property be caused by an insured peril before business interruption insurance may be collected.

- The difference between forms that are crafted around actual loss sustained and valued loss formats.

- The importance of the period of recovery or period of restoration to the length and, consequentially, amount of business interruption loss that may be recouped through the insurance policy.

- The difference between coverage for extra expense and expenses to reduce the business income loss.

- The implications for recovery in a partial suspension of business operations versus a complete suspension of operations.

One of the mantras of the insurance industry is that a majority of businesses fail to survive after sustaining major property damage. This is not because of a lack of appropriate property insurance but, rather, because of the consequential affects of a suspension of operations while the property is repaired or replaced. Many businesses are ill prepared to resume operations and regain customers even if they are able to rebuild the physical elements of the business.

This book explores the issues surrounding this phenomenon and illustrates methods that may be employed to better guarantee survival of these damaged businesses. Preparing ahead of time to prove a business interruption claim can go a long way toward ensuring good cash flow and complete claim recovery at the time of loss. It also helps to limit some of the distractions that occur when a large loss is suffered.

Endnotes

[1] Robert M. Morrison, et al, *Business Interruption Insurance: Its Theory and Practice* (Cincinnati: The National Underwriter Co., 1986), citing Grant v. Parkinson (1781) and other court records.

[2] Ibid., 4-5.

[3] Lord Peter Levine speech to Risk and Insurance Management Society (RIMS), New York City, October 24, 2003.

[4] FM Global coverage form, ©2004 Factory Mutual Insurance Company. All rights reserved.

Common Elements of Coverage

The Fundamentals of Standard Policy Forms

I SO provides several standard business income coverage forms, which are reviewed in this chapter to provide a framework for the types of coverage available. Individual insurance companies frequently deviate from the ISO standard. Manuscript forms, which may be available to larger accounts, are discussed in Chapter 3. There also is information on the Gross Earnings form, which some insurers still use, in Chapter 1.

Since it is not possible to discuss each potential coverage deviation in this book, the ISO form is used to illustrate the most important issues. Variations are discussed in general, with endorsements that may be used to broaden coverage introduced.

The ISO Form Options

The three standard ISO forms are:

- Business Income Coverage Form (And Extra Expense) CP 00 30

- Business Income Coverage Form (Without Extra Expense) CP 00 32

- Extra Expense Coverage Form CP 00 50

Each of these forms is coupled with a causes of loss form (basic, broad, or special). Together they determine whether and to what extent business income coverage will be available. ISO currently entitles its business interruption forms *business income coverage* and not *business interruption coverage*, as it often is referred to in the industry. The term business income insurance was coined in the 1980s by ISO when it introduced its simplified commercial property program. The name change denotes the fact that the insurance covers a loss of income and not merely an interruption of business. Both a business interruption and a loss of income must be present before coverage is triggered.

In addition, ISO supports a form that provides coverage solely for additional *extra expenses* that are necessary to either

1. avoid or minimize a business interruption by continuing business operations at the insured business's normal premises or at a different location or

2. to minimize the interruption of business if the insured cannot continue operations.

Extra expense coverage often is purchased by service businesses—such as banks or newspapers—that typically need to continue to offer services even after a direct property loss destroys or cripples their normal operations. They use alternative locations to continue operations or run the risk of permanently losing their customer base.

Many types of businesses need both business income and extra expense coverage. They may purchase the ISO Business Income Coverage Form (And Extra Expense) CP 00 30, which provides business income coverage along with extra expense coverage. This form couples ISO's business income coverage grant with extra expense insurance.

Each of the ISO business income forms may be written as a separate policy or as a separate coverage item on a direct property damage policy. As noted previously, they are used in conjunction with one of the ISO causes of loss (perils) forms. The basic causes of loss form (CP 10 10) provides coverage for eleven causes of loss, such as fire and windstorm, which are described in the form. The broad causes of loss form (CP 10 20) adds the perils of falling objects; weight of snow, ice, or sleet; and water damage to the causes of loss specified in the basic form. The special causes of loss form (CP 10 30) provides coverage for risks of direct physical loss that are not excluded or limited on the form.

Business interruption forms that are developed and offered by individual insurance companies may follow the ISO approach of providing a coverage form that is tied to a causes of loss form. Some incorporate the causes of loss within the coverage form. Either way, it is essential for practitioners to understand both the definition of coverage and the causes of loss that will activate it when instituting an insurance program and when a potential claim occurs.

ISO Forms CP 00 30 and CP 00 32

The difference between ISO's CP 00 30 and CP 00 32 concerns the provision of extra expense insurance. CP 00 30 includes extra expense and CP 00 32 does not. This discussion centers on the combined business income and extra expense form with the understanding that the extra expense coverage may be deleted by selecting CP 00 32.

The 2002 edition of ISO's forms define business income as:

a. Net income (net Profit or Loss before income taxes) that would have been earned or incurred; and

b. Continuing normal operating expenses incurred, including payroll.

For manufacturing risks, Net Income includes the net sales value of production.

The two items of this definition are tied together by the word *and,* which indicates that the net income (or loss) is coupled with continuing normal operating expenses incurred. This could result in no recovery for a business operating at a net loss if continuing normal operating expenses do not exceed that net loss. This was shown in *Continental Ins. Co. v. DNE Corp.,* 834 S.W.2d 930 (Tenn. 1992). DNE was operating at a net loss prior to a business interruption that was covered by a Continental insurance policy. The definition of business income mirrored the current ISO wording. DNE, however, argued that the two aspects of business income were independent and that it should be able to recover for normal continuing operating expenses despite the operating loss. The Tennessee Supreme Court disagreed, however, stating:

> . . . the interpretation advocated by DNE Corporation (i.e., ignoring "net income" whenever there is a net loss) would put the insured, in all cases when there is a net loss, in a better economic position from having had its business interrupted than it would have occupied had there been no interruption of its business operations. Such an interpretation would obviously be inconsistent with the purpose of providing insurance, as well as with the decisions in other cases involving similar issues. We therefore conclude that the amount of "business income"

under the insurance policy provision involved in this case should be determined by adding the amount of "net income" and the amount of "continuing normal operating expenses." Under this approach, if "net income" is a positive number (which will occur whenever there are net profits), the amount of "business income" will be the sum of two positive numbers, and the insured will be entitled to recover that amount. If, however, "net income" is a negative number (which will occur whenever there is a net loss), the amount of "business income" will be the amount of "continuing normal operating expenses" reduced by the amount of the net loss. If, as under the facts of this case, the amount of the net loss that would have been incurred had there been no business interruption exceeds the amount of normal operating expenses actually incurred, the resulting number is a negative number, and there can be no recovery for an "actual loss of business income."

Rental Value

The forms further state that coverage may be provided for business income including "rental value," other than "rental value," or only "rental value." Rental value is defined as business income that consists of

a. Net Income (Net Profit or Loss before income taxes) that would have been earned or incurred as rental income from tenant occupancy of the premises described in the Declarations as furnished and equipped by you, including fair rental value of any portion of the described premises which is occupied by you; and

b. Continuing normal operating expenses incurred in connection with that premises, including

(1) Payroll; and
(2) The amount of charges which are the legal obligation of the tenant(s) but would otherwise be your obligation.

This definition makes it clear that rental income may be insured under this business income form without the necessity of using a separate form (as with some previous editions). The insured also may recoup the fair rental value of the part of the premises that it occupies, that is, the amount the business would have to pay to rent comparable premises elsewhere.

Elements Necessary to Trigger Coverage

The ISO insuring agreement requires that three elements be present before coverage is triggered. There must be:

- Direct physical damage to or loss of property at the premises described in the policy declarations that was caused by a covered cause of loss,

- A necessary suspension of operations during the period of restoration, and

- An actual loss of business income.

Without any of these elements, coverage is denied.

Direct Physical Loss of or Damage to Property and Covered Cause of Loss

The ISO coverage grant states that the business income and/or extra expense loss must be caused by "direct physical loss of or damage to property at premises which are described in the Declarations." Further, the damage must be caused by or result from a covered cause of loss.

It is worth noting that the ISO form does not specify that the direct damage must be done to *insured property* but, rather, that it be done to property at the *premises described in the declarations* by a covered cause of loss. It appears from this wording that the coverage is broader than what is available on insurer forms that require the direct damage affect property that actually is insured on the policy.

This requirement for actual direct physical damage has been consistently upheld by the courts, and a mere slowdown of income because of uninsured causes is not sufficient to trigger the coverage. For example, a North Carolina appeals court held that the inability to access a business did not trigger business income coverage because no physical damage had occurred. In *Harry's Cadillac v. Motors Ins. Corp.*, 486 S.E.2d 249 (N.C. Ct. App. 1997), a severe snowstorm isolated Harry's dealership, and customers could not reach it for a week. There was no damage to property at the dealership's premises. The court ruled that business income insurance "does not cover all business interruption losses, but only those losses requiring repair, rebuilding, or replacement."

In *St. Paul Mercury Ins. Co. v. Magnolia Lady, Inc.*, No. Civ. A. 297CV153BB (N. D. Miss. Nov. 4 1999), the court ruled that a loss of earnings could not be reimbursed without direct physical loss or damage to the insured's premises. In this case a barge collided with a bridge near a casino-hotel owned by the Magnolia Lady. State authorities closed the bridge for three weeks, and the Magnolia Lady argued that the closure caused a dramatic decrease in the casino-hotel's business. However, the casino-hotel remained accessible and sustained no damage, so coverage was not available.

Questions often arise about whether business income coverage is available for businesses forced to shut down because of bomb or terrorist threats. Coverage typically is not triggered by mere threats of harm because there has been no physical damage.

Special Exclusions

The ISO causes of loss forms (CP 10 10, CP 10 20, and CP 10 30) each contain a section of special exclusions that are applicable to business income and extra expense coverage.

Included among these special exclusions is loss caused directly or indirectly by power or other utility service failure that does not result in a covered cause of loss. For example, a storm causes a power outage at a business insured for business income and extra expense. The lights and cash register won't work, and the business must shut down, but

Importance of Insured Causes of Loss

The causes of loss that are insured on the business income policy will determine when coverage is or is not available.

Large, complex businesses typically have access to the broadest of coverages, including coverage for catastrophic occurrences such as floods and earthquakes. However, less complex or midsize businesses may purchase ISO's special causes of loss form (former all-risk coverage) and flood insurance through the National Flood Insurance Program (NFIP). (Flood and earth movement are two of the perils excluded on the special causes of loss form.)

A flood damages the building and equipment, and business is suspended for three months during the cleanup and repair period. Since flood is an excluded cause of loss on the ISO form, business income and extra expense coverage is not available from that source. And the NFIP commercial property program does not offer business interruption coverage. So, while the direct damage might be covered by the NFIP policy, the business would be unable to collect business income payments during the period of restoration because the damage was not caused by a "covered cause of loss" as dictated by the business income policy.

no property at the premises is damaged. Business income/extra expense coverage would not be triggered because there has not been any direct damage by a covered cause of loss to property at the described location. In addition, even if a small fire developed and damaged property, the business would have to be suspended for at least seventy-two hours (the waiting period) before business income insurance is available. The waiting period is discussed in more detail later in this chapter.

Another exclusion prohibits business income coverage for losses caused by or resulting from damage or destruction of finished stock or the time to reproduce such stock. This exclusion does not apply to extra expense coverage. The exclusion is logical because businesses typically would insure stock under its property insurance and expect payment to flow from that section of the policy.

Losses that arise from direct physical loss or damage to radio or television antennas or lead-in wiring, masts, or towers also are not covered, but the exclusion may be eliminated with Endorsement CP 15 50, Radio or Television Antennas, Business Income or Extra Expense.

The fourth exclusion specific to business income and extra expense coverage excludes any increase in the amount of loss that results from a delay in restoration caused by interference by strikers or others and the suspension, lapse, or cancellation of licenses, leases, or contracts. However, if the suspension or cancellation of licenses, leases, or contracts can be directly related back to the suspension of business operations, the insurance will cover such loss that affects business income during the period of restoration. For example, a company has a six-month contract to produce widgets, but business is suspended during the first month of the contract because of a fire at the premises. Operations are suspended for four months. As a result, the buyer cancels the contract because she must have all the widgets within the six months of the contract period. The loss of business income from cancellation of the contract is subject to coverage for the four-month period of restoration. However, the business may not be successful in claiming business income losses into the future, past the period of restoration, that result from the buyer canceling the contract when the production schedule could not be met.

Any other consequential losses—aside from business income and extra expense—also are excluded.

Necessary Suspension of Operations During "Period of Restoration"

Necessary Suspension

Prior to the 2000 edition of its business income forms, ISO did not define the term *necessary suspension,* even though the earlier forms also included the requirement. Independently filed coverage forms may not include a definition, and some carriers still may be using older versions of the ISO wording. Thus, questions continue to arise as to what, exactly, a necessary suspension of operations entails.

Courts have been divided on what a suspension entails when the term is not defined in the form. In *American States Ins. Co. v. Creative Walking, Inc.*, 16 F. Supp.2d 1062 (E.D. Mo. 1998), the court found that necessary suspension meant a complete cessation of business operations. Creative Walking's premises were directly damaged because of a water main break, which left its premises untenantable. The company moved to a temporary facility a few weeks later and made the temporary facility its new headquarters. Creative Walking subsequently submitted a business income and extra expense claim to its insurer, stating a business slowdown for approximately eighteen weeks following the loss. The court ruled, however, that "If the insured is able to continue its business operations at a temporary facility, it has not suffered 'necessary suspension' of its operations." Creative Walking therefore was entitled only to compensation for the period of time prior to moving to the new location plus expenses incurred in the relocation.

A 1996 case, *Royal Indemnity Insurance Co. v. Mikob Properties, Inc.*, 940 F. Supp. 155 (S.D. Texas), illustrates a similar line of reasoning. Mikob owned and operated a three-building apartment complex. A fire completely destroyed one of the buildings, but the two other apartment buildings sustained only minor damage. Asbestos was found in the soot from the fire, and the area of the destroyed building was fenced off until its remains could be demolished and the area cleaned. As a result, tenants were not able to use amenities located near the damaged building. The tenancy rates at the two buildings that remained in operation declined. Royal paid Mikob the rental income that was lost from the closing of the one building but refused to cover a reduction in tenant occupancy in the other two buildings. Mikob argued that the reduction in occupancy levels did constitute a necessary suspension of operations and was covered by the policy on the basis of "mutual dependency"— that the complex was operated as a whole and was dependent on the amenities that became unavailable as a result of the fire. The court disagreed, however, stating,

> Even if the character of the apartment complex was adversely impacted by the fire, there was no "necessary suspension of operations or tenancy" in Buildings A and B. . .the amenities which attract customers may be affected by a covered loss, but if the insured premises are still operating, the business interruption clause does not cover a decrease in income.

Conversely, the court in *American Medical Imaging Corp. v. St. Paul Fire and Marine Ins. Co.*, 949 F.2d 690 (3d Cir. 1991) ruled that companies should not be penalized for mitigating their damages. American Medical set up temporary offices with reduced phone capacity after a fire caused smoke and water damages at its premises. The company claimed that the reduction in telephone lines at the temporary location caused it to lose nearly $1 million and to incur extra expenses. The court sided with American, stating that it was entitled to coverage because it had acted promptly to mitigate damages and that its operations had been suspended.

ISO sought to diminish the problems over what constitutes a necessary suspension with its 2000 form by including a definition, which continues to be used in the 2002 form. The ISO definition of *suspension* is:

a. The slowdown or cessation of your business activities; or

b. That a part of all of the described premises is rendered untenantable, if coverage for Business Income including "Rental Value" or "Rental Value" applies.

This definition, which clearly includes a slowdown in business activities, incorporates portions of loss that may previously have been denied, such as the loss of efficiencies and, hence, income because of fewer phone lines in a temporary location. Note that the second part of this definition requires only that a *part* of the *described premises* be untenantable in order to qualify as a suspension. If this definition had been included in the policy covering Mikob Properties, the outcome of the case may have been different.

Period of Restoration

Regardless of whether the term *suspension* is defined on the policy or not, it typically is time-bounded by the period of restoration. Some policies, as noted in other chapters of this book, may refer to the period of restoration as the indemnity period or recovery period. ISO defines the *period of restoration* to include the period of time that begins seventy-two hours after the direct physical loss or damage is caused by a covered cause of loss at the described premises and ends on the earlier of:

(1) The date when the property at the described premises should be repaired, rebuilt or replaced with reasonable speed and similar quality; or

(2) The date when business is resumed at a new permanent location.

The period of restoration does not include additional time needed to resume operations because of complying with ordinances or law or to test for or deal with pollutants.

Therefore, business must be suspended for at least three full days before coverage is triggered. Once the waiting period has elapsed, the insured is given a reasonable amount of time to repair or rebuild, during which business income and extra expense coverage is available. The question of what constitutes repair or rebuilding "with reasonable speed" is one that may be controversial.

Typically, delays in the restoration that are caused by the insurer or by general conditions may extend the period of recovery, but delays on the part of the insured business will not extend it. So, for example, if an insurer fails to act with reasonable speed to adjust the direct damage loss and, consequently, the business remains suspended for a longer period of time that it should have been, the period of restoration should be extended to reflect the insurer's delay. Catastrophes present another challenge to this standard. Building supplies and contractors may not be available after hurricanes or unchecked fires devastate a wide area. Even though the insurer may have adjusted the direct damage claims promptly, a business may not be able to engage a contractor quickly, and the suspension may last longer than normally would be acceptable. Such a situation should not adversely impact the insured business. However, if an insured simply fails to rebuild in a reasonable period of time, the period of recovery should be limited by a theoretical amount of time that should have been involved.

While non-ISO policies may not include the exact definition that ISO uses, they typically include a similar time boundary, such as a requirement to rebuild with "due diligence and dispatch." Such wording has similar impact as is seen in *Fireman's Fund Insurance Co. v. Mitchell-Peterson, Inc.*, 578 N.E.2d 851 (Ohio Ct. App. 1989) and *Duane Reade, Inc., v. St. Paul Fire & Marine Insurance Company*, (279 F.Supp.2d 235 (S.D.N.Y. 2003).

In *Mitchell-Peterson*, a restaurant was shut down after being severely damaged by fire. The St. Paul policy specified that the insured must restore the business with "due diligence and dispatch", but it was not reopened until some seven months after the fire. The court ruled that the amount of recovery time was unreasonable and that the insured had not been diligent in its recovery efforts. Business interruption recovery thus was fifty days shorter than the insured claimed.

Duane Reade involved a store that was damaged in the 2001 terrorist attacks on the World Trade Center. Its policy required that the property be rebuilt with "due diligence and dispatch." Duane Reade contended that its recovery period should incorporate the amount of time required to rebuild the entire WTC complex. St. Paul argued that the restoration period ended when Duane Reade could have restored operations at its locations other than at the WTC. The court ruled, however, that neither side was correct in interpreting the policy, stating that "Once Duane Reade could resume functionally equivalent operations in the location where its WTC store once stood, the Restoration Period would be at an end." Even though the drug store chain was operating at its other locations, business interruption recovery should be calculated based on the business recovery of the specific store that had been destroyed.

Actual Loss of Business Income

The third requirement is for an actual loss of business income since the ISO form is written on an *actual loss sustained* basis. This concept is discussed in the sections of Chapter 1 that deal with the actual loss sustained coverage.

~~As noted previously in the *DNE Corp.* case, the loss of business income is cal-~~culated by adding the net profit (or loss) with necessary continuing operating expenses and comparing that with what would have been earned *but for* the loss. The difference is the amount recoverable, subject to limits and deductibles. Since this is a two-item calculation, businesses operating at net losses may not be able to collect as much, or even any, payments.

While this coverage premise seems straightforward, the actual loss calculation is not. Calculating the amount of business income that has actually been lost is one of the most complex and difficult exercises in the world of insurance because it requires accounting acumen as well as a well-honed understanding of insurance coverage. In addition, items used to determine the amount of recovery may be subject to many variables, such as general economic conditions, strategic plans to expand or contract business operations, and the fact that resources that would have been channeled into business operations must be redirected to recovery efforts—a residual impact that probably cannot ever be completely quantified.

Further, the amount recoverable is not definitively established and listed on the policy. The Loss Conditions state that the amount of business income loss payable is *based on* the net income of the business before the direct physical loss or damage, the likely net income that would have been earned had the loss not occurred, the continuing expenses that are necessary to resume operations, and other relevant sources of information, including the insured business's financial records, bills, deeds, and contracts. Necessary expenses that reduce the amount of the business income loss also are paid.

Commercial property forms, on the other hand, use definitive terms such as we will "pay the value of lost or damaged property" or we will "pay the cost of repairing or replacing" the damaged property. Business income losses are *based on* a comparison of the level of income before and after the loss.

Proving the amount recoverable is further complicated if the policy includes a coinsurance percentage. In that case, a penalty will be assessed if the insured business has not purchased sufficient limits to meet the coinsurance requirement.

Subsequent chapters and claim scenarios provide specific examples of loss situations in which variables had to be accounted for in proving the amount recoverable. For example, the Hospitable Hotels claim scenario, which follows Chapter 6, includes many variables that could impact claim recovery, such as the historical level of snowfall, activities at nearby hotels, and the fact that reopening was delayed because mold developed as a result of the direct damage to the hotel. Each claim situation is different, and each requires intimate knowledge of operations, financial situation, and insurance coverage.

Extra Expense Coverage

Extra expense coverage may be purchased through form CP 00 30, Business Income (And Extra Expense) Coverage Form, and independently through form CP 00 50, Extra Expense Coverage Form. It covers the necessary expenses an insured incurs—again during the period of restoration—to avoid or minimize the suspension of operations and continue business at either the same or temporary locations or to minimize the suspension if the business cannot continue operations. Note there is no requirement to reduce the total loss *except* when the extra expenses are incurred to repair or replace property.

For example, a business suffers a serious fire, and restoration is expected to take six months. Assume the insured spends an additional $100,000 to set up operations at a temporary location and, by doing so, can continue operations during the reconstruction period. This $100,000 typically would qualify for payment under extra expense because it allowed the company to continue operations. However, consider an alternative business that suffers a similar fire. Assume that it unfortunately runs out of insurance limits for replacing business personal property that was destroyed in the fire. The insurance company will cover extra expenses incurred to replace that property *only* to the extent that doing so reduces the total business income and extra expense claim. So, if the overall business income claim is $1,500,000, but $100,000 is spent to buy personal property in order to resume operations, and the $100,000 expenditure decreases the overall claim to $1,425,000, the insured should be reimbursed $75,000 of the $100,000 expenditure, that is, the amount by which the extra expenditure reduced the business income loss.

Extra Expense insurance may be contrasted with the additional coverage of *Expenses to Reduce Loss* as provided in the business income form without extra expense (CP 00 32). In order to collect on this provision, the insured must prove that spending the additional money decreased the amount of the business income loss.

Additional Limitation

Forms CP 00 30 and CP 00 32 limit recovery for interruption of computer operations. If operations are suspended because of destruction or corruption of electronic data, or damage to electronic data, no business income coverage is available. This, of course, is a critical limitation for businesses that rely on computers for any substantive part of their operations. It points out the need to have a well-planned data recovery plan in place, including backup hot site and/or records that can be used to restore operations quickly.

A small amount of coverage ($2,500 per year) is given back under a later section of the ISO forms. This is discussed further in a later section of this chapter.

Payroll and the Business Income Forms

The definition of business income in the current ISO forms states that payroll is considered a continuing normal operating expense if it is disbursed during the period of recovery. However, ordinary payroll expenses are deducted from operating expenses for the purpose of applying the coinsurance condition because the form does not require that ordinary payroll be continued during the suspension. The insured business owner can determine at the time of the loss whether to continue paying ordinary wages or not.

Non-ISO forms may treat ordinary payroll differently, as did earlier ISO forms. Therefore businesses should discuss their continuing payroll needs when purchasing the coverage and include the conclusions when establishing the limit of coverage.

Accounting Documentation—Who Pays?

An insured business sustained a covered loss and made a business income loss claim. The insurance company requested accounting documentation to support the claim.

To comply with the request from the insurance company, the business requested that its accountant accumulate the data and provide a report to the company. The accountant charged the insured for their time, and this cost was submitted to the insurance company. The insurer disclaimed responsibility for the accountant's fees stating that the insured did not have the right under the policy to hire an accountant to prepare the records. If such assistance was required, according to the insurer, the company would hire its own accountants.

The business owner contended that his staff could not supply the type of documentation required so experts were necessary. The business owner considered the accounting bill covered as claim investigation expense.

There is nothing in the wording of the ISO business income form that obligates the insurance company to pay the insured's accounting cost to determine the extent of the business income loss. However, the form also provides extra expense coverage. Extra expense is defined as "necessary expenses you incur during the 'period of restoration' that you would not have incurred if there had been no direct physical loss." The accounting fees in question would not have been incurred had there been no loss.

The policy also requires that the extra expense be incurred to "avoid or minimize the suspension of business and to continue 'operations'." A case may be made for extra expense payments for the accounting costs. A policyholder could argue that the assistance of outside experts decreased the length of suspension and allowed the company to restore operations more quickly by freeing key management to focus on loss recovery rather than data gathering and loss development activities. Therefore, it seems reasonable to conclude that the accounting fees were an insured extra expense as intended under the policy.

Suppose the insured had been covered by ISO's Business Income Coverage Form (Without Extra Expense) CP 00 32. That form covers expediting expenses that are necessary to reduce a loss "to the extent they do not exceed the amount of loss that otherwise would have been payable under this Coverage Form." The insurer could argue that the accounting fees did not qualify as an expediting expense, although the insured may argue that they do qualify. The end result may depend upon the specific details of the situation.

Additional Coverages

There are four additional coverages included in the ISO forms. They are:

- Civil Authority

- Alterations and New Buildings

- Extended Business Income

- Interruption of Computer Operations

Civil Authority

This coverage grant extends business income (and extra expense) coverage to losses that a business incurs because a civil authority has prohibited access to its premises. The civil action must occur because a covered cause of loss has caused direct physical loss of or damage to property elsewhere. The ISO wording was argued in a 2003 case, *Assurance Company of America v. BBB Service Company, Inc.,* 593 S.E.2d 7 (Ga. Ct. App. 2003). BBB claimed loss of business income under the civil authority clause after a county hurricane evacuation order. The court of appeals determined:

> The Civil Authority clause in the insurance policy requires two things in order for BBB to recover lost business income: (1) that the loss was caused by a civil authority action which prohibited access to BBB's insured premises, and (2) that the civil authority action which prohibited access was due to the direct physical loss of or damage to property other than the insured premises.

At the bench trial, the parties stipulated there was an evacuation order and a resulting $30,000 loss of business income. Further, they acknowledged that property damage was occurring throughout the term of the evacuation, when hurricane winds were making landfall. The appeals court upheld that there had been actual damage to property other than at the insured's premises and that the policy did cover the lost business income.

Business income coverage is available after a seventy-two-hour waiting period and applies for up to three consecutive weeks after coverage begins. There is no waiting period for extra expense.

Alterations and New Buildings

This provision extends coverage to loss of business income sustained because of direct physical loss or damage at the described premises to new buildings or structures, whether complete or under construction; alterations or additions to existing buildings or structures; and machinery, equipment, supplies, or building materials on or within 100 feet of the described premises that are being used in the construction or are incidental to the occupancy of the new buildings. Extra expense coverage also is available. If the damage delays the start of operations at the new building, the period of restoration begins on the date that operations "would have begun" had the damage not occurred.

This last provision can be extremely important because a delay in project completion due to a covered loss can cause a serious consequential loss of business income for a company that is counting on using the new or altered quarters to generate revenue.

For example, an insured firm is expanding its suite of customized offices, intending to take on two more practitioners. The new offices are scheduled to be operational on January 1. There is a small fire on December 15, and the offices cannot be used until February. Extra expenses the insured incurs to speed up repairs so the offices can be completed should be covered under the basic insuring agreement. Business income that is lost from January 1 to February 1, along with extra expenses incurred during that time period, would fall within the additional coverage for Alterations and New Buildings.

Extended Business Income

This pays for additional loss of business income that continues past the time that the damaged property is repaired and operations resumed. The purpose is to support the business until it can regain the customers and level of business income that existed before the loss. The additional coverage does not apply to the loss of business income that results from unfavorable business conditions. For example, a business resumes operations during a time of general economic malaise and has a hard time reestablishing its customer base. It can claim extended business income for a period of time past the period of restoration but is only entitled to the amount actually lost because of the effect of the suspension—it cannot collect for general economic problems.

The standard ISO policy provides up to thirty days of coverage, but additional periods of coverage may be endorsed onto the policy.

Interruption of Computer Operations

This additional coverage provides a very limited amount of coverage—up to $2,500—to offset the limitation for interruption of computer operations, which was discussed previously. If operations are suspended because of destruction or corruption of electronic data, or damage to electronic data, the $2,500 of coverage is available if the damage is caused by a covered cause of loss or certain computer-related perils that are listed.

Newly Acquired Locations

Both forms allow the named insured to extend coverage to newly acquired locations if 50 percent or higher coinsurance is shown in the declarations. The amount of insurance available is $100,000 per location for both business income and extra expense combined.

Optional Coverages

The ISO forms include optional coverages, which are activated by appropriate entries on the commercial property declarations page. The three optional coverages that may be used as alternatives to coinsurance are:

- Maximum period of indemnity

- Monthly limit of indemnity

- Business income agreed value

Any one of them may be applied to any one item of business income coverage.

Maximum Period of Indemnity

This optional coverage deletes the coinsurance provision and substitutes a provision stating that the most the insurer will pay for loss of business income is the smaller of the amount of loss sustained during the 120 days immediately following the direct damage or the limit shown in the declarations. This option is most effective for businesses that are unlikely to suffer interruptions of more than four months since it is based on four months of expected operational experience.

Monthly Limit of Indemnity

This provision also deletes the coinsurance provision. It establishes a monthly limit of insurance, which can be either one-third, one-fourth, or one-sixth of the total limit of insurance shown in the declarations. This optional coverage mimics the earning forms that previously were supported by ISO, but the extra expense and other extended business income provisions of the current form also are provided.

Although there are monthly limitations on recovery, coverage applies for the entire period of time that it takes to resume operations—plus the extended period of indemnity (an additional thirty days). Recovery is limited, however, to the indicated fraction of the total limit during each thirty consecutive days after the beginning date of the loss.

For example, an insured purchases $200,000 of business income and extra expense coverage subject to a one-fourth monthly recovery. During each thirty-day period, the insured can collect no more than $50,000 until the entire limit is exhausted. Problems may arise if expenditures are higher in some months than in others. Under this scenario, a business may incur $60,000 in business income loss in month one, $40,000 in month two, $50,000 in month three, and $25,000 in month four. Since the monthly recovery is capped at $50,000, the insured is paid $50,000 in month one, $40,000 in month two, $50,000 in month three, and $25,000 in month four. Assuming there is no extended period of recovery, the insured can collect only $165,000 instead of the policy limit of $200,000.

The benefit, however, is that smaller, less complex businesses do not have to be concerned about coinsurance penalties under the monthly limit of indemnity provision.

Business Income Agreed Value

Once an insured submits an acceptable business income work sheet (see Chapter 4 Work Sheet Instructions), the coinsurance provision may be deleted from the policy and replaced with an agreed value provision. The agreed value must equal or exceed the appropriate coinsurance percentage for the rates being charged times the upcoming year's estimated business income and extra expense values. As long as the insured carries the agreed value, the coinsurance provision is suspended for the twelve months covered by the work sheet unless the policy expires before that time.

If less insurance is carried than the agreed value, the insured's recovery is reduced in proportion to the deficiency, regardless of whether the amount of insurance carried is adequate to satisfy the coinsurance provision.

Endorsements

ISO supports nearly 200 endorsements that may be used to customize business income and extra expense forms. Since space constrictions dictate that only a few be covered here, we will discuss those that tend to be used most frequently with the understanding that coverage is available—from either ISO or company-filed endorsements—for many of the other specific time element exposures that an insured business may face.

Dependent Properties

ISO offers endorsements that provide either business income or extra expense coverage for loss the insured may incur because a *dependent property* has sustained direct physical loss or damage from a covered cause of loss. There are four types of dependent properties:

- **Contributing locations**—Locations that the insured is dependent upon for the delivery of materials or services that are critical to the insured's business operations.

- **Recipient locations**—Locations that accepts the insured's products or services, such as the sole distributor for a specialized product.

- **Manufacturing locations**—Locations that manufacture products for delivery to the insured's customers under contracts of sale, such as the manufacturer of high-end outdoor furniture that the insured sells under its name brand.

- **Leader locations**—Locations that attract customers to the insured's business, such as the department store anchors in a shopping mall.

If any of these dependent properties cannot operate because of physical damage, the insured may sustain a loss of business income. The endorsements exclude coverage for physical damage solely involving the loss or damage to electronic data. The dependent properties must be listed on the endorsements' schedule of locations, but an additional .03 percent of the limit of insurance is available for each day that operations are suspended and an actual loss of business income arises because of physical damage to dependent properties that are not listed.

Tuition and Fees

Educational institutions use the tuition and fees endorsement. It limits business income coverage to tuition, fees, and other education-related income. Perhaps the most important aspect, however, is that it takes the sequence of school terms into account in discussing the length of time that coverage is available. The endorsement extends recovery for actual loss of business income into the next school term if property is restored thirty days or less before the scheduled opening of the next school term.

Utility Services

Coverage under each of the three main ISO business income and extra expense forms may be extended to include business interruptions that are caused by utility service interruptions to the insured premises. Once again, the interruption in service must be caused by direct physical damage from a covered cause of loss to the types of utilities described in the coverage schedule. Utilities that may be included are water, communications, and power. Coverage for power supply interruptions may include or exclude damage to overhead transmission lines.

One source of confusion that frequently arises when discussing this coverage is the requirement that the utility involved be interrupted by a covered cause of loss. Brownouts or blackouts typically would not be included unless they are caused by a covered peril, unless they are caused by one of the causes of loss insured on the policy.

Ingress and Egress

Ingress and egress coverage involves the ability to enter or leave the insured premises. While ISO does not offer endorsements specifically focused on ingress and egress, many carriers do provide the coverage. A recent court record illustrates the differences of opinion that may arise when discussing ingress and egress provisions.

In *City of Chicago v. Factory Mutual Insurance Co.*, No. 02 C 7023, 2004 WL 649447 (N.D. Ill. March 18, 2004), the city claimed business interruption payments as a result of the Federal Aviation Administration (FAA) closure of Chicago O'Hare International Airport following the September 11, 2001, airplane crashes in New York City, Arlington (VA), and Pennsylvania. The city claimed damages under, among other coverage provisions, the ingress and egress coverage provided by Factory Mutual. The city argued that the FAA's ground stop order was indirectly caused by "terrorist-inflicted physical damage to the World Trade Center and the

Pentagon." The city reasoned that the insurance contract limited insurable business interruptions to those caused by "direct physical loss or damage," but argued that the ingress/egress provision did not include the word "direct" in its discussion of physical damage requirements.

The court, however, cited the policy's overall provision that "indirect or remote loss or damage" was excluded by the policy. There was a provision that the kind of property covered by the policy had to be within 1,000 feet of city property. Thus the court ruled that the prevention of ingress or egress from the airports did not trigger the business interruption coverage since terms of the policy were not met.

This case, on its own, amplifies the crux of all coverage discussions: the exact wording of the entire policy will be considered when coverage is disputed, and the placement—or lack thereof—of individual words can mean the difference between acceptance or rejection of a claim.

A chart outlining the civil authority and ingress/egress issues that arose after the 9-11 terrorist attacks on America is posted at www.nuco.com/businessinterruption.

CHAPTER THREE

Planning for the Future

Customizing Coverage Using Manuscript Forms

S tandard (ISO) and company form policies account for the vast majority of policies issued in all major lines of insurance. However, in certain circumstances, policyholders, brokers, and/or insurers might conclude that such forms are not optimal. For example, standard or company forms might not provide the breadth of coverage that is needed for a particular business's exposures. They may provide too much coverage or may fail to address peculiarities of the policyholder's core business or claims handling practices.

Whatever the reason, when standard or company forms do not meet the needs of one or the other party, they might consider crafting a *manuscript policy*. Manuscript policies differ from standard and company forms in one important respect: they are not drafted solely by the insurer. They are customized insurance contracts that are—to varying degrees—the product of joint negotiation between the insurer and policyholder.

This chapter addresses considerations fundamental to the manuscripting process, from determining whether manuscripting ought to be pursued in the first place to drafting and negotiating policy terms.

The Manuscripting Process: An Overview

Drafting and executing a manuscript policy—often simply referred to as *manuscripting*—is a complex process comprised of several parts. First, the policyholder must determine that a policy scripted to suit his particular business and its situation is desirable and worth pursuing. Second, one or more insurers must be willing to consider assuming risk under a manuscript policy, if projected premiums are sufficient to warrant the extra effort. Third comes drafting and negotiating the policy terms desired. From beginning to end, this process can involve extraordinary effort by numerous individuals, foremost among them being the policyholder's risk managers and other employees, insurance brokers, and insurance company underwriters and claims persons. When necessary, insurance consultants, forensic accountants, and lawyers also are involved.

When a policyholder and one or more insurers agree to work towards a manuscripted policy, the ultimate goal is an insurance contract that unambiguously expresses the intent of the parties. But the process is not without peril. The insurer must be careful to avoid agreement on terms that would result in broader coverage than it wants to provide; correspondingly, the policyholder must avoid unintended limitations on coverage. The perils of poor drafting represent only one component of the manuscript policy calculus. Reaching agreement on a manuscript form is demanding for all involved, so it is typically available only to policyholders who pay high enough premiums to entice insurers to engage in a process that will, in all likelihood, expose the insurer to a broader (and potentially uncertain) set of risks. So the threshold question in manuscripting—beyond the obvious desire of the insured for the broadest possible coverage—is whether to pursue such coverage at all. Before even addressing questions about word choice, the parties must consider a host of other factors, which we now introduce.

Ten Important Considerations in Manuscripting Coverage

Parties who draft manuscript policies do so to tailor coverage for a particular set of risks. Like any other policy, a manuscript policy transfers risk from the policyholder to the insurer in exchange for a premium, and the policy is defined by its terms. Manuscript policies, however, also involve the parties in issues that may not arise in the context of standard and company form policies. It is beyond the scope of this book to identify every possible issue that could arise or to identify all of the ways in which parties could manuscript coverage for property and business interruption risks. So we summarize the fundamental considerations surrounding such policies. There are at least ten such considerations in manuscripting business interruption coverage:

1.   Availability of Manuscript Policies

Manuscript coverage is generally broader than standard or company form coverage. By its very nature, a manuscript policy may contain terms that are untested by litigation or unproven by long-term or widespread usage. Such terms therefore are uncertain in scope. Underwriting for these policies is time-consuming and labor-intensive.

As a practical matter, then, manuscript policies generally are only available to certain policyholders under certain market conditions. Most insurers will not even consider issuing such coverage unless the premium is large enough to justify the complexities and effort involved in underwriting and negotiating a form that, in all likelihood, will provide materially broader coverage than standard and company forms. Some insurers will not provide it at all.

These are simply the realities of the insurance industry marketplace. Indeed, one widely used online insurance glossary defines a manuscript policy as "[a]n insurance policy designed or tailored for a *large commercial insured*; a unique coverage written at the request of a broker or a risk manager." (Emphasis added.)[1] Even for the largest policyholders, manuscript coverage can be difficult to acquire, depending on the financial condition of the insurance industry. An unhealthy insurance industry may yield a hard insurance market, in which insurers are extremely reluctant to even entertain a discussion about manuscript coverage (except, perhaps, to say "No"). Conversely, a healthy insurance industry can mean a soft market, in which insurers are more likely to issue coverage and may even appear eager to do so (See the BI Policy Language comparison chart that follows). Finally, insurers may be reluctant to issue coverage on a manuscript basis with respect to particular risks, regardless of the premium or nature of the market.

Hard and soft are simply colloquial descriptions of the financial condition of the broad insurance industry or a segment of it. In a hard market, premiums are higher, coverage is more restrictive, and insurers are generally disinclined to issue coverage on a manuscript basis. A large earthquake, for example, could result in a hard market for earthquake coverage. A hard insurance market is a sellers' market, where the capacity of the insurance industry to accept risk has diminished in real terms, as may happen when capital is depleted after large losses are incurred, or in strategic terms, when capacity is restricted to only those risks perceived to be the most profitable. The hard market of 2001-2004, closely timed to the tragic events of 9-11, generated hundreds of billions of dollars of additional premiums across virtually all lines. Yet despite this obvious leveraging of capacity (some would argue that 9-11 actually created additional capacity when several new insurers were incorporated to take advantage of increasing prices), the insurance industry's loss estimate has remained a static $40 billion, dwarfing the additional premium collections.

It is often very difficult to obtain coverage on a manuscript basis in a hard market because, even with standard forms, higher deductibles and increased waiting periods are common; new limitations on coverage are issued frequently; and the availability of reinsurance decreases, which in turn further constrains the amount of insurance available. Insurers are likely to be conservative and relatively risk-adverse, and policyholders may have difficulty obtaining *any* insurance, let alone enough. This was certainly the case after 9-11, as manuscript policies all but disappeared from the commercial marketplace.

A soft insurance market is a buyers' market, as competition for policyholders increases. Premiums and deductibles fall, coverage is broader, and insurers may be quite willing to provide coverage on a manuscript basis. In a soft market, insurers are far more willing to write innovative coverage for new classes of risk or issue broader coverage on a manuscript basis.

The financial condition of the insurance marketplace provides a basic measure for evaluating the likelihood of obtaining manuscript coverage. It is not necessarily dispositive, however. Even in extremely hard markets, it may be possible to obtain coverage on a manuscript basis—for a high enough premium. Moreover, policyholders can take steps to help insurers understand their potential exposure under a manuscript form. Many policyholders retain experts, such as forensic accountants, to analyze and report on their exposures and give the underwriters some comfort regarding the risks that would be covered under the proposed manuscript form. In a hard market, demonstrating to the insurer that the manuscript form under consideration will not subject them to unusual or extreme risk is often an effective way to overcome an insurer's reluctance to proceed. Finally, insurers may be more willing to provide such coverage when the potential exposure is spread among many insurers, such as in a layered program with multiple insurers assuming relatively small shares of the aggregate policy limits or when the policyholder assumes substantial risk through self-insured retentions or deductibles. However, with each layer comes the prospect of objection to one or more proposed wordings, with the possible effect of an individual underwriter having veto power when terms depart from the standard form.

Of course, markets for all types of insurance are cyclical, subject to macroeconomic pressures and isolated circumstances. The best source of information on market conditions for business interruption insurance or manuscripted forms to address specific coverage areas is an insurance professional, such as an insurance broker.

2.   Difficulties in Drafting—and Agreeing—on Terms

In a perfect world, insurance is the perfect risk management strategy. In theory, an insurer and its policyholder could agree on an almost infinite variety of policy wordings, limited only by their imagination, public policy, and applicable laws restricting the scope of insurance agreements. In theory, there is no reason why an insurer could not agree to cover "all business interruption losses no matter how caused," with no limitation on such coverage. Practically, of course, it is highly unlikely that any clear-thinking insurer would agree to provide such coverage unless the premiums paid could also be proven perfect—a calculation beyond the scope of even the most sophisticated actuarial models.

As a practical matter, most insurers are hesitant to agree on wording that deviates substantially from standard or company form wording or to provide coverage that is dramatically broader than that provided by standard or company forms. There are two overarching reasons for this.

First, the hesitancy of insurers is prompted by their own reinsurance policies—policies they procure to offset part or all of the risk they will insure under a policy written directly for certain risks, such as property damage and business interruption. Therefore, insurers are often parties to reinsurance contracts that cover specifically delineated risks, while excluding others. It follows logically that it can be difficult to persuade an insurer to directly insure risks excluded under their own reinsurance contract. Put differently, to the extent that the policyholder would like to include new or broadened coverage in the manuscript form, the insurer will more likely accept such coverage if the coverage provided is in turn covered by their reinsurance contracts.

Second, insurers underwrite risks based on policy wordings, the policyholder's potential exposures, and the expected scope of coverage for such exposures. Standard and company form policies are issued to many policyholders over a broad geographic area, sometimes over many years. Correspondingly, standard and company forms are more likely than manuscript policies to have been subject to the degree of litigation and/or usage that provides both the underwriter and policyholder with some degree of certainty in determining the circumstances under which the insurance policy will respond to losses or liabilities. In short, like the law, insurance policies have a background of precedents and cases that provide a useful and reliable guide on how coverages will be interpreted—even if no dispute should ever occur. New and untested language may be far less certain in potential scope and application—precisely because it has been issued only to a single policyholder and lacks the legal precedent or usage to provide a reliable interpretive frame. Put differently, *a policy with untested wording does not necessarily put the insurer's assets at unreasonable risk, but it does make the underwriter's judgment of such risk more difficult and possibly more tenuous.*

Manuscript forms, then, do not often stray far from the wordings and provisions found in standard and company form policies. To illustrate this, one need look no further than a straightforward comparison of wordings found in standard forms, company forms, and a broker manuscript form concerning fifteen key provisions bearing on business interruption losses arising from loss of, or physical damage to, real or personal property. As you can see, the broker manuscript policy used in this example provided coverage that was arguably broader than the standard and company forms used in the comparison, but many of the selected provisions were no broader than the analogous standard and/or company form provision. This is not surprising. The further one moves from the standard or company forms currently used, the more difficult is it to attract insurers to agree to terms.

3.   Get Your Best Minds on the Case

Those with experience in manuscripting generally agree that the most important decision is to use the best available minds in the process, from start to finish. Risk management is a remarkably complex field, and few tasks in risk management are as difficult as drafting and negotiating an insurance policy that addresses the risk management objectives of both the insurer and the policyholder to the greatest extent possible. Listed below are some of the individuals that should be on the roster for a "best minds" team:

Policyholder Risk Manager and Other Employees

Policyholders often designate a risk manager or someone in a similar position as their go-to person on insurance issues. Some have sizeable risk management departments with numerous personnel. Because no one better understands risk management objectives than the company's risk managers, the policyholder should ask one or more people familiar with the facts bearing on those objectives to stay actively involved in the manuscripting process.

Insurance Broker

Insurance brokers can evaluate market conditions, identify insurers that may be willing to issue coverage on a manuscript basis, provide manuscript wording, and participate in the negotiation of the policy. Over time, a broker can develop a substantial understanding of the policyholder's operations and thereby can become an indispensable risk management resource for the policyholder. Many major insurance brokers also have developed broad manuscript forms that provide an excellent starting point in negotiations with insurers.

Insurance Company Underwriters

The underwriter sells the insurer's product, and in that capacity protects the insurer from assuming unreasonable risk. In addition to evaluating the risk and setting the premium, the underwriter will make the key wording decisions for the insurer in the manuscript process.

Insurance Company Claims Persons

An insurance adjuster may be invaluable in the manuscripting process by providing her opinion of the potential scope and application of proposed terms. Even policyholders can benefit from running language by the insurer's claims department.

Forensic Accountants

Any insurance policy is written with an eye to an uncertain future; the true value of customized wording is only realized at the point of claim. Thankfully, underwriters and policyholders can rely on past experiences in conceiving of that possible future, and claim preparation specialists such as forensic accountants know all too well what works and what doesn't, based on their experience with hundreds of claims in myriad industries and involving a wide cross-section of adjusters, auditors, and other claim experts. Although not necessarily specialists in insurance policy terms and conditions, forensic accountants who know the property and business interruption claims process can provide excellent practical advice when it comes to drafting manuscript policies. Carefully drafted manuscript wording that takes the real world of loss adjustment into account will give added comfort that the individual needs of a specific account are thoroughly addressed.

Lawyers

In-house and outside counsel with insurance coverage expertise perform a vital role in advising the policyholder regarding the potential meaning and application of terminology used in the manuscript policy, assisting with drafting, and participating in negotiations. Because of their familiarity with where disputes can arise, their knowledge of what factors can predispose insurers to favor a claim, and their knowledge of insurance contract law and policy provisions governing different types of claims, outside counsel are often indispensable in the successful completion of the manuscripting process.

4.   Understand the Risks—and Craft Language Appropriately

The presumption of manuscripting is that the needs of any one policyholder cannot be sufficiently addressed by the standard ISO or company forms. Each policyholder is rightfully presumed different, and the manuscripted insurance contract is customized or tailored to that policyholder's risk management objectives and profile without, as previously noted, unduly exposing the insurer to unwanted risk. Accordingly, the potential benefits and pitfalls of an effort to cover risk through a manuscript policy—to both policyholder and insurer—are unique to every policyholder-insurer relationship. No single manuscript form will fit all policyholders. Policyholder strategies for insuring risk vary widely, and policyholder insurance programs reflect this variability. Some policyholders have varied operations and/or operations located throughout the world. Some programs are multi-layered; some allocate substantial risk to the policyholder through self-insured retentions or deductibles. Some programs carefully allocate related risks among different types of policies (*e.g.*, boiler and machinery, all risk property and business interruption, etc.). Sometimes the policy periods among all policies and all layers of coverage in an insurance program will concur; at other times, they will not. In short, different policyholders face different exposures, both in substance and in magnitude. A manuscript policy is attractive for precisely that reason, as it can be designed to address a specific policyholder's risk profile and coverage needs. But a poorly conceived, drafted, or negotiated form can leave a policyholder with less desirable terms than those provided by standard or company forms, or it could leave the insurer with exposure beyond its wildest expectations. Not only can unclear or poorly qualified language create potential exposures on either side, but an incomplete understanding of risk management objectives can have disastrous consequences for either party.

Simply put, in an insurance policy, every word counts, and the smallest words can have the largest consequences. Consider the potential scope of coverage for business interruption losses arising from interrupted utility services in the following three (purely) hypothetical manuscript policy contexts:

Example 1.   *Policy covers business interruption loss arising from "damage to or destruction of property of any utility company within a five-mile radius of the Insured Property."* This wording would provide narrowly circumscribed coverage for loss arising from impairment to utility company property. However, if lightning were to strike a utility company six miles from the insured's property, no coverage would exist for business interruption losses arising from the event. Moreover, the "property damage" requirement further limits the coverage; if a utility employee were to cut power by inadvertently flipping the wrong switch at the substation, that simple flip of the switch would not provide a basis for seeking coverage for any losses arising from the cessation of power.

Example 2.   *Policy covers business interruption loss arising from "damage to or destruction of property of any utility company."* This wording does not provide a geographic limitation – that is, a lightning strike to a utility substation located on the other side of the planet could trigger coverage if the policyholder's business interruption losses can be attributed to that event. The requirement for property damage, however, still limits the coverage.

Example 3.   *Policy covers, without any qualification, business interruption loss arising from "impairment to any utility company activities."* This wording would provide business interruption coverage even in the absence of property damage to the affected utility, wherever the utility is located, and regardless of the nature of the utility problem. In this case, an inadvertent flip of a switch could by itself provide a basis for seeking coverage for any resulting business interruption losses. Such wording, while clearly favorable to the insured, would potentially put the insurer's resources at the mercy of the most benign and predictable utility impairments.

The previous comparison underscores the most salient point about manuscripting: the wording truly matters. Not one of these three formulations of utility service interruption coverage contains even twenty words. Yet they differ drastically in breadth, and agreement on any one of these formulations would have potentially critical consequences for coverage. An insurer that does not wish to subject its capacity to boundless exposure for impairment to utility operations should not carelessly agree to provide such coverage. Otherwise, a mere flip of the switch or even inclement weather could trigger an insurable business interruption loss. A policyholder whose business depends upon power delivered from utility operations six miles from its insured property cannot casually agree to a five-mile restriction. Otherwise, the policyholder will be without business interruption coverage if an otherwise covered catastrophic event knocks out the power facility and brings its operations to a halt.

5.   Use Standard or Negotiated Endorsements

Policyholders may find that they can as easily and expeditiously achieve their coverage goals by using standard or negotiated endorsements, rather than resorting to manuscripting an entire policy. An endorsement is a form attached to an insurance policy that alters the policy's coverage, terms, or conditions, and insurers are accustomed to using them to alter standard and company forms. Indeed, insurers and brokers generally have a number of standard form endorsements on hand, which they will use to customize policies to fit a particular policyholder. In the business interruption context, such endorsements include Extended Period of Indemnity, Ingress/Egress, Ordinary Payroll Included, Dependent Properties, Contingent Business Interruption, Attraction Properties, Consequential Damage, Interdependencies, Leasehold Interest, Service Interruption/Off-Premises Power, Extra Expense, and Rental Income.

Endorsements also may be manuscripted for a particular policyholder. For at least two reasons, insurers may be far more amenable to customizing a policy using endorsements than seeking to create a completely manuscripted policy. First, insurers are already comfortable with the use of endorsements. Second, altering coverage through an endorsement makes it easier for the insurer to gauge precisely how the coverage contrasts with a standard or company form.

6.   Expect to Spend Time When Manuscripting

It takes time to manuscript a satisfactory policy; it is generally not consummated overnight. Commonly, when a large commercial policyholder with complex operations needs high-limits policies that require participation by numerous insurers, the manuscripting process can take the better part of a year. A policyholder is well advised to start the process early. Moreover, given the enormous expenditure of time and labor often associated with manuscripting a policy, their best first step is usually to determine if a manuscript policy is even a realistic option, given the state of the insurance market and the size of the policyholder.

7.   Prepare to Handle Complex Claims

The overwhelming preponderance of standard and company forms predicts that many insurance adjusters are more familiar and comfortable with the language in those forms, and the terms within such forms already have a legacy of interpretation that can inform decision making once a claim is made. On the other hand, claims handling under a manuscript form can be far more challenging. Manuscript policy terms can be broader or otherwise materially different than standard or company form terms. Occasionally, this can result in claims decisions that seem at odds with the manuscripted policy language, as claims handlers may be predisposed to make decisions as if standard or company form terms were being used, especially if—as can be the case quite often—the claims handler does not carefully read the manuscript form when a claim is made. Another typical result of a claim may be a lack of decisiveness on the part of the claims handler—simply due to the novelty of the policy terms and the lack of clear precedent on the scope and application of terms. The obvious consequences can be delays in the claims process. In either event, the policyholder who is making a claim for coverage under a manuscript form—especially where that coverage typically would not be available under a standard and/or company form–should be aggressive in determining if the insurer is proceeding on the mistaken assumption that the terms are not as broad as they in fact are.

8.   Be Wary of a Lack of Uniformity

Manuscripting may yield a lack of uniformity in coverage. Many large commercial policyholders spread risk among numerous insurers in multi-layered programs, and sometimes a policyholder will not get every insurer to agree to the same manuscript wording or cannot obtain sufficient policy limits on a manuscript basis. In either context, a decision to go forward with a manuscript policy might entail variation among insurance policies in the program on any number of terms. Inevitably this leads to differences or gaps in coverage. This is not necessarily unusual or even something that should be avoided. Even multi-layered programs based on standard and company forms may contain some variability because different insurers use different forms, certain policies contain endorsements that other policies do not, and for other possible reasons. Moreover, from the policyholder's perspective, it is still better to have at least some policies that provide broader coverage than that which is available through standard or company form policies, even if not all the policies are identical and even if some of the policies are not manuscripted at all. Variability among policies, however, can definitely add complexity to the claims and dispute resolution process.

9.   Legacy of Interpretation Is Scant—and Dangerous

It can fairly be said that choosing a manuscripted policy to insure against risks the business faces nevertheless can involve the policyholder and the insurer in business conflict—itself a potential risk. As noted earlier in this chapter many key terms and provisions in standard forms—and to a lesser extent, in company forms—have a history that provides a benchmark for interpreting them. That history may be developed through broadly applicable statements about the meaning and application of policy terms (delivered, for example, through judicial opinions that serve as legal precedent or by insurance industry statements about the intended meaning of policy terms), or through a custom and practice between the parties.

On the other hand, manuscript terms may have no legacy of interpretation, which may in turn lead to uncertainty and engage insurer and insured in disputes. There is no history to guide the parties. Thus, the meaning and scope of a manuscripted policy may be relatively uncertain, making disputes more likely and their outcome less predictable. It bears emphasis that, even in the manuscript context, no amount of extraordinary care or effort by policyholders or insurers will eliminate every ambiguity and uncertainty. Thus, there is an inherent risk, for both sides, that always has to be recognized and accepted. No one can ever anticipate all the scenarios that may develop, and indeed in the real world the amount of time and attention given even to manuscripted language will be relatively small (even if it doesn't seem that way to the individuals involved in the process). When drafting the language, the parties will be thinking about one particular set of issues, but five years later an entirely different context will be the issue. Added to that, the individuals involved may change—the people who drafted the language may be gone, and even though they will have had some understanding about why they drafted the language a particular way, that understanding will be long lost later. Policyholders who do not wish to live with potential ambiguity in the policy language can take certain steps to minimize the likelihood of misunderstandings down the road. For example, they can ask the insurer for a written statement regarding the scope and application of a particular policy term, and insurers occasionally will provide it. Policyholders also may consider documenting the manuscripting and negotiation process and providing such documents to the insurer to create a contemporaneous record that supports the policyholder's understanding of the meaning of the policy terms. Such a record might some day prevent a dispute from evolving.

It is worth noting that ambiguity in policy language often inures to the policyholder's benefit. In the United States, for example, certain rules of construction generally favorable to the policyholder have been developed. These rules of construction (which may differ to some degree from state-to-state) generally include some variation of the following:

- Unambiguous policy language must be applied as written; that is, the plain and ordinary meaning of policy terms must be enforced; policy language must be read in its plain and easily understood sense; technical and strained interpretations must be avoided; a court may not find ambiguity where none exists; and courts are not allowed to rewrite plain and unambiguous policy language under the guise of interpretation.

- Exclusionary or limiting language must be strictly and narrowly construed against the insurer, and courts may not read into a policy any limitations on coverage that are not clearly embodied in the policy terms. In other words, if an insurer wishes to impose a specific limitation on coverage, it must use specific words to do so.

- Ambiguities are construed against the insurer; thus, if there are two reasonable constructions of the policy language, the policyholder's interpretation must prevail. This doctrine is often referred to as the *contra proferentem* doctrine, and the existence of this doctrine explains why it generally is unavailing for an insurer to allege that policy language is ambiguous.

- The policyholder's objectively reasonable expectations of coverage must be honored. This reasonable expectations doctrine can be a complicated concept. In some jurisdictions, the reasonable expectations doctrine can be used to defeat language that otherwise would seem to unambiguously exclude coverage. In other jurisdictions, courts use this concept as an adjunct to the *contra proferentem* doctrine—that is, when there are two reasonable constructions, the policyholder's reasonable construction will prevail. Courts often use this doctrine as a principle of equity rather than as a rule of construction, as a way of ensuring that the policyholder receives the coverage that it believed it purchased.

These rules make insurance disputes quite unlike other contract disputes. They infuse some degree of predictability into the dispute resolution process by, for example, supplying tiebreakers in the event of competing reasonable interpretations of policy language. The rationale for such rules is sometimes (but not always) stated to be that insurers who are experts in drafting policy terms generally issue policies on a take-it-or-leave-it basis. Put differently, the argument goes, insurers generally control the policy language and know full well how to draft policy language in order to unambiguously limit the insured risks. The burden for failing to employ clearer language, or to expressly exclude coverage for risks that the insurer does not want to cover, should fall to the insurer rather than to its policyholder.

Because the rules of construction appear to favor interpretation in favor of policyholders, it is worth noting that manuscript forms—exactly because they are crafted between two parties with a shared interest in the outcome of the manuscripting process—can complicate things. Insurers do indeed sometimes argue that pro-policyholder rules of construction developed to assist in resolving insurance disputes (in particular, the *contra proferentem* doctrine) should have no application with respect to specific policy terms drafted by the policyholder or jointly negotiated. Such an argument will not resonate with many courts, but policyholders cannot entirely discount the potential risk that a court will not apply certain pro-policyholder rules of construction to jointly drafted and negotiated policy terms. This risk, in theory, should not extend beyond terms jointly negotiated; and, insurers and policyholders will sometimes agree on terms that make explicit the applicability or nonapplicability of pro-policyholder rules of construction in the context of a manuscript policy.

10.   Don't Forego Routine Maintenance

For many policyholders and insurers, a manuscript policy is a living document that must be revised to reflect claims experience, new exposures, changes in corporate organization, changes in the law, and the like. It is not unusual for a manuscript form to evolve over a period of many years. As in the case with any yearly renewal of a contract, manuscript policies must be subjected to a stringent level of scrutiny by insurer and policyholder alike to ensure that wording changes are made to fit changes in circumstances.

Conclusion

The principal risk associated with manuscripting is self-evident. If a manuscript policy is not carefully planned, researched, and painstakingly drafted to reflect considerations that affect both parties, the end-product could not only fall short of providing the coverages desired in the first place, but it could even allow for undesirable or even catastrophic financial consequences from the perspective of one or both of the parties. Attention to detail and the involvement of the right people will allow both insurer and policyholder to avoid unwelcome surprises in the event of a business interruption loss (or any loss, for that matter) and to reduce to the extent possible ambiguity in the policy terms. Moreover, skillful drafting and negotiation can result in an insurance product quite unlike anything generally available in the marketplace—yet one that fully reflects the exchange that the parties bargained for without inadvertently subjecting one or both parties to potentially calamitous financial risks.

Endnotes

[1]*Rupp's Insurance & Risk Management Glossary* (Chatsworth: NILS Publishing, 2002). View online at http://insurance.cch.com/rupps/manuscript-policy.htm).

Figure 3.1: Business Interruption Policy Language Comparison Chart

Business Interruption Policy Language Comparison Chart

	ISO Form	HPR Form	Brokerage Manuscript
Coverage Trigger	Necessary suspension of operations caused by direct physical loss or damage to property at the premises described in the declarations	Necessary interruption of business caused by physical damage of the type insured to real or personal property of the type covered located at the described premises	Necessary interruption of business caused by loss, damage or destruction by perils insured against to real and personal property
Loss Insured	Actual loss of business income consisting of net income and continuing normal operating expenses	Actual loss sustained of gross earnings or of net profit and expenses that necessarily continue	Actual loss sustained of gross earnings or of net profit and expenses that necessarily continue
Period of Interruption	Begins seventy-two hours after loss and ends when damaged property could be repaired with reasonable speed and similar quality	Begins at time of loss and ends when damaged property could be repaired or replaced using due diligence and dispatch	Begins at time of loss and ends when damaged property could be repaired using due diligence and dispatch
Extended Period of Indemnity (EPI)	Begins when damaged property is repaired and ends the earlier of when operations are restored or thirty days (or selected time)	Begins when damaged property is repaired or liability otherwise ceases and ends the earlier of when operations are restored or thirty days (or selected time)	Begins when damaged property is repaired or liability otherwise ceases and ends the earlier of when operations are restored or one year (or selected time)
EPI Exception	No coverage for losses incurred as a result of unfavorable business conditions caused by the impact of the covered loss	None	None
Extra Expense	Necessary expenses incurred during the period of restoration that would not have incurred if there was no physical loss or damage to property	Reasonable and necessary expenses incurred during a period of restoration to temporarily continue as nearly normal as practicable the conduct of the business	Excess of the total cost during the period of restoration of the damaged property over and above the total cost that would have been incurred had no loss occurred
Rental Value	Actual loss of total anticipated rental income from tenant occupancy, tenant charges and fair value of insured's occupied premises.	Actual loss sustained of fair rental value of property occupied by the insured, income expected from rentals of unoccupied space and rental income from rented portions, less noncontinuing expenses	Reduction in rental value less charges and expenses that do not necessarily continue during the period of untenantability
Leasehold Interest	Net present value of rent differential plus unamortized lease acquisition costs, improvements and betterments, and prepaid rent	Actual rent payable for the unexpired term of the lease or lease interest for the unexpired term of the lease	Pro rata proportion of the insured's interest in bonuses or lease acquisition costs, improvements and betterments to real property, and advance rental payments

Civil Authority	Loss incurred after seventy-two hours and limited to three consecutive weeks when action of civil authority prohibits access to described premises due to direct physical loss or damage to property caused by a covered cause of loss	Loss incurred, not to exceed two consecutive weeks, when as a direct result of damage of the type insured against, access to described premises is specifically prohibited by order of civil authority	Loss sustained when access to real or personal property is impaired by order of civil or military authority following or in connection with a peril insured against
Ingress/Egress	None	By endorsement; actual loss sustained when access to insured locations is prevented due to loss or damage of the type insured against	Loss sustained when access to real or personal property is impaired following or in connection with a peril insured against
Contingent Business Interruption	By endorsement; actual loss of business income due to necessary suspension of operations during period of restoration when suspension is caused by direct physical loss of or damage to dependent property at a premises described in the declarations	Actual loss sustained during a period of interruption directly resulting from physical loss or damage of the type insured against to property of the type not otherwise excluded at direct supplier or customer locations	Loss resulting from damage to or destruction by the perils insured against of property that directly or indirectly prevents a supplier of goods and services, or property that prevents a receiver of goods and services from accepting the insured's goods and services
Service Interruption	By endorsement; loss of business income or extra expense at the described premises caused by interruption of service caused by direct physical damage by a covered cause of loss to specific types of utility services property	Loss resulting from physical damage of the type insured against to electrical transmission lines and other electrical equipment and steam and gas transmission lines outside the premises but within one thousand feet thereof when used exclusively by the insured	Loss resulting from the interruption of electricity steam, gas, water, sewer, telecommunications or any other utility or service resulting from damage to or destruction caused by an insured peril that prevents in whole or in part the delivery of such utilities
Consequential/Remote Loss Exclusion	Increase of loss caused by or resulting from suspension, lapse, or cancellation of license, lease or contract, unless suspension is directly caused by the suspension of operations, then coverage is provided for loss incurred during period of restoration	Increase of loss resulting from the suspension, lapse or cancellation of any license, lease, contract or order unless such suspension results directly from the interruption of business, then there shall be liability for only such loss as affects the insured's earnings during the period of indemnity	Increase of loss occasioned by the suspension, lapse or cancellation of any lease, license, contract or order except with respect to loss directly resulting from the interruption of business as affects earnings during the period of interruption

Published in the February 2002 edition of *Risk Management Magazine* . Compiled by John D. Dempsey and Lee M. Epstein.

Before a Loss

Establishing Business Interruption Limits

Even risk managers with a thorough understanding of business interruption insurance have difficulty with the question: "How much business interruption coverage does my company need?" In answering this question, the potential policyholder needs to differentiate between business interruption limits, that is, the amount of business interruption insurance coverage purchased by a company, and business interruption values, which is the estimate of the total financial impact that a certain product, plant, division, or operating unit could be faced with in the event of a property damage loss over a set period of time. Determining what those limits should be deserves a closer look, and this chapter offers that look—illustrating the concepts and calculations of limit and value using examples from Fortune 500 companies. We draw on examples chiefly from larger manufacturing companies, but the techniques and conclusions apply equally to companies in nonmanufacturing sectors and to smaller, less complex companies. As a practical matter, businesses may be unable to devote the resources needed to follow the procedure that we map out in its entirety. However, companies of all sizes may review the information with the goal of developing processes that will lead to coverage limits that offer appropriate protection.

Why Set Limits?

Setting limits is an important step in securing coverage. While it's tempting to think, "The more business interruption insurance, the better," such thinking is usually inaccurate. Setting limits greater than the company needs may actually amount to wasting corporate assets, insofar as the company is spending money on unnecessary premiums. Such assets could likely be deployed in better ways, including on insurance premiums for other legitimate risk exposures. Certainly it is prudent to ensure a safety net or cushion in insurance coverage—that is, assuring the company an added amount of coverage over and above any actual analysis or calculation derived from its business interruption value analysis. Indeed, most companies do exactly this.

Of course, setting business interruption limits lower than the amount of insurance required can present even greater problems, not the least of which is exposure to the risk of suffering an underinsured loss. For most risk managers, that possibility is a nightmare. And it needs to be said that even if a company has blanket property limits that end up being adequate for a loss incident, problems can still exist. Blanket limits may mean that there are no *sublimits* for direct property damage versus business interruption, or even no sublimits within certain time element exposures such as extra expense or civil authority. As long as the loss is under the limit, the loss will be paid. But even in such circumstances, if a policyholder reports inadequate business interruption values for a particular location, the result can be significant mistrust from the insurance carrier, as well as likely delays in reaching settlement on a loss and difficulties in renewing the policy.

Effect of Limits on Premiums

Although business interruption limits affect policy premiums, the impact of those limits generally varies with the size of the program; the smaller the program, the greater the impact of the limits on premiums. In many jurisdictions, calculating policy premiums for business interruption coverage for small companies purchasing a standard business owner's policy is set by statute, just as for homeowner's insurance. Therefore, the amount of business interruption limits matters in absolute terms in determining policy premiums.

Typically, for small companies, business interruption limits do equal business interruption values. These can be determined by using a business income work sheet, using a certain percentage as a coinsurance multiplier—usually 70, 80, or 90 percent. For large companies, however, the underwriting process, including the determination of premiums, becomes more an art than a science. Along with business interruption limits, several other factors play a role in the determination of policy premiums, including:

- Loss history

- Policy endorsements

- Retention and/or deductible levels

- Risk classification (e.g., office buildings vs. chemical plants)

- Premium history

- Competitive nature of insurance marketplace

- Stock market and other common investment vehicles

- Capacity of cedents and reinsurers

The final policy premium often results from a negotiation based on the factors above.

Determining Business Interruption Limits: The Traditional Approach

Small, less complex companies typically determine business interruption limits by using a business income work sheet. The current ISO work sheet is discussed at the end of this chapter. (For an example of the ISO Business Income Work Sheet, see Exhibit 4.1). Large companies are more likely to examine possible scenarios for losses, including a comparison of *maximum possible loss* and *maximum probable loss*,[1] and then are likely to base a decision on that scenario planning. Given the limitations of the business income work sheet, we recommend the latter, more analytical approach, described in detail in this chapter. First, though, we'd like to explain why we discount the business income work sheet for complex or larger businesses.

The Business Income Work Sheet—and Its Limitations

Advising clients on the completion of the business income work sheet continues to be a challenge for professionals in the insurance industry. Properly preparing it typically requires specific knowledge of insurance coverage as well as accounting policies and procedures. Although this chapter provides a general overview of the business income work sheet at the end, further review should be given to the policy governing coverage to ensure that the work sheet is completed accurately.

The business income work sheet may help small, less complex businesses with few locations to assess business interruption values for coinsurance purposes. The method of calculating the values depends on the type of coverage and/or the policy forms used. The two basic forms used to calculate business interruption values are the gross earnings form and the net profits form. For a gross earnings form, values are calculated on a deduction or subtractive basis; for a net profit form, these values are calculated on a build-up or additive basis. Although they contain different definitions of business interruption, both forms are designed to cover lost net profits and to pay for continuing expenses during an interruption of business.

Despite the different approaches to determining values, each should end with the same mathematical result.

The business income work sheet is a tool for the insured to assess its business interruption values when determining necessary coverage. The work sheet begins by establishing guidelines by which the form should be completed; and it requires that the calculations be performed on an accrual basis—which means that income and expenses should be accounted for in the period that they are incurred rather than when cash actually changes hands. Generally, the form will also require that all calculations be performed with generally accepted accounting principles (GAAP), to ensure that the individual reading the work sheet is operating under the same rules and assumptions as the individual preparing it. Finally, the work sheet typically requires that the user indicate the insured's method of inventory valuation, because beginning and ending inventory significantly affect the results of the work sheet.

Calculating Gross Earnings

To ultimately assess the insured's gross earnings, the business income work sheet begins with a calculation of the insured's historical and expected net revenue on an annual basis. The ISO work sheet is shown as Exhibit 4.1, and step-by-step instructions on completing it are at the end of this chapter. In general, it indicates that net revenue is the sum total of the annual net sales value of production from manufacturing operations and the total annual net sales from nonmanufacturing operations, including merchandising. Net sales is defined as gross sales, less any discounts given, any returns, bad accounts and collection expenses, and/or prepaid freight charges to the extent they are included in gross sales. To round out total revenue, the form requires the insured to include any other earnings derived from normal business operations, such as cash discounts, commissions, and/or rental income. This would typically be other recurring income that is included below net revenue on the insured's income statement.

Gross earnings is then derived by subtracting the following items from total revenue:

- Raw stock from which production is derived: The cost of the raw materials used in the manufacture of the goods sold.

- Materials used to convert raw stock into finished goods: The cost of supplies and materials used to produce manufactured goods, including the cost of services offered by the insured and the cost of goods sold by the insured but not produced by it. (An example would be software purchased from an external developer to be bundled with the sale of hardware.)

- Merchandise sold, including packaging costs.

- Services purchased from outsiders that do not continue under contract: These are costs incurred for services that are outsourced by the insured, such as assembly of parts, that do not continue under contract in the case of a business interruption. Therefore, if the insured's business is temporarily interrupted, this cost will be saved.

The net of total revenue and the expenses discussed previously render the insured's expected gross earnings. The amount of insurance required is assessed as a percentage of gross earnings, depending on the level of coinsurance the insured requires. With the work sheet, the insurance required—that is, the business interruption limits—is determined by multiplying calculated gross earnings by a coinsurance percentage chosen by the policyholder. Therefore, if the policyholder desires a specific business interruption limit, they simply divide this limit by the gross earnings calculation to arrive as the desired coinsurance percentage. So, using the work sheet requires the prior determination of business interruption limits by a different mechanism.[2]

The gross earnings calculation provides manufacturers with an annual total of the sales value of production, less the materials portion of cost of goods sold. It does not consider other potential discontinuing expenses during a business interruption loss. Typical business interruption policies cover the loss measured at gross earnings less other discontinuing expenses. Further, the calculation does not address the length of downtime expected for a company during a loss incident. Because the business income work sheet does not include discontinuing expenses and length of downtime, the gross earnings calculation is constrained in its ability to provide information helpful in setting business interruption limits. The work sheet requires an estimate of coinsurance required to adjust the calculated gross earnings so they equal insurance required.

A common policy provision for small companies, coinsurance is an agreement from the policyholder to maintain insurance in an amount equal to or greater than a percentage of the total insured value. If the policyholder does not do so, it assumes a portion of the cost of each loss. The extent of the insured's participation in the loss is known as the *coinsurance penalty*. The reciprocal of the coinsurance penalty is the *collectible percentage*. The collectible amount of the loss is calculated as follows:

$$\frac{\text{Insurance Carried}}{\text{Insurance Required}} \times \text{Amount of the Loss} = \text{Collectible Amount of Loss}$$

In some cases, the policy may contain endorsements for ordinary payroll. The effect of these endorsements and their inclusion on the business income work sheet is discussed subsequently.

Ordinary Payroll Endorsements

If the insured's policy carries no ordinary payroll endorsement or exclusion, the work sheet instructs the user to calculate the product of expected gross earnings and the percentage indicated by the coinsurance clause to be used (from 50 to 80 percent). However, when payroll endorsements are used to limit coverage for payroll expenses, additional steps are to be taken in completing the form.

> **Ordinary Payroll Exclusion:** The ordinary payroll exclusion would exclude payroll for employees that would not be retained during an extended business interruption. Payroll that typically would not be considered ordinary includes but is not limited to officer and executive salaries, department heads, and employees under contract. Ordinary payroll generally includes the payroll, benefits, FICA, union dues, and worker's compensation premiums for the employees in question; however, it does not include any benefits that would continue under a contract. If the insured's policy includes the ordinary payroll exclusion, the business income work sheet requires that the gross earnings be reduced by the ordinary payroll. The result is then multiplied by the insured's Coinsurance Clause percentage (80% – 100%) to determine the amount of insurance required.
>
> **Ordinary Payroll – Limited Coverage Endorsement:** In some cases, the insured's policy may cover ordinary payroll for a limited period of time during the interruption period (90 to 180 days). If this is the case, then the Business Income Work Wheet calls for the preparer to reduce gross earnings by ordinary payroll and then add back the largest amount of ordinary payroll expense incurred in the specified consecutive number of days. For example, if the insured's policy contains a 90-day ordinary payroll endorsement, the insured should determine in what 90-day period in the last twelve months it incurred the highest payroll expense; this amount should then be added back to gross earnings, less ordinary payroll as calculated above, to determine the basis on which to assess the insurance required.

Calculating a business interruption claim is usually more complex than the calculation above. Assessing the insured's required amount of insurance using the work sheet remains, at best, an educated guess. The form clearly does not take into account the full amount of expense that could discontinue during a business interruption. Admittedly, assessing what specific expenses would or would not continue during a business interruption period is an inexact exercise; but the work sheet may lead the insured to buy more coverage than is needed. Many see this omission of other expenses from the work sheet as providing a necessary cushion in the amount of business interruption coverage that a policyholder carries. However, a more comprehensive and thorough approach to assessing needed coverage is needed, especially when dealing with complex businesses.

The conclusion is clear. Companies (especially large ones) should not prepare business income work sheets unless they have a coinsurance provision in their policies. Further, the work sheet should be used only for coinsurance purposes, not as the sole method of determining business interruption limits. So, the question of how to adequately determine those limits remains. For large, complex companies, the answer lies in a comprehensive approach focused on a product-line basis.

Setting Limits

When determining the business interruption exposure for a large company, a risk manager faces a challenge that requires expertise in business interruption insurance and accounting, along with detailed knowledge of the company's operations. The complexity is easy to imagine. For example, in a manufacturing company, the risk manager would need to solicit input from various functions in the company, including purchasing, logistics, plant planning and management, engineering, marketing and sales, accounting and finance, and legal. The risk manager also must understand the variety of available business interruption policy endorsements (see Chapter 2). The sidebar at left gives brief definitions of some of the key endorsements discussed in that chapter.

A key variable that plays into the calculation of business interruption limits is the location of the company's property. For manufacturers, core locations include plants, warehouses, and distribution centers; for nonmanufacturing companies, locations might include warehouses, retail outlets, and office space. Many manufacturers have interdependent production facilities, which rely on each other for complementary parts and processes. Figure 4.1 illustrates an example of

Key Business Interruption Endorsements

Contingent Business Interruption—Coverage for losses resulting from damage to suppliers or customers.

Service Interruption—Coverage for losses incurred due to the interruption of utility service resulting from physical damage to the property that supplies the utility.

Civil Authority—Business interruption and extra expenses losses caused when access to property is prohibited by order of a civil or military authority.

Ingress/Egress—Coverage when access to a property is impeded but without the need for an order that restricts access to property. (Similar to civil authority).

Ordinary Payroll—Coverage for entire payroll for the insured except for executives, managers, other salaried employees and other important employees (essentially payroll for hourly personnel).

Extended Period of Indemnity—Coverage for business interruption and EE losses from the end of the period of restoration for a specified time period, typically ranging from thirty days to two years.

an automobile parts manufacturer with three interdependent plants that together make rack-and-pinion steering systems. Although the three plants are distinct properties, hundreds of miles apart, each depends on the other so the company can produce a saleable product. Any of the plants suffering a loss would significantly affect the operations of the others. Therefore, for the purposes of determining business interruption limits, this manufacturer should consider the three plants as one location.

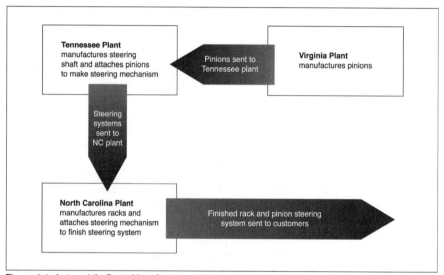

Figure 4.1: Automobile Parts Manufacturer with Interdependent Plants

We have developed four steps to evaluate business interruption exposures:

Step 1   Determine the Products and Locations to Assess

Step 2   Determine Length of Potential Downtime

Step 3   Determine Limits for Each Product Line

Step 4   Consider Limits by Product and Company Specific Attributes to Determine Total Company Limits

Step 1: Determine Products and Locations to Assess

Most large manufacturing companies produce many different product lines at numerous locations worldwide. Assessing business interruption limits for every production facility would be impractical. Rather, the risk manager should hinge the limit on products; as in Figure 4.1, multiple plants making one product are considered one location; therefore, the product line is the more important dimension. Of course, this raises the question: Which products are most profitable? In this case—barring readily available detail on profit by product line—one might safely assume that the 80/20 rule applies, and that 20 percent of a company's product lines generates 80 percent of its gross profit. Assessing coverage limits should focus on these most profitable product lines.

Working backward through the production process, the risk manager identifies potential causes of business interruption losses. The first step is a detailed map of each product's supply chain, that is, the network of companies and/or facilities that work together to procure materials, process those materials into finished goods, and distribute these finished goods to customers. Prepared with the help of purchasing, planning, and logistics, this map should include all relevant suppliers and locations, with a special emphasis on potential bottlenecks. A bottleneck occurs when the results of several stages and/or processes come together and flow through a single point. Not surprisingly, this point of intersection constrains the production process on the best of days; any damage at a bottleneck point can be devastating. In looking for bottlenecks, the risk manager must recognize that they can occur internally and externally.

Step 2: Determining Length of Potential Downtime

For the purposes of this discussion, downtime represents the period of restoration after a property loss. "Period of restoration" means the time that extends from the date of loss until repairs should be completed with due diligence and dispatch. However, as with any term used in these policies, the definition can vary by policy. As always, a company's management should read its policy and understand its terms. Companies are faced with almost as many issues affecting downtime after an incident as there are incidents themselves. To assess business interruption limits, the risk manager must focus on the loss incidents that could cause the longest downtimes at the relevant locations and the likelihood of those loss incidents.

Supplier Bottlenecks

The company's purchasing department provides expertise in finding supplier bottlenecks, which is important to assessing potential contingent business interruption losses. Attention must be paid to the percentage of particular materials from each supplier. In the automotive industry, only a few companies provide 100 percent of the vehicle frames for particular models. Should a key supplier incur damage that results in downtime, the automobile manufacturer would also suffer. Obviously, sole supplier agreements increase risk. When no single supplier provides a large percentage of a raw material, the exposure to this type of loss decreases.

Another major issue in determining downtimes in the supply chain is a company's ability to buy substitute materials from alternative suppliers. For example, a sole supplier of a key chemical product for a major consumer products company suffered complete destruction to its single manufacturing plant. As a result, the consumer products company faced an extended downtime for the plants producing many of its most profitable products. However, because purchasing was able to buy the same product from another supplier, most of the loss was mitigated. An up-front understanding of its options can help a company's minimize business interruption.

If the risk manager determines that damage to suppliers could result in significant losses for the company, he must consider buying contingent business interruption coverage that encompasses damages to his suppliers. Take the example of airline carriers: Should a fuel supplier suffer significant damage, the carrier would suffer a loss if an alternate supply were not available. But based on the number and dispersion of its customers, damage to a particular customer would not result in a business interruption loss, and contingent coverage for damage to customers is not practical or necessary.

Damage to Production Facilities

After understanding the company's supply chain, its risk manager turns to production processes. Here, each facility's plant manager and engineers provide invaluable information, since they are well aware of the potential causes of shutdowns. We suggest beginning the discussion by asking these experts to describe their worst potential loss situation—the one that could put them out of business. In such a discussion, the biggest risk will typically surface first.

One possibility for an extended downtime is severe damage to a plant's physical structure. For example, computer chip manufacturers require a clean room environment for production. Any damage to this environment results in a significant period of restoration—usually double that of a period for restoring an ordinary production facility of the same size. Geographical considerations may also cause extended downtime after damage to a factory or distribution center. In some geographical locations, there is a shortage of available construction labor, a problem exacerbated by large-scale disasters. After Hurricane Andrew leveled or severely damaged thousands of industrial and residential properties, policyholders faced considerable problems in overcoming the shortages of both labor and materials, extending many companies' downtimes significantly.

The risk manager must also research potential changes in building codes that might require that buildings be repaired with upgrades, typically in the area of fire protection. Resolving this issue requires two steps. First, the risk manager must factor in a potentially longer period of restoration in determining the maximum possible downtime for the location. Second, she should procure an endorsement to the property policy that covers any increased cost of replacement because of the code upgrades. Although upgrades usually affect older plants, recently constructed plants could also be at risk. During Hurricane Georges in Puerto Rico, a manufacturer of packaging materials for the pharmaceutical industry suffered severe damage at a plant less than four years old. In that four-year span, however, the municipality in which the building was located passed a new building code requiring sprinkler protection for manufacturing plants above a certain size—and the new code applied to this plant. Because the risk manager had considered the change in building code when procuring property and business interruption coverage for the facility, the company was able to rebuild the plant to its former size, while recovering all costs associated with the code upgrades, costs totaling more than $750,000.

Exposure from Damage to Machinery and Equipment

Damage to important machinery also creates the potential for extended downtimes for manufacturing facilities. And machinery can be seriously damaged in a discrete episode not harming the rest of the facility. The acquisition date on the Fixed Asset Schedule provides information useful to determining potential downtime from damage to equipment. With older machinery, the potential exists that it may no longer be made; replacing it would require a special order or a reconfiguration of other parts of the plant. Either scenario results in an extended downtime and greater loss that might be mitigated by purchasing and keeping on hand used spare parts or pieces of equipment that no longer are manufactured.

Any modifications to equipment should also be noted. Damage to already modified equipment may result in longer downtime. New equipment from the vendor would have to be modified—again, a time-consuming process under the best scenario. Given the pressure to mitigate a loss, the difficulties multiply as the down-time increases.

Exposure from Other Potential Causes of Downtime

Along with the downtime caused by damage to buildings and/or equipment, other events can lead to extended downtime for a plant; and the risk manager should discuss these with the plant manager. For example, for facilities that do not provide their own utilities, damage to the supply of power or water could cause significant downtimes. In this case, the risk manager must add the service interruption endorsement to the business interruption policy. Consideration should also be paid to purchasing backup power generation for the plants at greatest risk.

A remote location points to additional exposure. For example, the only access to an upscale resort in Northern California is a two-lane road winding through mountains. When this road was shut down for a month because of an avalanche, the resort was inaccessible when it suffered a loss. Because the risk manager had the foresight to purchase ingress/egress coverage, the company recovered proceeds for that loss.

Ordinary Payroll Considerations

Discussions with plant managers should also cover the need to retain employees through an extended downtime. When presented with the concept of ordinary payroll, the plant manager knows if the plant requires this coverage and for how long. Note that "ordinary" does not mean unimportant. Many production workers are highly trained and experienced employees who play a key role in the plant's success, yet their payroll would be considered to fall within the ordinary category. Losing these employees by not paying them during a downtime could severely hamper the plant's production after repairs are complete. Not only would the plant have to work through production issues after a cold restart of the plant, but it also would have to train new employees not familiar with the production process.

Training and geographic considerations weigh heavily in this decision. Where skilled assistance is harder to hire quickly, exposure to the loss of trained personnel can sharply increase. The damage to a key piece of machinery in an aluminum extrusion plant, the largest employer in a remote part of Pennsylvania, illustrates the importance of these considerations. Because the risk manager had purchased a policy with coverage for ordinary payroll, the company was able to pay employees during the downtime. If the company had lost these employees, they were likely irreplaceable because of the plant's location.

Other Exposures to Facilities Damage

Another job of the risk manager is assessing the adequacy of each plant's disaster plan, which should provide information useful in determining maximum downtimes along with approaches to mitigating losses. Along with obvious recommendations, such as keeping spare parts on hand for difficult-to-replace equipment, a disaster plan may also include creative ideas to reduce downtimes. For example, reciprocal agreements with other companies to use each other's facilities in the event of damage benefit both parties; by continuing production, the damaged company prevents the loss of sales and market share, while the partner company finds a profitable use for excess capacity.

Exposure from Damage to Customers

Damage suffered by key customers results in downtime if no others are available to purchase the finished goods earmarked for the damaged customer. Similar to assessing exposure from damage to suppliers, the customer assessment focuses on the relative percentage of production sold to a particular customer. If a few specific customers purchase a large percentage of a plant's production, then the plant is at risk for a business interruption loss should the customers suffer damage.

In late 2000, the major customer for a manufacturer of audiotapes, accounting for more than 80 percent of the manufacturer's sales, suffered a loss and was unable to take orders. No other customers were available to purchase the tapes at a profitable price. Because the risk manager had correctly assessed the chance of this scenario, the audiotape manufacturer was able to recover its business interruption loss under a contingent business interruption endorsement.

Step 3: Determine Limits for Each Product Line

After determining the product lines to be analyzed (Step 1), the risk manager has the information necessary to begin the process of determining business interruption limits for each product line. Step 3 can begin parallel to Step 2. Finance and accounting personnel serve as company experts for the analysis.

Contribution Margin

Contribution margin, a managerial accounting concept, represents the sales value for a product less costs that vary directly with production. For the purpose of this analysis we consider business interruption limits equal to the company's contribution margin for a particular product line plus any ordinary payroll coverage for the company facilities in the product line's supply chain. In most business interruption scenarios, the contribution margin exceeds the loss due to other saved expenses that do not vary directly with production. However, these other saved expenses are difficult to predict prior to a loss, particularly without knowing the type of incident. Therefore, using contribution margin serves as a practical approach that provides a slight cushion in determining business interruption limits.

Public financial statements are usually too broad for an analysis of limits. On the other hand, management accounting reports (prepared by finance departments) include specific information, including the sales, volume, and the profitability of each product line. Although the information would have to be analyzed, these management reports provide a basis for calculating contribution margin.

Analyzing Potential Sales Losses

Determining business interruption limits is a forward-looking exercise. The risk manager must consider any expected, significant changes in the sales of a product line. The contribution margin for each product line should be calculated by month for a period of two years before the loss. Analyzing the sales totals for this time period allows the risk manager to see the basic trend. After this cursory analysis, the risk manager meets with sales department personnel to discuss each product individually, focusing on the sales outlook for the product line for the coming year. Special consideration should be paid to new product lines or product lines in dynamic fields such as high technology. After meeting with sales department personnel, the risk manager will have projected sales for each product line for the coming twelve months.

Sales personnel can also provide information on whether the product line serves as part of a sales line. For example, a manufacturer and distributor of janitorial supplies provides a line of multiple products. If the company suffers a business interruption loss that prevents it from being able to deliver a particular product, such as floor cleaner, its customers will likely purchase the entire line of cleaning supplies from a competitor. As a result, sales for products produced at unaffected plants also suffer. The risk manager must appreciate this situation in the supply chain mapping in Step 1, which may result in additional locations to assess, as in Step 2.

Other topics to discuss with sales personnel include the capacity to make up lost sales after extended downtime. The uniqueness of the product line makes a difference here. Customers unable to find a reasonable substitute for the product are more likely to wait and buy extra quantities when operations resume, which amounts not to a loss of sales but only a delay in sales. A business interruption loss suffered by a software manufacturer illustrates this point. The company had expected to launch a new line of software, with no comparable competitive products, during the downtime. When production began after repairs were completed, the company partially mitigated the business interruption loss because consumers had waited to purchase the product.

Conversely, when a company cannot provide products to the marketplace, customers often purchase substitutes from competitors. A company selling commodity products often suffers sales losses after the downtime ends. Even after downtime ends, doubts about the company's ability to deliver can linger. As a result, customers do not purchase from the company again until it proves it can produce the product at the same level of quality as before the downtime occurred. In recognition of this situation, the risk manager must add the extended period of indemnity endorsement to the company's business interruption policy for a specified time period.

Analyzing Direct Variable Expenses

To translate monthly sales figures to monthly contribution margin totals for a product line, the company must analyze the product line's variable costs. For the purposes of setting business interruption limits, the analysis focuses on costs that vary directly with production and sales. Because other costs often do not continue during downtime, this conservative approach provides a slight cushion for the limits.

Costs that vary directly with production are found in the "cost of goods sold" section of profit and loss statements. These expenses include direct material costs, direct labor costs, and a portion of the production overhead (further analysis is required to determine this last expense). Finance and accounting personnel typically maintain detailed analyses on these costs that the risk manager can rely on in determining contribution margin per month. Certain costs, such as sales commissions and sales discounts, vary directly with sales dollars. Finance and accounting personnel will have a detailed understanding of these costs. Variable sales costs (compared to variable production costs) represent a much smaller deduction to sales in determining contribution margin.

All variable costs should be calculated as a percentage of gross sales dollars. To calculate monthly variable costs for a product, these percentages are applied to the monthly sales dollar totals. To determine monthly contribution margin for a product, monthly sales dollars are reduced by the calculated monthly variable costs. Figure 4.2 shows the product line of a powerboat manufacturer, representing a summary of this exercise. In this example, the powerboat line generates almost $83 million of contribution margin per year. To determine the business interruption limits for this particular product, the risk manager must consider the maximum potential downtime for the supply chain (step 2), keeping in mind that it could occur at various steps throughout the supply chain for this product.

Seasonal Sales

The risk manager must also factor in a product's seasonal sales. In the powerboat line example, the risk manager determines that the maximum potential downtime equals six months. Based on an average for six months, the contribution margin is $41.5 million. But this would be inadequate business interruption coverage if the six-month business interruption loss period begins in May. The risk manager must determine the contribution margin for the highest consecutive six-month period—in this case $53.6 million for May through October.

Figure 4.2: Calculation of Contribution Margin - Powerboat Line (000's)

	Gross sales	Variable production costs (40% of sales)	Variable sales costs (5% of sales)	Contribution margin
January	$7,500	$3,000	$375	$4,125
February	8,500	3,400	425	4,675
March	9,000	3,600	450	4,950
April	11,500	4,600	575	6,325
May	15,500	6,200	775	8,525
June	16,500	6,600	825	9,075
July	17,500	7,000	875	9,625
August	18,500	7,400	925	10,175
September	17,500	7,000	875	9,625
October	12,000	4,800	600	6,600
November	8,500	3,400	425	4,675
December	8,000	3,200	400	4,400
Total	$150,500	$60,200	$7,525	$82,775
Total for May through October				$53,625

Ordinary Payroll

The risk manager completes the assessment of the business interruption limits for this product line by adding any ordinary payroll coverage at the company
facilities throughout the supply chain for the product line (see Figure 4.3). In this
example, the supply chain for the production of the powerboat line involves components produced at plants in four different cities. Plants in two of the cities,
Huntsville and Savannah, require ordinary payroll coverage, while the plants in
Atlanta and Orlando do not. If a six-month downtime (the maximum possible for
the supply chain) occurs in May through October (the months with the highest
sales), the company would incur almost $2 million dollars in ordinary payroll cov-
erage. The risk manager adds this amount to the almost $54 million in contribu-
tion margin estimated for the same months to calculate required business interruption limits of $56 million for the powerboat line.

Step 4: Limits by Product and Company Specific Attributes

After determining the business interruption limits for key product lines, the
risk manager must combine all the results—a process that typically begins with
meeting high-level finance and accounting personnel to discuss the product-line
business interruption limit calculations and assess their reasonableness. Based on
feedback from this meeting, the risk manager may have to review and revise the
conclusions from Steps 2 and 3 before finalizing the business interruption limits for
the entire company.

Figure 4.3: Calculation of Business Interruption Limit – Powerboat Line (in 000's)

	Atlanta	Ordinary Payroll Estimate Huntsville	Orlando	Savannah	Total
May	-	$150	-	$175	$325
June	-	150	-	175	325
July	-	150	-	175	325
August	-	150	-	175	325
September	-	150	-	175	325
October	-	150	-	175	325
Total	$0	$900	$0	$1,050	1,950
Projected contribution margin for May through October					53,625
Total projected BI Limit					$55,575

Figure 4.4: Comparison of Business Interruption Limits by Product Line (000's)

Product Line	Business Interruption Limit
Business Products	*$700*
Consumer Products	*300*
Electrical Products	*200*
Medical Products	*500*
Pharmaceuticals	*300*
Total	*$2,000*

Finally determining what those limits should be for the whole company begins with a summary of the business interruption limits by product line (see Figure 4.4). This example shows the results of analyzing business interruption limits for a diversified chemical company with product lines in a wide variety of industries. In this instance, the company's five core product lines have business interruption limits totaling $2 billion. Should the risk manager set business interruption limits for the company equal to that of the highest product line ($700 million), the total of all product lines ($2 billion), or some amount in between?

The geographic dispersion of the plants in the supply chain plays a large role in the answer. If each product line has a key production facility in nearby locations, a catastrophic incident could cause business interruption losses for each product line simultaneously. In this instance, the risk manager may be compelled to set a business interruption limit of $2 billion.

Another important issue is the potential for one key supplier to affect multiple product lines. For example, if one supplier provides a chemical used in the business products, consumer products, and electrical product lines, the company business interruption limits would probably reflect some combination of the business interruption limits for these related product lines. Other key factors in this decision will be the percentage of the chemical provided by the supplier, along with the ability to purchase the chemical from alternative sources.

When determining business interruption limits, the risk manager should consult with a broker. Where the difference in prices of two policies—where one has a $700 million limit and the other a $2 billion limit—is negligible, the choice is easy. Where the price difference is large, the choice is more difficult.

Setting Extra Expense Limits

As detailed in Chapter 2, extra expense is generally defined as "expenses incurred above normal to continue operations during the indemnity period." Examples include:

- Temporary repairs to facilities

- Rental of temporary equipment

- Temporary warehousing costs

- Moving inventory to temporary locations

- Increased security for a damaged location

Extra expense is usually a small percentage of a total business interruption loss. Although determining extra expense limits is less important to an organization than setting business interruption limits, it can be more difficult, primarily in the need not only to understand the company's operations, but also to know exact circumstances of the actual loss event.

To determine extra expense limits, a risk manager may discuss the concept, along with several examples, with plant managers. However, information provided from each plant may vary significantly. One way around the problem is to avoid an extra expense sublimit in the property policy. If a sublimit does exist, special attention should be paid after a loss incident to categorize potential extra expense items as mitigating expense when possible.

The risk manager presents his final calculations to senior executives, particularly in finance and accounting. Any challenges to the results can be addressed by reviewing the limit-setting process along with the key variables. A secondary benefit of the risk manager's hard work is that the insights generated can help management prioritize capital expenditure for plants at greatest risk.

Endnotes

[1] Maximum possible loss denotes the total property value exposed to loss at any one location or from any one event. Maximum probable loss is the largest loss that is likely to occur.

[2] The Business Income Work Sheet also fails to consider other variables, such as seasonality, in its calculations. In such a case, the potential is high for being "underinsured" if a loss occurs during a busy part of the company's year.

A Guide
Completing the ISO Business Income Work Sheet[1]

Giving advice on completing a business income work sheet has always been a daunting task for insurance practitioners because it requires a specialized knowledge not only of time element insurance but also of accounting terms and procedures. This section takes you step by step through the five pages of the Insurance Services Office (ISO) Business Income Report/Work Sheet CP 15 15. A copy of the work sheet is shown as Exhibit 4.1. Additional value will be gained if this explanation is read while referring to the work sheet. Individual insurance companies may provide proprietary business income work sheets that may differ from the ISO form. However, the principal calculations and entries typically will be similar, if not identical, to those included in the ISO work sheet.

As discussed previously in this chapter, larger, more complex businesses should look beyond the work sheet when establishing business interruption insurance values. Even less complex businesses would benefit greatly by looking beyond the work sheet calculation to determine other business attributes that would affect the amount of business interruption insurance that is needed. However, the work sheet and this exercise provide starting points for establishing values.

ISO currently supports two editions of the work sheet: the 1988 and the 1995 editions.

DIFFERENCES BETWEEN THE 1988 AND THE 1995 EDITIONS

There are no earth shattering differences between the editions, but there are some variations. Despite the fact that ISO currently supports 2002 editions of its business income coverage forms, the 1995 edition of the work sheet is the most current format. In contrast with prior editions, it:

1.   Reminds insureds to add extra expense limits and extended business income limits, if purchased, to the business income coinsurance requirement.

2.   Calculates the cost of goods sold on a separate page from the rest of the calculations. The resulting figure for cost of goods sold is then inserted into the coinsurance calculation.

3.   Explains that the cost of merchandise sold by manufacturing risks is only "the cost of merchandise sold but not manufactured by you." This is assumed but not stated in the 1988 work sheet.

4.   Deducts the cost of services purchased from outsiders that do not continue under contract; power, heating, and refrigeration not continuing under contract; and ordinary payroll expense in a different order than the 1988 form. However, the final result is unchanged.

5.   Does not provide a place for calculating the amount of the ordinary payroll expense or the power, heat, and refrigeration deductions as does the 1988 work sheet.

PAGE ONE—THE GROUND RULES

The first page of the work sheet lays the ground rules for developing a dollar figure that will be used as a basis for calculating the coinsurance requirement for the business income insurance. The name asked for in the first line is the named insured, who must have an insurable interest in the loss of income. The location requested in the second line must show all locations that are to be insured and whether they are to be covered on a blanket or specific basis.

The form requires that the work sheet be completed "on an accrual basis." This means that income and expenses should be shown for the time period in which they are incurred as opposed to the time period in which the cash is actually transferred. For example, if a product were sold during the last week of the policy period, the income from that sale would be shown on the work sheet as being received during the expiring policy year. It would not be shown during the new policy year, when the cash would probably be received. Most companies accounting systems are set up on an accrual basis.

The work sheet should be completed in accordance with generally accepted accounting principles (GAAP). The principles embody broad guidelines and specific rules and procedures for reporting the financial activities of businesses. The primary purpose of GAAP is to make certain that those writing financial reports and those reading them do so with common understanding.

Since beginning and ending inventories figure predominantly in the completion of the business income work sheet, it is important that there be a clear understanding of the types of inventory valuation commonly used.

- The specific identification method is used when the inventory is made up of large, readily identifiable items such as automobiles. They are often identified in the inventory by serial number.

- The average-cost method is usually calculated on a weighted average cost basis. The total cost of the beginning inventory is added to the total cost of each individual purchase of supplies during the year. This total is divided by the total of the number of units in the beginning inventory and the units purchased during the year. The quotient is multiplied times the number of units in the ending inventory. When prices are rising, the inventory will be undervalued, and, when prices are falling, it will be overvalued.

- The first-in, first-out method (FIFO) assumes that the items purchased or manufactured first are used or sold first. During times of rising prices, the lower priced items are sold or used as supplies for manufacturing, making income appear larger.

- The last-in, first-out method (LIFO) makes the opposite assumption: the last items purchased or manufactured are the first ones used or sold. During inflationary periods LIFO will make income appear lower.

- Other types of inventory valuation methods include the base stock method, which assumes that there is an unchanging base of inventory below which it never drops. Only purchases over and above that base are used for current consumption. This method tends to undervalue inventory. The moving average method calculates a new average for the cost of inventory every time a purchase is made during the accounting period. This method works well when there is a large quantity of identical units, such as commodities. The simple average method divides the total unit price of all purchases by the total number of units purchased. It is not an accurate method because no weight is given to large purchases.

From time to time companies change their methods of valuing inventories. Should this happen during a business income insurance policy period, the insurance company should be notified and a decision made as to whether the inventory valuation method used in the business income work sheet should be changed. If such an agreement is not reached, a coinsurance penalty or a condition of over-insurance could result.

The agreed value coverage option replaces the coinsurance clause with a value agreed upon by the insured and the insurer. It is discussed in Chapter 2.

One point is worth reemphasizing: a deliberate understatement of values in the business income work sheet because agreed value is being used could be taken as a material misrepresentation and void the entire policy. This is because the business income work sheet becomes a part of the policy when the agreed value coverage option is chosen.

The premium adjustment form (ISO endorsement CP 15 20) converts the business income coverage into a type of reporting form. It allows the insured to carry a limit somewhat higher than the anticipated net income and expenses and to receive a return premium on the additional limits if they are not needed by the time the policy year is over. This has the effect of giving the insured leeway on meeting the coinsurance requirement. It does not replace the coinsurance clause as does the agreed value coverage option. The insured business must request additional limits of coverage if, during the policy term, a higher limit is required. The business income work sheet calculations required for this endorsement are those for the year immediately preceding the inception date of the policy. The premium adjustment endorsement contains an honesty clause similar to that found in most reporting forms, so the business income work sheet does not take on the characteristics of a warranty as it does with the agreed value coverage option.

PAGE TWO—TOTAL REVENUES

The second page of the business income work sheet begins the actual calculation of net income and expenses—the dollar figure on which the coinsurance requirement of the policy is based. Note that there are four columns on the page, two for manufacturing risks and two for nonmanufacturing risks. The first two columns use figures from the year immediately preceding the policy year to which the application applies. The second two columns require estimated figures for the actual policy year for which the insurance is to be effective. The amount of insurance required by the coinsurance clause is calculated based on the estimated figures in columns three and four.

As will be seen on page three of the work sheet, this form recognizes that a business may have both a manufacturing and a nonmanufacturing or mercantile exposure. These exposures may be combined on page three to develop one net income and expense base for calculating the coinsurance requirement.

> •   *A.* Gross sales should include total sales revenue for the twelve months immediately preceding the inception date of the policy. Income

taxes are not to be deducted, but sales taxes can be if they were shown separately from the sales price of the product.

- *B.* Manufacturing risks deduct finished stock inventory (at sales value) at the beginning of the year preceding the policy. This refers to finished stock already in existence at the beginning of the year, valued at the sales price that existed at that time. The policy is intended to insure the sales value of production that occurred during the year in question, while this stock was produced before the year in question. A mercantile risk does not require this deduction, because it does not manufacture the goods it sells.

- *C.* Manufacturing risks then add finished stock inventory (at sales value) at end of the year preceding the policy. Since finished stock inventory on hand at the beginning to the year has been taken out of the equation, this unsold inventory must have been manufactured during the year and, thus, is part of the insured value of production that occurred during the year. The inventory must be valued at the selling prices prevailing at the end of the year. This figure is carried over to column three on line B., which is finished stock inventory at beginning of the year to be insured.

- *D.* Gross sales value of production is the value of the actual revenue stream that was produced during the year, before certain sales and production costs are deducted.

- *E.* Deduct prepaid freight, returns and allowances, discounts, bad debts, and collection expenses from the gross sales value of production. These are items that, to this point, are included in the gross sales value of production but do not contribute to ultimate revenues. Some of them would not even have been incurred as of the time of completing the work sheet due to a short time since the sale had taken place; or as in the case of inventory on hand at the end of the year, the goods would not have been sold yet. Every effort must be made to estimate these numbers accurately and not on a conservative basis as is sometimes done by accountants. These items are also deducted from the gross sales of nonmanufacturing or mercantile companies.

- *F.* Net sales is the result of subtracting the expenses in step E from gross sales (step A) for *nonmanufacturing or mercantile companies*. Net sales value of production is the result of subtracting the expenses in step E from gross sales value of production for *manufacturing companies*.

- *G.* Add other earnings from business *operations* being insured (not investment income or rents from other properties) including commissions or rents, cash discounts, and other earnings. These are other earnings that derive directly from the operations being insured and that would be interrupted by an insured peril. Not included here would be speculative income that would not be expected to repeat in subsequent years. An example would be a cereal manufacturer that, due to an unusual fluctuation of wheat prices, was able to buy wheat at extraordinarily low prices during the preceding year.

- *H.* Total revenues is the sum of F, net sales, and G, other earnings. This figure represents all income from the insured operation from which is deducted some of the costs (but not all of them) of producing (or of buying merchandise in the case of mercantile operations) the goods that are sold.

Note that the only steps used for calculating total revenues for nonmanufacturing or mercantile operations are A, E, F, and G. The sales value of finished stock inventory at the beginning of the year and the end of the year are irrelevant for nonmanufacturing operations. Note also that the same calculations are performed for columns 3 and 4, but this time they are estimated for the upcoming policy year.

PAGE THREE AND FOUR—EXPENSES AND DEDUCTIONS

The third page of the work sheet develops expenses and deductions that may be subtracted from total revenues to produce the final figure—net income and expenses—on which the policy's coinsurance requirement is based. The total revenues entries from page 2 first are inserted for nonmanufacturing and mercantile operations. (All page numbers in this discussion refer to the work sheet.)

CALCULATION FOR NONMANUFACTURING BUSINESSES

To develop total expenses and revenues for *nonmanufacturing operations*, the cost of goods sold must be calculated as shown in the Supplementary Information section of page 4.

- Opposite inventory (including stock in process) at the beginning of the year (page 4), enter the cost of the nonmanufacturing inventory on hand at the beginning of the year.

- Opposite the cost of merchandise sold (page 4), add the cost of nonmanufacturing stock purchased during the year, including transportation costs.

- Opposite the cost of other supplies consumed (page 4), add the cost of packaging and wrapping supplies consumed, including the cost of supplies for transportations.

- These three items are added to develop the "cost of goods available for sale" on page 4.

- Opposite the line directing the insured to deduct inventory (including stock in process) at end of year on page 4, subtract the cost of nonmanufacturing inventory on hand at the end of the year.

- Opposite cost of goods sold (page 4), enter the total of the four items just listed, which will be the cost of goods sold for nonmanufacturing operations. This item then is entered as Item I on page 3.

- Opposite services purchased from outsiders to resell that do not continue under contract (page 3), add those services that pertain to nonmanufacturing operations. An example might be the cost paid to a contractor to install an appliance purchased by a consumer.

- The current ISO business income coverage insures ordinary payroll. If coverage for ordinary payroll is to be excluded or limited to certain job classifications or employees, endorsement CP 15 10 must be used. The ordinary payroll expenses that are to be excluded and any special mining property deductions that may apply should be entered on the work sheet under item I. Instructions for calculating special mining property deductions are on page 5.

- Opposite *J.1.,* Business Income exposure for 12 months, enter the result of subtracting the sum of costs of goods sold, services purchased from outsiders, and other coverage limitation numbers from total revenues. This yields net income and expenses from nonmanufacturing and mercantile operations. This is the figure on which the coinsurance requirement for nonmanufacturing or mercantile risks is calculated. If the risk also manufactures products, the figure is combined with net income and expense from manufacturing operations to produce combined net income and expenses in line J 2.

CALCULATION FOR MANUFACTURING BUSINESSES

The computations for *manufacturing operations* are as follows.

- *l.* Deduct the cost of the items listed on the work sheet (net of any discount received). See the special note on payroll coverage under the previous section dealing with nonmanufacturing risks. These are the only variable costs that may be deducted from total revenues to arrive at net income and expense from which the coinsurance requirement is calculated. There are other variable costs involved in production that are not allowed, thus making the amount of insurance required under the coinsurance clause higher than the amount that could be collected after a loss. Some of these disallowed variable costs are listed subsequently.

- Cost of goods sold (page 4): inventory (including stock in process) at the beginning of the year. This inventory is that of raw stock, factory supplies, and other supplies that are on hand at the beginning of the year. They will be going into the manufactured goods that will be sold during the year and, therefore, arc part of the costs of those goods.

- Add to that inventory the cost of raw stock, factory supplies, merchandise sold, and other supplies (including transportation costs) bought and consumed during the year. These also become a part of the manufactured goods that are included in the net sales value of production. The cost of merchandise sold refers to goods sold by the manufacturer but not manufactured by it. An example might be a computer hardware manufacturer that includes software, purchased from others, in the sales cost of the hardware. Should the risk contain nonmanufacturing or mercantile operations, the cost of merchandise sold may be placed in the second and fourth columns to be combined with manufacturing net income expenses in step *J 2.*

- Cost of goods available for sale is the sum of the inventory on hand at the beginning of the year and that bought and consumed during the year. However, not all the goods *available* for sale are sold during the policy year, which is the reason for the next step.

- Deduct inventory (including stock in process) at the end of the year. The purpose of the work sheet is to calculate net income and expenses derived from goods sold during the policy year. Any inventory of raw stock, factory supplies, and other supplies that are still on hand at the end of the year did not become part of the cost of the goods sold during the year and must be subtracted from the cost of goods available for sale that year. This figure should be carried forward to the third column as inventory (including stock in process) at the beginning of the next year.

- Cost of goods sold (page 3) is the sum of all the material costs that the work sheet allows to be subtracted from the total revenues calculated on page one. It is important to understand that the cost of goods sold as developed in the business income work sheet is not the equivalent of the term "cost of goods sold" as used in the financial reports of the insured. The latter contains other costs that are not allowed in the business income work sheet.

- Services purchased from outsiders (not your employees) to resell, that do not continue under contract. Often a part of the manufacturing process is contracted out to jobbers because it is more cost efficient than doing the process in plant—assembly of parts, for example. Similarly, mercantile operations might contract the installation of a product they sell. Usually the contract does not require that payments continue in the event of a business interruption. If that is the case, the cost of the contracts is added to the cost of goods sold as part of the sum that is subtracted from total revenues to develop net income and expenses. Should the contract provide that payments to the jobber continue in spite of a business interruption, the cost of that contract would be left in total revenues to be insured.

- The total is the cost of goods sold and services purchased from outsiders to resell subtracted from total revenues to produce net income and expenses. (Mining properties involve special situations. Page 5 of the work sheet includes special instructions for these types of exposures.)

- *J.1.* Business income exposure for 12 months (business income basis for coinsurance if a coverage modification does not apply) is the final result of the work sheet to which the coinsurance percentage indicated on the declarations page is applied. Coverage modifications that might apply are the agreed value coverage option, which would replace the coinsurance clause; the ordinary payroll limitation form CP 15 10, which is entered on page three of the work sheet; and the power, heat and refrigeration deduction form CP 15 11, which is also entered on page three of the work sheet.

- *J.2.* Combined (for firms engaged in both manufacturing and nonmanufacturing operations) is the step in which the net income and expenses for both the manufacturing and nonmanufacturing operations in one company are joined to provide one figure to use as a basis for calculating the coinsurance requirement.

CONTINUATION OF CALCULATION FOR BOTH NONMANUFACTURING AND MANUFACTURING EXPOSURES

- *K.* This section represents additional expenses that may be insured. ISO form CP 00 30, Business Income (and Extra Expense) Coverage Form provides coverage for extra expenses that are used to either minimize the business interruption or to continue operations. Businesses should determine how much extra expense coverage they anticipate would be needed in the event of a covered business interruption. Item K. 2. is the entry line for extended coverage of the time anticipated to regain pre-loss income levels. These amounts must be added to the total anticipated annual amount of the business income exposure. The 2002 edition of the ISO business income forms allot 30 days past the date that property should be restored to regain customers and stabilize operations. This is referred to as the period of extended period of indemnity or extended period of recovery. Insured businesses must take care to include in the calculation additional income for that period of time. In addition, some insurers may permit additional time for recovery. Insured businesses must enter sufficient income to reflect that additional period of time or a coinsurance penalty may be incurred.

- *L.* Total of J. and K., page 4. The figure in L. represents 100 percent of the estimated business income exposure for 12 months plus additional expenses the insured business anticipates. The work sheet directs the insured to determine the number of months needed to replace damaged property, resume operations, and restore the business to the condition that would have existed if the damage had not occurred. If the insured business believes it would take 12 months, the coinsurance amount selected should be 100 percent. If it estimates 6 months for recovery, the coinsurance amount would be 50 percent; 18 months would develop 150 percent coinsurance. The total of J. and K. is multiplied by the coinsurance percentage to determine the amount of business income insurance that should be purchased. Insurance companies establish the range of coinsurance levels they will offer, and that information must be used to decide upon the final coinsurance and limit.

Note that there is no space for this calculation under columns one and two. This is because the coinsurance must be calculated on the net income and expenses estimated for the coming policy year, which are developed in columns three and four.

OTHER INFORMATION

There are a number of possible coverage amendments that may impact the amount of insurance that should be purchased. Following is some additional information on selected amendments.

- If the ordinary payroll limitation form (CP 15 10) is attached, all ordinary payroll expenses may be deducted or limited. Ordinary payroll expenses are defined as those earned by employees who would not be kept on during a protracted period of business interruption. Those whose payroll would not be considered ordinary are officers of the company, executives, department heads, employees under contract, and any other employees specified by name or position in the policy. Ordinary payroll includes the payroll, employee benefits, FICA, union dues, and workers compensation premiums for the employees in question, but it does not include any benefits that would continue under a union contract.

- If 90 or 180 days is indicated for the ordinary payroll limitation, use the largest amount of ordinary payroll expense incurred during the specified number of days. Since these modifications to the ordinary payroll exclusion provide the option of covering ordinary payroll expense for either 90 or 180 days, the ordinary payroll for the time period chosen must be included in the calculation. If ordinary payrolls fluctuate in a predictable pattern during the year, use the three or six continuous months that produce the highest payroll.

- If the power, heat, and refrigeration deduction form (CP 15 11) is attached, deduct power, heat, and refrigeration expenses that do not continue under contract. These are examples of variable costs that, without this endorsement, would be included in the total net income and expense that is used for calculating the coinsurance requirement and, yet, would not be recoverable in a loss because they were not continuing expenses. This endorsement says that these expenses, if they are consumed in production operations, are not included in the net income and expense total used to calculate the coinsurance requirement. It serves to lower the amount of insurance that must be carried and is, therefore, deducted from net income and expenses shown on the first line. The deduction is combined with the ordinary payroll expense deduction if that endorsement is also purchased.

- Agreed value business income coverage may be activated if an acceptable business income work sheet is submitted to the underwriter. The agreed value option deletes the coinsurance requirement for the 12 months following coverage inception date or until the policy expires.

Mining properties present unique considerations for the business income work sheet. They are not discussed here.

ACCOUNTING VERSUS INSURANCE

There are a number of terms used in the business income work sheet that are either not used in the accounting profession or, if they are used, carry a different meaning. It is important for the insurance practitioner to recognize that these differences exist and to alert the insured to them. Simply transferring numbers directly from the insured's financial statements to the business income work sheet could result in the insured carrying too much or too little insurance.

- Sales value of production, found in lines D and F of page two of the business income work sheet, is a term not likely to be used by the insured in his or her accounting. Normal accounting procedures would have inventory valued at cost, but in lines B and C of page two, inventory is valued at sales value. This is because, on the business income work sheet, the assumption is that profit is earned upon completion of production. This assumption is not used, however, with respect to finished goods when adjusting a business income loss. In order to insure the sales value of finished goods, a selling price endorsement must be added to the property insurance that covers the inventory. Yet, the profit that would have been earned by goods that were unfinished when the loss occurred is insured by the business income coverage form.

- Inventory. Even after choosing one inventory valuation method over another, an insured may be motivated by tax or other considerations to be conservative or liberal in establishing the value of inventory. What might make sense from the tax perspective could be exactly the wrong decision for completing the business income work sheet. Inventories should be valued as closely as possible to their real value in the stream of production that would be interrupted in the event of a loss.

- Cost of goods sold are variable costs that would stop should production be interrupted. They are subtracted from total revenue on the business income work sheet to produce net income and expenses, the base on which the coinsurance requirement is calculated. The larger the value of cost of goods sold, the less insurance that needs to be carried. The business income work sheet limits the cost of goods sold to the difference between beginning and ending inventory plus the cost of the following items purchased during the policy year: raw stock consumed, factory supplies consumed, and other supplies consumed.

There are other variable costs that might or might not continue in the event of a loss. Whether they continue would depend on whether the loss were total or partial and the duration of the business interruption. For instance, a lease might specify that rent will abate if the building is unusable for more than 60 days. For 60 days, rent would be a covered continuing expense. If business remained interrupted beyond that time, rent would become a noncontinuing expense.

If the expenses are noncontinuing, no business income insurance recovery would apply to them, even though they were not used in calculating the cost of goods sold on the business income work sheet. Examples of possible noncontinuing expenses that would be included in accounting cost of goods sold but not on the business income work sheet cost of goods sold include ordinary payroll if the limiting endorsement is added; power, heat, and refrigeration expense; advertising expense; postage and telephone expense; travel expense; and maintenance expense. The first two items in the list, ordinary payroll expense and power, heat, and lighting expense can be subtracted from net income and expenses only if the applicable endorsements are attached.

Endnotes

[1] *FC&S Bulletins*, (Cincinnati: The National Underwriter Co., 2004).

POLICY NUMBER: COMMERCIAL PROPERTY
                                                      CP 15 15 06 95

BUSINESS INCOME REPORT/WORK SHEET

Your Name _____   Date _____

Location _____

_____

This work sheet must be completed on an accrual basis.

The beginning and ending inventories in all calculations should be based on the same valuation method.

APPLICABLE WHEN THE AGREED VALUE COVERAGE OPTION APPLIES:

I certify that this is a true and correct report of values as required under this policy for the periods indicated and that the Agreed Value for the period of coverage is $ _____ , based on a Co-insurance percentage of ____%.

Signature _____
Official Title _____

APPLICABLE WHEN THE PREMIUM ADJUSTMENT FORM APPLIES:

I certify that this is a true and correct report of values as required under this policy for the 12 months ended _____

Signature _____

Official Title _____

Agent or Broker _____

Mailing Address _____

CP 15 15 06 95   Copyright, ISO Commercial Risk Services, Inc., 1994   Page 1 of 5   □

Exhibit 4.1 Business Interruption Work Sheet

BUSINESS INCOME REPORT/WORK SHEET
FINANCIAL ANALYSIS

Income and Expenses	12 Month Period Ending ___		Estimated for 12 Month Period Beginning ___	
	Manufacturing	Non-Manufacturing	Manufacturing	Non-Manufacturing
A. Gross Sales.....................................	$ _____	$ _____	$ _____	$ _____
B. DEDUCT: Finished Stock Inventory (at sales value) at Beginning...............	– _____	XXXXXXXX XXXXXXXX	– _____	XXXXXXXX XXXXXXXX
C. ADD: Finished Stock Inventory (at sales value) at End.........................	+ _____	XXXXXXXX	+ _____	XXXXXXXX
D. Gross Sales Value of Production.....................................	$ _____	XXXXXXXX	$ _____	XXXXXXXX
E. DEDUCT: Prepaid Freight – Outgoing........	– _____	– _____	– _____	– _____
Returns & Allowances...............	– _____	– _____	– _____	– _____
Discounts..................................	– _____	– _____	– _____	– _____
Bad Debts...............................	– _____	– _____	– _____	– _____
Collection Expenses.................	– _____	– _____	– _____	– _____
F. Net Sales.......................................		$ _____		$ _____
Net Sales Value of Production........	$ _____		$ _____	
G. ADD: Other Earnings from your business operations (not investment income or rents from other properties): Commissions or Rents	+ _____	+ _____	+ _____	+ _____
Cash Discounts Received..............................	+ _____	+ _____	+ _____	+ _____
Other...	+ _____	+ _____	+ _____	+ _____
H. Total Revenues.............................	$ _____	$ _____	$ _____	$ _____

Income and Expenses	12 Month Period Ending ___		Estimated for 12 Month Period Beginning ___	
	Manufacturing	Non-Manufacturing	Manufacturing	Non-Manufacturing
Total Revenues (Line **H.** from previous page)..............................	$ _____	$ _____	$ _____	$ _____

I. DEDUCT:

Cost of goods sold (see next page for instructions).....................	– _____	– _____	– _____	– _____
Cost of services purchased from outsiders (not your employees) to resell, that do not continue under contract............	– _____	– _____	– _____	– _____
Power, heat and refrigeration expenses that do not continue under contract (if **CP 15 11** is attached)..	– _____	XXXXXXXX	– _____	XXXXXXXX
All ordinary payroll expenses or the amount of payroll expense excluded (if **CP 15 10** is attached)....................................	– _____	– _____	– _____	– _____
Special deductions for mining properties (see next page for instructions)...............................	– _____	– _____	– _____	– _____

J.1. Business Income exposure for 12 months......................................	$ _____	_____	_____	_____
J.2. Combined (firms engaged in manufacturing & non-manufacturing operations).............	$ _____		$ _____	

The figures in **J.1.** or **J.2.** represent 100% of your actual and estimated Business Income exposure for 12 months.

K. Additional Expenses:

1. Extra Expenses – form **CP 00 30** only (expenses incurred to avoid or minimize suspension of business & to continue operations).................			$ _____	$ _____
2. Extended Business Income and Extended Period of Indemnity – form **CP 00 30 or CP 00 32** (loss of Business Income following resumption of operations, up to 30 days or the no. of days selected under Extended Period of Indemnity option).......................			+ _____	+ _____
3. Combined (all amounts in **K.1.** and **K.2.**)...................................			$ _____	

"Estimated" column

L.   Total of **J. and K.** .... $ _____

The figure in **L.** represents 100% of your estimated Business Income exposure for 12 months, and additional expenses. Using this figure as information, determine the approximate amount of insurance needed based on your evaluation of the number of months needed (may exceed 12 months) to replace your property, resume operations and restore the business to the condition that would have existed if no property damage had occurred.

Refer to the agent or Company for information on available Coinsurance levels and indemnity options. The Limit of Insurance you select will be shown in the Declarations of the policy.

Supplementary Information

	12 Month Period Ending ___		Estimated for 12 Month Period Beginning ___	
	Manufacturing	Non-Manufacturing	Manufacturing	Non-Manufacturing
CALCULATION OF COST OF GOODS SOLD				
Inventory at beginning of year (Including raw material and stock in process, but not finished stock, for manufacturing risks).............	$ _____	$ _____	$ _____	$ _____
Add: The following purchase costs: Cost of raw stock (including transportation charges).........................	+ _____	XXXXXXXX	+ _____	XXXXXXXX
Cost of factory supplies consumed...	+ _____	XXXXXXXX	+ _____	XXXXXXXX
Cost of merchandise sold including transportation charges (for manufacturing risks, means cost of merchandise sold but not manufactured by you)......................	+ _____	+ _____	+ _____	+ _____
Cost of other supplies consumed (including transportation charges)..........	+ _____	+ _____	+ _____	+ _____
Cost of goods available for sale.............	$ _____	$ _____	$ _____	$ _____
Deduct: Inventory at end of year (Including raw material and stock in process, but not finished stock, for manufacturing risks)...............	− _____	− _____	− _____	− _____
Cost of Goods Sold (Enter this figure in Item I. on previous page)..........	$ _____	$ _____	$ _____	$ _____

CALCULATION OF SPECIAL
DEECUTIONS – MINING PROPERTIES

Royalties, unless specifically included in coverage	$ _____	$ _____
Actual depletion, commonly known as unit or cost depletion (not percentage depletion).............................	+ _____	+ _____
Welfare and retirement fund charges based on tonnage......................	+ _____	+ _____
Hired trucks	+ _____	+ _____
Enter this figure in Item I. on previous page...	$ _____	$ _____

CHAPTER FIVE

The Loss Adjustment Process

The Mindset of a Claims Adjuster

L oss adjustment. The very phrase conjures images of not fully recovering a loss. A policyholder may well ask a number of questions, such as "Why must a claim be adjusted and not simply be paid as is?" or "Isn't the whole purpose of insurance to pay claims?" or "Doesn't an insurance policy describe what a company will and will not get paid if it is unfortunate enough to incur a loss?"

After paying premiums to an insurance company for many years, it is understandable that most policyholders expect to be paid for their losses quickly—and with a minimum amount of work. Consequently, when policyholders learn that they have to prepare a claim that will withstand the scrutiny of adjusters and insurers, they are often taken aback. It seems obvious that a company's main priority after sustaining a loss or business interruption is not preparing an insurance claim but restoring the business as soon as possible; the company's top management may not see claims preparation as a vital immediate step.

Ironically, the effort to document, present, and negotiate an insurance claim can for many companies prove the toughest part of a recovery. While the company's goal most likely is to achieve the greatest recovery in the shortest possible time, the loss adjustment process can be long and arduous, often taking months, if not years, to complete. On its face, loss adjustment is simple. In reality, the process can involve a variety of participants, each with different interests and expertise, and can entail a tremendous amount of documentation and analysis. Rather than rubber-stamping a policyholder's claims, professional loss adjusters face constraints on approving what is filed, based on a justifiable belief that claims must be substantiated, investigated, or verified before asking an insurer to settle.

Understanding everyone's perspective during the loss adjustment process—including that of the claims adjuster, and by extension, the insurer—makes it easier for a company to reach its goal of a fair settlement in a reasonable period of time. This chapter seeks to demonstrate, in turn, the insurance company's typical perspective on a claim, the perspective of most policyholders, and the role of the claims adjuster in the claims adjustment process, including a look at some of the most common steps toward a better understanding on both sides in order to smooth the way to amicable settlement.

Ten Key Elements of the Loss Adjustment Process

✓ Investigating the incident
✓ Policy review, coverage analysis, and interpretation
✓ Mitigating the loss
✓ Estimating the loss and setting reserves
✓ Communicating
✓ Decision-making and authority
✓ Experts and advisors
✓ Compromising and negotiating
✓ Time management
✓ Organizing and documenting

Differing Perspectives

"What's the Loss, Where's the Proof?"

The Insurance Company's Perspective

Each insurance company has its own philosophy about claims and claim handling; that philosophy can evolve from year to year and can even differ from office to office. For the purposes of this book, we address the two fundamental perspectives in the terms that are used by the two parties: insurers and insureds. Insurers call the loss process the loss adjustment process, whereas policyholders call it the claim recovery process. And understanding the claims process from either perspective depends on understanding the underwriting process.

The purpose of insurance underwriting is twofold: first, to control and identify the types of losses paid, and second, to reduce the possibility of paying a claim—or at least to reduce the amount paid on routine or nuisance losses (that is, small losses that happen frequently, such as one-hour power outages). Underwriters do this by assessing the risk of loss with respect to each potential insured. The greater the risk, the higher the premium; and at some level of risk the underwriter will recommend that coverage not be provided at all. But losses are inevitable; they cannot be predicted or prevented. While claims obviously represent a significant cost to the insurer, in reality insurance companies need claims to sell more insurance. Without the sense of real risk or recorded actual losses to companies, there would be no need for insurance and therefore no market. But losses do occur, despite policyholders' best efforts to prevent them from happening. Precisely for this reason, insurers will always have a product to sell. Insurance companies are businesses just like any other: they exist to make money for their owners or shareholders.

Overall, most insurance companies enter the claims process with the intent to honor their contractual policy requirements. It is rare to find or establish the intent not to pay a valid claim. But how can insurance companies be sure the policyholder's claim is valid? Many of us have heard some variation of the story of a person who, having had five compact disks stolen from his car, instead claimed that ten were taken? And what about the leather jacket in the back seat? Or stories of contractors giving two repair estimates—one being the actual charge and the other inflated to "cover the deductible"?[1] At the other end of the spectrum are honest policyholders who—without fully understanding the coverage—submit costs that are clearly not covered by the policy.

As a result, insurance companies have implemented a method of processing claims that is best described as a "trust but verify" policy. In effect, they say to policyholders: "We believe your business was damaged by this event, but you must prove and document the damages to the extent they are covered by the insurance policy." In fact, the insurance company has a fiduciary duty to confirm whether the policyholder's claim is covered. Put differently, the insurer is prohibited from using this verification role as a quest to challenge, reduce, or deny an otherwise valid claim. That said, it is equally as natural for insurers to seek to verify claims as it is for policyholders to seek the highest possible recompense for the loss in accordance with their reading of the policy.

"Here's My Claim, Cut Me a Check"

The Policyholder's Perspective

When a loss occurs, the policyholder wants to be paid completely and quickly. However, the reputation of some insurance companies has left people wary of the claim recovery process. Among skeptical policyholders, three attitudes are common. First of these attitudes is best expressed as "Hey! You owe me." Large corporations often want to say, "Look, XYZ Company has paid insurance premiums for twenty years. Now we've experienced our first large loss. Our claim is $20 million; please wire-transfer the money to our account." In this circumstance, the company's underlying premise is that its insurance policy is like a bank account: premiums are deposits, and a claim is simply a withdrawal. Companies adopting this attitude frequently take offense when the insurance company requests supporting documentation for their claim.

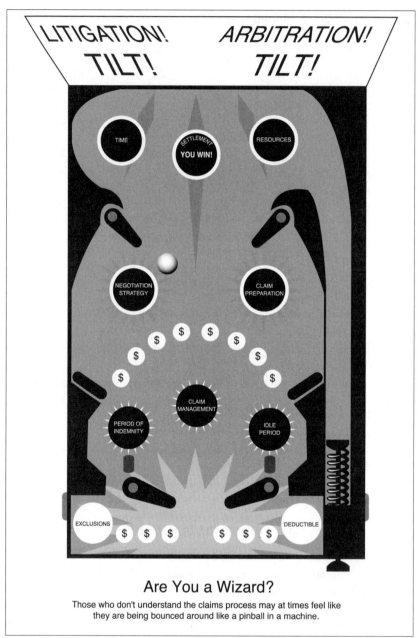

Figure 5.1: Claims Pinball

The second prevailing attitude can be summed up as "You're not going to cheat me!" This stance reflects the following line of reasoning: "All insurance companies are greedy and will do everything possible to not pay our claim. They'll drag the process out as long as possible and make it as painful as possible so that we will just give up. Therefore, we are justified in advancing the most aggressive claim possible." Clearly, this position creates an adversarial relationship from the beginning; the lack of trust from the policyholder will create its mirror-image in the insurance company.

A third attitude—less cynical, more appropriate, and therefore perhaps the most common of all—is the thinking, "Be fair, be diligent, but please be quick." The majority of companies making a claim seem to say to their insurers, "We had a loss. We know you need to perform due diligence. But we want only what is owed to us under the policy, so do your claim audit quickly and pay us. Don't make this claim a full employment opportunity for your experts."

The main point to take away from this discussion of perspective is that communication between the two parties to a claim is essential. Policyholders need to accept their responsibility for identifying all the losses and providing adequate support for their damages. They should anticipate being challenged on items that are not supported or are not credible—for when gray areas exist, the best documented position usually wins. But the insurance company and policyholder do share goals. Both want to mitigate the loss, see the business return to normal operations, and resolve the claim as quickly as possible. Both parties typically want to maintain positive, professional relationships—including a continuing business relationship after the settlement. An insurance company's best salesperson, after all, is a satisfied customer who appreciates the value of insurance from a particular carrier.[2]

The Adjuster

Few other jobs include people with such a dramatic range of education, background, experience, and training as insurance claim adjusters, who range from highly experienced, well-trained professionals with engineering, accounting, or law degrees to first-day, on-the-job trainees without a college diploma. There are two types of adjusters in today's market. Staff adjusters are employees of the insurance company, and independent adjusters work for a third party not owned by the insurance company.[3]

Often, the question arises as to which is better. Many different answers are possible, each depending on circumstances of the case. Some insurance companies require the use of their own staff. Some insurance companies have excellent training programs; others have little to no training whatsoever. For larger losses and for shared or layered insurance programs, however, an independent adjuster is usually preferred. We will discuss the merits and drawbacks of each type as we discuss the adjuster's role in the loss adjustment process.[4]

An adjuster's title typically reflects seniority or authority: adjuster, senior adjuster, general adjuster, executive adjuster, and senior executive adjuster. (Unfortunately, when it comes to titles, there are no industry standards, so a senior adjuster at one company may be more seasoned than a senior executive adjuster at another.) Usually, the estimated size of the loss will dictate the seniority level of adjuster; however, loss size is a matter of perspective. To some insurance companies, a $100,000 loss would be very large indeed, and an executive general adjuster would handle that claim. To other companies used to managing larger claims, the same $100,000 loss would be assigned to a trainee, while the most experienced adjuster would be given claims in the $10+ million category.

Selecting an Adjuster

Claims adjusters are the eyes and ears of the insurance company, essentially working on behalf of the insurance company to investigate the facts associated with a loss, determine the application of coverage to those facts, and negotiate settlement of the claim. Many facets of the adjuster's job are not immediately apparent to the policyholder, who does not see what goes on "behind the scenes" between the adjuster and the others, such as underwriters.

Part of acquiring insurance coverage is determining who will adjust a claim. Though they may not know it, companies often have considerable discretion in who will do this. Most will closely review the amount and type of coverage and its price when selecting an insurance company, but few consider the insurance company's skill and speed in handling or adjusting claims. A good, experienced adjuster can make all the difference in whether the loss adjustment process goes smoothly or becomes a study in frustration. Some adjusters have the policyholder's best interest in mind; others throw up roadblocks to settlement at every opportunity. Some adjusters are knowledgeable, learn fast, and make quick decisions; others are uninformed, unwilling to learn, and evasive.

Certainly if the adjuster assigned to a case is unresponsive, indecisive, or combative, the policyholder has a right to ask for a replacement. Securing a replacement, though, can be difficult. It is therefore important for a policyholder to determine if it can select its adjustment firm before a loss, even before selecting an insurer or renewing an insurance property program. It pays to discuss performance measures for the adjuster with a broker, risk manager, or claims consultant when looking for an insurance provider. If the insurance company uses an independent adjustment company, a company reviewing coverage and selecting an insurer will do well to research these adjusters also, and then to select one with a reputation for fairness, thoroughness, and skill. It is prudent to look closely; even within the same organization, as the abilities of individuals vary greatly.

The quality of the relationship between the policyholder and the adjuster, developed early on, often determines whether or not the adjuster will become an advocate in the claims recovery process, promoting an equitable settlement in a reasonable period of time. The sophistication of the adjuster should correlate to the sophistication of the policy, whether it is a standard Insurance Services Office (ISO) policy or a broader manuscript. Without a doubt, a red flag should go up in the insured's mind if an adjuster says, "I've never seen a policy like this before."

Initial Notice of Loss

As part of their job, all adjusters perform similar tasks and produce similar reports. When policyholders call the insurance company's claim hotline to report a loss, adjusters might even answer the phone and take down the information themselves. More likely, the call will go to an administrative clerk who advises the policyholder that someone will be calling back. Basic policy information is pulled from a computer database, and notification is sent to the claims department to assign an adjuster, whether staff or independent. Adjusters are assigned based on experience and other factors, such as geography; and, once assigned, he will call the policyholder to gather additional information and determine if a visit to the location is necessary.

> **Read the Policy, So Get it First!**
>
> We often mention the importance of reading the policy in other sections of this book. Just as important is simply getting a copy of the policy. Some policies are not issued for weeks or even months after the premium is paid and coverage is bound; the delay can be especially problematic if a loss occurs before the policy arrives. Some of the largest insurance disputes from 9/11 are over whether a specific policy was in force on the date of loss. In today's electronic age, waiting thirty, sixty, ninety days or more for an insurance policy is mind-boggling.

Often, the adjuster will not have a copy of the insurance policy at this point in the process; therefore, she will not know whether coverage is in force or the amount of the deductible. A certified copy of the policy may take days, or even weeks, to get to the adjuster. In fact, sometimes a policy is not available when a loss occurs, and everyone must wait for it to be issued (see sidebar, "Read the Policy, So Get It First!").

With the policy in hand, the policyholder needs to read and review it to generally understand coverage, deductibles, and any sublimits. And after a loss, the policyholder should definitely read the policy again, listing questions, concerns, or issues before making any phone calls.

After the initial discussion with the policyholder, the adjuster may have to file the first report. Some companies require this report within twenty-four hours after notification of the loss; others allow thirty days. Given that there may be one insurance company or many, the purpose of the first report is to notify underwriters of the loss. This first report briefly describes the claim and sets an initial estimate of loss or loss reserve.

Loss Estimates/Reserves

Loss estimates are always a major point of discussion. The main purpose of the initial loss estimate is to identify the approximate magnitude of the loss, allow underwriters to assign appropriate resources to the claim, and make appropriate financial arrangements. Notwithstanding its status as an initial estimate of the loss, or *loss reserve* as deemed by the insurance carriers, preparing such an estimate can be demanding for the adjuster. The final settlement will be compared to an initial loss estimate, the estimate on the books at sixty or ninety days, the estimate on the books at the end of the policyholder's fiscal year, or at all of these points. This comparison might be made for each loss the adjuster handles, or it might reflect an aggregate assessment of all the files handled in a year.

Either way, since this estimating activity is typically part of the adjuster's performance rating, the adjuster's skill in estimating losses can impact his compensation. Some people erroneously believe that adjusters initially will set the loss reserve high because it is easier to reduce an estimate than to increase it. In reality, an accurate estimate is always preferable.[5] Adjusters are measured on the difference between the initial lost estimate and the final settlement; a small difference is better than a large one, whether the change is on the plus or minus side.

Precisely because of the pressure that insurers place on adjusters to accurately estimate the loss, the policyholder should provide information to the adjuster early and often. Good information allows the adjuster to adequately manage the loss reserves. Many insurance companies require a comment on the adequacy of loss estimates in the adjuster's report every thirty days or on a routine basis; but if new information becomes available that will either increase or decrease the loss exposure, the adjuster should be advised as soon as possible. Reserves or estimates can always be changed; such changes are expected. Major problems can occur, however, if an adjuster has to significantly change a loss estimate a long time after it has been posted and after the adjuster has confirmed and reconfirmed the reserve as accurate. Such a situation can call the adjuster's competence into question and, ultimately, can hurt his performance review. In other words, bad information from the policyholder can sometimes negatively impact the overall claim recovery process and even the final settlement. It can create anxiety in an adjuster about accuracy, inviting her to argue in the future what may otherwise be a legitimate adjustment to the claim.

Loss Adjuster's Report

Most insurance companies require that a loss adjuster's report be sent to them every thirty days, particularly if the loss is large. Through this report, the adjuster passes on information about the loss and claim to interested parties (see Exhibit 5.1, The Loss Adjuster's Report, at the end of this chapter). If the loss is large enough, a copy of the adjuster's report will be reviewed not only by claims, underwriting, operations, and sales but will go all the way to the CEO, as well as to other participating insurance companies and reinsurers. Supporting documentation, such as consultant's reports, photographs, or other claim documents, may be included with the loss adjuster's report.

While the loss adjuster's report transmits facts, observations, and issues associated with the claim, it still in large part reflects the adjuster's subjective point of view and is a function of how such information has been imparted. Often, new information emerges throughout the claim process that replaces prior assumptions or possible misinformation. It can be very difficult to overcome incorrect information that might be included and just as difficult to get the adjuster to issue

> **Advanced Loss Management Skills**
> A highly experienced insurer or claims accountant hired by the insurer to prepare the claim will include enough initial information for an early loss estimate to present to the loss adjuster, so that such information can simply be inserted into the loss adjuster's report.

a new report revising or retracting an old one. This should not preclude the policyholder's conveying a change in information once it is known; however, it is in the policyholder's best interest to work with the adjuster and to provide accurate, up-to-date information in a timely way. Communication should be frequent and followed up by confirmation in writing. If nothing else, good record keeping during this process provides backup to the policyholder should the loss adjuster's report not adequately or accurately reflect the claim.

Top Three Ways an Adjuster Can Assist with Your Claim

Experience – Most experienced adjusters will likely have worked on similar claims. They will have dealt previously with many of the issues or problems being experienced on the current loss and can provide advice to help avoid problems or pitfalls—especially as they relate to ideas surrounding loss mitigation and the restoration of the property to its former state (i.e., judgments on whether to repair or replace).

Advance Payments – A good adjuster typically will help gather appropriate documentation and request advance payments early in the process and will set up a schedule to keep advances flowing. This helps the insured with cash flow and prevents delays or additional costs associated with financing or other cash flow issues.

Advocacy – Frequently, underwriters or other insurance company personnel do not understand the facts or particular issues associated with any given claim. In such circumstances, the adjuster is often the best person to argue a coverage position or other claim issue for the insured. He or she can be a terrific advocate for the insured, explaining and documenting the issue and building the comfort level of the insurer.

Top Three Ways an Adjuster Can Obstruct the Claim Process

Indecision – It is not uncommon that adjusters have decision-making taken out of their hands. Where adjusters have limited authority, they cannot and often will not take a position on questions or issues. When this occurs, almost every question from the insured seems to be answered with the same refrain: "I don't know. Let me check with the underwriters."

Inaccuracy – For whatever reason, in some cases adjusters will not devote the effort necessary to understand the issues or problems associated with certain losses. In the worst case, they could make an uninformed decision early on, sharing that inaccurate position and related information with underwriters. Unfortunately for the claimant in such circumstances, adjusters who do this put themselves in a difficult situation because subsequent changes to their position make it clear they made a mistake. This normally results in lengthy negotiations, focused based on personal misjudgments rather than factual information.

Lack of Interest –Many adjusters hire consultants to handle all the work and have little involvement in ongoing discussions. This results in their not returning phone calls, missing important meetings, and the inability to themselves discuss the loss in great detail to underwriters. Often, as a result of their disengagement, such adjusters will lose interest in the claim.

Loss Investigation

Insurance companies are required to investigate the validity of any claim and to pay valid claims to the extent coverage is afforded by the policy. The loss investigation should determine the cause and origin of the loss, the application of coverage to that loss, and whether any subrogation is likely. The investigation should also quantify the loss exposure wherever possible and provide information necessary to set loss reserves. The investigation period is usually fairly short, averaging less than thirty days. However, complicated situations that include personal injury or highly technical losses may take much longer.

The adjuster can be thought of as the project manager for the loss investigation. Many adjusters carry a very heavy load of files; having more than 100 open files is not uncommon. When faced with small or straightforward losses, adjusters may complete the entire investigation themselves. Other adjusters may be senior enough to handle only a few large claims. Sometimes, much of the workload is passed to consultants to allow the adjuster plenty of time to manage the process and resolve issues. Adjusters can't be experts in every field, of course. Even if they were, they wouldn't have the time to handle all aspects of a loss investigation. For more complex claims, consultants and specialists—ranging from accountants and engineers to metallurgists and contractors—may be brought in (see Chapter 6 for a description of claims professionals inside and outside of the insurance company).

At the end of the investigation, the adjuster should discuss with the insureds the coverage provided by their policy, along with coverage issues (such as exclusions or limits) that may come into play, loss mitigation efforts, timelines, and interruption periods. When an adjuster does state a position on an issue, the policyholder should get this opinion in writing, or, at least, should confirm the understanding in writing. Of course, the policyholder does not have to agree with the adjuster at this point, but it is smart to get actual or potential issues on the table. Some adjusters may discuss all these issues only if they are asked; others are fairly straightforward. Even then, they may refer the policyholder to someone else or say, "I'll get back to you." Faced with this suggestion, and recognizing that an adjuster without authority to make decisions can create a frustrating claim recovery process, a policyholder should seek the decision-maker, making every effort to resolve issues as they arise instead of waiting until the end of the process. Open communication from both parties is particularly important throughout the loss adjustment process.

Following the initial investigation comes preparation of the claim, the step during which property damage is repaired, costs are qualified and quantified, and supporting documentation is compiled. The adjuster continues to monitor the loss, usually through consultants, and keeps underwriters informed through loss adjustment reports. Depending on the size and complexity of the loss, weekly or monthly meetings between the adjuster and her team are a good forum for discussing issues and keeping the lines of communication open.

Reinsurance and Shared/Layered Programs

Reinsurers are insurance companies that insure other insurance companies. Often, multiple insurance companies participate in a large, corporate insurance program. They may share the loss from the first dollar over the deductible. Or they may have layered coverage, so that one insurance company covers up to a point, then other insurers come in when the value of the claim increases (See Exhibit 5.2: Shared/Layered Insurance Program). Both these variations—multiple insurance companies and reinsurers—can create special problems for an adjuster. When a loss occurs, it can happen that the insurance companies no longer form a cohesive team providing seamless coverage for their policyholder; instead, they become squabbling competitors that can't agree.

Even one dissenting insurance company can hold up settlement indefinitely. Multiple insurance companies may not concur on the choice of adjuster and end up hiring more than one. Sometimes, these adjusters cannot agree either. Even if they all eventually agree, the adjuster must go to each company separately to collect the payment amount. This scenario is complicated further when multiple insurance companies hire multiple adjusters, who also cannot agree. The overall impact of all these obstacles can result in significant and continuing delays in advance payments or the final settlement.

Dealing with Catastrophes

Catastrophes such as hurricanes and earthquakes create a special situation since they typically cause many losses at the same time, thereby taxing adjusters, their consultants, and the insurance industry in general. Adjusters specializing only in catastrophes provide support during these times.

After a catastrophe, the loss adjustment process can either be expedited or delayed by the sheer number of similar claims occurring at the same time in the same place. There is usually a window in which certain claims can be settled in an expeditious manner; such claims tend to involve property damage and inventory issues and are less likely to be business interruption claims. At other times, claims could be delayed not just because of a shortage of resources but because insurers want to take a consistent position on equivalent claims. Even claims for losses not caused by or related to a catastrophe can be delayed because of the burden placed on the insurance companies by the catastrophe.

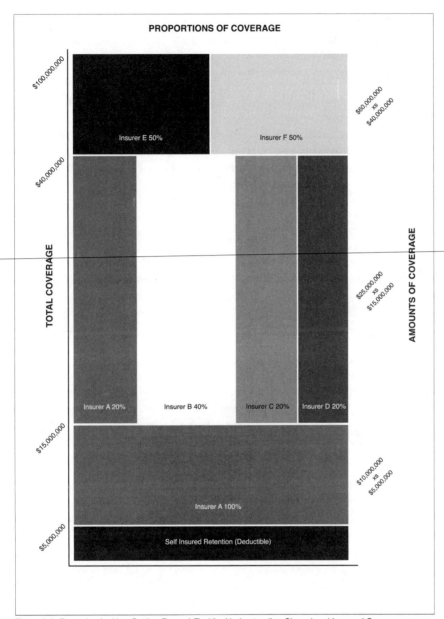

Figure 5.2: Example of a Line-Setting Form: A Tool for Understanding Shared and Layered Coverage

Seeing Red about Theoretical Recovery Periods

Catastrophes create some complicated claims positions for both insurer and insured—especially when tackling an issue such as theoretical recovery periods. In such circumstances, many different variables can affect how a claim can be presented, defended, and resolved.

For example, when the Red River flooded and inundated the city of Grand Forks, North Dakota, the entire business district suffered extensive damage. To make matters worse, the power company had not shut down power to the entire area; electrical short circuits in the system due to the rising flood-waters caused a fire that further damaged substantial amounts of property in the area. As a result, city leaders redlined an area including the business district, precluding any reconstruction work until final plans could be made to construct retaining walls and take other measures to prevent future floods from causing similar damages.

The vast extent of damages, coupled with the relatively remote location of Grand Forks, created a situation in which there simply were not enough contractors or materials to undertake cleanup, repair, restoration, and replacement. These factors created controversy as to what period of time was appropriate for businesses in the area to complete their recovery efforts—and by extension the period of indemnity. In one significant situation, a policyholder's entire operations were located within three buildings located inside the redlined zone. All were flood-damaged, and some had experienced fire damage as well. While the company's representatives were able to visit the sites to assess the damage, they were unable to remove major equipment for repair or to begin other recovery efforts at the properties. When the policyholder began discussing these issues with the loss adjuster, it was distressed to learn that the insurance company's view was that the redlining issues (which they felt were not technically "code" changes as covered under the policy) were irrelevant to the loss adjustment. Furthermore, the adjuster's construction expert had ignored the geographic lack of resources and materials in preparing his estimates of cost and timing for reconstruction activities. Accordingly, the adjuster intended to impose a theoretical recovery period on the BI claim, beginning with the date the floodwaters receded and concluding a mere six-to-eight weeks from that date.

The policyholder had already begun plans to move most of its operations outside of the flood plain of the Red River. In the process of trying to line up architects, engineers, and contractors for that purpose, the policyholder had determined that it was impossible to even procure the necessary resources to begin this work within the time period allotted by the insurance company for theoretical complete restoration of the damaged properties. War over these issues was brewing when the parties agreed to meet to discuss a more amicable resolution. The policyholder pointed out that the redlining issues should be appropriately considered code changes, because they created new rules for access to loading docks and other areas, due to the soon-to-be-constructed levees and retaining walls. In addition, the policyholder made a compelling argument regarding the availability of contractors and materials. Finally, the policyholder pointed out that construction in the new location was being done using methods that were likely to reduce the actual cost of replacement of the property. These arguments were successful in gaining some additional time with regard to the theoretical restoration period—or indemnity period—and a settlement was ultimately negotiated.

The Value of Time—A Complex Calculation in the Loss Adjustment Process

Often, the most urgent issue for companies suffering a loss is time. How much time is covered under business interruption insurance? Calculating this period is precisely where adjusters typically spend a lot of their own time. Insurance policies use multiple terms, including period of indemnity, period of interruption, period of liability, and period of restoration. Some policies use and define multiple periods, and often one period is used for the business interruption itself and another for the extra expense. (Extra expense coverage typically applies to the actual and necessary expenses that the insured incurs to either avoid or minimize the interruption.) Finally, both U.S. and non-U.S. forms now address the business interruption timeframe differently and with different wording.

Adjusters and other insurance professionals frequently use the variety of terms interchangeably. In reality, they can have very different meanings. For example, the period of indemnity and the period of restoration can mean very different things. In some policies, the period of indemnity is the time required for all damaged property to be repaired to a condition equivalent to that before the loss, with "due diligence and dispatch." Seemingly simple enough, this definition can raise many questions, including, "What type of property damage? Is it only the insured property or is it property of the same type?" and "Is it only for property owned by the insured? What about property not owned by the insured but used by the insured, such as leased equipment or buildings or a utility-owned transformer?" Other questions inevitably arise as well, such as "What is equivalent condition?" and "What if the new property is an upgrade of the old?" Lastly, the very terms of policies frequently come into dispute, such as "What is due diligence and dispatch? According to whose standards? What if the insured proceeds with due diligence and dispatch, but the landlord does not?"

In other policies, the period of indemnity is limited to a specific time, such as twenty-four months. In these policies, business interruption losses can be claimed during the entire time, even after repairs are complete, as long as the business is not meeting preloss expectations. The period of restoration is typically estimated in the beginning of the claim recovery process, but final settlement is usually not reached until after the restoration is over and the insurance company and policyholder agree that preloss business operations have been restored.

Determining time periods and coverage can be very complex. Take the claims from the events on September 11, 2001, for example. Say a tenant of the World Trade Center incurred damage to property, such as office equipment and supplies, and that property can be restored or replaced quickly. But the office space itself is another story. What is the period of indemnity in this case? Does the fact the World Trade Center cannot be rebuilt exactly as it was have an impact? These types of questions are being argued in the courts because many policy definitions were unclear and didn't account for such a situation.

Here is an example of a more complex period definition, taken from an FM Global property policy:

A. The PERIOD OF LIABILITY applying to all TIME ELEMENT COVERAGES, except GROSS PROFIT and LEASEHOLD INTEREST and as shown below or if otherwise provided under the TIME ELEMENT COVERAGE EXTENSIONS, and subject to any Time Limit provided in the LIMITS OF LIABILITY clause in the DECLARATIONS section, is as follows:

1) For building and equipment, the period:
   a) Starting from the time of physical loss or damage of the type insured against; and
   b) Ending when with due diligence and dispatch the building and equipment could be:
      (i) Repaired or replaced; and
      (ii) Made ready for operations;
          under the same or equivalent physical and operating conditions that existed prior to the damage.
   Not to be limited by the expiration of this Policy.
2) For building and equipment under construction:
   a) the equivalent of the above period of time will be applied to the level of business that would have been reasonably achieved after construction and startup would have been completed had no physical damage happened; and
   b) due consideration will be given to the actual experience of the business compiled after completion of the construction and startup.
   This item does not apply to COMMISSIONS, PROFITS AND ROYALTIES.
3) For stock-in-process and mercantile stock, including finished goods not manufactured by the Insured, the time required with the exercise of due diligence and dispatch:
   a) to restore stock in process to the same state of manufacture in which it stood at the inception of the interrup-

tion of production or suspension of business operations or services; and

b) to replace physically damaged mercantile stock.
This item does not apply to RENTAL INSURANCE.

4) For raw materials and supplies, the period of time:
a) of actual interruption of production or suspension of operations or services resulting from the inability to get suitable raw materials and supplies to replace similar ones damaged; but
b) limited to that period for which the damaged raw material and supplies would have supplied operating needs.

5) If water:
a) used for any manufacturing purpose, including but not limited to as a raw material or for power,
b) stored behind dams or in reservoirs, and
c) on any Insured Location
is released as the result of physical damage of the type insured against under this policy to such dam, reservoir or connected equipment, the Company's liability for the actual interruption of production or suspension of operations or services due to inadequate water supply will not extend beyond 30 consecutive days after the damaged dam, reservoir or connected equipment has been repaired or replaced.
This item does not apply to RENTAL INSURANCE.

6) For physically damaged exposed films, records, manuscripts and drawings, the time required to copy from backups or from originals of a previous generation. This time does not include research, engineering or any other time necessary to restore or recreate lost information.
This item does not apply to RENTAL INSURANCE.

7) For physically damaged or destroyed property covered under DATA, PROGRAMS OR SOFTWARE, the time to recreate or restore including the time for researching or engineering lost information.
This item does not apply to RENTAL INSURANCE.

9) If an order of civil authority prohibits access to the Insured Location and provided such order is the direct result of physical damage of the type insured against under this Policy at the Insured Location or within 1,000 feet of it, the period of time:
a) starting at the time of physical damage; but
b) not to exceed 30 consecutive days.

As illustrated, defining the period of insured business interruption can be complicated. Imagine the number of questions that can be developed based on the listed definition.

Gross Profits/Extended Period of Indemnity

The time periods discussed previously are typical of U.S. insurance policies. Many European or Canadian insurance policies define the period of indemnity as a specific time period not related to repair of physical damage. Here is an example:

> The period beginning with the occurrence of a peril insured against and ending not later than 36 months after the waiting period during which the results of the business shall be affected in consequence of the destruction or damage by a peril insured against, and shall include such time as necessary to restore the Insured's business to the same level that would have existed had the loss not occurred.

Basically, this period starts with the physical damage and includes all loss that occurs during thirty-six months, without taking into consideration when the repair work is completed. Some U.S. policies have copied this type of coverage to a certain extent, by providing an Extended Period of Indemnity clause, such as the one shown here:

> EXTENDED PERIOD OF INDEMNITY: The GROSS EARNINGS coverage is extended to cover the reduction in sales resulting from:
>
> 1) The interruption of business as covered by GROSS EARNINGS;
> 2) For such additional length of time as would be required with the exercise of due diligence and dispatch to restore the Insured's business to the condition that would have existed had no loss occurred; and
> 3) Commencing with the date on which the liability of the Company for loss resulting from interruption of business would terminate if this Extension had not been included herein.

While this particular clause does not include a specific time limit, the norm ranges from thirty days to two years. The limit may be included in the definition or listed in another section of the policy. Typically, the extended period of indemnity does not start until the period of indemnity ends, so the requirement remains to determine that period.

What about Expenses?

Many terms are part of a claim recovery process: for example, extra expense, expediting expense, mitigating expense, increased cost of working, or expenses to avert business interruption. Many insurance professionals, including adjusters, use these terms interchangeably and, more often than not, incorrectly. The confusion comes from the fact that different policies define these terms differently.

"Expenses to avert business interruption" are those incurred to reduce BI losses otherwise payable, but these costs cannot exceed the amount of business interruption that they reduce. "Expediting expense" is property damage coverage that allows for the additional costs of expediting permanent repairs (for example, transporting parts by air freight rather than cargo ship).

"Extra expense" is the cost of continuing business operations as near normal as possible and practical, often without a requirement to reduce BI loss that would have been payable. Many times, extra expense is considered money to help maintain market share. In many policies this coverage is very broad and can be a powerful tool to be used by the insured to continue serving and satisfying good customers. Unfortunately, many people fail to understand this coverage. When choosing extra expense coverage, a policyholder should ensure they understand it.

Fair Claims-Handling

Sometimes it seems that the claims recovery process could benefit from a referee. Every state in the U.S. has laws that prohibit unfair or deceptive claim settlement practices. These laws vary from state to state, but most are similar and based on the model developed by the National Association of Insurance Commissioners (NAIC). The following list of unfair or deceptive practices is summarized from the State of Texas insurance regulations as prepared by the Texas Department of Insurance.[6]

> No insurer shall engage in unfair claim settlement practices. Unfair claim settlement practices means committing or performing any of the following:
>
> 1. misrepresenting pertinent facts or policy provisions relating to coverage(s) at issue
>
> 2. failing to acknowledge with reasonable promptness pertinent communications. An acknowledgement within 15 days is presumed to be reasonably prompt.

3. failing to implement reasonable standards for prompt investigation of claims.

4. not attempting to effectuate prompt, fair, and equitable settlements of claims submitted in which liability has become reasonably clear.

5. compelling policyholders to institute suits to recover amounts due by offering substantially less than the amounts ultimately recovered in suits.

6. failure to maintain a complete record of complaints.

7. failing to provide claim forms when the insurer requires such forms as a prerequisite for claim settlement.

8. not attempting to settle promptly claims where liability has become reasonably clear under one portion of the policy in order to influence settlement under other portions of the policy coverage.

9. failing to provide promptly a reasonable explanation for denial of a claim or for a compromise settlement.

10. failing to affirm or deny coverage of a claim to a policyholder within a reasonable time. The reasonable submission of a reservation of rights letter by an insurer to a policyholder within a reasonable time is deemed compliance.

11. to refuse, fail, or unreasonably delay offer of settlement under applicable first-party coverage on the basis that other coverage may be available or third parties are responsible for damages suffered.

12. attempting to settle a claim for less than the amount to which a reasonable person would have believed she/he was entitled by reference to an advertisement made by an insurer or person acting on behalf of an insurer.

13. undertaking to enforce a full and final release from a policyholder when, in fact, only a partial payment has been made.

14. failing to establish a policy and proper controls to make certain that agents calculate and deliver to policyholders or their assignees funds due under policy provisions relative to cancellation of coverage.

15. refusing to pay claims without conducting a reasonable investigation based upon all available information.

16. failing to respond promptly to a request by a claimant for personal contact about or review of the claim.

17. to delay or refuse settlement of a claim solely because there is other insurance of a different type available to satisfy partially or entirely the loss forming the basis of that claim.

18. a violation of the Insurance Code.

19. requiring a claimant, as a condition of settling a claim, to produce the claimant's federal income tax returns for examination or investigation by the insurer unless the claimant is ordered to produce those tax returns by a court of competent jurisdiction, the claim involves a fire loss, or the claim involves a loss of profits or income.

Requirements in Case of Loss

Most policies include a list of requirements that a policyholder must follow in case of loss. We have included an example from an FM Global property policy.

REQUIREMENTS IN CASE OF LOSS:

The Insured will:

1) Give immediate written notice to the Company of any loss.
2) Protect the property from further loss or damage.
3) Promptly separate the damaged and undamaged property; put it in the best possible order; and furnish a complete inventory of the lost, destroyed, damaged and undamaged property showing in detail the quantities, costs, actual cash value, replacement value and amount of loss claimed.
4) Give a signed and sworn proof of loss to the Company within 90 days after the loss, unless that time is extended in writing by the Company. The proof of loss must state the knowledge and belief of the Insured as to:
   a) the time and origin of the loss.
   b) the Insured's interest and that of all others in the property.
   c) the Actual Cash Value and replacement value of each item and the amount of loss to each item; all encum-

brances; and all other contracts of insurance, whether valid or not, covering any of the property;

d) any changes in the title, use, occupation, location, possession or exposures of the property since the effective date of this Policy.

e) by whom and for what purpose any location insured by this Policy was occupied on the date of loss, and whether or not it then stood on leased ground.

5) Include a copy of all the descriptions and schedules in all policies and, if required, provide verified plans and specifications of any buildings, fixtures, machinery or equipment destroyed or damaged.

6) Further, the Insured, will as often as may be reasonably required:

a) exhibit to any person designated by the Company all that remains of any property;

b) submit to examination under oath by any person designated by the Company and sign the written records of examinations; and

c) produce for examination at the request of the Company:

(i) all books of accounts, business records, bills, invoices and other vouchers; or

(ii) certified copies if originals are lost,

at such reasonable times and places that may be designated by the Company or its representative and permit extracts and machine copies to be made.

How to Succeed in the Loss Adjustment Process

- *Document your claim*—Poorly prepared and supported claims waste time and result in less-than-satisfactory settlements.

- *Claim what you lost*—Overstated or exaggerated claims invite additional scrutiny, hurt credibility, complicate and delay review, and seldom result in a greater recovery.

- *Be organized*—Lack of organization results in reduced recovery.

- *Stay flexible*—There may be no clearly acceptable correct result to a business interruption claim. There may be only a number that is acceptable or agreeable to both parties.

- *Expect the unexpected*—Expect significant scrutiny for all losses not immediately provable.

- *Stick to the facts*—Facts win negotiations.

- *Be aware of egos*—Individuals, including employees and adjusters, will often act in their own interest.

- *Don't try to fool people*—Insurance companies, adjusters, and consultants hired by adjusters are claim experts and are not likely to be fooled. Only a fool would attempt to fool them.

- *Be in control*—Cooperation, planning, and control are the policyholder's best tools.

Flattened Flooring Plant Betterment Issues

Tough issues in managing claims can lead to difficult settlement questions—and some unfortunate results. For example, a major manufacturer of sheet vinyl flooring suffered a disastrous explosion in its production plant when gases built up in the oven due to a ventilation problem. The explosion completely destroyed the production facility. The oven, which cured the various layers applied to the base felt sheet during manufacture, was an antiquated piece of equipment that could not be replaced with like kind and quality. In fact, its manufacturer no longer existed, and the blue prints for the equipment were lost. As a result, the manufacturer was confronted with the prospect of having to replace their older, oven-based technology.

Such a change, however, represented a significant betterment to the processes that had been destroyed. The company's dilemma was that there was no coverage for betterments and improvements in the insurance policy. Furthermore, there was a downside to those betterments; the new technology had such radically different operating characteristics that literally *none* of the product formulations that were proven on the old equipment would work on the newer equipment. Finally, all the ongoing research and development related to developing formulations that worked on the old equipment were rendered obsolete. In short, the company was back to square one on its product lines, which had to be completely redeveloped.

Accordingly, the company was faced with a significant business interruption issue that was complicated by a muddy property damage scenario. The insurance companies initially responded by asserting a theoretical replacement period based on rebuilding the original equipment, which excluded all of the time required to reformulate the products. The policyholder retained counsel and demanded mediation.

At the end of the day, the insurance companies agreed that the original equipment could not be rebuilt, as there was no longer any means of doing so in the absence of original "as-built" blueprints. However, they refused to compensate the policyholder for the full value of the replacement equipment due to the betterment issues. A negotiated agreement was reached as to the BI period, in light of the long duration of the recovery period under both the rebuild and replace scenarios. To reach closure, a lump sum payment was negotiated and the loss settled. Unfortunately for the company, however, it was never able to recover from this disaster, and the plant was ultimately closed.

Conclusion

Thousands of property and business interruption claims are settled and paid every year without major issues having arisen—and without recourse to litigation. Some insureds are very satisfied with the claim process, and with their final settlement. Conversely, some insureds find the process frustrating, or feel that they were significantly under-compensated for a loss. Many aspects of a policyholder's satisfaction with the claims process relate to the adjuster's expertise, her ability to hire capable advisers and/or consultants, and—let it be said—to his or her personality and management of the adjustment process. These factors can hugely impact the policyholder's experience. A more satisfied insured will typically convey that the claims process went smoothly, that good communication was maintained throughout, and that they recovered in good measure what they felt they were owed.

Sadly, this satisfaction appears to be in growing jeopardy, as more authority is stripped from adjusters, the use of shared and layered insurance programs increases, workloads continue to increase, and claims become progressively more complex. The number of satisfied insureds could markedly decrease due to the combination of these factors. An insured that understands the process, though, will have the ability to control it, overcome most frustrations, and reach the ultimate goal of the fair settlement they feel they are owed.

Endnotes

[1] In the insurance industry, "moral hazard" relates to the susceptibility of loss as the result of the moral lapse of the property owner. A dishonest policyholder may be better off after a loss. If a loss is $10,000, but the insurance policy pays $20,000, the insured has no incentive to prevent the loss and, in some circumstances, may invite or cause it. Examples of moral hazard range from the intentional (a building owner setting a fire) to negligence (leaving sensitive equipment in damaging conditions because the insurance policy will pay to replace it with state-of-the-art models).

[2] Many times, the policyholder has contact only with the adjuster. In these cases, it is well to keep in mind that behind the adjuster are claims managers, underwriters, sales people, operations people, and corporate executives. Add the fact that many large-company insurance programs are shared among multiple insurance companies and reinsurance companies; these parties may disagree on what is covered or which policy applies. While all are contractually obligated to pay claims, each wants to make sure it is paying only the appropriate amount. Complete documentation and timely communication from the policyholder go a long way towards building the comfort level required for insurance companies to sign the check.

[3] Although they are called "independent," these adjusters are hired and paid a fee by the insurance companies and do not work directly for the insured. Some states do permit public adjusters to represent insureds in negotiating certain elements of claims.

[4] Also discussed in Chapter 6: The Claim Recovery Process.

[5] It is this process—and the fact that insurers need to post a reserve on their books for statutory financial statement purposes—that motivates the adjuster to get her accountants involved with the policyholder immediately after a loss. Sometimes, the adjuster may even show up with those accountants at the policyholder's place of business. Insureds should not feel rushed by this activity, but rather should take a reasonable amount of time to review and prepare their own loss estimates before handing over their books and records to a third party. Chapter 9 includes a discussion of the policyholder's duty to cooperate with the insurer after a loss.

[6] This is only a summary to show examples of the types of practices that represent unfair claims settlement practices. Copies of the insurance regulations for individual states should be available from each particular state's Department of Insurance.

Exhibit 5.1: Sample Loss Adjuster's Report

Manufacturers Insurance Co.
13442 So. Imperator Lane
Orange, CA 92465

LOSS ADJUSTMENT MEMORANDUM

To:	Haight Lawsses
From:	Norman Conquest
Re:	Bio-Steam Innit Facility
	Loss Adjustment Report: Business Interruption (Explosion)
Date:	June 1, 2004
Event date:	March 16, 2004

Distribution
Dawson Leigh, V.P., Adjustment Division
Mark T. Worth, V.P. Actuarial Division

Estimate

	Net Amt.	Gross Amt.	Deductible		Est. Date
Property Damage	$ 10,611,289	$ 10,867,000	$ 255,711		12.21.2004
Bus. Interruption	$ 29,948,307	$ 30,670,000	$ 721,693		12.21.2004
Extra Expense	$ 937,646	$ 960,242	$ 22,596		12.21.2004

Executive Summary
An explosion occurred in the propellant-mixing area at this rocket-motor manufacturing facility. The Insured's current claim is $375,000,000 for a six-month shutdown, due to replacement of all mix bowls. We have requested additional supporting documentation; however, our current measurement is based on a 30-day shutdown to perform repairs to the mix bay.

Action Requested
Please review the attached documents and process this request for advance payment in the net amounts of $5,000,000 Property Damage and $15,000,000 Time Element.

Discussion
The Bio-Steam Innit facility manufactures propellant for various military and commercial rocket motor assemblies. The propellant mixture is composed mainly of ammonium perchlorate, aluminum dust, and a polymer-based binding agent. These materials are mixed in a 1,000-gallon batch mixer. Total propellant mixing capacity at the facility is 1.3 million gallons per year. The mixing area has gone through a series of upgrades and modifications over the past five years. The facility has a history of fires and explosions; however, explosions are inherent to a propellant manufacturing facility. Damage-limiting construction, reinforced concrete walls, explosion relief panels, high-speed deluge fire-suppression systems, and remote operator controls are all designed for the occasional fire or explosion. These systems are designed to limit damage from any fire or explosion to a confined area, to limit the downtime associated with repairs.

Mixing Incident: March 16, 2004
On March 16, 2004, the mixing line was in normal operation when an explosion occurred in the Mix Bay. The Mix Bay contains the 1,000-gallon batch mixer. Typical batch mix time is 8 hours. The explosion occurred in the Mixer, rupturing all 14 rupture disks which are designed to limit damage to the mixer by relieving internal pressures during an explosion. The high-speed deluge nozzles did not function, and neither did the nine automatic sprinklers in the ceiling, due to impact damage to an 8" cross-main water supply line used to supply both systems. Explosion relief panels on the wall and roof operated, but the frames were damaged due to over-pressurization.

The Fire Chief of the City of Innit issued a Cease-and-Desist order to Bio-Steam on March 17, 2004, in his words, "Due to the persistent, chronic, and ongoing pattern of frequent and severe explosions." The Order was rescinded on May 15, 2004, contingent on compliance with a new safety action plan.

Coverage
Bio-Steam claims the replacement of the mix bowls, the lead time to acquire frames for the explosion-relief panels for the building, and the changes required by the City of Innit to rescind the Cease-and-Desist order. The long lead-time item in this loss is the replacement of the mix bowls. Cracking was found in the bowl involved in the explosion as well as other bowls not involved. It was determined the cracking was due to fatigue and was not due to the incident. This is supported by the Metallurgist's report. The Exclusions on page 12 of 24 in the Manufacturer's Insurance Company Policy No-UA 2783 state the following:

> "This Policy does not insure against:
>
> deterioration, depletion, rust, corrosion, erosion, wear and tear, inherent vice or latent defect; all unless physical damage not excluded by this Policy results, in which event, this Policy shall cover only such resulting damage..."

Manufacturers Insurance Co.

As such, replacement of the mix bowls is not recoverable under the policy because the fatigue cracks are excluded by the above. The time required to repair the uninsured damage to the mix bowls (fatigue cracks) is not a recoverable cost under the MIC Policy. The physical damage to the mix bowls was not physical damage of the type insured against, and therefore the Policy is not extended by the Gross Earnings Endorsement—defined in the Gross Earnings endorsement as the following:

> "In determining the indemnity payable under the Endorsement; the Period of Interruption shall be:
>
> (1) The period from the time of physical damage of the type insured against by this Policy to the time when with due diligence and dispatch physically damaged buildings and equipment could be repaired or replaced and made ready for operations under the same or equivalent physical and operating conditions that existed prior to such damage, not to be limited by the day of expiration named in this Policy. This period of time does not include any additional time required for making change(s) to the buildings, structures, or equipment for any reason except as provided in the Demolition and Increased Cost of Construction provision."

The fatigue cracks in the Mix Bowl were not physical damage of the type insured against; therefore, the time required to repair the fatigue cracks does not extend the Period of Interruption. The time required to perform repairs to the insured physical damage was determined to be 30 days. This period ended on April 15, 2004. Changing the production process to avoid the 22 weeks of downtime associated with repairing the uninsured fatigue cracks is not a recoverable cost and did not mitigate the insured loss. If Bio-Steam had discovered the fatigue cracks prior to the March 16, 2004 explosion, production would have been shut down for 22 weeks for replacement of the bowls, or the production process would have had to be changed. None of these costs are associated with the March 16, 2004 explosion and are not recoverable under the MIC Policy.

Bio-Steam advised us during our April 18, 2004 meeting that explosion relief vent panels for the mix bay were not immediately available after the loss and that this impacted Bio-Steam's ability to restore production. Chickasawa Building Systems Invoice No. 1297 for the replacement of the panels appears to indicate the panels were delivered prior to April 16, 2004. Invoice No. 1296 from Chickasawa Building Systems indicates temporary 26 Gauge Vee Rib Wall panels with explosion fasteners were used in other areas of the facility. These invoices indicate the replacement panels were available prior to the time required to repair the physical damage in the mix bay. In addition, the invoices indicate temporary wall panels were adequate for operation. The additional claimed delay falls into an Idle Period as described the Gross Earnings Endorsement as follows:

> "This Endorsement does not cover:
>
> **IDLE**   1. any loss during any period in which goods would not have been produced, or
> **PERIODS**   business operations or services would not have been maintained, for any reason
>   other than physical loss Or damage of the type insured against to which this
>   Endorsement applies;"

As such, any costs associated with downtime due to the lack of panel availability is not a recoverable cost because the mix bay could not operate due to the fatigue cracks.

Any additional costs associated with changes to the facility as outlined in the Plan of Action developed by the City of Innit and Bio-Steam are not recoverable under the MIC Policy. We have reviewed the points raised in Luther Gradgrind's May 13, 2004 letter with regard to the Demolition and Increased Cost of Construction provision of the MIC Policy. Our position remains as stated in our letter of May 5, 2004.

Loss Measurement

Our analysis of the incident is based on the MIC Policy, which takes into consideration the experience of the business before the loss and the probable experience after the loss had no interruption to production occurred and had no changes to the process been made. We projected the production for the mixing operation based on production levels prior to and after the loss period. Had no changes been made to the process, production levels would have returned shortly after repairs to the mix bay were complete.

The May 3, 2004 Claim Summary presented by Hunnicutt & Spelenger states on page 2, "If Bio-Steam had returned to its prior manufacturing process . . . use of the prior start-up curves might be appropriate." Our projection is based on returning to the manufacturing process that was in effect at the time of loss. Our projection is also based on operating at capacity to make up lost production as required by the policy. The projection described in the May 3, 2004 Hunnicutt & Spelenger Claim Summary uses average production taken over a time period that includes the month of August when the mix bay was shut down for the maintenance. This does not reflect production levels that could have been reached in order to make up lost production.

As indicated in the attached schedule, titled "Production & Inventory Analysis," the projected production capability would have returned the inventory to a level greater than 100,000 during the week of April 20, 2004. Reference the attached schedules for a summary of the computed claim and the amounts recoverable under the MIC Policy.

Typically, the Loss Adjuster's Report is used to notify the insurers of the initial loss estimates as well as any changes to the loss estimate. If one report is created for multiple insurers, this section may actually prorate the estimate for each insurer based on their percentage participation in the insurance program.

Executive Summary—Provides a quick overview of the type of loss that occurred and any particular issues.

Action Requested—Describes anything the adjuster is requesting from the underwriters. It may be a request for settlement authority or a request to make an interim or final payment. Here is a list of typical requests:

- Payment request
- Estimate or reserve change
- Settlement authority
- Authority to hire consultants
- Coverage review or analysis
- Review of consultant's reports
- Subrogation or legal review
- Specific coverage or measurement issues

Discussion—Covers the loss and the adjustment activities; description of the facts, loss mitigation activities, consultant's findings, etc. The intent of this part of the memo would be to describe everything about the loss and everything that was being done following the loss. It should provide the information necessary for underwriters to make decisions and to accept or reject the items listed in the Action Requested section. This section of the report may be lengthy and may reference other support documents and summary schedules.

Coverage—Lays out the insurance coverage that is applicable to the particular loss including deductibles, any exclusions that apply and any limits or sub limits that may apply. It is here so the individual reader does not need to refer to the policy while reading the memo.

Measurement—Discusses the adjuster's measurement of the loss or the basis for the loss estimate; may also discuss issues or disagreements between the adjuster's measurement and the insured's claim. For instance, there may be a discussion on sales projections during the period of indemnity if the adjuster disagrees with the projection claimed by the insured.

Settlement strategy—Discusses what the adjuster is doing to resolve the claim. If there is a difference between the adjuster's measurement of the loss and the insured's claim, there may be a discussion of the difference and how much money above the adjuster's measurement they think will be required to settle the claim. This gives the underwriters an opportunity to weigh in on the strategy and if they think something different should be done.

Next steps—Lists tasks to be completed and possibly a timeline. It could be a listing of items the adjuster is waiting for or an estimate of when the next interim payment will be requested.

The Developer
Setting Up the Claim

Blue Island, off the coast of Southern California between Los Angeles and San Diego, was the site of the first amusement park ever built on the west coast. Built in 1921, the Blue Island Amazement Park contained all the traditional rides and the largest midway of any amusement park in North America at the time. The park included a 100-room, bungalow-style motel with a themed restaurant, as well as a boat dock and yacht club. Adjacent to the property was Sonny Beach, a quarter-mile stretch of beach accessible from the park.

During the Depression, the Blue Island Amazement Park fell into disrepair and decrepitude. After the attack on Pearl Harbor in 1941, the U.S. government decided to strengthen the country's war resources on the west coast, and Blue Island was purchased so the Navy could run underground pipelines from a refinery forty miles away to Sonny Beach, the site of a temporary fueling station. Blue Island and Sonny Beach were used by the government from 1945 through 1979, then put up for auction in 1980. At the time of the auction, all information regarding the land's use (including the underground pipelines) was disclosed to all parties.

Sold at the auction in 1980, the land was held until real estate values started to climb. In 1998, the owner sold Blue Island, and the land on which it was built, to New York real estate billionaire Marty Graw, who wanted to raze the facility and build California's first beachside casino and resort. Marty's prior project had been the conversion of an industrial lakefront property in Colorado, called Happy Mountain Mills, into the Happy Mountain Resort and Casino, which opened in January of 1999. Happy Mountain was a huge success. With more than 3,000 slot machines and 200 gaming tables, it was the largest casino ever built in Colorado. In its first year of operations, the casino generated more than over $100 million in revenue.

By 1999, Marty and his company, Two Pay Inc., had secured all approvals needed to build the new casino on Blue Island and were ready to begin construction. Less than two years after acquiring the property, Marty had completed demolition of the amusement park—except for its 300-foot Ferris Wheel, which served as the centerpiece of the casino's main drive. He had converted the Blue Island Motel to temporary office space for on-site crew and had converted and renovated the Sonny Side Yacht Club to sell permanent slips and provide yacht tours for VIPs. In addition, Graw's team had fully restored the Blue Island Restaurant and added high-end retail space.

The *pièce-de-la-resistance*, however, was the completed construction of the Blue Island Casino, a 150,000-square-foot casino with 2,500 slot machines, over 200 gaming and poker tables, and a 1,500 seat amphitheater for entertainment and meeting space. At a Year 2000 Millennial New Year's party for the grand opening of the Blue Island Casino, Marty revealed plans to also build a 500-room, high-rise hotel adjacent to the casino on the site of the old Blue Island Motel. The total cost of Graw's project was more than $175 million.

In early 2000, the same time Blue Island Casino had opened, Happy Mountain expected 30 percent casino revenue growth over the next three years. Marty had similar expectations for Blue Island. While the two casinos were in different states, they enjoyed similar clientele and a tourist draw from surrounding recreational facilities. With both casinos open and enjoying success, Marty could focus on his latest venture, a reality television show centered on the high-stakes world of commercial real estate, "The Developer."

PLAYING THE BLUES ON BLUE ISLAND

Exactly as planned, less than a year after the Blue Island Casino opened, construction began on the Blue Island Resort Hotel. Unfortunately, as construction progressed, oil spots began to appear throughout the development, and at 6:30 in the morning on Monday, July 2, 2001, a fire started when sparks from an outside contractor's torch hit a puddle of oil that had been developing from a crack in the casino's parking lot.

The fire quickly ignited the landscaping and spread throughout the casino. It blazed uncontrollably until fully 80 percent of the casino building and the Ferris Wheel were destroyed. A large smoke cloud hung over the facility for hours and soot fell over the newly renovated restaurant and retail space. Fortunately, the casino was relatively empty and no one was injured. It turned out afterwards that in the previous few weeks, the Domestic Oil Refinery of California (DORC), which had originally designed the pipelines for the government in 1945, had shut off the pressure to the old underground pipeline system. This caused an implosion in the pipes that sent hundreds of gallons of oil slowly percolating upwards through the subsoil, eventually breaking ground in the building site.

PUT YOURSELF IN THE PICTURE

It is January 3, 2003. The reconstruction of Blue Island Casino has been completed. Unfortunately, Two Pay was unable to replace Blue Island Casino's marquis Ferris Wheel; it was a 60-year-old design and the last of its kind. But the casino is open for business.

You have been hired by Two Pay to assist in calculating the property damage and business interruption claim. Two Pay's broker has been handling the claim thus far. On completion of its Blue Island Casino, Two Pay had procured comprehensive property insurance, including endorsements for business interruption, from its broker. Two Pay also had complete commercial general liability insurance. To date, the insurance company has been reluctant to advance cash, suggesting on more than one occasion that the DORC has some liability for the destruction of the casino. Luckily, Two Pay has hit the jackpot with its new reality television show, "The Developer," and has plenty of cash to float the cost of rebuilding.

Due to the cleanup and remediation of the property required during the reconstruction, the existing casino was relocated to a temporary off-site facility for a period of eighteen months. Two Pay is looking to recuperate the following out-of-pocket costs as a result of the fire:

Two-Pay feels that its property damage claim is fairly simple. It seeks all property damage costs and the cost to rebuild the casino. Graw has stated that he believes these costs are reasonable given that the casino was essentially destroyed and that the total cost of rebuilding was less than the project's original cost. He has also indicated that Two Pay was unable to obtain a valuation on the Ferris Wheel, but feels that $5 million is a fair number since it was a one-of-a-kind item; replacement cost for a new Ferris Wheel would have been $1.1 million. The casino replaced the Ferris Wheel with a fountain featuring Morpheus, the Greek god of dreams. The cost of the fountain was $1 million and is included in the building reconstruction costs above.

Two Pay's executive team believes that due to the public's negative perception of the "Oil Slick Casino" and increased competition in the area, it will take at least a year after the Blue Island Casino reopens before it is back to its previous revenue growth. Graw feels strongly that Two Pay should be compensated for that loss. The company's best estimate of Blue Island Casino's expected revenue had the incident not occurred is in the three-year strategic plan prepared in 2000. The policy covering this claim states that the business interruption claim should be based on net sales lost, less saved expenses.

Two Pay has provided you and the claim adjuster, Will Naughtpeigh, with the Blue Island Casino's profit and loss statements prior to the incident, 2000, and six months ended June 30, 2001, as well as the Casino's three-year strategic plan revenue, developed in late 2000 for the years 2001 through 2003. Also, Two Pay provided its profit and loss statements during the period that the casino was relocated to the temporary facility, July 3, 2001, through December 28, 2002. For comparative purposes, the company added profit and loss statements for the casino operations of its sister casino, The Happy Mountain Resort and Casino, from 1999 to 2002. Those statements follow:

Figure D-1

	Cost
Emergency Clean-up	$ *1.2*
Temporary Facility	*15.0*
Site Remediation	*20.5*
Building Reconstruction	*97.6*
Equipment	*14.0*
Labor	*3.8*
Landscaping and Roads	*2.5*
Advertising	*3.5*
Ferris wheel	*5.0*
Other	*11.0*
Total	$ *174.1*

Figure D-2

		2000		6 Mos. Ended 6/30/01
Blue Island Casino				
2000 - 2001 Actual				
(In Millions)				
Total Revenue	$	75.0	$	45.0
Cost of Sales		25.0		15.0
General & Administrative		10.0		6.0
Sales & Marketing		7.0		3.7
Other		10.0		6.0
Total Expenses		52.0		30.7
EBITDA	$	23.0	$	14.3

EBITDA = Earnings Before Income Taxes, Depreciation, and Administration

Figure D-3

		2001		2002		2003
Blue Island Casino						
2001 - 2003 Strategic Plan						
(In Millions)						
Sales	$	93.8	$	112.5	$	135.0
Cost of Sales		30.9		37.1		44.6
Labor		11.6		13.2		14.9
Sales & Marketing		7.3		7.6		7.9
Other		11.2		12.4		13.7
Total Expenses		61.0		70.3		81.1
EBITDA	$	32.7	$	42.2	$	53.9

Figure D-4

Blue Island Casino Loss Period (In Millions)	6 Mos Ended 12/31/01	2002
Total Revenue	$ 10.5	$ 24.7
Cost of Sales	3.7	8.6
General & Administrative	4.5	9.0
Sales & Marketing	1.0	3.2
Other	3.0	5.0
Total Expenses	12.2	25.8
EBITDA	$ (1.7)	$ (1.1)

Figure D-5

Happy Mountain Casino 1999 - 2002 Actual (In Millions)	1999	2000	2001	2002
Total Revenue	$ 95.0	$ 123.5	$ 142.0	$ 156.2
Growth		30%	15%	10%
Cost of Sales	29.5	38.3	44.0	48.4
General & Administrative	15.2	18.2	20.5	22.6
Sales & Marketing	9.0	9.0	9.4	9.8
Other	14.3	16.1	17.8	19.6
Total Expenses	67.9	81.6	91.8	100.4
EBITDA	$ 27.1	$ 41.9	$ 50.2	$ 55.8

THE DEVELOPER

QUESTIONS
AND ANSWERS

1. What issues might Two Pay have with indemnity for this incident?

    •   The insurer may suggest that it should not have to pay the claim since other parties contributed to the fire. However, property insurance policies are first party policies that allow for recovery against the insurer for insured property. If the insured suffers losses that are not covered by the property policy, they could sue the wrongdoers separately. Also, if the property insurer seeks to recover against the wrongdoers separately, they could subrogate the matter on behalf of the policyholder.

2. As an adviser on this claim, how and to whom would you advise Two Pay, Inc., to proceed with the submission of its claim?

    •   It may be in the best interest of the company to proceed with its claim to its own insurer, while simultaneously pursuing other avenues of indemnification. Ultimately, the insurer will want to reduce the claim by any dollars Two Pay receives from other sources, and it may speed recovery. Therefore, Two Pay could calculate the claims it has against all parties (which will likely be similar in nature and amount) and inform all parties of its intentions.

3. From the insurance company's perspective, what coverage issues (depending on the policy) might affect Two Pay's property damage claim?

- **Plural indemnity.** The insurer may prefer to determine who is responsible, and may require Two Pay to exhaust all other potential sources of recovery, before even considering (let alone paying) the claim. Such an approach, however, might be risky. Generally, collateral sources of recovery, such as potential third-party claims or contractual indemnity, will not limit or negate the insurer's independent obligation to its insured to promptly adjust and pay covered claims. Thus, the insurer should fully evaluate the possibility that such an approach could expose it to claims from the insured (e.g., breach of contract, bad faith) before embarking on such a course. Such an analysis would include a review of the policy language and applicable law.

- **Policy limits and exclusions**. Two Pay's recovery from the insurance company might be limited based on potential limits to coverage (e.g. landscaping) or exclusions for certain items (e.g. retraining of labor or site remediation).

- **Dual recovery**. Two Pay appears to be making a claim for both the value of the Ferris Wheel and the cost of building the fountain. The insurer would likely see this as an attempt at dual recovery. Further, it would likely not pay the "value" of the antique Ferris Wheel, as recovery would likely be limited to replacement cost.

- **Property damage claim—advertising**. The insurer may not pay advertising costs outside of those incurred in the normal course of business and may not consider additional advertising as property damage. However, should this amount mitigate a business interruption loss or should Two Pay have extra expense coverage, the amounts would be recoverable.

- **Property damage claim—other costs**. The insurer will likely question the validity of $11 million in *other costs* without further description and support.

4.   How should Two Pay calculate its business interruption claim?

- There may be several different calculations to consider.

- Consider the best way to present the BI claim based on the context provided in the reading (lost revenue less saved expenses).

- Discuss/think about what is the most appropriate period of loss (time to rebuild v. time to recover prior revenue performance).

- Focus on a reasonable estimate of the casino's expected revenue and expenses to compare to actual results.

- If the company expects to recover continuing losses, estimate the casino's actual performance for the next year to compare to projections.

5. How would the insurer and/or the adjuster view Blue Island Casino's revenue projections? What approach would the adjuster take to project the casino's revenue during the loss period?

- The insurer may consider the revenue projections as aggressive given world and economic events that may have affected the casino's performance.

- Additionally, the insurer may look at the results from the Happy Mountain Casino and see that actual revenue growth from 2000 to 2002 did not match expectations (30 percent).

- To project revenue, the insurer may take historical results and apply some growth percentage that it deems reasonable based on economic factor and comparable property data. Also, depending on the policy the insurer will likely end the loss period after eighteen months.

6. What factors should Two Pay's claim adviser consider in estimating the casino's projected revenue for the loss period?

- The effect of both 9–11 and war in Afghanistan on the U.S. tourism industry

- The effects of a changing national and local economy on the casino's results

- Changes in supply and demand for Two Pay's casino product during the loss period

- Happy Mountain Casino's revenue and cost expectations and actual results

- Industry growth and profitability

- Are there any losses from the reality TV show that would have been earned had it not been for the loss?

7.   How should Two Pay measure its saved costs during the loss period?

- Estimate expenses that would have been incurred based on the information that is given and compare to those that were actually incurred.

- How those expenses are estimated and the results will vary depending on the methodology used. Typically, when preparing a claim, one would consider the insured's historical profitability, industry profitability, the profitability of similar products (in this case the Happy Mountain Casino), the nature of the estimated expenses (variable, fixed or some mix), and/or changes in economic and industry factors, like inflation or changes in the competitive market.

8.   What other lost income claim might Two Pay, Inc,. have against other parties?

- Two Pay should claim all losses not covered by their property damage insurance policy. This would include losses beyond the covered business interruption period, losses due to the market's negative perception of the casino after the incidents, and losses for delays around the development and operation of the hotel.

An Inferno of Losses

Giovanni Donatello's self-founded company, Creative Comedia, specialized in detailed, beautifully crafted toys, figurines, and other collectibles. Two years ago, Giovanni sold the company to The Wilton Brothers Co., one of the largest toy and game producers in the world. The company was a particularly attractive acquisition for three reasons. First was the quality and uniqueness of the products. Second was Donatello's patent on Reformall, a versatile rubber/clay type material that could retain its shape for 100 years, yet was also easily recycled into another form. Third, Creative Comedia had won the contract to make merchandise for four of the prior year's smash-hit movies.

The sale of Creative Comedia to Wilton Brothers gave Donatello much greater research and development resources, a 50 percent increase in production and distribution capacity, and the largest sales network in the industry. The deal immediately paid off when the soon-to-be-hit movie, *Space Voyage from Earth*, signed Wilton Brothers and Creative Comedia to handle all the merchandising. Immediately, Reformall became the basis for what was conceived as one of the world's greatest marketing promotions. Creative Comedia promised a 25 percent price reduction on a new toy in exchange for the return of an old one, which itself could be recast in an efficient, cost-effective recycling process.

The sales potential for a franchise like *Space Voyage from Earth*, with an anticipated three movies and a five-part mini-series, was obvious. Collectors would have an incentive to buy more and more merchandise, trading in duplicates and out-of-favor toys and action figures. The deal with *Space Voyage from Earth*—with the first movie in the series due to be released in December of 2002—was signed by Wilton Brothers and the movie's producers in 2000. At the time of the signing, a few slight anomalies were still being worked out in the formula for Reformall. Yet, Donatello envisioned that more than five million units would be shipped for each movie, with a sales value of over $5.00 per unit for each of the three movies and another ten million units for the five-part series, for a total of twenty-five million units or $125 million in sales.

TROUBLE IN TOYLAND

On January 2, 2002, an explosion occurred in the #2 mixer of the Reformall factory in Provo, Utah. The cause of the incident is still under investigation. Repair and/or replacement of the mixer was projected to take between six and nine months. The explosion pushed back the qualification test of Reformall from March 1 to April 1. The risk manager at Wilton Brothers, Rollyn Dice, told Donatello there was no need for him to visit the plant site; he had also informed his insurance carrier, Production Mutual, of the loss by email, describing: "a minor fire with some property damage, but no business interruption." Then, he added, "Can you come out and take a look?"

On April 1, the Reformall was finally being mixed again in an auxiliary testing mixer. Just as production began to ramp up speed, a crane moving the old mixer #2 collapsed. "That big old crane just collapsed as soon as it started to get going," said Mike Foreman, the production manager. The platform and various crane parts went flying into the auxiliary mixer, causing a second explosion and delaying the qualification test even longer. "This Reformall product is sure causing us quite a challenge," added the laconic Foreman, in a quote that made the local news.

Because of these two unfortunate incidents, the producers of *Space Voyage from Earth* began to worry. With a prerelease marketing blitz planned for early October, the producers were concerned that Wilton Brothers would not be able to make the merchandise in time. Wilton Brothers was able to "toll" or rent out another mixing facility from a California clay manufacturer in bankruptcy reorganization; and another product test was planned for July 1. The producers used this extra time to ask for some changes in the merchandise specifications.

If anything, July 1 turned out to be worse than April 1. Another crane, being used to dismantle a neighboring building on the same property, actually fell onto the mixing facility as a result of a minor explosion occurring during the mixing of the Reformall. Said the security officer on site, "That darned crane just crunched over the top of that old mixing building." As might be expected, the testing date got pushed back again. The State Safety Board began an investigation and released a statement: "The minor explosion is under investigation, but it could be related to the use of a toxic dye recently added to the manufacturing process and not in the original specifications submitted as part of the plan for leasing the facility." These changes were the ones requested by the producers after the first crane event.

On July 15, 2002, the producers for *Space Voyage from Earth* signed a contract with Acme Toy Company to make their promotional merchandise. They also filed a breach of contract lawsuit against Wilton Brothers, noting "failure to produce, loss of market, manufacture's default, environmental hazard and other complaints."

PUT YOURSELF IN THE PICTURE

You are newly hired treasurer for Wilton Brothers, brought in two months before the second incident, to help the company bring its business to the next level. For twenty years you've worked with a leading manufacturer known for its cross-functional team work, research and development, and product innovation. Years ago, coincidentally, you also handled a "bet-the-farm" business interruption claim for that company—and through teamwork (including functional departments, impacted customers, third-party claim consultants, the insurance company, and the broker), your company settled a claim in a way that left everyone comfortable with the process and its outcome.

As soon as you're on board at Wilton Brothers, you see that the company's growth over the past few years came from acquisitions and that the acquired companies continue to work in isolation. The CFO suggests that the company is "leaving money on the table" by not integrating its new businesses and sharing information across divisions. Now you're faced with a major business interruption that affects the viability of the entire enterprise. And your problems aren't over.

Mix-up in the Mix House

Just as you're about to pick up the phone to contact Rollyn Dice, the company's risk manager, Dice sends you an email: "The insurers are willing to pay only $2 million on our claim because the mix house was not a named location in our policy. I think it's a good settlement offer because we have a renewal in a few weeks and the broker is telling me it will be a tough market this year. Besides the insurers really don't know the whole story, so I think we should take it. Can you authorize me to settle the claim?" You pick up the phone and dial Dice. Your first question: "Rollyn, why on earth isn't this a named location?" He responds: "Well, our broker never submitted that information because they only send our updates to the carrier once a quarter. That's their policy."

No sooner is this exchange over than you receive a copy of the legal complaint filed by the producers of *Space Voyage from Earth*. The claim is for more than $50 million in lost costs and sales. You feel like you just landed on a different planet yourself. Clearly it's time to put some heads together.

Comedia? Or Tragedy?

You call a meeting of the following people to discuss the matter and decide on a strategy. First on the list is Giovanni Donatello, President of Creative Comedia; second is Rollyn Dice. Others invited are Mike Foreman, Director of Production & Manufacturing; Julie Juris, Deputy General Counsel; and Ian Accurate, your Director of Budgeting and Planning. On Thursday morning, everyone gathers in the boardroom—and you're amazed at the level of cheerfulness. Donatello, Mike, Rollyn, and Ian all act as if they just hit the jackpot. As you enter the room, Donatello is holding up the front-page story in *The Wall Street Journal*: "New Contract for Wilton Brothers Makes Up Lost Sales for Old: Dante Resurrects Donatello from Inferno of Losses." Julie, however, is quiet; she seems upset.

You pick up the article and begin to read. Hearing of Creative Comedia's loss of business, Donatello's cousin, Dante Bonatello, had signed a contract giving Creative Comedia all the production rights for merchandise from Dante's new, monumental film release, a five-movie version of the poet Dante's *The Divine Comedy*. The series is expected to appeal to teenagers, academicians, artists, and religious moviegoers. "No need for a meeting anymore, eh!" says Donatello. As people start to leave the room, you say, "Hey, wait a minute, guys. Not so fast."

Just at that moment, your assistant brings in a message. "The insurance adjuster and his accountant are in the lobby. They say they need to tour the plant today and want to meet about the loss." She hands their cards to you, you pass them to Donatello, and the company's president reads two names: Norman Conquest, Insurance Adjuster, and Kurt Mudgeon, Accountant. Then she asks, "Should I have them wait in your office?"

Other Key Facts

Wilton Brothers has a worldwide property and business interruption policy with many of the endorsements others may characterize as "the bells and whistles." It's a substantial, detailed policy, containing many layers with slightly different wording in each. At one of the bottom layers is the statement: "Business Interruption for only scheduled locations," while in another place one can read, "All risk for all insurable property." The policy also states that "the company shall operate with due diligence and dispatch to restore operations and mitigate its loss; any make up in production shall be considered in establishing the loss." The business interruption time period has no limit, but rather states "when repairs are complete and business returns to normal, had no loss occurred."

The business interruption section also includes the following: "... [I]n order to predict what sales would have been, the company shall consider the historical performance of the insured, plus any adjustment needed to consider any current business environment that existed at the time of the loss." The policy also has a clause for consequential loss: "We will pay for consequential loss for related or 'sister' products that are impacted as a result of the insured event." Too, the policy has a clause for exclusions pertaining to cancellation of contracts: "is not covered unless as a direct result of the insured event."

The contract with *Space Voyage from Earth* would maximize production for Reformall but not other material. While the contract did not specifically say it required Reformall in the products supply, that idea was understood between the parties.

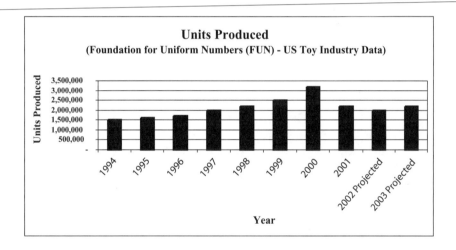

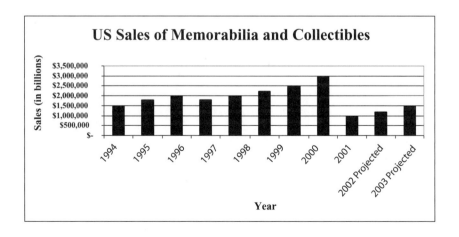

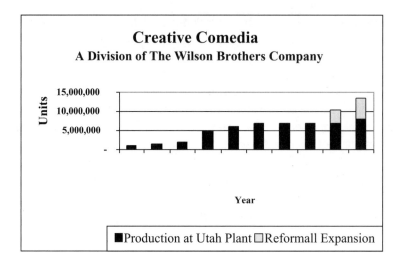

AN INFERNO OF LOSSES

A R E A S   O F

D I S C U S S I O N

1.   How in the world would you deal with the above situation?

   a)   Ask the insurance adjuster to perform an investigation of the situation and write a report. This is the most cost-effective way to deal with the situation.

   b)   Sue the insurance company, your customer, and broker.

   c)   Ask the insurance company what it's willing to pay for.

   d)   Prepare a summary and timeline of facts and events in order to decide what to do.

2.   Does The *Wilton Brothers* Company have a valid claim for business interruption?

   a)   No, the contract was cancelled and that's excluded in the policy.

   b)   No, as the entire operations were not suspended.

   c)   No, *Reformall* is not even a proven product.

   d)   Yes, but valuation of the claim may be a challenge.

3.   How do the crane crunch and crane collapse impact the insurance claim?

   a)   No impact, as the event would have happened anyway.

b)   The loss period would simply be "extended" to include this time, since there is no time limit to the business interruption endorsement.

c)   To the extent that the events are related to the initial cause of loss, they would be covered.

4.   If the loss period is extended because of the general contractor should that be included in the claim?

a)   Yes, this is part of the loss.

b)   Yes, and the company would then "subrogate" against its customer.

c)   No, there is no relationship between change orders and a cause of loss for an insurance claim.

d)   Maybe, this is an extremely interesting situation where legal advice is needed.

5.   How does the lawsuit by the producers impact the claim?

a)   No impact.

b)   Some impact as it would limit the insured claim to be no greater that the $50 million dollar amount of the lawsuit due to state law requirements.

c)   Is a separate issue from the property and business interruption claim, but has many elements of similar facts that may need to be considered by the insured prior to making a claim.

6.   Can The *Wilton Brothers* Company put forth a claim for all other Space Voyage from Earth movies and TV series if the contract covered only one movie?

a)   Yes.

b)   No.

7.   Is the contract for The Divine Comedy merchandise considered "makeup" production? (Explain) How would you develop a claim estimate?

What are some of the issues that will be raised by the insurance company and their experts?

a)   What is the production history of the facility; what was planned for production during the current year?

b)   Capacity of the facility and other plants to produce the product.

c)   Was property a named insured or not? Is this an issue?

d)   How necessary was the Reformall to this sale?

e)   Were there other issues that caused the producers to go somewhere else?

f)   If there is a loss, what would be the minimum and maximum claim esti-mates (for reserve purposes)?

g)   Was the industry for these products shrinking or going away?

h)   What was the market share of The Wilton Brothers Company doing in this industry?

i)   What were its competitors doing?

What experts may be used in this situation to prove or critique a claim?

a)   Cause and origin engineering expert to understand cause and extent of losses.

b)   Accounting expert to quantify claims.

c)   Possibly a toy and or "memorabilia/collectible" expert or even a movie production expert.

d)   Insurance coverage lawyers.

e)   Subrogation attorneys.

Suggested Answers

1.   d)

2.   d)

3.   c)

4.   d)

5.   c)

6.   Discussion item. See pages 146 and 147.

7.   Certainly "The Divine Comedy" merchandise is not makeup of the "Space Voyage from Earth" merchandise because it is a different movie, different product, and did not use Reformall. Further it can be construed that this production is merely an indirect consequence of the loss. Since indirect losses are not covered, indirect gains should not be credited. This portion of the claim would and should be closely scrutinized by the insurance carrier as possibly other facts may contribute to a theory of makeup.

Claim by the Insured

Wilton Brothers chooses to file a business interruption claim that includes losses for the three *Space Voyage from Earth* movies, as well as for the five-part mini-series. The company persists in its belief that handling the merchandise for the first movie would have all but guaranteed they would have handled merchandising for the remaining movies. The claim, as a result, is for twenty-five million lost units, valued at their selling price less saved expenses. Saved expenses are estimated at 25 percent for The Wilson Brothers Company. This would yield a claim value of approximately $94 million.

The contract with Dante does not require the use of Reformall. Therefore, Wilton Brothers could use its available capacity to fill this contract in addition to the *Space Voyage from Earth* contract. Therefore, these would not be considered "make-up" sales.

There would also be a claim for property damage and extra expense from the initial explosion in the #2 mixer, as well as from the two crane collapses which were which were a result of the initial explosion.

Rebuttal by the Insurer

In the view of the insurer, there is no business interruption loss for Wilton Brothers. The Reformall, still in development and testing, had never actually been used in production. Therefore, it was not certain that its product launch would have been successful. The market for this type of merchandise was also on the decline. In addition, the contract was for one movie for a total of $25 million, and the Wilton Brothers Company had make-up sales of approximately $90 million from Dante Bonatello after the *Space Voyage from Earth* contract was cancelled. The Dante contract was for three million units per movie, at an average sales price of $6.00 per unit for each of the five movies.

However, there would be a claim for property damage and extra expense from the initial explosion in the #2 mixer, as well as from the collapse of the first crane, which was being used to remove this mixer. The insurers are only willing to pay $2 million on the claim because the mix house was not a named location under the policy.

An Arbitrator's Likely Stance

Called to arbitrate this difficult, multi-faceted claim, a likely position on the part of an arbitrator would be that the business interruption claim should include losses for the first *Space Voyage from Earth* movie since the contract only included it. There was no guarantee that The Wilson Brothers Company would get the remaining contracts. These additional contracts would depend on the success of the Reformall launch and the success of the products marketed with the first movie. The claim, therefore, would be for five million lost units. These units would be valued at their selling price less saved expenses. Saved expenses are estimated at 25 percent for Wilton Brothers, yielding a claim value of approximately $19 million.

The contract with Dante does not require the use of Reformall; therefore, Wilton Brothers could use its available capacity to fill this contract in addition to, and not instead of, the *Space Voyage from Earth* contract. Therefore, these would not be considered "make-up" sales.

There would be a claim for property damage and extra expense from the initial explosion in the #2 mixer, as well as from the first crane collapse since the crane was being used to remove this mixer. The second crane collapse was a result of Wilton Brothers using materials with specifications different from originally planned, which resulted in the explosion and collapse. Coverage for the second crane would be a function of the property policy wording.

CHAPTER SIX

The Claim Recovery Process

Building the Team, Knowing the Plan

For many executives, each day brings some type of business interruption— whether caused by inclement weather keeping people from work or by training programs that impact productivity; whether triggered by a power outage, the delivery of the wrong raw materials, an equipment failure, or a strike; whether coming from the company's own operations, from its supply chain, or from the marketplace. While these types of business interruptions might require work-arounds, and while they're certainly nuisances, they usually have little or no insurance impact due to the event's size or nature.

But when a major disruption—a fire, explosion, flood, or other disaster— brings business to a halt, a company needs to respond quickly and appropriately. Immediately, there's the need to safeguard assets or save lives. An insured that has never experienced a large property damage and business interruption insurance claim can often be overwhelmed not only by the overall claim process, but by the sheer number of people that may be involved and the planning necessary to move things forward. This chapter takes a close look at the Who's Who of the process and at the planning involved:

Which people, with what skills, belong on the claims team?

Consider for a moment a circumstance not unlike that faced by many in a business interruption loss. Think of yourself as the Plant Manager of CruiseHomes, Inc., a manufacturer of recreational vehicles. You've been with the company for many years, and you know you face significant issues at your plant. Productivity has fallen, employee turnover is high, and—as your plant uses a just-in-time manufacturing process to assemble the RVs—you and your management team believe that inventory levels are problematic.

You and your staff have been working extra hours to remedy the problems. Then, suddenly, a fire breaks out in your plant, causing significant property damage and other significant losses. Three of your best employees suffer minor injuries, and, while not all your equipment is damaged, you certainly don't have the ability to make any more RVs. And you have a lot of cleanup to do.

Of course, your initial goal is to safeguard assets and assess damage. Immediately after the loss, you will need to assemble a claims team and develop a plan to better understand the loss. Your team will consist of at least one member for each discipline within your company, including accounting and finance, risk management, engineering, production, operations, and sales and marketing. For larger or more complex losses, it will also typically include outside consultants with significant claims experience not usually available in your company. This team will investigate all aspects of the loss, identify and evaluate opportunities to mitigate it, review options for repairs, select vendors to complete such repairs and monitor progress, evaluate available insurance, and work with insurance company representatives to answer questions and negotiate a settlement when insurance coverage is available.

Of course, the composition of any specific claims teams will differ based upon a specific type of business and the nature of the loss. The collective efforts and knowledge of your claims team will greatly impact your plan to obtain information about the loss, to better understand what happened and its potential financial impact, to act to mitigate the loss, and, in the end, determine what is covered under the policy. Every claims team, therefore, needs to address similar fundamental questions:

1. What was the cause of the incident?

2. In what ways can we mitigate the loss?

3. Were any third parties impacted for which we may have liability?

4. Should government agencies, such as OSHA, be notified?

5. How will this impact our brand reputation and market position?

6. How do we manage the loss while staying focused on our business?

The engineers on the claims team often work with local fire authorities or with *cause and origin* experts hired by the insurance company. They will report the status of their investigation and findings to the entire team. This information will be important to others—to assess the possibility of subrogation, monitor the impact of action by civil authorities, and consider specific ramifications for the coverage.

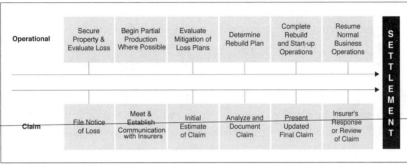

Figure 6.1: Insurance Recovery Chart

The claims team also addresses all insurance issues, including ensuring a thorough analysis of coverage, arranging meetings with insurance adjusters, working with the insured's broker, and establishing a protocol among members of the team. Decisions made early in the claim recovery process can make or break the outcome. For example, it may be tempting to put the claim on the back burner because management believes that all issues are straightforward and a reasonable settlement is at hand. But companies that procrastinate in forming a claim recovery team to manage the claim process, review policy provisions, and develop a comprehensive, well-documented claim can quickly fall behind in dealing with the insurer. In fact, without a dedicated and skilled claim recovery team and a clear plan, the whole process can stagnate or, in the worst cases, come to a grinding halt.

The question remains. In our hypothetical case, you are the Plant Manager for CruiseHomes. Who should you have on your claims team? And that's not the only question to ask. Others include:

- Do we expect this claim to be significant?

- How complex will it be?

- Do we have anyone internally who has sufficient time available to lead this effort?

- Who can we count on to provide an independent assessment of coverage?

- Is it possible that this claim will involve questions for production? finance? engineering? sales? engineering? other?

With a dedicated claims team, the company can be assured of a better process, of having the right people with the right expertise and skills working in a systematic way within a timetable of milestones toward a well-defined purpose.[1] Note also that some policies provide coverage for claim preparation fees, which facilitate the selection of qualified outside consultants to assist in preparing the claim. Individual policies must be reviewed to determine whether such expenses are covered. Even when claim preparation fees are not covered by the policy, consideration should be given to selecting the qualified consultants. The work product of the claims team—that is, the claim itself—will be reviewed and scrutinized by the insurance company's adjusters, accountants, underwriters, coinsurers, reinsurers, and other experts.

For this reason, two things are critically important. First, the claim recovery team must receive input from every relevant department in the company. Second, the claim itself must be a stand-alone, well-documented road map of the financial loss, with comprehensive supporting analysis. Let's take a look at the people or departments that play a role on a claim recovery team.

The Insured's Resources

Claims Manager/Leader

It is best to have one group or individual take responsibility for coordinating all efforts involved in the claim. For large or complex claims, this leader may be someone outside your organization or someone internally who has significant claims experience; either preferably will have experience with similar claims in your industry. The individual must have sufficient authority to manage the team and make critical decisions throughout the adjustment process.

Risk Management

In some cases, the risk manager acts as the main internal company contact, with chief responsibility to work closely with the Claims Manager to ensure strong communication among members of the claims team and with the insurance company's team. The risk manager should have a relationship with the insurance broker and/or the insurance company account representative and should know the insurance policy and the extent of coverage.

Financial Management

At least one member of the company's financial management team should be actively involved in the claim. This person (or persons) should help assess the overall impact of the loss, evaluate options for business recovery, oversee cash requirements, ensure appropriate distribution of requested documents, maintain a good understanding of claim activities, play an active role in claim negotiations, and work to ensure proper accounting and tax treatment of the loss and related insurance recoveries. In addition, the representative(s) from financial management often help to identify all appropriate resources within a company to ensure that the full impact of the loss can be quantified.

Operations Management

To recover from a shutdown, production may have to work overtime or in adverse conditions. Operational questions that impact the claim can include: Is the company still operating in a partial capacity? Can other locations gear up to help mitigate the loss? What inefficiencies will likely result from the incident? Can any production be outsourced? What is the best deployment of employees in the post-loss environment?

Clearly, the Chief Operating Officer and others involved in operations (e.g., the plant manager for a manufacturing operation, the hotel manager for a hotel) need to be involved in the claim process. Not only can they mitigate operational losses during the interruption period, but they can also answer property damage repair questions, such as whether to upgrade or expand capacity in tandem with repairing or replacing damaged property. They also provide a strong perspective on how the business would have performed had it not been for the loss.

Marketing/Sales

After a property damage loss, the Sales and Marketing department(s) primarily concentrate on maintaining customer confidence and relationships. They can also play an important role in developing claim projections, often providing qualitative data to help understand projected sales. For example, the Director of Sales may indicate that he expected sales to increase significantly because several significant proposals were pending as of the date of the loss. Marketing will know whether any new product introduction has been delayed as a result of the loss, as well as the effort (including time and money) to restart the launch once repairs are completed. The perspective from both contributors could impact the claim.

Inside Counsel

Sometimes, a company's in-house or general counsel is in charge of the insurance program. In some cases, counsel even leads the claims team. A Corporate Legal Department often will play an important role in coverage interpretation and will oversee claim negotiations and any resulting disputes, as discussed in Chapter 9.

Outside Resources

In our experience, most companies fail to recognize the full extent of effort needed to prepare and support a large claim. Even a company with a sophisticated, fully staffed claim recovery team likely needs specialized expertise at some point in the recovery process. Outside professionals can supplement the team, providing theoretical and practical knowledge, claims experience, and the ability to coordinate how the claims team operates in order to get the job done. Developing a qualified claims team that includes specialized expertise is a solid business strategy, likely leading to a quick and equitable settlement. Outside resources that often are needed follow.

Legal Counsel

Regrettably—but, of course, not unexpectedly—policyholders and insurance companies do not always agree on every aspect of the claim. While relatively few claims are actually litigated, a dispute can trigger the need to retain outside counsel who specializes in insurance coverage and claims. Such counsel often can add value before any dispute materializes, as noted in Chapter 9.

Claim Accountants/Consultants

Because of the financial and investigative nature of establishing, negotiating, and settling claims, and because of the complexity of coverage under contemporary insurance policies, it is no surprise that a cadre of professionals has emerged to help policyholders with large property damage and business interruption claims. Typically, these individuals work at major accounting or consulting firms and are retained as advisers not only to augment the capabilities of the policyholder's in-house staff, but also to bring knowledge and experience from many years of handling other claims. More than likely, these individuals are experienced in specific issues or problems that typically arise in complex claims and will in some circumstances already have developed a solution.

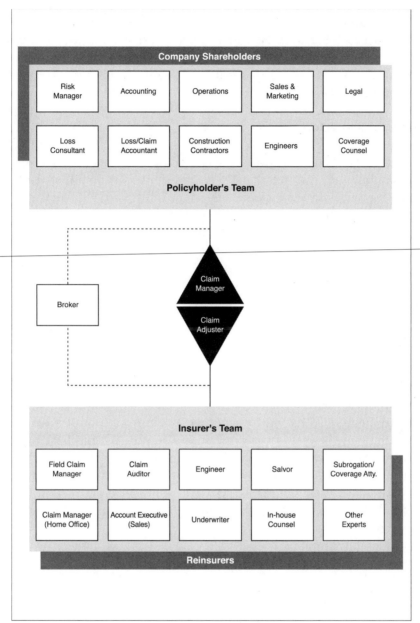

Figure 6.2: The Claims Team on Both Sides

The Insurance Company's Team

Let's look at the insurance company's team.

Claim accountants/consultants generally represent only policyholders. Perhaps their greatest contribution to the claim recovery process is a healthy dose of independent, audit skepticism. In fact, a company's corporate governance standards likely mandate hiring only advisers that have an arms-length distance from the insurance representatives.[2]   •

Engineers/Contractors

Often, a loss results in or includes physical damage that requires rebuilding. For most companies, the resources required for this effort come from contractors or engineering firms. When an engineer/contractor is hired as part of a business interruption recovery, a higher level of documentation for fees and expenses is usually needed. For example, the insurance company typically will play a part in deciding the scope of damage (and any changes to the scope down the line), the pricing of the repairs, and the timetable for the completion of construction. On larger losses, it often makes sense to hire an outside and, hence, objective expert to handle the analysis and management of a critical path for the project.

Insurance Brokers

Brokers are independent insurance professionals whose primary function is to help companies identify their coverage requirements and then find the best fit among potential insurers. While brokers, by definition, act as a conduit between insurer and policyholder, some may function as an advocate for the insured on claims, and some brokers formally offer claims services as part of the services offered to policyholders. There may be limits, however, on how far brokers are able or willing to go on the policyholder's behalf, given the importance of their relationships with insurers from whom they earn commissions or fees when placing policies. Brokers therefore often must walk a fine line between the insurer and the policyholder in an effort to avoid alienating either constituency. More often, brokers act as a go-between or coordinate advance payments or meetings, and they tend to be most effective in this role.

Claims Adjuster

The adjuster may be an employee of the insurance company or an outside adjuster hired by the insurance company. The claims adjuster investigates all aspects of the loss, prepares periodic reports to the insurers, establishes and monitors claim reserves, and works to settle the claim. Adjusters for large business interruption claims are usually highly skilled and have experience with other large business interruption claims. Large corporate insurance programs may include a provision that permits an insured business to choose the adjuster. A company should take advantage of this feature when it is available. However, it is well to remember that while outside adjusters are often called "independent adjusters," they are paid by the insurer to protect their interests and do not represent the insured. The loss adjustment process is discussed in Chapter 4.

Claims Manager/Examiner

An employee of the insurance company, the claims manager supervises adjusters. When adjusters are independent, the claims manager hires or assigns them to specific losses; in turn, the adjusters periodically provide written reports to the claims manager.

In many cases, the claims manager's role is simply to act as a conduit for information, as someone who facilitates communication by passing the adjuster's reports on to others. At other times, though, the claims manager has final authority on how a claim is adjusted and can overrule decisions or agreements made by the adjuster. If this is the case, the policyholder needs to involve the claims manager in all meetings and copy her on all correspondence. Obviously, in the rare circumstance where an adjuster has no authority and must go to the claims manager to get an answer to every single question, the process can be frustrating—and exhausting—for the insured.

Loss Accountants/Auditors

When a claim includes large-scale physical damage and/or business interruption, an adjuster will likely retain outside accountants for two reasons. First, they will seek professional assistance when there is insufficient time to review and deal with all the documents in the claim. Second, they will resort to experts when the business interruption calls for accounting expertise and analysis. For the most part, these accountants work at boutique CPA firms that specialize in insurance work. They may not be independent. In cases in which the insurer retains such advisers, they represent that insurer's interests.

Engineers/Contractors

For technical or complex claims, adjusters often engage independent engineers to evaluate the *cause and origin* of a loss. They also may use an engineer or contractor to evaluate the scope of repairs and the cost of construction. Finally, these consultants may also be used to identify and document any subrogation opportunities for the insurer. The insured would be wise to match this expertise on its own claim recovery team.

Salvors

Usually brought in by the insurance company to dispose of damaged assets that have residual value, salvors are also used to inventory damaged goods. A representative from the insurance company should always be present during salvage operations, since the salvor and the insured often disagree about what is damaged and what is not. Any items triggering a disagreement should be set aside for further discussion with the adjuster. To get a quick advance on a large claim, the insured company may receive an advance payment from the net sale proceeds of the salvor, with the final claim settlement adjusted by the salvage amount.

Subrogation Attorneys

If the insurance company thinks a third party caused or contributed to a loss, it will likely hire a subrogation attorney to pursue recovery from that third party. An example of this circumstance would be a fire caused by faulty electrical equipment, because the insurer would likely pursue recovery from the manufacturer or installer of that equipment—and possibly both. If there is subrogation on a claim, the policyholder might be required to cooperate with the insurer to facilitate the insurer's recovery from the third party. Sometimes, however, this additional work pays off; the insured might be able to recover uninsured items, such as the deductible or other losses for which the insured did not obtain an insurance recovery.

Restoration Companies

After fire or water damage, an insurance company will often recommend that a company hire a restoration specialist to make the cleanup quick and efficient. Given today's litigious environment, this is a smart idea. Although the recommendation comes from the insurer, the insured signs the contract. Good business practices dictate that the policyholder and adjuster agree on scope and cost up front.

Other Specialists

Depending on the nature of the business and the loss, other technical experts may be hired by the insurance company to assist the adjuster. For example, economists evaluate the economic conditions to support or refute the business interruption claim. Other experts may be retained to evaluate the cause and origin of the loss, the scope of damage, and any other variables that might impact the claim amount.

The appropriateness of using consultants is recognized by many insurance companies, which include coverage for Claim Preparation Fees or Professional Fees in their policies. Such coverage typically reimburses a company for using an outside accountant or consultant to help prepare the claim. These costs are not reimbursable on all policies, so it is important to check on whether a specific insurer offers the coverage before claims occur. It also is worth noting that fees incurred on the insured's behalf by public adjusters, attorneys, or brokers are not usually covered under these provisions.

Planning—And Managing That Plan

Among the first items that will be developed by your claims team is the plan to mitigate the loss, work with the adjuster, rebuild the plant, and develop the claim. That plan needs to be developed quickly and must be updated regularly throughout the claim process. Here are some items that should be included in your plan:

Ownership from the Top and Good Project Management

Executive management should be sufficiently involved in a business interruption claim to ensure that the company's interests are well represented. The claim process requires sophisticated management from high levels over a fairly long period of time. The efforts of diverse people, from inside and outside the company, need to be coordinated. Communication and commitment are essential. But the good news is this: the claim

---

Why use outside claims accountants/ consultants?

For several reasons, companies will resort to outside claims advisers, including accountants and other knowledgeable experts:

· To gain expertise not available inside the organization—that is, expertise that's often erudite and particular to the process.

· To increase speed and efficiency.

· To eliminate guesswork in building a case for a claim.

· To level the playing field with the insurance company.

· To make one's conclusions clear, fair, reasonable, credible, and defensible.

· To play devil's advocate with the management team to ensure credible positions.

· To help manage expectations along the way, including those of the insured and the insurer.

· To help ensure an equitable settlement, providing both sides with the right type and amount of expertise.

· To ensure continuity toward resolving the claim, since large property and BI claims can take years to resolve, during which time company employees will leave or change jobs within the organization. Outside consultants bring consistency and stability to the process.

process can be extremely rewarding even while challenging. The collaboration of many groups that don't normally work together can be a valuable lesson for a company—a lesson with impact far beyond the claim recovery process itself.

Crisis Management

Any large-scale catastrophe or other event typically triggers a substantial first-party insurance claim. Simultaneously, it may implicate numerous collateral concerns and exposures, in which case the insurance claim must be considered in the context of an overall crisis management plan. And while a detailed discussion of proper crisis management techniques is beyond the scope of this book, it is worth highlighting some of the key issues that a policyholder might consider when it finds itself in a crisis management mode.

In general, in the aftermath of a catastrophic event, a policyholder must be able to make informed decisions based on a holistic understanding of what has transpired. Decisions need to be made about matters ranging from how to manage any third-party investigations to how to communicate with relevant constituencies, including workers, regulators, politicians, the public, and the media. Recognizing this, the policyholder should promptly take appropriate steps to understand all the ramifications of the event to the fullest extent possible. Such ramifications can include the possible types of civil and/or criminal claims against the policyholder, the policyholder's own claims against third parties (including its insurers), potential evidentiary issues and disputes, and likely key witnesses and documents.

In the event of a large-scale catastrophe or any other event that implicates multiple exposures, it is advisable to seek legal and expert advice from individuals with experience in handling responses to such events. Nevertheless, policyholders should be prepared to answer some important questions after such an event, including:

- Does the organization have an overall game plan for managing the situation?

- Do crisis management team members have defined roles, including a control person or persons in charge of the management exercise and a designated spokesperson?

- Is there a clear chain of command for such circumstances?

- Does the organization completely understand the facts?

- Has the organization anticipated and analyzed its potential legal exposures arising under federal and state statutes, contracts, and common law tort theories?

- Does the company have a handle on its public message? What themes can the policyholder use to manage public perception? Are these themes consistent with its overall strategy (including insurance recovery strategy)?

- Are protocols in place to ensure that the legal, risk management, and crisis management teams work in a strategic, coordinated fashion? (For example, an insurer potentially may use a public announcement that an insured's business has not been harmed by the incident in connection with the business interruption claim.)

- Has the organization established (and is it managing) points of contact with regulators?

- Does the organization have the right team interfacing with outside parties?

- Has the organization established protocols for document control and retention with due consideration of privilege?

- Is there an internal cost code to track all time and expenditures incurred in relation to the insured event?

- What outside expert services will the organization need?

- Has the organization identified potential deficiencies in reporting mechanisms, taken necessary steps to minimize nonprivileged communications on important substantive issues, and worked towards creating an accurate record that is consistent with its themes?

- Is the organization prepared for on-site document reviews and witness interviews by insurance company representatives or by state or federal authorities?

- Has the organization coordinated any local, state, and federal political components?

- Has the organization fully analyzed risk transfer issues (e.g., insurance, indemnity)?

A number of these concepts are discussed in other sections of the Policyholder's Predispute Checklist, which is covered in Chapter 9.

Developing a Critical Path

As noted at the beginning of this chapter, the road back from loss means developing a timeline and a critical path. After a loss, the first focus for a company's operational group will be to determine how long it expects the operations of the business to be interrupted. The group must then consider the ways in which it can mitigate the interruption. Equally important, the team must establish both the projected time it will take to repair the facility as it was (for insurance purposes), and how long it may actually take should improvements or changes in configuration extend that time period.

All these issues relate to establishing a critical path to recovery. The accountant will need to know the length of expected downtime in order to calculate the loss; the adjuster wants to know if certain time periods may be idle periods—that is, if periods of time within the period of indemnity are not insurable; and, production, sales, and marketing will need to know how to plan work-arounds during the period of interruption.

Systematic Data Gathering and Claim Documentation

One of the key variables in the claim recovery process is the company's ability to provide financial information in a user-friendly format, so that the insurer can more readily understand and accept the claim. Time and time again, companies fail in this regard, delaying the whole process and jeopardizing their success. A systematic, six-stage approach is useful for this process.

1. **Identify** – This first step entails the *discovery* of information and records vital to preparing the claim. Usually, the claims manager or team leader prepares a *document request list* to be filled in by appropriate team members. Typical accounting records, such as production reports and monthly financial statements, will be of critical importance. Information and data might be readily available or might be archived.

2. **Meet** – Shortly after a loss, key members of management should be interviewed to discuss their respective insights into what would have happened had the incident not occurred. Information gathered during these meetings is often critical to ensuring that a claim reflects all aspects of a loss. Insights gained from these meetings should then be scrutinized to ensure that all parties are in agreement and that adequate documentation is available to support the insured's positions. Certainly in this setting, both the team leader and individual members should play devil's advocate with one another's positions, to establish the veracity and plausibility of scenarios and ensure credibility. For example, in one such meeting shortly after a significant fire at a Midwest manufacturing company, the production manager indicated that he expected a significant increase in production before the fire. His insights seemed credible and supportable. However, after a follow-up discussion with the sales manager, it was determined that the additional product, if produced, would likely not have been sold.

3. **Obtain** – At the outset of the claims preparation process, data gathering might seem the simplest task. In reality, it is often frustrated by people's busy schedules—including their additional responsibilities as a result of the interruption itself. Conversely, if the document request list is assigned to personnel who may have time but who perhaps lack either understanding of what is sought or access to it, the claim recovery process can grind to a halt. When it comes to obtaining key information, senior management has to drive the process.

4. **Accept** – Leadership and the claims team must examine all available information with an objective and informed point of view. All information presented must be reliable and credible; accounting records will need to be corroborated by information from other areas in the company, such as operations or marketing and sales.

5. **Interpret** – Part of the success of a claim will rely on the presentation of much disparate information in a single, focused argument for coverage. Since a company's information on the loss and its financial and practical implications will likely come from various departments and analyses, the team leader will have to assemble and organize it into a readable, user-friendly format. From there, the team should analyze the information to understand what it means and how it should be used.

6. **Implement/Present** – Finally, every claim needs to be organized according to convention and industry practice, with the level of detail appropriate for supporting the findings. Policyholders should provide data promptly, but they should take steps to understand the data themselves before forwarding it to others.[3]

The Insurer's Practice

In its turn, the insurance company validates the claim by performing its own analysis, asking questions about what is being gathered and presented, and when necessary requesting more data and information. The company would do well to anticipate the likely requests and to promptly provide answers throughout the process.

Negotiate

One of the best tools for reaching agreement is an interim analysis of the claim from the insurance company—an analysis that shows those items approved for payment and those still in question or requiring additional documentation. In the *Preliminary Report, Standard Letter and Schedule*, Exhibit 6.1, note that, while the claim amount exceeds $8 million, only $4 million has been approved for payment. Communication like this is a perfect opportunity to resolve open issues.

Communicate

Another effective element in a successful claim recovery process is regular meetings between the two teams—that of the insured and the insurer—to discuss the claim, review progress reports, and resolve issues as they emerge. Through such meetings, the two parties can come to understand and respect each other's points of view early in the process, increasing the likelihood of an amicable settlement dramatically.

A Positive Claim Recovery Process

From our experience, the questions asked and the analysis performed for a business interruption claim often result in significant findings outside the scope of the insurance claim. For example, after a fire caused damage to a chemical producer, the claims team determined that much of the loss could be made up at another plant location. After the claim was settled, management permanently consolidated production lines that resulted in significant savings.

Many positive experiences can actually develop from large, complex claims. In one instance, a multinational medical products company developed a better, less expensive product as a result of losing its supply of a raw material due to an explosion at one of its plants. In another circumstance, a U.S. manufacturing company discovered that an overseas finance manager had been taking kickbacks from contractors when the adjuster noted that the price of repairs was up to 20 percent higher than what was typical in that marketplace. And the list goes on.

A comprehensive coordinated claims team and a well-defined plan can ensure that all aspects of a loss are quantified and included in a comprehensive, well-documented claim that holds up against the scrutiny of the insurer. The result of this effort can lead to a more expeditious and reasonable settlement.

Endnotes

[1] The claim process is discussed in detail in Chapter Five: The Loss Adjustment Process.

[2] For more information on the composition of the claims team—and in particular how best to involve advisers in the process, review Daniel T. Torpey, "The Shackleton Approach: Effective Leadership Throughout the Claims Process," on www.irmi.com/Expert/Articles/2002/Torpey08.aspx.

[3] As discussed in Chapter 9, a policyholder might consider asking the insurer to execute a confidentiality agreement encompassing sensitive information provided to the insurer during the adjustment of a loss, and both parties might consider taking various steps to protect themselves in the event that disputes arise, such as including counsel in important claim-related communications in order to make such communications "privileged" and therefore generally protected from forced disclosure.

Sharp Accounting, LLP
Certified Public Accountants
900 Pine Street, New York, NY 11001
(212) 555-1111

Adjustment Business Services, Inc.   April 11, 2005
123 William Street
New York, NY 10038

Attention: Mr. Les Lowenbrau   Re: Northern Frozen Foods
                                                Rochester, New York
                                                Loss – July 7, 2004
                                                PRELIMINARY REPORT

Gentlemen:

In accordance with your request, we have analyzed certain records and other pertinent data of the above insured to determine loss under insurance coverages in force on the date of that loss.

The schedules accompanying this report present our findings. Since the procedures we employed in our analysis differ from generally accepted auditing standards, this report is designed solely to assist you in evaluating the reasonableness of the claim and should not be used for any other purpose. Amounts contained in this report represent expenditures reported on the insured's books and records as of December 31, 2004. Expenditures represent amounts paid by the insured. Expenses incurred through December 31, 2004, but not yet paid, will be recorded by the insured in subsequent months.

We have deferred for your review and consideration certain claimed expenditures. These expenditures are summarized on Schedule 1 under the caption "Held For Discussion". The following is a brief explanation of the "Held For Discussion" categories:

NOT LOSS RELATED – Included under this caption are various types of expenditures that may not be related to the loss of July 7, 2004. These expenses are detailed on the supporting schedules.

NO SUPPORT – Claimed expenses that have not been fully documented by the insured are included herein. Once the requested documentation has been received and analyzed, we will transfer the expenditure to its appropriate category.

RESIDUAL VALUE – The acquisition cost of equipment purchased during the period of loss is included under this category. The amount of residual benefit the insured may have for this equipment is deferred for your consideration.

NOT EXTRA EXPENSE – This category includes expenditures that may not represent an extra expense to the insured.

DEFERRED – Included under this caption are certain expenditures requiring additional information or your approval with respects to the insurance coverages. This category will be adjusted once the additional information has been received.

Should you require any additional information, please contact either John Frick or Peter Frack.

Respectfully,
Sharp Accounting, LLP

Copy: John Smith – Claims Manager

Exhibit 6.1: Preliminary Report, Standard Letter

Northern Frozen Foods - Rochester, New York
SUMMARY OF LOSS: Loss - July 7, 2004
Schedule 1

CATEGORY	Sched. No.	As Claimed	Held For Discussion						As Proposed
			Not Loss Related	No Support	Residual Value	Not Extra Expense	Deferred	Total	
Business Interruption									
Sales Less Non-Continuing Expenses	2	$550,000	$50,000	$ -	$ -	$ -	$ -	$50,000	$500,000
Total		$550,000	$50,000					$50,000	$500,000
Extra Expense			0						
Freight	3	1,800,000	-	50,000	-	60,000	-	110,000	1,700,000
Co-Packers	4	900,000	170,000	12,000	-	-	-	182,000	700,000
Process Purchases	5	900,000	10,000	11,000	-	-	240,000	261,000	650,000
Golden Continuing Expenses	6	800,000	60,000	-	-	-	-	60,000	750,000
Production Inefficiencies	7	600,000	650,000	-	-	-	-	650,000	600,000
Overhead & Variable Expenses	8	650,000	-	-	-	-	-	-	-
Outside Storage	9	750,000	140,000	270,000	-	-	-	410,000	500,000
Additional Labor & Supply Costs	10	750,000	3,000	-	-	30,000	390,000	423,000	200,000
Travel Costs	11	100,000	-	10,000	-	6,000	-	16,000	80,000
Temporary Line	12	100,000	-	-	50,000	-	-	50,000	45,000
Estimated Saved Costs - Dallas		-	-	-	-	-	1,300,000	1,300,000	-1,300,000
Utilities Savings Loss		200,000	-	-	-	-	200,000	200,000	-
Depreciation - Dallas		150,000	-	-	-	-	-	-	150,000
Claim Preparation Fees		250,000	-	-	-	-	-	-	-
Total		7,950,000	1,033,000	353,000	50,000	96,000	2,130,000	3,662,000	4,075,000
Grand Total		$8,500,000	$1,083,000	$353,000	$50,000	$96,000	$2,130,000	$3,712,000	$4,575,000

Exhibit 6.1 Schedule: Preliminary Report, Summary of Loss

Hospitality Industry
Hospitable Hotels, Inc.
Avalanche at The Lake Tahoe Hospitable Hotel

I.   BACKGROUND

A publicly traded corporation based in Chicago, Hospitable Hotels, Inc., owns and operates fifty upscale and luxury hotels throughout the United States. The company has experienced significant growth over the past ten years as it has increased its portfolio of quality properties through strategic acquisitions and improved operations. This has been accomplished through a combination of strong management and a commitment to necessary capital renovations and improvements.

Hospitable Hotels owns two properties in Nevada, approximately forty miles apart. They are the Lake Tahoe Hospitable Hotel and Spa, with 520 rooms and 210 suites, and the Reno Hospitable Hotel and Casino, a 648-room hotel in the heart of Reno.

The Lake Tahoe Hospitable Hotel and Spa is located within walking distance of Lake Tahoe and caters primarily to vacation travelers. During summer months, discerning guests visit The Lake Tahoe Hospitable for the ultimate in a relaxing getaway. For winter months, the hotel services the skiing enthusiast—who can choose from slopes at Heavenly, Alpine Meadows, and Kirkwood. Located on Lake Tahoe's exquisite south shore, the hotel also offers extraordinary culinary options and nightlife. The property provides limousine service for casino gambling at Caesar's Tahoe and Harrah's Lake Tahoe casinos.

With amenities of a slightly different order, and catering specifically to large corporate groups, The Reno Hospitable Hotel and Casino offers over 5,000 square feet of meeting space, a large ballroom, and five restaurants. After purchasing the property three years ago, Hospitable has invested over $5 million in renovations, including significant enhancements to the lobby, restaurants, spa, and guest rooms. In the short run, the renovations caused a decline in the hotel's occupancy and average daily room rate, as corporate groups shied away from a hotel under construction. However, with renovations nearing completion, Hospitable Management predicted strong revenue and earnings growth.

Fire in the Snow: The Incident

On January 1, 2005, an avalanche occurred on a New Year's Day that no Hospitality guest who witnessed it would ever forget. The Lake Tahoe property suffered significant damage as a result, and federal ski marshals investigated, concluding that fireworks that culminated a day-long New Year's Eve festival must have caused the avalanche. Western Pyrotechnics, Inc., a national fireworks provider, was believed to be responsible.

Fortunately, no guests were injured as a result of the avalanche; however, the avalanche caused significant damage to Heavenly Ski Resort and blocked access to Route 50. It also badly damaged the west wing of The Lake Tahoe Hospitable Hotel, including 280 guest rooms, the lobby, and the spa. Most of the damage was caused by the accumulated horizontal pressure and weight of snow against the walls of building structures. A nearby luxury hotel, the Western Lakes Conference Resort, also suffered significant damage.

Clearing the Way to Recovery

Two weeks after the incident, Route 50 finally reopened for traffic. Heavenly remained closed for two months. The Western Lakes Conference Resort, forced to close as a result of the avalanche, did not reopen until January 2006.

The Lake Tahoe Hospitable also struggled in the aftermath of the avalanche. After the incident, some guests who could not be accommodated at The Lake Tahoe Hospitable Hotel were shifted to The Reno Hospitable Hotel and Casino. As a result, operations at The Reno Hospitable Hotel and Casino were better than expected.

The Lake Tahoe Hospitable remained open at partial capacity while repairs were being made, but understandably, the hotel struggled to secure additional bookings while undergoing repairs. Consequently, occupancy remained below projected levels for most of 2006. Worse, a Grand Reopening Party for the hotel, scheduled for June 30, 2005, at a cost of $500,000, was postponed when mold was detected in many of the guest rooms, causing the date to be pushed back to September 30, 2005.

Immediately following the incident, Hospitable Management called an emergency meeting in Chicago and appointed you, as Corporate Risk Manager, to assemble a team and ensure that Hospitable recovers fully under its insurance policy.

ESTABLISHING COVERAGE

Hospitality Hotel's Commercial Property Policy, with IOU Insurance, is effective July 1, 2004, to June 30, 2005, and includes the following clauses:

1. **Deductible**

   In the case of loss or damage covered under this policy, this company shall not be liable unless the Insured sustains loss, damage, or expenses arising out of any one occurrence greater than $500,000.

2. **Period of Indemnity**

   In determining the indemnity payable under this policy, the period of indemnity shall be the period of time commencing with the time of the physical damage of the type insured against to the date at which physical damage is repaired with due diligence and dispatch.

3. **Extended Period of Indemnity**

   This coverage is extended to cover the reduction in sales or additional costs incurred commencing on the date that repairs can be completed with due diligence and dispatch and ending no later than ninety days thereafter.

4. **Ordinary Payroll**

   Covered for a period of up to thirty days immediately following the interruption.

5. **Walked Guests**

   This policy covers the actual expenditure incurred beyond those normally incurred in relocating guests to another hotel.

6.   Idle Period

This policy does not insure against any loss during any idle period, including but not limited to when production, operation, services or delivery of goods would cease due to any reason other than the physical loss or damage insured by this policy.

7.   Experience of the Business

In determining the amount of net profit, charges, and expenses covered here-under for the purpose of ascertaining the amount of loss sustained, due consideration shall be given to the experience of the business before the date of damage or destruction and to the probable experience thereafter had no loss occurred.

8.   Contingent Business Interruption Coverage

This policy also covers the actual loss sustained and/ or extra expenses resulting from the interruption of business due to damage to: (1) The facilities of suppliers of the Insured, and (2) The facilities of customers of the insured.

9.   Extra Expenses

This policy is extended to cover such necessary Extra Expenses incurred by the Insured in order to continue as nearly as practicable the normal operation of the Insured's business following damage to real or personal property.

10.   Civil Authority

This policy is intended to cover the actual business loss sustained during the period of time, not exceeding ten days, when as a direct result of a covered peril, access to the premises is prohibited by order of civil authority.

11.   Ingress/Egress

This policy is extended to cover the loss sustained, limited to a sixty-day period, when as a direct result of a peril insured against, ingress to or egress from real or personal property is thereby prevented or hindered.

12. Claim Preparation

This policy covers the actual fees payable to accountants or other professionals for preparing insurance claims. Coverage will not include the fees and costs of attorneys, public adjusters, and loss appraisers.

ADDITIONAL FACTS

In December of 2004, as part of normal yearly budgeting and planning, both Hospitality Hotels in Nevada prepared comprehensive monthly budgets for 2005. The following summarizes projected occupancy and average daily rates for both properties:

The Lake Tahoe Hospitable Hotel

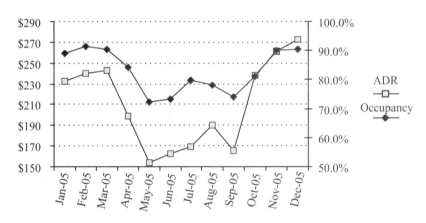

The Reno Hospitable Hotel and Casino

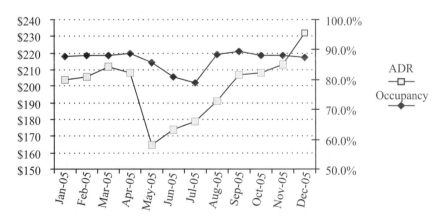

Occupancy at The Lake Tahoe Hospitable Hotel during winter months is highly dependent on the level of snowfall in the area. In 1997, occupancy in November was only 62 percent, when virtually no snow fell before Thanksgiving. The following year, occupancy rates for the month were a record 89 percent after a Halloween snowstorm dumped thirty-five inches of snow. And in November 2005, resorts in the Lake Tahoe area experienced record-breaking snowfall.

Hourly employees at The Lake Tahoe Hospitable Hotel are members of the National Hotel Workers Union. After the avalanche, the hotel laid off fifty-two hourly employees and paid a total of $248,000 in severance under the terms of the collective bargaining agreement.

In November 2005, The Reno St. Jacques, located adjacent to The Reno Hospitable Hotel and Casino, converted to condominiums.

YOUR OBJECTIVES

In the emergency meeting called by Hospitable Management, you are bombarded with questions and issues that must be addressed immediately:

1. Hospitable's **Chief Executive Officer** wants to understand all aspects of coverage. In particular, he wants to understand Hospitable's total exposure for uninsured items.

2. The Lake Tahoe Hospitable Hotel **General Manager** indicates that the current staffing is too high for the postloss expected occupancy. He is concerned, however, that if he lays off employees now he will have trouble replacing many later when repairs are complete and the hotel returns to occupancy levels projected before the incident.

3. The Lake Tahoe Hospitable Hotel **Director of Sales** is concerned that bookings after the avalanche are down, which will result in lower sales for the following year. What do you tell him?

   Hospitality's **Corporate Treasurer** is extremely concerned that cash flow will be impacted if the insurance does not make a significant payment soon.

4. The Lake Tahoe Hospitable Hotel **General Manager** indicates that several guests have demanded recovery of personal items lost after the avalanche. Others seek reimbursement of costs incurred when they moved to other hotels the day after the avalanche.

5. The **Chief Financial Officer** feels compelled to report to shareholders concerning the expected claim and likely recovery. He wants a preliminary property damage and business interruption analysis done as soon as possible and indicates that he would like the claim settled prior to the Stockholder Meeting in March. He wants your assurance that you can get that done. He also asks you to develop property damage and business interruption claims and let him know as soon as possible what data will be needed. He states that he believes that a reasonable settlement would be a recovery of net profit "at least 10 percent higher" than amounts included in the hotel's budget.

6. Hospitable's **Asset Manager** for the two Nevada properties indicates that the Tahoe location would have had a tremendous year had the avalanche not occurred, since renovations were complete and bookings were strong. In addition, the hospitality industry overall is poised for a strong year.

7. Hospitable's **General Counsel** believes that suit should be filed against Western Pyrotechnics, Inc., to recover damages.

8. Hospitable's **Controller** asks how certain costs, such as management fees, intercom any charges, and depreciation will be treated in the claim.

Hospitable Welcomes the Adjuster

The following day, the insurance adjuster arrives with accountants hired by the insurer. They have additional concerns:

1. The **Adjuster** indicates that she needs to book a reserve and asks you for a rough estimate of the total loss amount for property damage and business interruption.

2. The insurer's **Accountants** request monthly financial statements for the prior three years and budgets for Lake Tahoe property. They indicate that they plan to review these documents to develop a rough estimate of loss. They want your concurrence that this makes sense.

3. The insurer's **Accountants** indicate that they will be working to estimate and calculate make-up of lost sales at The Reno Hospitable Hotel and Casino and need monthly financial statements for the prior three years as well as budgets for that property.

In a follow-up meeting six months after the avalanche, you also learn that:

1. The **Insurance Adjuster** mentions the amount of the reserve that he established. He explains the importance of establishing appropriate reserves. Hospitable's **Chief Financial Officer** becomes irate, indicating that the reserves are woefully inadequate.

2. The **Adjuster** indicates that damage caused by mold was significant and that costs associated with mold remediation was not covered under the policy. Neither was the time required to eliminate the mold.

3. The **Asset Manager** points out that the significant snowfall in the area has resulted in higher occupancy and average daily rates than had the avalanche not occurred. The **Chief Financial Officer** concurs. The **Insurance Adjuster** indicates that loss projections should be based on data available prior to the incident. The **Chief Executive Officer** looks to you to resolve the issue and walks out. The **General Counsel** threatens to sue.

4. The **Corporate Treasurer** chastens the **Adjuster**, indicating that cash advances have not been timely or adequate. The **Adjuster** retaliates by indicating that she and the **Insurer's Accountants** have not received all necessary data that was requested.

5. Lake Tahoe Hospitable Hotel's **General Manager** is concerned that the opening date of the hotel has slipped several times and that several important corporate accounts are irate because the hotel cannot accommodate their functions.

6. The **Chief Executive Officer** indicates that he needs a thorough update for next week's Board Meeting.

7. Everyone looks to you. As **Corporate Risk Manager**, you have been focusing on many other issues, including the upcoming policy renewals. You point out that the policy provides coverage for professional fees.

CLAIM SCENARIO

Hospitality Industry
Hospitable Hotels, Inc.

REVIEW

GENERAL

1. Outside claims assistance should be used when:

    A. The claim amount may be sizable.

    B. The claim is expected to be complex.

    C. The insured does not have previous claims experience.

    D. The policy provides coverage for Claim Preparation.

    E. All of the above items should be considered.

2. One of the first steps after a loss is to:

    A. Notify your broker and insurance company.

    B. Review your policy in detail and summarize key provisions.

    C. Assemble a team of all applicable disciplines (e.g. Risk Management, Finance, Operations, etc.)

    D. Gather pertinent data, such as historical operating statements and budgets.

E. Work with engineers to estimate time to complete repairs.

F. All of the above.

3. The Insurance Company adjuster initially wants the insured's optimistic assessment of the impact of the loss so that he can establish reserves.

A. True

B. False

4. In preliminary discussions with Hospitality Management, one of the most important issues is to manage everyone's expectations.

A. True

B. False

5. It is a requirement under most policies that cash advances be made on a timely basis to cover property damage costs, extra expenses, and business interruption losses.

A. True

B. False

HOSPITABLE'S ISSUES

6. Projected revenue in the business interruption claim should take into account which of the following:

A. Historical Occupancy and Average Daily Rates.

B. Budgeted Occupancy and Average Daily Rates.

C. The expected impact of the recent renovations.

D. Record snowfall in the area.

E. The expected impact of the conversion of the Reno St. Jacques to condominiums.

    F.   Overall trends in the hospitality industry.

    G.   The expected impact of the closure of Route 50.

    H.   All of the above.

    I.   A through F only.

7.   Severance paid under the Collective Bargaining Agreement should only be paid to the extent that Ordinary Payroll is covered under the policy.

    A.   True

    B.   False

8.   The property policy should respond only after the insured has sought and exhausted recovery from Western Pyrotechnics' liability insurance carrier.

    A.   True

    B.   False

9   A business interruption claim should not be prepared until the indemnity period has ended and actual postloss data is available.

    A.   True

    B.   False

10.   Without specific coverage for mold, the cost to remediate the mold is not covered under the property damage claim and the time to remediate the mold should be excluded from the business interruption claim.

    A.   True

    B.   False

11. Hospitable's claim projections should be based upon the level of occupancy that would have been achieved had The Lake Tahoe Hospitable Hotel and Spa not been damaged, not including the fact that the nearby Western Lakes Conference Resort was damaged from the avalanche.

    A. True

    B. False

12. Losses incurred after the June 30, 2005, expiration of the policy are not covered by the IOU Insurance policy.

    A. True

    B. False

CLAIM SCENARIO

Hospitality Industry
Hospitable Hotels, Inc.

A N S W E R S

1. **E.** All of the above should be considered.

    In general, an insured should seek outside claims assistance if the claim is expected to be sizable and/ or complex. A sizable claim requires claims assistance to ensure that all amounts are fully recovered. A complex claim requires the expertise of an experienced claims consultant to ensure that all areas are addressed early and quantified in accordance with their insurance policy.

    An insured without prior claims experience should seek outside assistance, especially if the claim is expected to be sizable and/ or complex.

2. **F.** All of the above.

    After a loss occurs, it is important that the insurer be provided notice. (This is also required under most policies.)

    Reviewing your policy early can help avoid problems later. A claims team, consisting of all areas impacted, is extremely helpful. (One role that your outside claims professional generally fills is to oversee the claims team and report back to management.)

    Your outside claims professional will generally provide you with a preliminary list of data to begin assessing your loss.

Engineers or outside contractors should be consulted early and should continue to be a part of claims team.

3.   **B.** False.

The Insurance Company Adjuster initially wants your realistic assessment of the potential loss. He prefers to understand the overall possible exposure rather than an optimistic assessment of the loss.

If the final loss is lower than the initial assessment, the adjuster will be able to adjust accordingly.

4.   **A.** True.

Managing the expectations of everyone in the process is critically important. The insured needs to understand early on that the adjuster and her accountants will challenge all aspects of your loss. That is their job.

Similarly, it is important to manage the adjuster's expectations as well. If, at times during the process it becomes apparent that the adjuster is underestimating the loss, it is best to work to resolve differences.

5.   **B.** False.

Cash advances to allow an insured to cover property damage, extra expenses, and business interruption losses are not usually required under a policy.

Best Practices in the industry usually mean that insurers provide cash advances for property damage and extra expenses that have been incurred, even if not yet paid. Business interruption losses are usually advanced to the extent that the insurer's accountants concur with the calculations.

6.   **I.** A through F only.

The policy requires that due consideration be given to the experience of the business before and after the loss. Therefore, any items that would have impacted operations at the hotel should be considered.

However, the closure of Route 50, which may have resulted in lower occupancy, was due to the avalanche itself and should therefore not be considered.

7.   **B**. False.

Severance paid under the terms of a Collective Bargaining Agreement is a contractual obligation and should therefore be covered in full.

8.   **B**. False.

The property insurer is responsible to the insured in the event of a loss. The insurer can subrogate against the liability carrier, if appropriate. The insured can join the property insurer to recover uninsured losses, such as the deductible.

9.   **B**. False.

A preliminary claim should be prepared shortly after a loss to provide some quantification of the possible loss. This preliminary claim should clearly explain all assumptions used, such as expected period of indemnity, etc. All preliminary documents should be clearly marked as "Preliminary – For Discussion Purposes Only."

10.   **B**. False

Courts have generally ruled that mold exclusions do not apply when mold occurs as a direct result of an insured peril.

Property insurers are also required to complete repairs correctly and in a timely fashion to ensure that mold does not develop.

11.   **B**. False

Courts have generally ruled that the insured cannot benefit from the incident. In this case, the insured may indeed argue that their occupancy and average daily rate would have been higher as a result of damage to a competitor caused by the incident. However, without specific policy wording to the contrary, claim projections likely should be based upon the occupancy and average daily rate that the hotel would have achieved had the incident not occurred. They should be based on assumption that the competitor was not damaged as well.

12.   **B**. False

Property damage and business interruption claims are *occurrence-based* policies. The expiration date of the policy has no impact on the indemnity period.

NaviPorte and Grisham Industries
Simon's Awkward Position

Simon Grisham, Chief Executive Officer of Grisham Industries, was a man used to knowing where things were. In fact, he prided himself on it. Today, though, with a guest standing beside him in the middle of his brand new 250,000-square-foot production facility, Grisham couldn't find what he was looking for: the NaviPorte—his latest hand-held gadget—a product that Grisham Industries literally could not keep on its shelves.

Simon Grisham was an electrical engineer by training and an avid golfer. During one of his many vacations, he had played a course in Florida that attached Global Positioning System (GPS) tracking devices to its golf carts, so golfers could know their location on the course. Alongside some research that he had been conducting at his current employer, this gave Simon an idea. Using similar technology, he could develop a portable navigation system that would show the user her location anywhere in the world—and provide directions to any published address. And it would be compact enough to fit into a briefcase or purse.

In 1991, Simon Grisham set off to follow his dream. He purchased the research and rights from his current employer and started his own company with one goal: to develop a personal, lightweight, portable navigation system. Over the next five years, he saw and read about many products similar to his in the market, but almost all of them were software or CD-ROM based devices. Many were produced specifically for automobiles and could not be removed for use outside them. Simon knew he had a product that would be successful.

By late 1996, Grisham Industries had twenty-five employees. Simon had conducted several interviews on his new product but was always careful not to give too much away. Then, his idea took another turn. One day, on an airplane, he overheard a fellow traveler complaining that he was tired of carrying a cell phone, a pager, and a PDA. This got him thinking about how he could further improve his product.

By December 1999, Grisham Industries had a prototype of its product, the NaviPorte, a production facility near the Gulf Coast that was 90 percent completed, and over 250 employees. At heart, the NaviPorte was still a portable navigation system that needed no software, was usable on a global basis, and, like many other navigation systems, was searchable for locations such as restaurants, hotels, airports, etc. But unlike other navigation systems, it was light enough to be carried by the user. In addition, through partnerships with service providers and a major computer manufacturer, the NaviPorte could also serve as a PDA with email and instant messaging capability, as well as a cell phone, a pager, an MP3 player and a satellite radio receiver. The NaviPorte, a triumph of micro engineering and technology, was the all-in-one device the market was searching for. Resulting demand was expected to be enormous.

In March of 2004, after much press and publicity, Grisham Industries unveiled the NaviPorte at the Consumer Gadgets Hype-It-Conference in Los Angeles. Though full production would not begin until June, by the end of the conference, Grisham Industries already had orders for 5,000 units. The most popular feature of the NaviPorte was the manufacturer's ability to customize the device to the user's specifications. For a modest price, the consumer could get the basic portable NaviPorte; after that, however, Grisham Industries could fully customize the NaviPorte depending on what the consumer wanted.

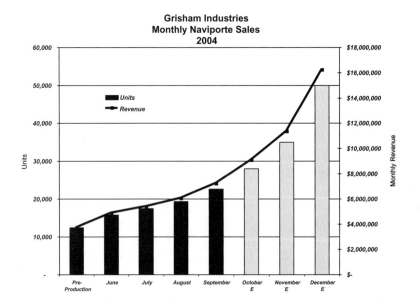

Grisham Industries
Monthly Naviporte Sales
2004

In June, Grisham Industries began scheduled production on the NaviPorte and started taking orders from its Web site and its call center at the production facility. In seven to ten days, Grisham Industries could take an order, build a customized NaviPorte and send it to the consumer. This not only resulted in satisfied customers but also significantly reduced inventory; since NaviPortes were largely built to fill specific orders, Grisham Industries held little finished goods inventory. By the end of September that year, Grisham Industries had sold and delivered over 85,000 units. Technology analysts were predicting that from October through the holiday season, Grisham Industries would sell more than 110,000 units worldwide, despite the entrance of a similar product from a large computer manufacturer. Then disaster struck.

CONVERSATIONS WITH AN ADJUSTER

It's not surprising that Simon couldn't find a finished NaviPorte that fateful morning on October 2, 2004. The man with him was an insurance adjuster, and the two were standing in fully eight inches of water, staring at the rubble and wreckage strewn throughout the facility. Two nights before, on September 30, 2004, Hurricane Senta had ravaged the Gulf Coast. With winds in excess of 120 miles per hour and massive flooding, the entire area around Grisham Industries' production facility was wiped out. Half the new facility's roof was peeled off, exposing the interior of the production facilities and the company's call center to wind and water damage. By most accounts, it would be well into 2005 before the area was restored to normal.

As Simon stood staring into the darkness after the storm had passed, he knew he could not be back in production by the holidays. With competitors lurking behind him, Grisham Industries would never recover those sales. And it would take months for Grisham Industries to catch up to its competitors. He knew he faced worrisome months ahead. What he didn't anticipate was the next question from Jason O'Shea, the adjuster for Koen Insurance: "So let me understand the situation, Mr. Grisham. Are you telling me you have no finished goods inventory you can sell? No retail outlets?"

After building its Gulf Coast production facility, Grisham Industries had obtained comprehensive property and liability insurance coverage through its broker. The coverage was offered through a standard U.S. Form policy, with no extended period of indemnity. (For an explanation of the difference between U.S. and European Forms, see Chapter 5.) The policy covered business interruption, including all ongoing labor costs.

So, Simon Grisham spent the better part of that October morning explaining his business to the adjuster. He explained that the NaviPorte was a customized product sold over the Internet and through the call center, and while many of the parts needed to meet orders were lying about the building, the production facilities would be down until mid-January 2005. In the meantime, Grisham Industries had no way to assemble new product. All new orders would go unfilled or to competitors until January 15, 2005. The adjuster and Simon ultimately agreed that the adjuster would work directly with the contractor managing the repairs to ensure all costs were captured correctly, and Simon would find a third party to assist with the calculation of the business interruption claim.

BUSINESS INTERRUPTION CLAIM

Simon Grisham contacts you about his claim, providing you a copy of the policy, historical financial statements, internal sales projections, and external sales projections prepared by *Tech Monthly*, a noted technology industry publication. Grisham indicates that he believes that *Tech Monthly's* projected sales in units are a bit aggressive, but he is unsure because he is not a retail expert. He asks that you help him with Grisham Industries' business interruption claim, assuming that there will be no sales of NaviPortes from October 1, 2004, through January 15, 2005.

You have the following information:

Figure N.1: Grisham Industries' Monthly Financial Statements, 06/01/04 – 9/30/04

Grisham Industries 2004 Profit & Loss *(In Millions)*				
	Jun-04	**Jul-04**	**Aug-04**	**Sep-04**
Sales	$ 4,890	$ 5,392	$ 6,061	$ 7,227
Cost of Sales	1,956	2,087	2,394	2,732
Labor	1,027	1,078	1,206	1,425
Sales & Marketing	750	525.0	544.0	599.0
Other	432	142	151.0	144.0
Total Expenses	4,165	3,832	4,296	4,900
EBITDA	$ 725	$ 1,560	$ 1,766	$ 2,327

Figure N.2: Grisham Industries Unit Sales and Avg. $/Unit (Projected), 4th Qtr. 2004

Grisham Industries
Unit and Price Projections
Q4 2004

	Units	Average Price
October 2004	26,500	$ 315
November 2004	32,000	$ 315
December 2004	45,000	$ 315
Total	103,500	

Figure N.3: Tech Monthly's Unit Sales and Avg. $/Unit (Projected), 4th Qtr. 2004

Tech Monthly
Unit and Price Projections - Naviporte
4th quarter '04

	No. of Units	Price
October 2004	28,000	$ 320
November 2004	35,000	$ 325
December 2004	50,000	$ 325
Total	113,000	

In further conversations with Grisham you determine that the company plans to retain all of its employees to avoid losing ground to its competitors. Most of the employees will be on-site three to four days per week, assisting with cleanup and bringing the business back on line. Further, due to advertising contracts, Grisham Industries will continue to incur approximately half of its expected sales and marketing costs to run ads in newspapers and magazines informing consumers of the disaster and assuring current customers that their service will continue.

CLAIM SCENARIO

NaviPorte and Grisham Industries
Simon's Awkward Position

Q U E S T I O N S

1. What factors contribute to Grisham Industries ability to mitigate its losses?

2. As Grisham Industries' claim adviser, what approach would you take to calculate its business interruption claim?

3. If Grisham Industries' policy were written on a European form, how might the claim be different?

4. How would you help manage expectations for Grisham Industries' shareholders, management, and insurance company throughout the process?

CLAIM SCENARIO

NaviPorte and Grisham Industries
Simon's Awkward Position

DISCUSSION

1. What factors contribute to Grisham Industries ability to mitigate its losses?

   a) It appears unlikely that Grisham Industries will be able to generate new product to fulfill orders due to its lack of finished goods inventory.

   b) Grisham Industries should investigate the possibility of setting up a temporary production facility that would mitigate its loss.

2. As Grisham Industries' claims adviser, what approach would you take to calculate its business interruption claim?

   a) The claims adviser should meet with Grisham Industries management to understand the likely level of sales had the incident not occurred. Any and all pertinent data available, including historical operating statements, projections done by outside sources, and internal projections should be considered. The claims adviser should investigate the status of outstanding orders. In addition, orders that come in after the indemnity period should be considered.

   b) Historical data and projections should also be used to calculate projected costs had the incident not occurred. Management should be consulted to understand the likelihood that historical trends would have continued had the incident not occurred.

3.   If Grisham Industries' policy were written on a European form, how might the claim be different?

    a)   The wording of the specific policy should be reviewed in detail. However, in general, the European Form provides for coverage based upon the overall recovery of operations, subject to a specified period of time (e.g., twelve or twenty-four months). The United States Form typically provides coverage until the date that repairs are or reasonably could have been completed.

4.   How would you help manage expectations for Grisham Industries' shareholders, management, and insurance company throughout the process?

    a)   This loss could either put the company out of business or become a testament to the importance of both a well-prepared and evidenced property and business interruption claim and a fair, equitable settlement. How do you ensure the latter and not the former? First, it will be important to have an all-hands meeting with the insurer, the broker, attorneys, executive management—and loss consultants as needed, to discuss the options available to (1) mitigate the loss, (2) maintain cash flow, (3) rebuild the facility, and (4) retain employees and keep customers (market share). This can only be accomplished through a team effort and open communication among all the parties.

CHAPTER SEVEN

Calculating the Business Interruption Loss

A Challenging Task

In legal contracts and insurance policies, *business interruption* means the financial impact of a disruption of operations over a period of time. Perils causing a business interruption may include fires, floods, explosions, hurricanes, and tornadoes, but they are not limited to these. The purpose of business interruption insurance is to put the insured in the same financial position it would have been in had no loss occurred, subject to specific endorsements in the policy. Business interruption insurance is typically purchased as an endorsement to property insurance; and under most policies, physical damage or loss caused by an insured event and resulting in business interruption meets the requirement for coverage.[1]

Every company that experiences a business interruption loss seems to seek some magical formula or easy mechanical method to quickly value and settle its claim. But there is no magic bullet; no automatic formula can be used in situations where each loss can be very different from the next. Determining the amount of a business interruption loss can be one of the most challenging tasks in the world of insurance. Calculating value requires forecasting what a business might have done had it not been for a certain event. This forecasting can be optimistic, pessimistic, and/or realistic. Even before addressing how the insurance coverage would apply to the equation, one can see where disagreements might develop. However, be aware that any conversation regarding the quantification about the loss can rarely be restricted to only the numbers. The length of time, or "indemnity period," and the coverage endorsements always play a critical role in determining the amount of the claim.

All business interruption losses share three elements that need to be addressed in developing a claim: the *duration* of the loss, the *coverage* in effect at the time of that loss, and *quantification* of the loss. This chapter focuses on the latter.

Figure 7.1 illustrates the most basic example of a business interruption calculation where projected results were compared to actual, with a slight adjustment for a nonloss related item.

Figure 7.1: Basic Example of a Business Interruption Loss

	Projected	Actual	Difference	Adjustment	Claim
Net Sales	$2,000,000	$1,200,000	$800,000		
Variable Expenses	1,200,000	700,000	500,000		
Fixed Expenses	400,000	400,000	-0-	25,000	
Net Income	$400,000	$100,000	$300,000	$25,000	$325,000

In this basic example of a loss calculation, projected results are compared to actual, with a slight adjustment for a nonloss related item. Few claims are this simple.

Few claims are this simple. Calculating a business interruption loss can be extraordinarily complicated because many claims have gray areas either in the application of coverage or in measuring the loss. The success or failure of a claim ultimately depends on the ability of the practitioner preparing the claim to understand fully the insured's business and the impact of the loss, to interpret and apply coverage, to calculate the impact of the business interruption, and to provide adequate support for the claim.[2]

This chapter discusses the mechanics of preparing a business interruption claim. At the outset, it is worth emphasizing that the process and events that lead up to that final claim document are anything but mechanical, as they are iterative and require a substantial number of probing questions.

The first steps in evaluating a business interruption loss come within a few hours, days, or weeks of the event. Usually, a company's boardroom will be filled with representatives from accounting, marketing and sales, production, legal, and risk management to discuss the impact of the loss and potential short- and long-term financial effects of the event. These meetings constitute the early stages of developing a claim, and many key questions are asked, including:

• What sales were expected during the loss period?

- Are historical sales trends a good indicator of what would have happened?

- How quickly can we get back into production—partial and/or full?

- Will this event delay the introduction of any new products?

- How do we plan to mitigate the loss by use of other plants or temporary facilities?

Other meetings, similar in composition to this initial one, will be required as the claim theory is further developed and documented. Moving past the process, let's get into the calculation itself, beginning with some terminology common in business interruption insurance.

Common Business Interruption Terminology[3]

In many U.S. insurance policies, business interruption is defined as either (A) or (B):

Gross Earnings Form		Business Income (or Net Profits) Form
A. The reduction in "gross earnings" less charges or expenses that do not continue during the interruption of business.	OR	B. Net income (net profit or loss before income taxes) that would have been earned or incurred plus continuing normal operating expenses incurred.

Whether the policy is a **Gross Earnings Form** or a **Business Income Coverage Form,** which may be referred to as a net profits form, the claim calculation should be exactly the same because both forms measure the same value. (See Chapter 2 for a general discussion of these forms.)

For simplicity, this chapter focuses exclusively on the **Business Income (Net Profits) Form.** However, in practice, an accountant would use either the gross earnings approach or the net income approach. Often, the claim preparer for the policyholder and the claim auditor for the insurance company will agree on an approach early in the process.

Following are common terms encountered in the preparation of a business interruption claim. Many are simply accounting terms used in an income or profit-and-loss statement. For example, an income statement may include the term "fixed expenses;" in business interruption calculations, these relate to "continuing expenses"—expenses that are ongoing during the loss period. While these expenses may include many fixed costs, they usually comprise a portion of both fixed and variable costs.

Definitions of Important Terms in Business Interruption Claims

Income Statement	The statement of revenues, expenses, gains, and losses for the period ending with net income (or loss) for the period. The income statement formula of revenue less cost of sales less operating expenses (exclusive of income taxes) equals net income/(loss) before income taxes. The cost of sales and operating expenses are comprised of both variable and fixed expense components (exclusive of income taxes).
Revenue	Sales of products, merchandise, services, and earnings from interest, dividends, rents, and wages; transactions resulting in increases in assets.
Cost of Sales	The total cost of goods sold during a given accounting period, determined by ascertaining for each item of sale the invoice and such other costs pertaining to the item as may have been included in the cost of goods purchased.
Expenses	Outflows or other use of assets or incurrences of liabilities (or both) during a period as a result of delivering or producing goods, rendering services, or carrying out other activities that constitute the entity's ongoing major or central operations.
Operating Expenses	Expenses incurred in conducting the ordinary major activities of an enterprise, usually divided into two categories: selling expenses and general and administrative expenses. Examples include: · Payroll and payroll taxes · Rent · Utilities
Net Income (Net Profit or Loss before Income Taxes)	Revenue less cost of sales less operating expenses. The term "net income" is sometimes referred to as "net profit" in insurance policies and legal documents.
Variable Expenses	Expenses that vary directly, sometimes proportionately, with business volume.

Fixed Expenses	Expenses that do not vary with business volume. Examples include: · Rent · Property taxes · Interest on bonds · Certain portions of selling and general overhead · Depreciation
Continuing Expenses	Normal operating expenses that are incurred during the period of loss. Examples include: · Rent · Utility costs (electric, water, gas, and telephone) · Payroll and payroll taxes, if employees were paid during the period of loss
Noncontinuing Expenses	Expenses that are not incurred during the loss period. Examples include: · Sales commissions · Bad debt expense · Credit card transaction fees · Sales discounts · Payroll and payroll taxes, if employees were not paid during the loss period · Raw materials, if not producing any product
Gross Earnings – Mercantile Form	The sum of total net sales plus other earnings derived from operation of the business less the cost of merchandise sold, including packaging, materials, and supplies consumed directly in supplying the service(s) sold by the insured, as well as service(s) purchased for resale that do not continue under the contract.[4]
Gross Earnings – Manufacturing Form	Net sales value of lost production plus other operating income plus net sales of outsourced products less raw material and packaging costs of manufactured products; materials and supplies consumed; services purchased from outsiders not under contract; and cost of outsourced products sold.

Common Elements of the Business Interruption Calculation

Early in this chapter, we described the key elements of a business interruption claim as duration of the loss, coverage in place, and quantification. Before focusing more on the quantification portion of the claim, we should discuss the important attributes of time and coverage.

Time

Any business interruption calculation requires the determination of the time period or duration of the calculable loss. Under a business interruption policy, compensable time is the **period of indemnity** or the time it would take, with due diligence and dispatch, to replace the damaged property with property of like kind and quality and for business operations to return to normal.

Here is fairly typical policy language concerning the time period:

> PERIOD OF INDEMNITY – The PERIOD OF INDEMNITY applicable to all TIME ELEMENT coverage is the period starting from the time of physical loss or damage of the type insured against and ending when with due diligence and dispatch the building and equipment could be repaired or replaced and made ready for operations under the same or equivalent physical and operating conditions that existed prior to the damage.

Yet, businesses commonly continue to experience losses beyond the point of physical repairs; therefore, insurers typically offer as an extension of coverage an **extended period of indemnity**. Here's how that extension is typically defined in a policy:

> EXTENDED PERIOD OF INDEMNITY – Coverage is extended to cover the reduction of sales resulting from the interruption of business for such additional length of time as would be required with the exercise of due diligence and dispatch to restore the Insured's business to the condition that would have existed had no loss occurred, subject to a maximum of 180 days. This period commences on the date on which policy liability would terminate if this extension had not been included herein.

The duration of the loss period can be debated by insured and insurer, especially in extenuating circumstances such as changes to the replaced property or the efficacy of new machinery in returning operations to preloss efficiency levels.

No matter what the type of manufacturing, determining operating levels—before and after a business interruption—is extremely important, addressing the following questions:

- How is performance measured?

- How long did the plant operate at the stated rate before the loss?

- Is the rating achieved only at certain peak operating times of the year?

- How long will it take to return to the preloss performance levels?

To answer and resolve any uncertainty, these steps may be taken:

1. Identify a qualified, dedicated claims team (see Chapter 6).

2. Prepare a comprehensive, well documented claim.

3. Bring in an accounting expert to measure the pre and postloss efficiency.

4. Keep the loss open until the preloss efficiency rating has been reachieved by the insured.

Sometimes, but not often, there is an opportunity to settle the business interruption claim early in the process.

Quantity

To calculate the lost units or sales, the insurance company or policyholder has to answer this question: *How would the entity have performed during the loss period or indemnity period?* A policy typically addresses this question with somewhat vague language, as this sample shows.

> EXPERIENCE OF THE BUSINESS - In determining the amount of net profit, charges and expenses covered hereunder for the purpose of ascertaining the amount of loss sustained due consideration shall be given to the experience of the business before the date of damage and the probable experience thereafter had no loss occurred.

What type of information does one look for to determine sales lost during the indemnity period? How does the policyholder apply this policy language in the measurement of its loss? The answers to those questions reside in several sources of data in the policyholder's organization, including budgets, forecasts, industry trends, and historical operating and financial performance. In a nutshell, one must derive the sales that would have occurred "but for" the loss itself. The actual sales achieved during the indemnity period is subtracted from the "but for" amount to arrive at the claimed lost sales (see Exhibit 7.2).

Figure 7.2: Lost Units/Sales, Projected & Actual

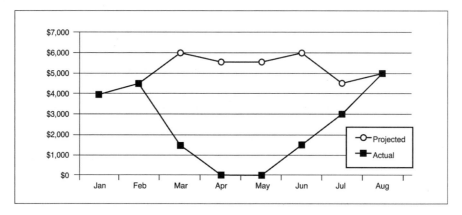

Here are variations to consider in these calculations.

Budgets and Forecasts Versus a Base Period

One way to begin the estimation is through the use of projections and budgets. Their applicability depends on several factors. For example, sometimes budgets are used as stretch targets that generally fall short of actual performance. In some instances, budgets are understated so management can always meet or exceed budgeted figures, since in many organizations this comes with a financial incentive.

Also, the accuracy of historical actual performance to the respective projections or budgets should be evaluated. Base period data should be compared to budgeted performance for the same period to calculate the average percentage of budget typically achieved. The percentage thus attained—call it the accuracy percentage—should then be applied to the budget that covers the loss period to determine what performance could have been anticipated during the period of indemnity. Depending on the nature of the business, key members of management should be interviewed to gain a full understanding of the level of sales that would have been achieved had the incident not occurred. Some questions include:

- Are historical sales a good indicator of what would have been achieved had the incident not occurred?

- Do internal forecasts and/or budgets accurately reflect the level of sales that would have been achieved had the incident not occurred?

- Were you expanding or reducing capacity in any way or introducing new products?

- Were there any recent changes in the competitive marketplace (e.g., the closure of a competitor's business)?

- Did you enter into any significant additional sales contacts recently?

- Is there any interdependency between the damaged location and other insured locations?

- Do you expect that other insured locations will be able to make up some of the loss at the damaged location?

However, although projections and budgets are good starting points when determining actual or "but for" performance, they are not always the complete story. When a budget or forecast is not a true reflection of performance during the loss period, the insurance company and policyholder need to establish a base period to project the lost sales. A base period can be a week, a month, seven months, a year, etc. The rule of thumb is that the base period is often close to or similar in length to the period of interruption and representative of its characteristics. In other words, if the loss period is six months or less, then a base period of six months to a full year is often employed.

A few other considerations arise in determining the proper length of time to use as an historical basis. For example, one company's performance might be constant throughout the year, while another's is seasonal. That distinction is important. Does the company anticipate any significant changes in future performance? That question should be asked. Finally, it is necessary to consider any anticipated increases or decreases in market demand, as well as the projected potential impact of a planned expansion or new product launches.

Seasonality

Using a representative base period is especially important when the company's performance is seasonal. In these cases, the actual-to-budgeted performance may fluctuate significantly during the course of a year. As a result, a period of one month, three months, or even six months before the loss may not be representative of company performance if the indemnity period contains the peak season.

For example, in the Greater Mass Hat Manufacturing (GMHM) case study (at the end of this chapter, beginning on page 207), the production and sale of the company's core product—woolen hats—changes with the season. If the GMHM facility were shut down only during the winter, it would make no sense to project lost sales for woolen hats since their production would have been completed before the cold weather set in.

Future Changes in Performance

When evaluating projections or budgets, the policyholder must also anticipate changes to future performance due to improvements or other situations. In the GMHM case study, for example, the manufacturer had planned to expand its production facility in 2004. So, calculating "but for" performance based on data for periods subsequent to July 2003 would not be representative of GMHM's performance after the planned expansion. If a consistent production amount per square foot is supported, and if the planned expansion is fairly certain to proceed, a case may be made that "but for" production should be adjusted for the greater square footage.

Market Conditions/Consumer Demand

Also important to consider when using projections or budgets are market conditions during the indemnity period. For example, if GMHM were one of only two hat producers in the U.S., and if its competitor went out of business just one week after the beginning of the business interruption, the budgeted projected sales for GMHM should be reevaluated to include the likely surge in demand caused by altered competitive conditions (assuming GMHM had the capacity to take advantage of the opportunity).

Launch of a New Product/Planned Expansion

When the "but for" production calculations include a planned event with an unknown outcome, it can be difficult to substantiate the loss claim. Insurers will likely reason that revisions to projected performance are speculative at best. In these situations, it is helpful to demonstrate past performance in similar projects, whether an expansion, acquisition, or entry into a new market. If a precedent is not available, the debate will likely be more intense. Insurers will certainly and closely examine the feasibility of the planned event. The following scenario with Lester's Sticky Buns illustrates the debate that can surround an unknown "but for" calculation.

A Sticky Wicket for Sticky Buns

For sixty years, Lester's Sticky Buns operated in a prime location in St. Louis. But when a Donut Delights opened two miles away, the impact was powerful, culminating in a 15 percent drop in business for Lester's. The owner began looking for innovative ways to lure customers back. Could a new location be the answer?

A great corner property directly across the street from the shop's current location—a spot never previously developed—came on the market. Lester's seized the opportunity, purchased the property, and began construction. The company's plans included doubling the dining capacity, adding a drive-through window for service, adding a donut oven to expand its product line, and introducing a line of healthy breakfast choices including an egg-white omelet inside a multigrain bagel shaped like the St. Louis Arch.

Everything went well until disaster struck—and it wasn't Donut Delights. On the second day of the new store's opening, a tornado swept through the neighborhood.

Luckily, the owner carried business interruption coverage. But what is his loss? To project the loss of sales, the owner has to consider several pieces of information: sales projections prepared by the marketing company that reviewed Lester's business plan; sales forecasts given to the bank to obtain financing for the new location; and the growth in the donut industry as a benchmark for the new products. The calculation was challenging; so was the evaluation of the claim.

Value

The business interruption value can be calculated using either of the following methods, since both yield the same result:

Business Interruption Value = Net Income Plus Continuing Expenses
OR
Business Interruption Value = Gross Earnings Less Noncontinuing Expenses

As a practical matter, however, the business interruption value is often expressed as a percentage of sales; and the loss is determined by multiplying the net value of lost sales[5] by the business interruption value percentage.

The identification of expenses is important, no matter what method is used, since expenses directly impact business interruption value. Expenses come in two types: **continuing**, which are fixed costs (they must be paid even when a company is not operating at normal capacity) and **noncontinuing**, which are variable costs (they usually relate to production or sales activities and are not incurred during the period of interruption).

Typical Continuing Expenses	*Typical Noncontinuing Expenses*
• Mortgage or rent payments	• Raw materials
• Salaries	• Maintenance
• Insurance	• Direct labor and other hourly wages
• Advertising	• Shipping or freight
• Property taxes	• Bad debt expense
• Interest on bonds	• Sales discounts

Whether an expense is continuing or noncontinuing is not always clear-cut, since some could be either depending on the company's business and the specifics of a particular loss. Consider these examples:

- Advertising can be a continuing expense since it is planned far in advance and budgeted at the beginning of the year; like depreciation, it is a sunk cost allocated over the course of the year. But advertising would be a noncontinuing expense if the policyholder stops or cuts back on its use because of the loss.

- Some expenses can have both a fixed and variable component. When this occurs, the appropriate portion of the expense should be allocated to each category, whether continuing or noncontinuing. For example, a company might have a fixed fee for telephone service; this would be paid even during the loss period. But the additional charges incurred by employees during the normal course of business—such as long distance charges for calling customers or suppliers—would be a noncontinuing expense.

Determining whether an expense is continuing or noncontinuing can also depend on the circumstances of the business interruption claim. Some factors potentially affecting the outcome include type of company, nature and extent of the loss, period of loss or interruption, and company contracts.

Analyzing continuing and noncontinuing expenses can become challenging in a production loss environment where a portion of the plant's operations are suspended (interrupted), yet production continues for other products. An example of this would be in steel mills or casting plants where a furnace or a finishing line may go down. There is still an ability to produce product—but at an inefficient rate. This inefficiency is a loss to the company's gross margin and should be included as part of the claim.

Some business interruption policies also include coverage for ordinary payroll or wages paid to an hourly workforce. Without this explicit coverage, payroll expenses could be classified as a noncontinuing expense. To get reimbursement, policyholders with ordinary coverage must continue to pay their hourly workforce. Ordinary payroll coverage is a good idea for companies needing to keep a skilled workforce during the loss period. Also, this coverage saves the policyholder the costs of hiring and training new employees once operations resume.

To claim hourly wages as a continuing expense, the policyholder still needs to do some calculation. Perhaps the company will choose to let some workers go, thereby lowering the payroll amount. Or the ordinary payroll amount may increase because of postloss inefficiencies. In some instances, it may be more representative to show ordinary payroll as a separate calculation outside business interruption value. This would make it easier to separate the actual hourly labor costs and benefits paid during the period of indemnity and the extended period of indemnity. If ordinary payroll were treated as a separate component, it would be shown as a noncontinuing expense in the business interruption value since it would be captured elsewhere.

Documenting a Business Interruption Claim

With a business interruption claim, the burden of proof is on the policyholder—and a claim is only as good as the policyholder's documentation. Not only does documentation move the claim recovery process along more quickly and smoothly to a successful settlement, it also expedites advance payments from insurance companies. Poor documentation can mean significant delays every step of the way.

What Documentation Is Required?

A policy does not contain a punch list of required documentation to support a claim. The type and amount of documentation needed is case-specific. Obviously, the larger and more complex the loss, the more documentation required to support the policyholder's position. Likewise, the adjuster and accountants will have their own expectations, again based on the facts and circumstances of each loss. In the end, the documentation has to answer their questions without overburdening them with excessive or irrelevant information.

Initially, the policyholder will decide which documents are relevant and sufficient, so that the claim can stand on its own with supporting detail and assumptions. See the following business interruption document checklist to get an idea of what is typically required to get the process started.

A typical claim packet can be substantial. A large property damage claim can generate enough documentation to fill numerous three-inch binders and/or significant hard-drive space, with final files resembling those in Exhibit 7.3.

Typical Business Interruption Document Checklist

✓ Monthly profit and loss statements
✓ Monthly inventory reports
✓ Monthly production reports
✓ General ledgers
✓ Cost accounting reports
✓ Sales and production forecasts
✓ Budgets
✓ Invoices and purchase orders
✓ Details of any loss related accounts
✓ Claim narrative

Figure 7.3: Case Files for a Typical Claim

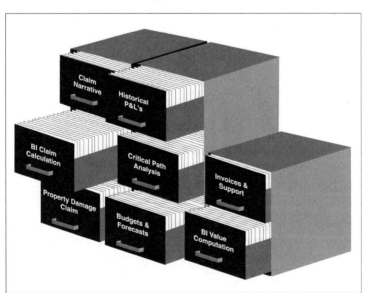

Qualitative information—both oral and nonfinancial, including minutes from meetings relating to the loss, transcripts from investor's calls, and information in the media—can also be important to supporting a business interruption claim.

While they do not specify documents required, policies do give insurance companies the right to audit and inspect the policyholder's books and records.

What Level of Detail Is Reasonable?

The scope of the documents usually covers not only the loss period(s) but also several months or even a few years before. Typically, the length of the indemnity period dictates how much historical information is required to support the loss: the longer the indemnity period, the greater the documentation. Nevertheless, both parties need to decide the reasonableness of a request in light of both its applicability and the availability of information.

Case Study—Greater Mass Hat Manufacturing

We can examine the principles and processes of calculating a business interruption loss by walking through a detailed case study involving the Greater Mass Hat Manufacturing Company (GMHM). Accounting data and other supporting information for this case study is located at the following Web site: www.nuco.com/businessinterruption.

GMHM specializes in the production of trendy baseball caps and ski hats, fashionable with the under-twenty crowd. The company operates two facilities in the U.S., one in Massachusetts and one in Southern California. The facility in Boston produces both baseball caps and ski hats; the facility in California produces only baseball caps.

As a result of a July hailstorm, GMHM suffered physical damage to its Boston plant—specifically a destroyed roof, damaged manufacturing equipment, and ruined work-in-process and finished-goods inventory. At the time, management thinks the damaged facility will be up and running again in five months, which translates into the loss of an entire production and sales season for the ski hat line as well as lost production of baseball caps.

GMHM expects to recover *all* property damage and time element losses under its "all risks" policy written by Boston Insurance. Meanwhile, to mitigate its losses, the company moves the production of ski hats to the California facility; the plant's conversion (from baseball caps to ski hats) requires two weeks and costs $155,000.

Production commences on August 1, as planned. The California plant's production of baseball caps is outsourced to a competitor, Ohio Cap Company (OCC), under a contract calling for a monthly volume of 30,000 units at a price of $24 each. While this puts GMHM in a loss position since it sells the caps for $22, this strategy is necessary for the company to maintain its market position with department store customers nationwide. OCC begins making baseball caps for GMHM on August 1.

The Situation

The Boston plant makes 65,000 baseball caps and 50,000 ski hats during each month of their respective production seasons: baseball caps are produced from January to July, and ski hats are produced from August to December. At the end of each manufacturing season, production is halted for the two-week conversion of the line. The facility in California, making only baseball caps, produces 70,000 units per month. Its machinery had never been configured to allow for the production of ski hats.

At the time of the storm, the inventory in Boston consisted of 5,565 ski hats in finished goods, 11,440 baseball caps in work-in-process, and 36,214 baseball caps in finished goods. Water from the storm damaged 55 percent of the baseball caps (6,292 work-in-process and 19,918 finished goods) and 100 percent of the ski hats. However, the damaged finished goods were salvaged and sold at 50 percent of their original price. Five thousand of the baseball caps had been left over from a special promotion; there was little likelihood these could have been sold under any circumstance.

The Boston plant's budget for ski hat sales depends on forecasts for snow in the Northeast. If the average snowfall is less than anticipated, sales average a 1 percent drop for each monthly two-inch shortfall. The year of the storm, GMHM anticipates a snowfall of 100 inches from October through January.

Workforce Issues

The employees in Massachusetts are members of the United Federation of Hat Workers Union. Under terms of a collective bargaining agreement, if they are laid off they receive $1,000 for every week of service up to twenty weeks. And, in October the union went on strike for one month, thereby cutting that month's production to 15 percent of normal levels.

Market Issues

As a result of the incident, one of GMHM's largest customers, which had purchased $500,000 of ski hats over the prior three years, removes GMHM from its preferred supplier list, citing concern over the company's ability to meet delivery schedules. This customer shifts all its business to a competitor for the next four years (total sales loss to GMHM of $2.0 million).

The Price Tag

Facility Cleanup Costs

GMHM uses salaried employees, unable to work while the plant is closed, for cleanup. Despite high absenteeism during this time, the company does not force employees into cleanup duty; employees not reporting for work do not receive wages. The plant manager informs the insurance company that GMHM is saving $200,000 by using salaried labor rather than outside contractors. An additional $30,000 is saved in wages of absentee employees.

Total wages paid to employees during the facility cleanup is $175,000, a figure that does not include $45,000 in overtime. (In the prior-year same period, overtime wages equaled $12,000.) In addition, all employees who do at least eighty hours of cleanup are given a $250 gift certificate to a local home improvement store. In total, GMHM spends $6,250 on these.

Cleanup supplies are another cost. The company spends $2,500 on mops, buckets, towels, and other cleanup materials. Four heating fans are required to expedite the evaporation of water from the facility: two are on hand; two need to be bought. The GMHM plant manager contends that the two new fans might also be useful in normal operations to control temperatures during the colder months. Each fan costs $1,200.

Property Damage Repair Costs

GMHM's own engineers (corporate and local plant) repair the plant's machinery, including specialized hat machines. Given they had designed the original equipment, these professionals are best suited for the job. The amount of annual salaries the engineers receive during the repair period totals $40,000. (Note: the engineers are not compensated for overtime.) By late July, the repair team realizes that the machinery is irreparably damaged. To this point, the repair effort has cost $250,000 for various replacement components, none of which can be safely reused.

GMHM immediately contacts GEMAX, Inc., to purchase replacement machinery for $900,000. GEMAX agrees to deliver the new equipment in six weeks, after which GMHM needs two more weeks to modify the machinery to produce both baseball caps and ski hats.

After the machinery is installed and modified, the corporate engineers begin work on the reconstruction of the factory. The Boston plant agrees to pay, through internal cost allocations, $50 per hour for each corporate employee. Annual engineering salaries equate to an average hourly rate of $20 per hour (although the engineers are not compensated on an hourly basis). Additionally, the Boston plant agrees to pay the repair team's living and travel expenses. While negotiating rates and costs with the corporate engineering department, the Boston plant manager also receives a quote from a local construction firm, Tea Party Construction (TPC), of $40 an hour. However, prior experience at the Boston plant showed TPC tended to run over budget and had difficulties in meeting aggressive project timelines.

The estimated time period to restore the facility to its original design and performance is twenty weeks. Over the reconstruction period, the GMHM plant incurs charges for twenty-five assigned engineers for 300 hours each. Additionally, each engineer incurs $7,500 in travel expenses.

In total, material costs for repair and reconstruction total $1,950,000 (exclusive of labor and a fire suppression system). GMHM engineers estimate that $500,000 of this is directly related to the expansion of the manufacturing and packaging areas, an expansion originally planned for 2005 but logically made part of the repair effort. Before the loss, the GMHM facility manufacturing area was 10,000 square feet; the packaging and order staging area was 5,000 square feet. After the reconstruction, these areas would expand to 15,000 and 10,000 square feet respectively. Corporate engineering prepares a formal estimate indicating that this change would extend the facility reconstruction project by three weeks.

When the facility was originally built, all manufacturing plants smaller than 20,000 square feet required the installation of A-rated fire suppression systems, while those larger than that required B-rated systems. Shortly before the storm, these standards had changed, and B-rated systems were required for *all* new manufacturing facilities regardless of size. While the old plant was grandfathered under the old fire code, the new facility requires a B-rated system. GMHM's original A-rated system had cost $150,000; a new A-rated system would cost $175,000, while a new B-rated system would cost $300,000. The installation of either system adds one more week to the reconstruction schedule.

Time Element Claim

Mitigating and Extra Expenses

The policy contains the following language with respect to extra expense:

> EXTRA EXPENSE – The recoverable EXTRA EXPENSE loss will be the reasonable and necessary extra costs incurred by the Insured to temporarily continue as nearly normal as practicable the conduct of the Insured's business.

Period of Indemnity

GMHM's "all risk" policy contains the following clauses with respect to the length of the applicable coverage period.

> PERIOD OF INDEMNITY – The PERIOD OF INDEMNITY applicable to all TIME ELEMENT coverages is the period starting from the time of physical loss or damage of the type insured against and ending when with due diligence and dispatch the building and equipment could be repaired or replaced and made ready for operations under the same or equivalent physical and operating conditions that existed prior to the damage.

> EXTENDED PERIOD OF INDEMNITY – Coverage is extended to cover the reduction of sales resulting from the interruption of business for such additional length of time as would be required with the exercise of due diligence and dispatch to restore the Insured's business to the condition that would have existed had no loss occurred, subject to a maximum of 180 days. This period commences on the date on which policy liability would terminate if this extension had not been included herein.

The following dates represent key events related to GMHM's business interruption.

July 1— Storm strikes GMHM's Boston facility, suspending operations.

July 15 — Facility cleanup is completed.

December 31— Facility reconstruction is completed after twenty-four weeks: twenty weeks to rebuild the plant, three weeks for the expansion, and one week to install a fire suppression system.

January 15 — Two weeks required for modifying the specialized machinery from GEMAX.

January 31— Quality control testing complete; production line is back in operation.

Calculating the Business Interruption Loss

Schedules were provided by GMHM to assist in the preparation of a business interruption claim. The complete schedules are found at www.nuco.com/business-interruption.

Schedule 1	2002 Budget versus Actual Production
Schedule 2	2002 Monthly Inventory Data
Schedule 3	2002 Sales Data
Schedule 4	2003 Budget versus Actual Production
Schedule 5	2003 Monthly Inventory Data
Schedule 6	2003 Sales Data
Schedule 7	Profit and Loss Statement 2002
Schedule 8	Boston Facility Inventory Schedule at Date of Loss
Schedule 9	Inventory Cost Data
Schedule 10	Important Dates
Schedule 11	Average Annual Snowfall in Greater Northeast Region
Schedule 12	Insurance Claim Suspense Account Data
Schedule 13	External Contractors versus Employees with Hourly Wages

Other Considerations

The outsourcing contract with OCC gives that company access to GMHM's markets and customers. And, as it turns out, OCC's production costs are more efficient and cost-effective than GMHM's. Not surprisingly, OCC attempts to seduce GMHM's customers with deep discounts and long-term deals.

Once management becomes aware of OCC's intentions, GMHM decides to remove OCC as quickly as possible from its supply chain. The only way to do that is to restart an old, moth-balled production line in the California plant. The one-time cost: $750,000. The revived line can achieve the same production volumes as OCC (30,000 caps per month) and can continue to be used even after the Boston facility is back up and running.

The refurbishment of the line starts in late August, and GMHM begins producing baseball caps in mid-September. The contract with OCC is cancelled with a penalty of $75,000. GMHM also starts an advertising campaign—at a cost of $18,000—to maintain market awareness of its product and to rekindle relationships with consumers.

Discovering that OCC's lower costs derived in great part from the company's use of a Radio Frequency Identification system to ship products faster and cheaper, GMHM decides to implement RFID in both plants at a cost of $84,000. This amount is included in the insurance claim.

Questions

Put yourself in the picture. How would you answer these questions?

1. What assumptions can GMHM employ when determining the claim amount?

2. What amount can GMHM claim for business interruption?

3. What amount can GMHM include for:

   a.   Ski hats finished goods

   b.   Baseball caps finished goods

   c.   Work-in-process

   d.   Cleanup of the facility

   e.   Facility repair and reconstruction

   f.   Extra expense

4. Can GMHM recover the lost sales to customers? If so, for what time period?

5. Should salaried payroll costs required for repairs be covered?

6. What are the ramifications of the employee strike that occurred on October 1?

7. Should management salaries be included in the claim?

8. What additional data would be useful in developing the claim?

Given all these variables, what is the total amount GMHM should claim? How might GMHM's claim figure differ from the insurance company's? Why?

From the beginning of the business interruption claim preparation process, financial and market information needs to be gathered and analyzed. This table shows the types of documents GMHM needed to prepare and support its business interruption claim:

Type of Information For	*What Time Period?*
Preloss budget/forecast data for both the Boston and California facilities	Monthly from January 1, 2002, through February 29, 2004
Actual production data for both the Boston and California facilities	Monthly from January 1, 2002, through February 29, 2004
Expected order data from GMHM's order processing system for both the Boston and California facilities	Monthly from January 1, 2002, through February 29, 2004
Sales orders that received the promotional discount of 15% following the restart of the production facility	For the two-month period following the restart of the production facility
Actual sales for both the Boston and California facilities	Monthly from January 1, 2002, through February 29, 2004
Profit and loss statements for GMHM as well as both the Boston and California facilities individually	Monthly from January 1, 2002, through February 29, 2004, as well as annual statements
Finished goods and work-in-process inventory records for both the Boston and California facilities that also include the damaged product at the Boston facility	Inventory information as close to the date of loss as possible
Contract with OCC for production of baseball caps to mitigate loss N/A	N/A

The Solution

Not surprisingly, the two parties come to different conclusions. The GMHM claim is aggressive, perhaps even naïve since management does not completely understand the intricacies and wording of the business interruption policy and claim recovery process. The insurance company's position is just as aggressive but in the opposite direction.[6]

Some of the more serious points of dispute follow

GMHM submits a claim for the business interruption associated with the loss of sales from ski hats and baseball caps. Here are the salient points in this claim calculation. Supporting documents and schedules are located at www.nuco.com/businessinterruption.

- In the solution presented (**Schedule B**), Boston Insurance is reflecting a period of indemnity adjustment for the increased time associated with building a larger plant, which effectively lengthens the loss period.

- The planned rate of gross profit differs from the actual rate of gross profit, a relatively common occurrence in a business interruption claim. As part of the negotiation process, the two parties must figure out why the rates differ (e.g., changes in product mix) and whether they are consistent with budgeted and prior periods. Large unexplained differences between the planned versus actual rate of gross profit calculation can point to fundamental errors (e.g., misclassified costs fixed versus noncontinuing or extra expense items buried within noncontinuing costs). For an example of the impact of product mix see the notes on Schedule D.

The adjuster and the insured's accountants can and often do classify costs differently, and the effects can be readily demonstrated. While each expert may have reasons for believing that her classification is correct, the impact on the claim calculation can be material.

The reasons for the differing classifications need to be discussed and resolved. For example, in this case study, prices were kept constant; however, price fluctuations can be a point of disagreement in many types of claims for commodities. Prices can increase as a result of the interruption itself. Is this increase in price to the benefit of the insurance company or the policyholder? Each case must be assessed independently.

No matter what approach is taken, the answers should be consistent. Policy wording usually dictates the preferred approach. Any material difference in the calculation under different approaches points to different assumptions, policy interpretations, or a mathematical error. For example:

Schedule B is a top-down (revenues less noncontinuing expenses) three-column approach.

Schedule C calculates the gross profit on a per unit basis and calculates the total number of lost units to arrive at the same answer.

Schedule D is a top-down gross profit approach based on information taken directly from the income statement; it calculates a rate of gross profit that is equal to that utilized on **Schedule E,** which employs a bottom-up approach.

The calculation in this case is done on a production basis, which assumes that each unit of lost production equals a lost sale[7]—a true assumption in this case because of the marketplace demand for the product. For example, GMHM lost a major customer for the remainder of a four-year contract. The company should put together a claim under its extended period of indemnity coverage to reflect this loss. (Note: More information is required for such a claim.)

Areas of Dispute and Negotiations of Lost Profit Claims

It is common in business interruption claims for the respective accountants of the insured and insurer to disagree on the components that comprise the business interruption claim calculation. For example, in the GMHM case the insurer's accountants may challenge the overall lost volume, the classification of continuing versus noncontinuing expenses, the valuation of damaged inventory, and the issue of saved expenses. These disagreements do not doom a settlement; rather, they are areas where further documentation and information may need to be collected so both sides can find common ground and agreement.

All claim professionals will tell you the key to resolving these items is effective communication and the exchange of quality information. A second key factor is up-to-date market analysis that can come into play when determining the accuracy of management budgets and current market conditions. The purpose of the coverage is to put the company back into the same position but for the insured loss. If new competitors enter the marketplace, or the fickle tastes of teenage consumers changes from baseball caps and ski hats to headbands and nose piercing, these factors must be taken into account when quantifying the loss.

Inventory Claims

For every type of inventory, the amount recoverable depends on the policy wording.

- **Finished goods claim, ski hats**—presented on **Schedule M**. In this case, the ski hats are valued both at selling price and cost.

- **Finished goods claim, baseball caps**—Boston Insurance makes an adjustment in its calculation for obsolete inventory. The policyholder should not expect to make recovery for items that should have been written off prior to the loss. The valuation of inventory is done on two bases: selling price and cost.

- **Work-in-process claim, baseball caps**—presented on **Schedule O**. WIP is commonly valued at selling price less nonincurred costs. The valuation presented here is at cost.

Settlement Issues in Inventory Claims

One situation that is not an area of dispute but does require separate consideration is when damaged inventory is valued at net selling price (sales price less discounts). When the policy pays for damaged inventory at net selling price, the amount of profit paid as damaged inventory must be deducted from the business interruption claim.

Aspects of the GMHM claim that may create settlement issues include:

- The existence and valuation of obsolete inventory.

- The assessment of WIP at 30 percent complete by Boston Insurance and at 50 percent complete by GMHM—the reasons for this difference need to be investigated further.

- If salvaged goods had a warranty or guarantee associated with them, the validity of these associated items can become void once they're damaged and salvaged.

- The insured does not want to compete against its insurer in selling its own goods. For this reason, the insurer may be restricted in the markets that it can sell in or be required to remove all labels and tags that associate the product with the insured. These types of issues can be addressed via specific policy wordings regarding warranties or labels and brands; however, if they are not, they can become the subject of disagreements between the parties.

Property Damage—Cleanup Costs (Schedule P)

The primary difference between the calculations of GMHM and Boston Insurance is the treatment of compensation expense. Coverage for compensation of employees is provided for under ordinary payroll cover. If the insured had used outside contractors to perform these activities, then this expense could be included under extra expense.

- A claim for payroll expense needs to be presented correctly within the context of the coverage provided by the policy.

- Boston Insurance makes an adjustment for overtime, the argument being that the overtime expense normal for the period should be deducted from the claimed amount. The argument could go either way on this point.

Property Damage Repair Costs

At issue here is the treatment of the allocation of costs to the original structure. The policyholder must understand an insurance company's position about what would be covered and what would *not* be covered when rebuilding to specifications different from the original. Agreement prior to the actual execution of the rebuild project would be preferable.

Labor costs are also an issue in this calculation. GMHM attempts to allocate labor to this project at a rate greater than actual cost; the insurer calls this into question. When looking to recover labor costs, getting quotes to perform a project is critical. The adjuster plays an integral role here. The insurance company will favor the most reasonable cost for the project. To avoid disagreements on coverage down the road, both sides should discuss labor/contractor costs up-front and openly. The settlement position for labor costs associated with property damage is subject to negotiation in this case.

Time Element Extra Expenses

The 45,000 baseball caps produced under the OCC contract were effectively purchased at retail from OCC and then sold to GMHM key customers. The increased cost associated with this strategy could be defended, since a loss of customers could easily trigger the extended period of indemnity coverage and increase the insurance company's overall payment.

The mitigating strategy then shifted to the refurbishment of an older production line—an action that could easily represent an enduring benefit to GMHM. Boston Insurance assumes this to be the case and allows only 50 percent coverage.

Conclusion

GMHM's claim to the insurer and the adjuster's response to the claim are shown in the suggested solution. The settlement of the claim can now be narrowed down to differences between the adjuster and the insured. During settlement discussions, representatives of the insurance company must be available to authorize and agree to settlement offers. If differences between the insured and the insurance company adjuster cannot be resolved, legal counsel may have to get involved. As its claim calculation makes apparent, GMHM was aggressive on some aspects of the submission and potentially understated other aspects; for these reasons, an expert claim preparer may be better able to present the claim to support the insured's interests and ensure a smooth recovery.

The business interruption claims approach should ideally facilitate settlement. Experience indicates that major disputes in business interruption claims center mainly on policy wordings and their application. If the parties can agree on the intention of the policy wordings, the calculation, negotiation, and settlement of a business interruption claim, though complex, is achievable.

Because a business interruption claim involves the *subjective* estimation of what would have happened had an incident not occurred, different parties commonly take very different approaches and arrive at very different results. It is important that the insured establish a solid rationale for all assumptions used in the claim and provide adequate documentation. The insured and insurer should establish a workable process to address differences and to move towards a reasonable settlement.

Endnotes

[1] Boiler & Machinery (B&M) policies are another form of property insurance specific to large industrial machines (boilers, etc.); these also include endorsements for business interruption. B&M coverage may be excluded from a property policy.

[2] Claims are typically prepared by the insured or an outside claims consultant. Most policyholders choose to use an outside claims consultant when the claim is expected to be either large, complex, or both.

[3] Please note that this section relates only to the U.S. Form

[4] Segal, Joseph, "Valuing Damages." Argonaut Publishing, 1991.

[5] Or, the net sales value of the lost production if the calculation is performed on a production basis.

[6] There are always gray areas in any business interruption claim, and settlements are reached via negotiation. The ultimate settlement amount depends greatly on the specific wording of the policy in effect.

Obviously, if a position cannot be supported by policy wording, it won't be defensible. But some settlement positions can be considered good business decisions by both parties and should be part of the settlement agreement.

[7] This assumption must be proven true or false *before* one decides on a production-based claim approach.

Hindsight Versus Foresight
Measuring Expected Operations

There can be little argument that the exercise of calculating an insured's business interruption loss is speculative in nature. Uncertainty is the market-maker of insurance, for no one can know the future—or what losses will occur, if at all. This is the fundamental tenet of both seeking insurance and underwriting it.

However, there has long been discussion as to the appropriate method by which to measure the insured's expected operations had an incident *not* occurred. The two primary schools of thought in this argument can be categorized as those who lean to hindsight and those who favor foresight.

Those who subscribe to the hindsight school of thought believe that during the period of loss, all internal and external factors that may have impacted the insured's theoretical operations must be taken into account. With this model, an insured's loss cannot truly be measured until operations resume or the period of loss is complete. Clearly, however, this approach can slow the process and will leave a final settlement open for months—or even years.

Those who pitch their tents in the foresight camp believe that the insured should be compensated based on the results during the period of loss that were expected at the time of the loss. Further, they hold that little if any attention should be granted to postloss events.

The argument between the two schools of thought crystallized when the wording in policies began specifying that the insured should be compensated for the "Actual Loss Sustained." Because events subsequent to the incident will affect the insured's ability to generate revenue and profit, the "hindsighters" theorize that the insured could not truly predict the future results of its business prior to the incident.

For example, in the case of the Wilton Brothers's contract with the film producer (see the extended claims scenario, "Inferno of Losses," which begins on page 137), multiple events could have delayed the development and therefore the sale of the insured's toys. The theory of hindsight holds that all of those events affected the insured's business, irrespective of the insured incident, and should be factored into the calculation of the business interruption claim.

The foresight theory argues that while many events *could* have affected the insured's operations, it is impossible to determine what would have occurred if the insured's business had not been interrupted. Because there is no actual experience upon which to base the expected performance, the entire exercise is speculative; trying to factor in every change from wind patterns to nuclear war is an exercise in futility. Moreover, the foresight theorists argue that the insured's expectations, based on the knowledge of the insured's capabilities, industry, and marketplace, are the best proxy for the expectations of the business and that the intent of the policy is to return to the insured the income that would have been realized based on those expectations.

In reality, business interruption claims are usually settled using part of both theories. Foresight predominates while the claim is first estimated. As the months go by and operations come online, actual results are applied against any sales projected, resulting in an amount for net loss. An insurer is unlikely to settle a claim without first determining the external factors that might have affected the insured's ability to do business. In the case of the Wilton Brothers' toys, for example, had the movie been a flop and the merchandising fallen flat, it is unlikely that the insurer would be willing to settle the claim on expectations that were in place prior to the incident's occurring.

Frequent Questions

An entire book is insufficient to address all the possible scenarios, variables, and contingencies in which a business interruption can lead to a loss. An almost unlimited number of issues can develop in determining such loss. However, some interesting questions and some standard answers have developed over the years and reviewing them will benefit many readers.

Q.   What if my company could maintain sales, but only by substitutng a product of lesser quality? Do I still have a claim?

A.   Typically, under a business interruption claim, you will be insured for net lost sales less the costs of sales, less noncontinuing expenses. However, if you spend a dollar to save a dollar, that is covered. Faced with the need to fill orders with product of lower quality, a manufacturer should still calculate a loss-of-margin claim and present it to the carrier. Of course, managers will appreciate that lower quality products can impact your brand and its reputation in the marketplace—and that, too, entails certain business risks.

Q.   What if I continue to manufacture the same product, but it costs me more to produce the product due to overtime. Are my plant inefficiencies claimable?

A.   Production inefficiencies caused by or directly attributable to an insured interruption typically are covered.

Q.   What if I spend more than a dollar to save a dollar? What if, for instance, I incur excess freight costs to get a product to a customer and it is an economic loss for me?

A.   Extra expense coverage would be needed in such situations. Extra expense coverage usually insures you for "the cost to continue operations as normally as possible." However, such coverage does not include the cost of replacing property unless the replacement reduces the loss that otherwise would be payable.

Q.   How do I know the insurance company is treating me fairly?

A.   Insureds often ask this question—and gauging how to answer it can be difficult. Do you agree with how the insurer is adjusting the claim? Are you consulting with others in your organization on their responsiveness? Are the questions they are asking thoughtful and informed by an understanding of your business? Have you sought an independent review of your claim issues by a qualified third-party such as an accountant or attorney?

Q.   When do I submit my claim?

A.   When to file a final claim with the insurer is a function of the length of your indemnity period, the size of the loss, and other considerations affecting how and when you receive all the necessary data and documentation you need. However, there is a great benefit to insureds who estimate their claim for the insurer as soon after the loss as is reasonable. This opens the avenue of communication to discuss the loss in more detail. You should plan to review that calculation with the adjuster and the insurer's accountant. From that point, you should plan on preparing a more comprehensive claim that is filed with the insurer, then updated and modified on a regular basis. Remember, too, that a long indemnity period should not mean deferring any communication with the carrier; instead, you will want to communicate early and provide information on a regular basis.

CHAPTER EIGHT

The Top Ten Common Disputes in Business Interruption Claims

Perspectives from the Field

Many sources explain business interruption insurance coverage with variations of the same inadequate description, which goes something like this:

> The business interruption policy is supposed to do for the policyholder what the business would have done, but for the loss.

It is unfortunate that this description is used so often, because one would need a mind-boggling host of endorsements or extensions of coverage to make it even close to accurate. In fact, most basic business interruption coverage specifically excludes types of damages that are a natural and common result of otherwise covered perils. A short list of these would include remote and consequential losses, penalties, interest, and extra expenses under some policy forms.[1] And while many policies now routinely include coverage for ordinary payroll, contingent and interdependency business interruption, service interruption, civil authority, and ingress/egress, they often come at an increased premium.

Business interruption insurance is complex and difficult, and disputes are to be expected. Some disputes surface so frequently that they have received substantial comment and analysis in the industry press. This chapter summarizes many of these disputes with the goal of providing insight into ways to avoid them altogether.

Confusion Abounds

Because business interruption insurance addresses the uncertainty of predicting the future, and because the majority of such policies are written to cover policyholders in many different industries, the wording of such policies tends to be general rather than precise. This often results in a degree of built-in ambiguity—in many cases, policyholder and insurer may advance competing interpretations of the same language, both of which are reasonable. In other cases, the parties may have dramatically different views regarding the scope of coverage simply because one or both of them have not taken the time to read the policy itself. Disputes frequently turn on disagreements about the meaning of a policy's terms, and such disputes have fueled thousands upon thousands of lawsuits. Not surprisingly, the starting point for such litigation is frequently the claim of both policyholder and insurer that their respective interpretations are based on the "clear and unambiguous" policy language, which if true suggests that the language at issue is at best *unclear* and *ambiguous*. Further complicating the situation, interpretations can change over time, as the facts and circumstances of an actual loss may alter the relative importance of different policy terms. Indeed, both parties may view the same facts differently, with the coverage outcome dependent on which side's version of the facts is closer to reality.[2]

Claims Philosophy

The claims philosophy of the policyholder or the insurance company can also trigger disputes. An organization's claims philosophy is often driven by the personality of senior management, the claims professionals, the risk manager, or even in some cases by outside coverage counsel. Claims philosophy may be influenced by previous experiences on policyholder losses, the size of the loss and its impact on the company, the behavior of participants in the loss adjustment process, or the size of the insured. At one end of the spectrum are those who view coverage strictly and narrowly; at the other are those who view coverage as broadly as possible. There are even some individuals (from both the insurer and policyholder ranks) whose notions regarding the scope of coverage are not even remotely connected to what the policies say.

Policyholders with an unduly conservative claims philosophy ("we'll take whatever the insurer will pay us") are less likely to experience disputes; if gray areas are encountered, they may be willing to concede a lack of coverage to the insurer, or, more likely, not even raise the question of coverage in the first place. The cost for this perspective may be that legitimate, recoverable losses are left on the table—which is not a good outcome. Policyholders with aggressive philosophies will likely have more disputes, will view any gray issue as an ambiguity that should be construed in their favor, and will be more than willing to litigate to maximize their recovery. Here there is greater risk and potentially greater reward. An unduly aggressive philosophy ("We'll spare no expense to pursue questionable claims, as long as there is a remote possibility of recovery") may not reflect rational decision-making from an economic standpoint and carries with it the risk of antagonizing the insurance market and making it more difficult to obtain coverage in the future. Likewise, the insurer's claims philosophy may impact whether the claim will be characterized by peace or by disputes.

The substantive bases of most disputes can be separated into three primary categories:

Coverage: What is or is not included in the policy?

The proliferation (e.g., manuscript, broker, and company) and complexity of forms mandate a careful review of each policy on virtually every loss. With multiple insurance companies on a program, changing players at renewal time, and shifts in the market affecting coverage availability and terms, the possibilities abound for confusion about what is and what is *not* covered.

Compounding the problem are one-size-fits-all policies, generally constructed to address manufacturing exposures yet sold to entities in virtually every industry. After September 11, 2001, risk managers and claims professionals struggled to interpret such policies for financial services firms whose business losses were not reflected precisely in a manufacturing policy that discusses sales, cost of goods sold, production, and inventory.

Also, policies written for large companies with national, multinational, or international operations will often contain different coverage provisions and valuation procedures for different locations (provisions that either conflict or appear to be conflicting), voluminous endorsements (which are frequently not indexed and almost never cross-referenced within the body of the policy), and myriad (sometimes complex) deductibles applicable to different coverage scenarios. Poorly defined or undefined terms also can make an accurate understanding of the policy a challenge. As a result, nearly every large business interruption claim involves a contentious policy interpretation, which can lead to litigation or another time-consuming and expensive dispute resolution process (such as arbitration). Many of these claims settle without an ultimate resolution of the proper interpretation of the disputed policy terms, but, rather, with a final number that both insured and insurer can live with, given the risks and expense of proceeding all the way to judgment in a legal forum.

Quantification: How should the business interruption claim be calculated?

Quantification, or "the quantum" as used by some professionals, is the term used to identify the calculation of a business interruption claim. Quantifying what a business would have done had an incident not occurred is very difficult. A comprehensive business interruption claim must reflect the sales that would have occurred were it not for the incident and the relevant cost savings as a result of the incident. In this area differences in the views of the policyholder and the adjuster can be significant and usually result in the hiring of a claim accountant by the adjuster. The claim accountant reviews, critiques, and audits the insured's claim and, ultimately, develops the insurer's own calculation of the loss, which may deviate from the insured's calculation.

Claim accountants for both the insurer and insured must work to understand all aspects of an insured's business and develop comprehensive projections for what would have happened had the incident not occurred.

Timing: How long is the business interruption period?

Many people on both sides of the equation will agree that disputes over the business interruption time period are the most controversial. From such disagreements arise the biggest dollar differences between the insurer and insured. Why is this so? One reason may be that this issue—"How much time should be used to measure the business interruption loss?"—overlaps so many others. The applicable time period is often, as a matter of policy wording, measured by the time needed to rebuild a damaged facility. The amount of time to clean up a loss site from a fire or insured event and rebuild or restore operations to normal can be subjective, thus engendering disputes between the insured and its insurers on the critical path to get operations back up and running. Such disputes can greatly influence the accounting issues as well. That is, although production may be back, the accountants may disagree as to whether such production is at the preloss level. As you can see, time-related disputes may fuel (or be fueled by) issues relating to (1) coverage or policy wording and (2) engineering and quantification.

Naturally, some of the issues discussed in this chapter will overlap the three categories discussed previously, but generally it is safe to characterize these issues as relating to questions and confusion around (1) Coverage, (2) Quantification, and (3) Timing. Because there are ten of them, we simply identify them as the *Top Ten.*

The Top Ten Disputed Issues

What types of disputes do policyholders encounter most frequently?[3] While new types of disputes often emerge as case law, insurance policies, and adjusting practices change over time, these old standbys have endured the test of time and continue to frustrate insurance companies and policy-holders.

1. Period of Indemnity and Period of Restoration
2. Overhead
3. Necessarily Continuing Expenses
4. Sales Projections
5. Makeup, Offsets, and Residual Values
6. Idle Periods
7. Nonbudgeted Events and/or Delays in Budgeted Events
8. The Depreciation Issue (or, Lost Income Versus Lost Cash Flow)
9. Number of Occurrences
10. Other Consequential or Remote Losses

Honorable Mentions
Some issues that did not make it into our Top Ten list include:

·   Rental Income Versus Business Interruption Coverage
·   Civil Authority Clauses with Muddy Definitions
·   Lost Sales Versus Sales Value of Lost Production
·   Extended Period of Interruption
·   Future Earnings on New Clients
·   Damage to Property Not Belonging to Policyholder
·   Leasehold Interest in Leasehold Improvements
·   Valued Policies
·   Business Interruption Claims by Not-for-profits

The Top Ten

1.   Period of Indemnity and Period of Restoration

Property and business interruption insurance policies are indemnity policies. That is, they are designed to compensate a policyholder for damage to, or loss of, assets resulting from perils the insurance company agrees to insure. To insurers, indemnity generally means that a policyholder should not profit from its loss but should simply be put back into the same position it would have been in, but for the loss, consistent with the exposures for which coverage was purchased and subject to limitations specified in the insurance contract. To policyholders, indemnity typi-cally is defined by the policy. For example, replacement cost coverage in property damage losses reinforces that the policy pays out what is defined in the policy: no more, no less. (Note: Replacement cost coverage allows the policyholder to purchase a new asset at the current replacement price, not at the depreciated or actual cash value of the asset at the time of loss.)

Under basic U.S. business interruption coverage, the period of indemnity usually ends at the conclusion of the period of restoration of the lost productive assets—that is, when the damaged property has been, or *theoretically should have been*, restored, repaired, or replaced. It is not uncommon for policies to set outside limits on this time period. For example, a policy might define the period of indemnity as being the period of restoration or one year, whichever is shorter.

Endorsements or coverage extensions can be purchased to extend this period of indemnity to include a period of time subsequent to the restoration of the damaged or destroyed property. That extended coverage may be for a defined period of time (e.g., twelve months) or may state that it ends when the business is restored to its preloss level of activity or profitability. These "Extended Period of Indemnity" provisions begin when the normal period of indemnity ends, so the total period of indemnity measured from the date of loss will vary based on how long it takes, or *theoretically should have taken*, to restore or replace the damaged property.

Note the critical difference between the times required to restore the *assets* versus the *business*. Lack of clarity regarding the exact meaning of "restoring the business" creates one of the common disputes in connection with the period of indemnity. Unfortunately, most policies do not provide any definition of the term *business*, nor of what would constitute its restoration. As a result, most parties agree on a measure that is usually based on the company's sales volume or profitability at the time of the loss. In addition, we have seen arguments that restoring the "business" is a measure of productive capacity, market share, number of customers, and/or other volumetric or scale measures.

But some disputes surrounding the period of indemnity are more commonplace and hotly contested than those driven by the restoration of the business. In fact, several of our Top Ten (including makeup, offsets, idle periods, and partial suspension—covered in detail in this chapter) have implications for the period of indemnity. But three additional sources of dispute—theoretical periods of recovery or property restoration; incurred versus paid expenses; and outside economic factors—require a few words now. While we discuss these separately, they are often interrelated in actual experience. For example, the widespread damage of a hurricane can affect the economy of a local community, as well as the availability of resources to rebuild. This will affect the length of the actual and/or theoretical rebuild period, as well as the length and extent of business interruption.

Theoretical Versus Actual Periods of Recovery

Although many insurance policies do not clearly address the issue, most adjusters, in the absence of clear direction to the contrary, will assume that a restoration period (and by extension, the period of indemnity) should be limited to the lesser of the actual time required to restore the lost/damaged property or the theoretical time in which a policyholder could have restored the property using due diligence and dispatch.[4]

This either/or provision is intended to protect the insurance company from extra costs that could be associated with a protracted or excessive recovery process. These extra costs might include ongoing expenses, the inflation of replacement cost, additional business interruption, and loss adjustment expenses. Under the appropriate application of the concept, this limitation is quite reasonable because some policyholders may find themselves in a postloss economic situation where rebuilding all lost property immediately is neither desirable nor economically necessary.

However, in some instances, insurance companies have asserted unrealistic timeframes for recovery. In one case, an insurance company asserted that reconstruction of a policyholder's lost buildings could be accomplished in six to eight weeks. The buildings had been completely flooded and then had sustained significant fire damage as a result of an electrical short-circuit. In fact, a massive flood had devastated the entire area, and the company was unable to retain a contractor or find materials for the rebuilding process within the period of time allotted by the insurance company for the complete rebuilding effort. The insurance company's argument was based on a theoretical rebuilding period, which resulted in a very short period of indemnity. In defense of insurance companies, positions this extreme are not common.

The theoretical rebuilding period of the World Trade Center complex is a contemporary example of these types of disputes on a large scale. While insurers may look back at the timing of building the original World Trade Center complex (see Figure 8.1) as a proxy for the current rebuilding period, what is left out of this equation is the fact that when the original World Trade Center buildings were constructed, they essentially stood alone with few buildings around them. Now, development and skyscrapers surround the area where the complex once stood. The mere logistics of moving building materials and resources through the crowded streets and buildings surrounding the site will have a significant impact on the amount of time required to rebuild the complex. Thus, simply looking at the prior build time can be false logic.

At the root of many of these disputes are the concepts of due diligence and dispatch, the policyholder's obligation to take reasonable efforts to reduce the loss payable by the insurance company, and the policyholder's reasonable expectations for sufficient time to analyze its options in determining how best to proceed with the rebuilding effort.

Not surprisingly, insurance companies may reason that the best course of action is the one that results in the lowest cost. Also of no surprise is the position of most policyholders that they should not have to suffer additional uninsured loss or act with incomplete or ill-considered plans to restore or replace lost assets hastily for the convenience and benefit of their insurance company. They may believe that this would improperly transfer the risks attendant to the loss back onto their shoulders, thereby nullifying some of the benefit of purchasing insurance in the first place.

At the end of the day, it is wise for policyholders to act reasonably and expeditiously in finalizing whatever restoration or replacement plans they intend to execute. And they should keep good records of decisions made and the rationale for making them. Although not always easy or practical, regular and open communication with adjusters minimizes disputes over the appropriateness of actions intended to impact the period of restoration and/or indemnity.

Incurred Versus Paid Expenses

When a policyholder buys goods or services in connection with restoring its assets, it will likely do so under some type of financing arrangement. That expense is *incurred* at the time the goods or services are purchased, but may be *paid* a month, or sometimes several months, later. The expense is accrued for payment— as accounts payable—under accrual accounting at the time the obligation is incurred. When the actual payment is made (i.e., when cash is disbursed), the payable balance is reduced and so is the company's cash. This, of course, is Accounting 101, and most disputes do not revolve around these concepts. Insurance companies generally recognize accounts payable and other accrued expenses as legitimate expenses to be considered in the extra expense and business interruption calculations, although they will often require proof of payment of those items before settling the loss.

The issue becomes significantly more complex and contentious when the dollar obligations are large and extend for a significant period beyond the time required for restoration or replacement of the damaged property (or restoration of the business when there is extended period of indemnity coverage). Consider the

Figure 8.1: World Trade Center Planning and Construction Timeline 1960-1973

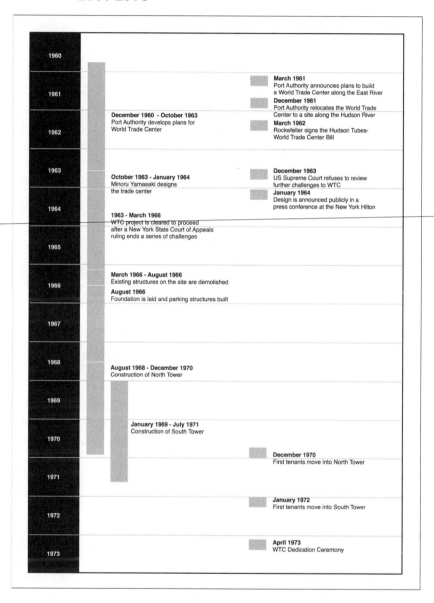

This timeline illustrates milestones during the building of
the original World Trade Center in New York, NY.

situation of many major financial institutions after September 11. While most institutions had backup facilities for vital operations, thousands of employees were displaced by the damage to, or destruction of, the buildings. Assuming that there would be a high demand for office space, some companies took unusual measures—from occupying entire hotels to entering five- or ten-year leases—to assure they had sufficient temporary space to accommodate employees as quickly as possible and to minimize their business interruption losses during their reconstruction or relocation periods. As it turned out, more space was available than expected in the New York real estate market, and most institutions were able to relocate their work forces to permanent space fairly expeditiously. Unfortunately, these institutions then had unneeded space under long-term leases they were obligated to pay. And the soft, post-9-11 real estate market has made subleasing virtually impossible.

The obligation for these leases was generally *incurred* during the period of indemnity for these companies, but the *payment* of these obligations will occur over time. At this writing, these specific issues have no clear resolution, although most companies have asserted claims for the present value of the tail on these residual lease obligations. A very strong case can be made, based on both insurance policies and simple logic, to support the validity of these claims. As a practical matter, the leases could have been terminated—and the expense of doing so rightfully claimed—within the indemnity period. Insurance companies argue that the payment of lease expense occurs over time, notwithstanding when the obligation was incurred, and that the portion of the expense paid after the indemnity period should not be recoverable.

The ultimate resolution of these issues may well provide new case law, but, for the immediate future, the prudent course is to evaluate the language of the insurance contract and to reasonably and consistently position claims.

Outside Economic Factors

Outside economic factors may influence the period of time during which a business interruption policy or extended period of interruption coverage should apply. This is particularly true of seasonal or trendy businesses and of losses that result from major catastrophes affecting large geographic areas or industries. Disputes in this area generally arise from separating the impacts that are directly related to the property damage (usually clearly covered) from those that are related to general economic conditions or other factors (that may be covered only under special extensions or endorsements). Unfortunately, separating these impacts can be highly theoretical, and the econometric or other modeling techniques used to do so are complex. Concurrent causation comes into play, a theory that policyholders have put forth and won in the courts except in cases where the policy language clearly excludes it.

Resolution usually comes from developing compelling fact-based and case-based arguments about why and which factors would rightfully extend the period of interruption. As a general rule, the more closely the extension of time can be directly related to the damaged property or restoration thereof, the more compelling the argument. While some policyholders and some adjusters might be tempted to rely substantially or exclusively on trend-line analysis, such a rudimentary approach is increasingly unreliable in complex losses or in situations where broad economic impacts result from a large-scale event. Claims practitioners, risk managers, and insurance companies should all become better versed in the more sophisticated and accurate techniques for evaluating the interrelated impacts of multiple or large loss events.

2.   Overhead

Overhead is an accounting term describing costs incurred in the operation of the business that are incidental to the production process. Generally, there are three categories of overhead: (1) those directly associated with plant operations, such as heat, light and power, lease costs, and insurance; (2) general selling and administrative costs attendant to the production, sales, and delivery of product; and (3) particularly in larger organizations, corporate costs incurred for the benefit of multiple operating units (none, some, or all of which might be impacted by the insured event), including debt service, executive management compensation, investor relations costs, and corporate advertising.

The first two categories of overhead do not give loss preparers and adjusters much difficulty at the conceptual level, although arguments do arise over the *necessity* of incurring some of these costs during a period of a suspension of operations. However, the applicability of corporate overhead items to a business interruption calculation is often a matter of considerable debate. In large part, the discussion centers on the method (or lack thereof) of allocating these costs to business units. Unlike production-related or plant-level overhead, whose allocation is usually tied to production activities or volumetric measures, corporate overhead is often not allocated according to the relative use of resources by a given business unit.

As a result, insurance companies are predictably unenthusiastic about including in business interruption loss calculations the continuing costs of corporate activities that only indirectly relate to the lost sales of a divisional or affiliated operating unit. This is particularly true when corporate overhead is not allocated to all business units or operating entities. To be clear, in most instances, the debate is not about whether the company should be entitled to recover its continuing (fixed) expenses, but rather over how much of these expenses should be attributed to the operations affected by a covered loss.

One thing is certain: the sales of a divisional or operating unit contribute to the corporate overhead (allocated or not) of an organization. On that basis alone, it is appropriate to include some of the corporate overhead in the business interruption calculation. After that general assertion, things become very fact-specific. If a company's method of allocating corporate overhead ties those costs to the operating unit in a meaningful way, debate is less likely. Unfortunately, that is not often the case. The more complex and indirect the allocation methodology, the more likely that insurance companies will balk at inclusion of these overheads as a continuing expense.

Risk management professionals likely to confront this issue would be wise to spend some time understanding the company's allocation methodology. Further, if any overhead included in a claim is calculated on a basis different from that used for the normal corporate overhead allocations for the affected unit, an explanation (with detailed support) should be prepared to justify the divergent treatment.

3.   Necessarily Continuing Expenses

Whether one is dealing with a gross earnings form or a Business Income Coverage (BIC) form[5] for the business interruption calculation, the question of which expenses must necessarily continue during a period of suspension of operations will often prompt disagreement and debate.

The calculation of business interruption losses (see Chapter 7) entails the determination of "necessarily" continuing expenses. In accounting terminology, continuing expenses are equivalent to fixed costs, most often measured on one-year cycles. Conversely, in business interruption insurance terminology, continuing expenses generally refer to those that continue during a period of interruption. The difference can be significant, particularly for relatively brief interruptions during which virtually all expenses may continue.

This all seems very straightforward—so where's the dispute? Several factors can drive a debate about necessarily continuing expenses:

- Were they really necessary to continue—and how is that proved?

- Did they in fact continue?

- For how long should they continue?

- How should continuing expenses be calculated when there is a partial resumption of operations?

Necessity is a qualitative principle that depends on one's perspective. Policyholders will often see necessity where insurance companies do not. In many cases this difference stems from the object of the necessity. Policyholders may view necessity through the prism of what is best for the business without consideration of what the policy is really intended to cover. Alternatively, insurance companies may view necessity through a filter of what is required to reduce losses otherwise payable.

Insurance policies will sometimes clarify the terms "necessarily continuing expenses" with language such as "expenses incurred to continue the operation of the business as normally as is practicable"—a clarification that can confuse, rather than enlighten, because the term practicable is seldom, if ever, defined. The definition of normal can also be a question of perspective and objectives. Accordingly, policyholders should be prepared to build a case for the necessity of the expenses to be incurred—a case that is as grounded in the policy as possible. Being able to demonstrate that absent these expenses, losses otherwise payable would have been higher enhances the prospect of recovery.

Sometimes, merely demonstrating that an expense continued can be a challenge. Basic trend-line analysis can be fraught with erroneous assumptions. Consider an example of a company that experiences a catastrophic loss at a time when its key markets are depressed and when it is in the midst of headcount reductions and other cost-cutting measures. A straight trend-line analysis will indicate a reduction in plant supervisory salaries and benefits and, perhaps, general administrative expenses. The insurance company might conclude that these saved (non-continuing) expenses reduce the compensable loss under the business interruption formula; however, this conclusion may be erroneous. Reduction of these expenses in the aggregate may have had nothing to do with the catastrophe if the event did not affect the need for supervisory personnel or general administrative expenses. Rather, the reduction may have resulted from ongoing cost-cutting measures and/or responses to outside market conditions. A more sophisticated analysis is required to separate the catastrophe-related losses from the market-related ones. The analysis is even more complex when the scale of the catastrophe impacts the larger environment.

The duration of an interruption can generate questions about the necessity of continuing certain types of expenses for the full loss period. For example, some insurance companies would suggest that during long closures, a policyholder should cease noncontractual advertising until product can once again be manufactured or supplied. While the policyholder may contend that such expenditures are necessary to preserve market visibility and protect market share (or facilitate its recovery postloss), the insurance company may contend that, because these expenditures will do nothing to reduce losses during the covered loss period, they should not be incurred. Well-constructed policy language will make clear whether expenses to protect market share are recoverable, but absent such clear language, this is fertile ground for dispute. Much of the resolution of such a dispute rides on the quality of the policy language, the persuasiveness of negotiating positions, and the policyholder's relationship with the loss adjuster. Ultimately, such disputes might have to be resolved in some judicial proceeding pursuant to the applicable rules of construction.

Of course, all potential disputes become more nettlesome if there is a partial resumption of operations. For example, if a damaged, four-stage production process can be repaired in phases, a company may be able to resume some but not all operations. Accordingly, it will incur some expenses in full measure even though only some less-than-final product can be made. Depending on the level of these expenses, the costs may be substantial during the period of partial operations. Policyholders will seek to recover those continuing expenses that flow to the income statement (the classification of inventoried costs is not as contentious), while insurance companies may reason that they should not be incurred until salable product can be produced. Once again, policyholders are well served by showing the benefit of incurring these expenses—for example, through a shortened business interruption period.

Overall, it is important that the necessity of expenses be supported, particularly with an analysis of how they reduce losses otherwise payable (e.g., expense to reduce the loss) or are covered by plain language in the policy regardless of any loss reducing benefits (e.g., extra expense). Being expeditious minimizes the potential for disputes, as does clear communication with loss adjusters.

4.   Sales Projections

Most business interruption policies contain language like this: "Due consideration shall be given to the experience of the business before and after the loss in evaluating the lost business income." In many cases, the most direct manifestation of this "due consideration" revolves around projecting the insured's expected revenue had the incident never occurred and accurately and fairly setting the performance standard of the business. Not surprisingly, insurance companies and/or their experts generally elect conservative sales projections, while policyholders paint a rosier picture of their prospects. In fact, the two perspectives often can result in a difference of 50 percent or more from the claimed amount. When straight trend-line approaches are applied to some industries, the disparity can be even wider.

One of the chief difficulties is identifying a representative period for modeling what would likely have occurred during the period of interruption. For short loss periods or for very stable and nonseasonal industries (such as certain commodity or utility businesses), a basic trend-line analysis may be acceptable, but most businesses are not that simple or steady. Accordingly, selection of the base period can have a significant influence on the size of the claim.

First, a representative period should be essentially free of any major or one-time aberrations. For example, the bankruptcy of a key supplier or customer would likely be an extraordinary event that skews the results of a base period. Only the normal ups and downs of a business should be included in the base period. Similarly, a surge of sales from a one-time promotion would need to be considered in defining a base period. Most practitioners would also agree that the greater the time between the loss period and the base period, the less reliable a correlation. Having said that, comparing periods for a seasonal business might require going back several years.

Start-up businesses and new product lines present similar problems. Without history, trend-line analyses are simply not germane, as there is no representative period of sales on which to base the insured's projection. But this certainly does not mean that there are no losses or that they should be heavily discounted because of the lack of actual experience. Sophisticated policyholders will build a strong case for their loss claims based on budgets, projections, market studies, and even actual results, if applicable.[6]

These losses can become much more complex when a company loses competitive advantage or market opportunity as a result of the business interruption. Insurance companies may assert that these losses are consequential and remote, thereby denying coverage for their financial impacts. Recovery depends heavily on establishing as direct a causal link between the property damage and the loss of income as possible.

The conclusion is unavoidable. Arriving at the right answer depends on considering many company-specific and industry-specific factors. In looking at the disputes and challenges that might arise, simply recognizing the perspectives of each party to the process offers guidance as to how to prepare. Documenting and supporting sales projections will help resolve disputes that may arise around the business interruption calculation.

5.   Makeup, Offsets, and Residual Values

Insurance adjusters have to evaluate loss claims in at least two ways. First, they may dissect the policy, reading it carefully to determine the coverage parameters. Second, they may look for potential makeup, offsets, and residual values that can be applied to reduce the aggregate quantum of the losses. Let's take a closer look at the latter.

Makeup (a term not often found in the text of an insurance policy) refers to a situation in which the performance of the business after restoration of operations exceeds the normal trended results. Adjusters and accounting experts use this excess performance to reduce the amount of measured losses. In other words, the apparent losses during the period of interruption that are made up for after restoration through excess performance are not considered losses at all, but rather *deferred* sales or earnings.

Insurance companies typically think they are entitled to these positive, subsequent makeup sales or earnings as credits against the losses measured during the interruption period. Interestingly, should results worsen postloss as a result of damage done to contracts or reputation during the interruption, insurance companies often will *not* agree that business interruption coverage extends to a recovery of those subsequent losses. An inherent difficulty in measuring makeup, even if one were to concede that a makeup credit is appropriate, is that crude trending techniques are inadequate to identify and quantify precisely what part of the postloss sales was deferred and what was simply a boost in sales that would have occurred anyway.

This issue may be of particular significance when a loss occurs immediately before a seasonal sales surge, new product introduction, previously planned major promotion, or other event that would drive postloss sales higher. Unfortunately, as many September 11 claimants have found, adjusters sometimes take the position that a "sales dollar is a sales dollar" and accord no significance to the cause or nature of the additional postloss sales. This approach simplistically takes a total sales trend line and assumes that any sales above that trend line (which is most often not determined on a very scientific basis) are extra sales subject to a makeup credit against claimed losses. This approach is often wrong and can be averted by better educating adjusters about the nature of the business, that is, whether sales can actually be made up or if a lost sale is just that—a lost sale.

Offsets (which again is a term seldom, if ever, defined in the insurance policy) represent another means of reducing measured losses. While the makeup concept is most often applied on a product-specific basis (i.e., the subsequent sales of the same product are evaluated against the claimed losses in that product), other *offsets* may include sales of substitute products or alternative models from the same division or other related companies within the policyholder's portfolio.

Again, this analysis is often based on simplistic trend-line analyses that may give little or no weight to the actual causes of increased sales. An example of offsets on the expense side of the equation would be actual *or assumed* sublease income on a temporary lease taken to accommodate people during a period of interruption (particularly where the term of the temporary lease may extend beyond the defined period of indemnity).

Residual values represent a credit against claimed losses pertaining to the assumed ongoing value of temporary assets obtained during a period of restoration that will be retained by the policyholder after the loss period ends (assuming they are not salvaged, which would generate a salvage value credit). In the case of residual values, the determination of the amount of the credit is heavily dependent on the methodology and assumptions employed to value the retained assets.

One of the greatest problems is the lack of agreed-upon procedures for determining residual values. In fact, many policyholders find it impractical or cost prohibitive to salvage temporary assets after the loss and may, therefore, retain assets that are of no value to them on an ongoing basis. However, even if they are of some notional value, measuring that value is virtually impossible. For example, what is the value of improving temporary space under a lease term that exceeds the period of restoration of the damaged property? Similarly, how should one measure the value of temporary telecom cabling within a facility under repair? Frequently, the cost of removing and salvaging such equipment exceeds the amount that could be gained from selling it. The question is whether an insurance company should get a credit against claimed losses for the residual value of these temporary assets, when the policyholder neither needs nor wants them any longer and would not have acquired them but for the loss?

Most practitioners on both sides of a claim would agree that a policyholder should not earn a windfall from its loss (that is, policyholders should not obtain a recovery that is not permitted by the policy). They would also agree that, if certain events or activities mitigate the losses suffered, these should be considered in judging the amount due from insurance, at least where such considerations are supported by the policy language. But while everyone might agree to this principle, there is little agreement on measuring the makeup, offset, or residual values. The severity of disputes could be mitigated if both parties agreed that any makeup or offsets should be directly attributable to the loss suffered and that residual values should be determined using generally accepted valuation methodologies.

6.   Idle Periods

The concept of idle periods is not difficult to understand, but it is often applied in ways that surprise policyholders. Most people understand an idle period to be any time when normal operating activity would have ceased whether or not a loss occurred. For example, closures due to holidays or for normal maintenance, due to planned equipment upgrade or installation, or due to relocations or labor strikes (where specific coverage has not been purchased) are usually not disputable idle periods. In these cases the parties usually agree that the loss measurement should be reduced by the amount of loss caused by the idle period (essentially, this involves adjusting the trend-line analysis to reflect the expected idle period).

However, policyholders are surprised when an insurance company argues that the idle-period concept also applies when concurrent losses occur or when there are multiple causes of loss. Consider an insurance policy that covers wind and water damage, but excludes flood damages. The policy also contains an idle period clause that states:[7]

A. This policy does not insure:

   a. Any loss during any idle period. Idle period includes but is not limited to any period when goods would not have been delivered or received due to:
      i. physical loss or damage not insured under this policy on or off of the described location.
      ii. planned or rescheduled shutdown.
      iii. strikes or other work stoppage.
      iv. any reason other than an insured loss.

Assume a hurricane damages the roof of a manufacturing plant and that heavy rain entering the plant significantly damages critical manufacturing equipment. Assume further that it will take three weeks to replace the equipment and make repairs to the roof. Finally, assume that related inland rains form a flood, which sweeps through the plant three days after the hurricane itself, causing more damage to the facilities and equipment—damages that would take two weeks to repair and/or replace. What should the period of indemnity be? How should the idle period clause be applied?

Figure 8.2: Two Views on Idle Periods

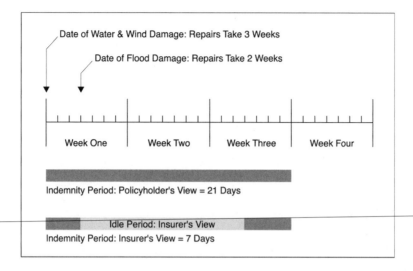

The answers to these questions are interdependent but not straightforward. The actual period of indemnity would be three weeks. But because of the idle period clause, some insurers may take the extreme position that the *effective* indemnity period is only one week (see Figure 8.2: Two Views on Idle Periods). The insurance company might conclude that the flood event does not qualify. In that scenario, because damage caused by the flood results from an excluded peril, its two-week repair/recovery time represents an idle period—a period of time during which revenues and earnings would not have been generated because of a noncovered event. Most policyholders would reason in response that the flood damage, by virtue of being a subsequent event, is irrelevant to the covered loss triggered by the wind and rain damage. Who is right?

Once again, much depends on the specific language of the idle period clause and perhaps other provisions of the business interruption policy, as applied to the facts of the loss events. In this example, both components of the loss resulted from the same hurricane. The flood damage would not have occurred but for the same event that caused the wind and water damage. As such, the excluded flood damage should not supersede the initial trigger of coverage due to the wind and water damage (the idle period argument seems more compelling if the subsequent flood had been caused by a separate event). The policyholder would contend that the flood damage represents a supplementary element of physical damage that either (a) does not cause any additional business interruption because the plant was already closed due to the previous covered physical damage or (b) should be considered concurrently with the covered loss. Policyholders typically contend that the fact that coverage does not extend to the flood peril does not negate the coverage afforded for losses resulting from the covered wind and rain damage.

Those insurers aggressive about idle period clauses tend to assert that the number and/or sequence of events are irrelevant. They would assert that any losses incurred during a repair period for assets damaged by a noncovered peril are excluded under the idle period clause.

Suffice it to say that there is plenty of room for argument on this issue, but because most business interruption losses are settled out of court, there is not a deep enough pool of case law on the issue to lend much clarity or give special weight to either point of view.

7.   Nonbudgeted Events and/or Delays in Budgeted Events

In many cases, corporate budgeting is an annual ritual. In some companies it is long on process and content but short on substance and practical value. Unfortunately, adjusters always seem to turn to the budget and use it as a principal tool in evaluating business interruption losses because they often consider it to be the best available information about the policyholder's expectations.

Some annual budgets are living documents, adjusted for changing circumstances and market conditions over time and used as integral management tools in the day-to-day operation of the business. Other budgets may be used for capital allocation and/or investment decisions at the beginning of the year but are seldom (if ever) consulted or adjusted after that. Still other budgets have different purposes, which may reflect contradictory expectations if not prepared by the same people (e.g., production budgets versus strategic planning budgets). Unfortunately, loss adjusters may not recognize these distinctions and, without adequate explanation from the policyholder, may rely on the wrong one. Here again communication is key.

As previously discussed, the measurement of a business interruption loss requires the projection of anticipated results. But because loss periods seldom line up cleanly with budget periods (typically monthly), the timing of specific events (anticipated or not) can have an important impact on loss measurement. Hence, there are two predominant budget issues in measuring loss:

(1) **The timing and impact of nonbudgeted events**. Obviously, nonbudgeted events are not included in budgeted projections. For companies using fixed annual budgets or budgets that only change quarterly or semiannually, the disconnect can be meaningful. Monthly budgeting can mitigate this concern but cannot eliminate it. Adjusters will generally accept that not all things may end up in the budget, but

the weight they will attribute to nonbudgeted events will usually be directly proportional to the sufficiency of support. Policyholders, either in the ordinary course of business or as a fundamental activity in the loss development process, would be wise to keep good records of these events, down to specific dates and/or times.

(2) **The impact of a loss on the timing (usually a delay) of budgeted events.** Delays of budgeted events (such as cost reduction programs, new product introductions, or sales initiatives) can cause even more complex problems. Adjusters are typically skeptical of the timing and amount of impact. Frequently, an adjuster will require proof after the fact—a demonstration of the results realized after the delayed program is actually implemented—before imputing any such savings into the business interruption loss measurement. Unfortunately, the postloss results may not really reflect what would have happened had the opportunity been captured when intended. For example, new product introductions may succeed or fail based on market-sensitive timing.

8.   The Depreciation Issue (a.k.a. Lost Income Versus Lost Cash Flow)

Some policies address whether depreciation should be treated as a continuing or a noncontinuing cost for the business interruption period. Most policies remain silent on this topic, making room for another insurance debate. Before getting into this discussion, remember that whether the policy is silent or merely ambiguous on this issue, undefined terms often are construed by judges in favor of the policyholder. That said, the depreciation debate is never black-or-white for the insurance industry as a whole, as each policy and loss can be unique.

The combat over depreciation has been long and arduous, and the arguments on each side heated and subject to flaws—not surprising for an issue driven significantly by the interpretation of what the business interruption policy is supposed to do for the policyholder. As with all insurance disputes, the facts of each case and the language of each insurance policy (including use of the applicable rules of construction to unclear terms) should be dispositive.

In both gross earnings and business income coverage (BIC) forms,[8] the issue hinges on whether depreciation on destroyed assets should be reflected in the business interruption calculations as a continuing expense (i.e., one that does not abate as a result of the loss). This gets tricky because depreciation expense is really an accounting convention that recognizes that a productive asset loses value as it is used over time and that this loss in value should be recognized as an expense over the asset's useful life rather than all at once at the time of purchase. Thus, the depreciation of any asset is reflected as an expense over multiple accounting periods. But it is a *noncash* expense—cash is not paid out as the expense is recorded.

Therein lies the rub. If depreciation of destroyed assets were treated as a non-continuing expense, it would be deducted from gross earnings in calculating the business interruption loss. Similarly, under the BIC form, it would *not* be added back to net income because it is not a continuing expense. Thus, under both forms, if the depreciation expense were treated as noncontinuing, the claim is decreased. The converse is true if depreciation is treated as a fixed or continuing expense, in which case the amount of the claim would increase. In asset-intensive companies, like large manufacturers with newer equipment and/or facilities, the value of the depreciation expense can be substantial. So can its impact on a claim.

Why would any policyholder believe that depreciation should continue on an asset that was destroyed? How can there be any value to depreciate? The common answer includes several components.

Policyholders reason that if the business interruption policy is supposed to do for them "what the business would have done, but for the loss," then it should generate the cash flow that would have been earned during the business interruption period. Therefore, because depreciation is an accounting convention and, thus, a noncash expense, a policyholder must be compensated for it as a continuing expense. Otherwise, the recovery will fall short of what was lost, and the policy will not meet its stated or assumed objectives.

Furthermore, policyholders often assert that replacing lost assets with new assets can negatively impact the financial results of operations under generally accepted accounting principles. The depreciation of the new, higher valued assets will cause a higher level of expense to the organization than existed preloss and will reduce net income and/or have negative tax consequences. These impacts will in turn affect common stock values and may affect borrowing capacity and the pricing of acquisition transactions.

In the end, policyholders may reason, the mere reimbursement of replacement cost for the lost asset under the property policy does not compensate them for the full business interruption impact of the loss. Interestingly, insurance companies are not very receptive to recognizing these higher levels of depreciation expense in measuring losses when the replacement of significant assets occurs early during a lengthy period of interruption or during an extended business interruption coverage period.

Finally, many policyholders argue that in the process of determining coverage requirements and pricing, the values they report to the insurance company include depreciation expense on the assets they are protecting. Insurance companies seldom adjust these values in any way to reflect the fact that when losses are paid, depreciation on destroyed assets will not be considered part of the business interruption loss. Thus, from the policyholders' perspective, they have paid a premium for a business interruption value that is overstated by the depreciation expense that they will not recover under their policy. Obviously, the validity of this position depends on each policyholder's business interruption work sheet and the methods used by insurance companies in pricing the policy. As a practical matter, many policyholders have not taken the time to do a good job of defining their business interruption values, and insurance companies have not spent much time validating them. But as a matter of principle, it seems that the loss measurement ought to be consistent with the values insured.

Conversely, almost any insurance company will say that destroyed assets cannot be depreciated because they no longer exist. This logic is difficult to ignore on its surface. Furthermore, a carrier may say that the policyholder is already being compensated for the lost assets through recovery under the property policy. This may be true, assuming that (1) *all* of the depreciation relates to loss of covered assets; (2) the policyholder has adequate replacement coverage without limitations; and (3) the full amount of the replacement cost claim is paid. Also, in this argument, insurance companies generally ignore the existence of a deductible and of other noninsurable items.

Some insurance companies may say that it is irrelevant whether depreciation was included in the values to be insured during the policy underwriting. Some may also question whether it is even meaningful to determine an appropriate amount of depreciation to include in business interruption values, as the level of depreciation changes with acquisitions, disposals, and accelerated depreciation methods, and no one at the time of underwriting could ever accurately foresee the extent of assets that might be destroyed in a loss. Furthermore, the pricing of premiums is not strictly related to the values insured and may reflect a number of other risks and considerations with respect to a specific policyholder. Finally, the policy affords coverage of lost "business interruption value"—a term not equivalent to cash flow.

To add to the complexity of the matter, a question also arises about how to value depreciation for an insurance claim. Would it be valued as it is for tax purposes, as it is under Generally Accepted Accounting Principles (GAAP), or as it is under physical (economic) valuation methods?

In these areas, case law is evolving. As we have noted, specific policy language can impact the strength of the coverage arguments either way. In any event, the depreciation debate continues, remaining a frequent sore spot in the claims recovery process.

9.   Number of Occurrences

A discussion about the number of occurrences is usually a discussion about deductibles. Policyholders might view connected events as one occurrence to avoid having more than one deductible applied. However, where the policyholder has small (or no) deductibles or relatively low limits, positing more than one occurrence may become the preferred course to increase the amount of the potential recovery. Insurance companies will generally take the opposite view for similar reasons. Thus, there is no true policyholder or insurer position on this issue; either party may take either a multiple or single occurrence position depending on the circumstances.

How occurrences are counted can be driven by how one views the loss. While not synonymous, "loss" and "peril" are often used interchangeably. A peril is a risk against which one buys insurance; a loss results from the occurrence of a peril. Some events present numerous perils (causes of loss)—some of which may be insured and some of which may not.

For example, a hurricane presents the perils of wind damage, water damage, flood, service interruption, and ingress/egress problems. The hurricane itself is not the peril. Counting occurrences means evaluating the proximity of the events causing loss to the insured perils. Recall the example used earlier in this chapter. A flood occurring three days after a hurricane (but caused by the hurricane) is likely to be considered part of the same occurrence as the original wind damage. But if that flood were caused by a separate storm, it would likely be considered a separate occurrence. This is relatively straightforward. Having seen this fairly often, people have over time moved towards consensus on how to interpret these types of causes and effects in counting occurrences. Under this example, where two storms occurred, the main dispute that may arise is which of the storms caused the damage. This will, in turn, impact the number of occurrences, deductibles, and limits in play.

Consider perhaps the most notable and complex occurrence case in history: the events on September 11, 2001. By now, rehearsing the details of that day seems unnecessary—but it is crucial. Precisely because two teams of terrorists, having overtaken two airliners from different airlines, attacked the two largest buildings of the World Trade Center in September 2001, a dispute arose in addressing claims. Policyholders maintained that the attacks were two separate occurrences—a critical argument given the coverage limits of their insurance policies. Certainly, each tower was attacked, the attacks occurred more than twenty minutes apart, and the two towers fell at different times. But the insurance companies argued, in part, that because the attacks were orchestrated by a single organization as a coordinated event, they represented one occurrence—a sequence of related events. Focusing primarily on the respective policies' language and the intent of the parties, the courts deemed that under some policies, the attacks were indeed one event; under others, the courts judged that they might be two events. The wording of the respective policies was dispositive to the rulings. The definition—or lack thereof—of the term "occurrence" and which wording actually applied were generally considered the most significant issues in measuring losses for which the insurance companies were ultimately responsible.

10.   Other Consequential or Remote Losses

Other consequential or remote losses are nearly always contentious. They often involve detailed analyses of causation of the losses, and different stakeholders may have widely different interpretations of how directly attributable the losses are to the physical property damage that is generally a prerequisite for business interruption coverage. Typical language follows:[9]

A. Additional Time Element Exclusions:

1. This policy does not insure:
    a. Any increase in loss due to:
        i. Suspension, cancellation or lapse of any lease, contract, license or order
        ii. Fines or damages for breach of contract or for late or noncompletion of orders, or for penalties of any nature
        iii. Any other consequential or remote loss.

The fact that there are rarely, if ever, definitions for these terms enhances the potential for disputes. Most insurance professionals rely on custom, previous experience, or personal perspective in determining whether a given loss is excluded by the other remote or consequential loss exclusion. While there will undoubtedly be many opinions and perhaps examples that would modify the following definitions, these are fairly commonly accepted in practice.

Other consequential losses are those that (1) may ultimately result from a ripple effect of the physical damage but not directly attributable to it (i.e., these losses may be related to, but not be caused by, the physical damage) or (2) are directly attributable to the physical damage but are excluded from coverage. For example, after a catastrophic event, a manufacturer cannot make product A. But the public incorrectly perceives that the company cannot make products B and C either—even though these products were not impacted by the event. In fact, the marketplace might even be concerned about the overall future viability of the manufacturer. These perceptions, in turn, result in a cancellation of contracts or lost sales not directly attributable to lost production of product A. Insurance companies will cover the lost earnings for product A but will generally not allow coverage for the lost sales of products B and C. Loss of market share, cancellation of leases, increased operating costs for other reasons, and loss of goodwill are other common examples of losses generally considered other consequential losses. In an "all risks" policy, there can be a complete lack of clarity as to what other consequential losses are excluded unless they are itemized.

Remote losses are generally identified as those occurring in locations not directly suffering the physical damage or where direct attribution to the covered physical damage cannot be established. For example, damage to the retail location of a clothing company might result in reduced production of sport coats, thereby hurting the plant's productivity and profitability. Policyholders can protect against such remote losses by acquiring interdependency coverage, which addresses losses incurred up and down a supply chain.

Note that the exclusion refers to other consequential and remote losses but is silent about consequential and remote *gains.* Policyholders may be (and many have been) distressed to learn that their insurance companies have no reservations about viewing consequential and remote gains as offsets against losses suffered as a result of an insured peril. Many lawyers for policyholders will emphatically advise that this disparate treatment is neither equitable nor justified by anything in the insurance contract.

The other consequential or remote loss issues integrate a number of concepts described in this chapter. Let's consider the World Trade Center attacks once more. Should policyholders measure losses that result directly from the loss of property as a result of the specific covered peril (fire, collapse, explosion, etc.) that destroyed their property? Or should they measure losses that are a direct result of the events (the terrorist attacks) that gave rise to the perils that caused the loss for most claimants? Had the planes not exploded, perhaps the towers would not have burned and fallen. It was the perils of fire and collapse that caused many of the covered losses.

Many insurance companies evaluating 9-11 losses from financial institutions have sought to offset losses measured during the period of time the markets were closed with consequential gains that resulted from a surge in the markets subsequent to their reopening a week after the attacks. These market gains are broadly thought to be the result of investor concerns about future terrorist activity and its impact on the U.S. and global economies. In fact, detailed analysis showed that there was a "flight to quality" by investors who chose to move assets into more conservative and safer investments. Rather than pent-up demand, this signified changed investor behavior triggered by fear of terrorism. Policyholders in general do not believe the resulting spike in activity was simply makeup trading attributable to the property damage that precipitated the market closure.

Policyholders point out that virtually all of the foreign markets experienced a surge in trading both during the four days of the U.S. market closure *and* during the ensuing few weeks immediately after the U.S. markets reopened. In most major global markets, this spike in activity exceeded the increased volume that occurred in the U.S. markets during the week after the closure, which further supports the premise that the U.S. and international market moves were driven by global economic concerns rather than by pent-up trading demand. Thus, policyholders would have experienced the consequential gains *and* losses that characterized the markets after they were reopened, regardless of whether or not they suffered physical damage. That is because these *consequential* gains and losses can be said to have resulted from the event of terrorism, not the physical damage to the World Trade Center and surrounding property that precipitated the market closure.

In large part, the insurance companies have posed that the post 9-11 market surge was "makeup" and have not addressed or acknowledged consequential gain arguments. Some insurance companies have even considered using the remote gains in the global markets as offsets to U.S.-originated losses. The basis for these positions appears to be the premise that a dollar is a dollar and that the consequential nature of the cause of the increased revenues when the markets reopened does not matter. However, if insurance companies contend that consequential *gains* are to be included in the equation, why do they not believe the same for consequential losses attributable to the same facts and circumstances? The approach to how consequential gains and losses are considered should at least be consistent.

Because both remoteness and the degree of consequentiality are subject to judgment and perspective, the "remote and consequential loss exclusion" continues to vex policyholders and frustrate many otherwise quick and amicable settlements.

Honorable Mention

The following dispute-triggering variables occur less frequently but can still put a wrench in the works.

Rental Income Coverage Versus Business Interruption Coverage

Some policyholders, depending on the nature of their business and the evolution of their policies, find themselves with both rental income coverage and business interruption coverage. Disputes sometimes arise out of how to measure losses when both types of coverage might arguably apply. Consider a real estate company that principally owns and manages apartment buildings. If one of the properties suffers a fire that damages both rental units and common areas or amenities, which coverage should apply first?

Rental income coverage is intended to cover the loss of rents during the period of restoration. The coverage frequently is for *gross* lost rents or *net* losses if the deductions are specifically identified. Business interruption coverage covers lost earnings, and the measurement formula is typically either **lost gross profit – non-continuing expenses** or **lost net income + continuing expenses**. Thus, the measurements for lost rental income and lost business income may give different results.

Policyholders with both types of coverage may find it beneficial to run the numbers both ways to see what works best, assuming their policy language sheds no light on how they are to be interpreted relative to each other. Newer BIC forms have eliminated this potential ambiguity.

Civil Authority Clauses with Muddy Definitions

Before 9-11, most practitioners had rarely focused on these clauses. After 9-11, these clauses are central to *very* substantial claims. From one policy to another, the language is inconsistent. The gravest disputes arise with those that do not provide clear guidance on

- whose property damage can trigger the coverage

- how proximate the property damage has to be to the locations where losses result

- who or what constitutes a civil authority

- what form the notice of closure must take

- how long the coverage applies

- whether the damaged property must be of a type insured by the policyholder

Some 9-11 policyholders took the position that losses suffered as a result of the airport closures across the country (for example, retail locations in airports, rental cars, ticket sales, and hotel bookings) should be recoverable under civil authority clauses. Insurance companies disagreed. Ultimately the courts may be asked to decide many of these cases.

Lost Sales Versus Sales Value of Lost Production

Newer business income coverage forms do not contain the term "sales value of lost production," but older, gross earning forms (still in use) do. As a result, the distinction between lost sales and sales value of lost production can generate problems. "Lost sales" is a relatively simple income statement comparison of the sales line to see the impact of a closure on sales. "Lost sales value of production" is a more complex analysis. The essential difference is in whether and how inventory is factored into the computation.

Before just-in-time (JIT) management philosophies became vogue, manufacturing companies commonly kept large inventories of both raw materials and finished product. For most, JIT concepts and advanced technologies made planning the manufacturing process much more efficient and less inventory-intensive. Either way, under gross earnings forms, inventory usage is germane to the business interruption calculation. Policyholders will typically try to shore up sales (prevent lost sales) by using inventories to meet critical orders. If this is successfully done and no sales are lost, there is really no business interruption claim; but there may be an extra expense claim associated with replacing the depleted inventory.

However, if no inventory is available, or if it is insufficient to prevent a loss of sales, then the measurement of losses will begin with a calculation of the sales value of the lost production. So, first the lost production must be determined; then an appropriate sales value (price per unit) must be attached to it. It is not hard to see the potential for disputes about whether and how inventory should be used, what the planned production would have been, what the sales price per unit should be, and which deductions from that sales price are appropriate.

Extended Period of Interruption

This coverage is designed to protect policyholders against business income losses that are suffered during the period of time between restoration of damaged facilities and complete recovery of the affected business. This is usually measured in terms of sales, profitability, and/or production volumes. The greatest arguments generally arise over the cause of the reduction of sales during this period.

Once again, a great deal depends on specific policy language, but typically insurance companies will adjust such claims on a basis that the reduced sales must be directly attributable to the physical damage and its impact on specific products. Given that the coverage sometimes applies for a period of up to one year from the restoration of the property, there is plenty of room for disputes over factors impacting the total recovery of sales, profits, or production volumes.

Future Earnings on New Clients *(expected to be obtained during the interruption period)*

Insurance companies will emphatically assert that there is no coverage for losses that fall outside of the business interruption period, including loss of future earnings on new clients that would have been obtained during this time. They may further argue that, where it exists, the "other consequential and remote loss" exclusion expressly excludes such lost orders and contracts from coverage, except to the extent they result in lost sales within the business interruption period or any extended period for which coverage was purchased. Generally speaking, a policyholder has to climb a steep hill to obtain any recovery for these losses.

However, when a policyholder can demonstrate that the loss of new clients, orders, or contracts was a direct result of property damage—e.g., the computer system to take orders, open customer accounts, or process contracts was destroyed—the arguments for valuing these losses may be more successful. In this event, the losses are not indirect or remote from the physical damage, but rather are clearly and directly caused by it. Insurance companies are still likely to balk at paying losses that extend beyond the indemnity period (through discounting of those future estimated lost income or gross earnings), but the directness of the causation may open the door to greater recovery in this area.

Damage to Property Not Belonging to the Policyholder

Conventional wisdom dictates that there must be damage to the policyholder's property before business interruption insurance will respond to a loss. However, a careful reading of each individual policy is necessary because the language varies substantially. Some policies may say "damage to property at a premise described in the Declarations" and others may say "damage to property of a *type* insured under this policy." Both circumstances would represent significantly broader coverage than a form that says "damage to property insured under this policy."

A business interruption policy might refer to "the property" but, if it does not expressly state that "the property" must be that in which the policyholder has an insurable interest, it may be quite difficult for the insurer to justify denial of a claim on the basis that it was triggered by damage to *third-party property* that interrupted the policyholder's business.

Leasehold Interest in Leasehold Improvements

A dispute that surfaces from time to time is related to measurement of the value of leasehold interest in assets (leasehold/tenant improvements) added during the term of a long-term lease. Generally, the dispute is not one of coverage but rather of valuation.

Having said that, coverage questions may arise when construction conventions change. For example, many landlords have over the years significantly reduced the nature and/or extent of improvements that come with the building. Current construction conventions often do not include bathroom accoutrements, perimeter heating, sprinkler systems, escalators, and other improvements that were commonplace a number of years ago.

A careful review of the policy language may help sort out to whom such assets belong in the event of a loss. Insurable interest is often cited as a prerequisite to recovery, but some policies include coverage for interests that might arise out of the terms of the lease, from a responsibility to insure the assets, or by a provision within the policy. Insurance companies want to pay for lost assets only once—not once each to the landlord and the tenant. Consequently, disputes can arise when it is not made clear how the insurance is to apply to the leasehold or tenant improvements. Leasehold interest, as applied to assets, is most often determined on a *pro rata* basis calculated using the remaining years on the lease and the total lease term. This may or may not have any bearing on the useful life of the assets, but in most leases the improvements revert to the landlord upon expiration of the lease. While many insurance companies view this fact as determinative, many policyholders do not, and disputes will continue to arise over who should receive the insurance recovery for these assets.

Valued Policies

Valued policies are a relative rarity these days but some continue in circulation. The essence of a valued policy is that it pays a predetermined amount for each (usually) day or hour that a business is completely suspended because of an insured cause of loss. In the loss adjustment process, use of these forms can prevent many disputes because the measurement process is for all intents and purposes superseded by a predetermined loss amount for the valued time period.

But it is not hard to see that this, in turn, shifts many of the disputes from the adjustment process to the underwriting process. The policyholder and insurance company must agree on the time period value, and this analysis is subject to the same qualitative judgments inherent in projecting "but for" results. For example, to determine the values, one might consider line of business/product profitability, expectations for growth in revenue and profits, new product introductions, or cost reduction programs.

Disputes arise when the valued policy requires (as most do) the consideration of the prior and likely subsequent experience of the business in determining loss payable, thereby opening up the potential for adjustments to the valued policy amounts based on actual experience, which may differ materially from expectations at the time the policy was underwritten. This brings back the subjectivity of projecting "but for" results, undermining the apparent (but illusory) simplicity of a valued policy.

Business Interruption Claims by Not-for-profit Organizations

How can a not-for-profit organization have a loss of income? A fair question! Generally speaking, the not-for-profit must demonstrate that it lost fund-raising dollars or that it continued to incur fixed expenses during the period of interruption. The issues become far more complex when government or other grants or programs fund the not-for-profit and the monies are provided under the mandate that they be spent for the designated purpose or returned if unused. In these cases, if it never receives the money and never expends it for the intended purposes, the not-for-profit has not lost anything (excepting fixed costs that would have appropriately been charged to the program under the grant). The party suffering a loss would be the ultimate participant, not the not-for-profit. Of all these challenges to the not-for-profit claimant, perhaps the biggest is proving permanent loss of fund-raising revenues.

Endnotes

[1] In the absence of extra expense coverage, many common loss-related extra expenses may be unrecoverable unless they can be proven to have reduced other losses otherwise payable.

[2] For example, both insurer and policyholder may plausibly view certain costs as comprising either "extra expense" or "expense to reduce the loss," and the parties may be motivated to take a certain position depending, for example, on the existence of higher policy limits for one type of coverage than for the other type of coverage.

[3] These are not ranked in any particular order.

[4] The terms "due diligence and dispatch" are seldom, if ever, defined in the insurance policy. Consequently, these terms often result in disputes as well. However, parties often agree that the concept is one of reasonableness and prudence in the behavior of a policyholder in expeditiously restoring its property to preloss conditions.

[5] These coverage forms are described more fully in Chapter 2.

[6] For example, "same as" studies of new product introductions or start-ups—studies already reviewed and evaluated by bankers and/or other capital providers—may be used.

[7] From a 1999 Allendale Mutual Insurance Company Form GEY2K.

[8] Sometimes referred to as "top down" and "bottom up" forms, respectively. The gross earnings form measures the loss of gross earnings and deducts noncontinuing expenses (also known as saved or variable expenses) to determine the business interruption loss—from the top down. Alternatively, the BIC form determines lost net income and adds back continuing expenses (also known as unabated or fixed expenses) to determine the business interruption loss—from the bottom up.

[9] From Allendale Mutual Insurance Company policy GEY2K.

High Octane Refinery
Due Diligence Required

High Octane Refinery owns several refineries throughout the world. One of its facilities was built in 1970 near New Orleans, Louisiana. The New Orleans facility, which refines sweet premium crude oils received primarily by sea from Saudi Arabia, functions primarily as a "tolling" operation, processing crude oil for customers for a fee. When built, High Octane's New Orleans Refinery, known to its refining crews as HONO, had an initial output of up to 150,000 barrels of oil every day, processing low-sulphur premium crude into low-sulphur gasoline, diesel fuel, heating oils, light naphtha, and liquid petroleum gas, referred to in the trade as LPG.

Modernized in 1995, High Octane implemented measures at HONO to increase its refining capacity and improve environmental and economic efficiencies. These modernizations included adding a second distillation unit with the capacity to distill 150,000 barrels of oil a day—increasing the refinery's total output of distilled crude to 300,000 barrels per day. Other improvements included redesigning process units to eliminate bottlenecks in production and achieve higher throughputs. The company also installed new heat exchangers to reduce fuel and utility consumption.

The fundamental process of refining crude oil relies on "cracking" the crude: by heating crude to controlled temperatures in what is referred to as a distillation column, different grades of oil and fuel products can be siphoned off or captured in liquid form or as gases. The resulting products can be further refined through a combination of chemical processes. A simple representation of the distillation column shows the typical process flow, and the outputs of crude at different temperatures:

Figure R.1: Crude Oil Distillation Column

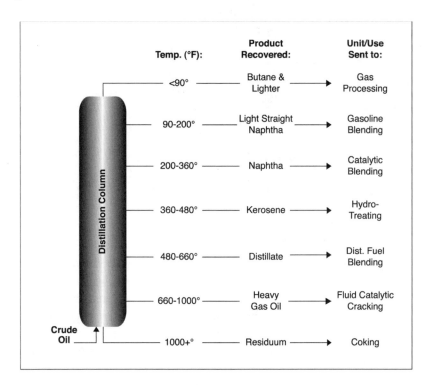

	Temp. (°F):	Product Recovered:	Unit/Use Sent to:
	<90°	Butane & Lighter	Gas Processing
	90-200°	Light Straight Naphtha	Gasoline Blending
	200-360°	Naphtha	Catalytic Blending
	360-480°	Kerosene	Hydro-Treating
	480-660°	Distillate	Dist. Fuel Blending
	660-1000°	Heavy Gas Oil	Fluid Catalytic Cracking
Crude Oil	1000+°	Residuum	Coking

While High Octane Refinery has an established network of customers, demand for its products fluctuates based on seasonal needs. During low-demand months for gasoline and heating oil—from August through October and from March through May—the plant operates at 70 percent of capacity. During high-demand months, the plant operates at 95 percent of capacity. Preventative maintenance is scheduled annually during low-demand months.

FIRE IN THE HOLE: THE INCIDENT

On December 1, 2003, a fire broke out near the older distillation column unit, CDU #1. The explosion that followed severely damaged the column and injured several workers who had sought to control the fire. CDU #1 was immediately shut down for three weeks by OSHA, which during that period conducted a thorough investigation.

Two days later, on December 3, HONO's management team held an emergency meeting of its accounting, engineering, procurement, production, and sales staff. At this meeting, the company's CFO, Tom Walsh, stressed the urgency of beginning repairs and resuming operations—especially in light of the currently favorable market conditions. "It's vital we get this column running again, guys," Walsh said. "We're facing a 50 percent loss of production, and it can be devastating to the company."

Everyone appreciated the gravity of the situation in a month where the plant faced a continually high demand. However, the engineering team leader had some bad news for HONO.

"Tom, CDU #1 needs to be completely rebuilt. And it won't be cheap," said Greg Caliper. "I talked to an equipment vendor we've used in the past, and the representative says they can do the job. But he quoted $8 million for the entire project—including design, engineering, fabrication, installation, and testing of the equipment. They have a backlog now. The representative is confident they can complete all the work in five months, but to get it done faster they'll need an additional $600,000. Then they can knock off three weeks. I asked them to put together a formal bid, and they're doing that now."

After Greg sat down, there was a short silence. Everyone in the room knew exactly what was meant by four-to-five months of output at half the plant's full capacity. Then Jennifer Gogetti, HONO's Procurement Director, quietly gave her own report and announced her principal concern: what to do about the crude shipment schedule.

"Our current delivery schedule was negotiated with the Saudis three months ago," said Gogetti. "It was based on a combined throughput of 90,000 to 95,000 barrels of daily throughput. But now that CDU #1 is down, we can't possibly process or store all that arriving crude. But our supply contract includes a $50,000 penalty if we refuse or reject a crude shipment—and we're staring down not one, but multiple penalties if we can't take the crude." Gogetti winced as she reported this. "We should be prepared to incur these penalties, as well as demurrage charges, if a tanker is held up in a port for longer than the required period of time. But I've no way to estimate how much this could be yet."

Dan Widgeon, the production team manager for HONO, amplified Gogetti's concerns. "CDU #2 is running at 95 to 99 percent capacity right now. Spare capacity won't be available until March. But even then," noted Widgeon, "the unit's total capacity is limited to 50,000 barrels per day. We simply can't process the excess crude."

Then it was Tom Walsh's turn. "Folks, we have to get a handle on what's possible—and what's not. Dan, I need you to work with Jennifer and the sales staff to put together a revised optimization model—a Linear Process Optimization model—to address this current decrease in our throughput. That LP should give us a good feel for the P&L impact of these additional constraints. Our actual results historically have been very consistent with those generated by our monthly LP runs; so it should be helpful in measuring the financial impact of the fire."

After a few quiet nods of agreement, and with everyone in a somber mood, the operations meeting at HONO was adjourned. Just afterward, Tom called his risk manager. "Jack? I'm afraid we have a significant loss exposure. Why don't you bring a copy of the business interruption policy and come to my office? Let's start getting into some of these details."

Half an hour later Jack was in Tom's office with a stack of papers.

"Here's what we've got," Jack began. "Our insurance carrier is Groenen Loudlee in New York, and I've put together a summary of the relevant policy provisions." Jack handed Tom a spreadsheet.

Type of Coverage	Form Used	Amount	Deductible	Indemnity
Business income	Gross Earnings	$200,000,000	10-day waiting period	12 mos.
Extended coverage	Gross Earnings	$15,000,000	n.a.	6 mos.
Extra Expenses	Yes		n.a.	

"We need to contact our carrier as soon as possible to advise that we intend to file a business interruption claim," Jack added.

"All right," Tom replied. "Keep me posted, Jack".

VISIT

On December 10, Jack received a phone call from the insurance adjuster, Michael Crawford. Crawford explained that he had been appointed by the insurance company to handle the claim and would like to visit the site with an engineer and an accountant. "My goal is simple," Crawford told Jack on the phone. "I want to meet with the refinery's personnel to discuss the scope of information we'll need to quantify your business interruption loss." They agreed to meet two days later.

When Crawford arrived, Jack began the meeting by providing an update on the status of the investigation. "OSHA's investigation is expected to take longer than we'd originally thought," he began. "This will obviously delay the cleanup and site preparation activities for the CDU column contractor."

"Jack, the policy doesn't have a civil authority provision," replied Crawford. "In my opinion, any delay beyond what otherwise would reasonably be required for a similar investigation will not be covered."

"Well, I have to disagree with that, Mike," was Jack's rejoinder. "OSHA's in here doing what they believe they require. It's a standard investigation that's a little more complicated is all."

"I have a different question," interjected the insurance engineer, Mr. Steelman. "I know a contractor in Mexico that fabricates refining columns and instrumentation. I made some preliminary inquires, and I was told that they could do the job for approximately 20 percent less than your current contractor quoted you and in just sixteen weeks. I think this is a viable alternative, as it will save the insurance carrier money on both the property damage and business interruption sides."

Now it was the plant's engineer's turn to disagree. "Mr. Steelman," he replied. "I have to challenge that. Fact is, we've dealt with that contractor before. And the problem we ran into, frankly, is that their work is inferior quality, and they have serious issues with the instrumentation compatibility. I agree that going with that company might shorten the time to rebuild, but I've got to tell you there's a high probability we would experience a substantial loss of productive time due to equipment failure during the ramp-up. I can pretty much guarantee it." Mr. Steelman demurred. Clearly, he was unconvinced.

Then the agenda turned to accounting for different aspects of the interruption. The insurance accountant, Stan Ledger, introduced himself. A soft-spoken man, Ledger explained his role and his general method in approaching the loss calculation.

"Ideally, I would like to leave this meeting with a general agreement on the loss methodology," Mr. Ledger suggested. "I plan to use average daily throughput rates and the final product yields before the loss in order to calculate the estimated production during the interruption period. Obviously, the figure will have to be adjusted for beginning inventories. And, since I'll be using preloss production figures, I'll also use the preloss average monthly finished product prices to value the net output. The goal is to be completely consistent."

Ledger continued. "I've also put together a list of the accounting documentation that I'll need to prepare the calculations. I hope this won't be too much trouble." He passed a piece of paper to Jack.

"Thanks, Mr. Ledger," replied Jack, as he took the document offered. "I'll forward your request to our accounting department. But I do hope we can further discuss the issues your team has brought up during today's meeting, internally, before we commit to anything. Shall we have lunch?"

After the insurance adjuster and his companions departed, Tom Walsh stayed quietly thinking in the meeting room for some time.

"Clearly," he thought, "we disagree with the insurance company's team on several key issues. I know the fire is having an economic impact on the refinery, and I think I know how to measure this impact. This insurance team, however, seems to be looking at the situation from a totally different angle."

Walsh then picked up the phone. "Jack, what do you say we bring somebody in to help us prove our case?"

"I know just the person," came the reply.

Solving a Puzzle

You assisted Jack previously on other claims, and he trusts your professional opinion. After getting off the phone with his CFO, Jack dials your number, and you agree to meet. As you prepare for the meeting, you review Jack's questions; and, as you begin to read more deeply, you realize this promises to be an extremely interesting case. What follows are Jack's questions, and some considerations about the possible answers.[1]

Questions:

1. The refinery's losses can be difficult to measure. Based on **Fig. R.1: Crude Oil Distillation Column**, what are some internal and external factors that contribute to the complexity of the loss calculation?

2. If a contractor offers an incentive to expedite work, how would you generally evaluate the cost of expediting such work, in the context of the business interruption coverage?

3. How could Linear Process Optimization models (LPs) be used to determine the value of the loss? What might be some of the drawbacks to using such models? What are some of the steps in due diligence that a claims adviser could take to ascertain the usefulness of the LP model if he chooses to use one to quantify the loss?

4. What is the significance of the lengths of the periods of restoration offered by the two contractors' alternatives? How would their significance change if it were a Gross Profit (European) policy?

5.   What arguments could be made to refute the use of the preloss data (the average production rates, prices, etc.) for the loss calculation? Could you find any inconsistencies within his intended approach? How would your finding change if it were a sales-based calculation?

Possible Answers

1.   Based on **Fig. R.1: Crude Oil Distillation Column**, what are some internal and external factors that contribute to the complexity of the loss calculation?

Internal factors

  •   Complexity of the plant (including the existence of processing plants downstream)

  •   Location of the loss in the production process (i.e., the largest business interruption exposure if a distillation column unit (CDU) is affected, versus a decreasing business interruption exposure as the loss location gets further down the production stream)

  •   The capacities of the distilling and storage units, etc.

External factors

  •   The type of crude oil, since modern refineries are typically built to refine only a particular grade of crude

  •   Ownership of the crude oil (i.e., questions about processing oil one owns rather than "tolling")

  •   The means of the crude's delivery (tankers, oil pipeline, etc.), and the ownership of those means

  •   Availability of alternate sources for supply (both for crude and for intermediate distillates)

2.   If a contractor offers an incentive to expedite work, how would you generally evaluate the cost of expediting such work, in the context of the business interruption coverage?

A possible answer: Business interruption policies don't usually cover expediting expenses except to the extent that they reduce the loss.

3.   How could Linear Process Optimization models (LPs) be used to determine the value of the loss? What might be some of the drawbacks to using such models? What are some of the steps in due diligence that a claims adviser could take to ascertain the usefulness of the LP model if he chooses to use one to quantify the loss?

A possible answer: An LP model calculates the theoretical (optimal) profit margin for the refinery based on the input variables and process constraints. Because the damage to a process unit alters one or more of the input variables and/or constraints, the comparison of the outputs with and without the effects of the damage will yield the loss. In practice, however, the claims professional cannot rely solely on the LP model—if at all. One of the drawbacks of optimization models is that they often do not incorporate inventories; therefore, care must be exercised in applying them.

Some of the due diligence steps that may be taken are:

- Understanding the inputs used in the model

- Review LP outputs for prior fiscal periods, comparing them to actual results from operations

- Ensuring the integrity of the variables and constraints used as inputs for the model.

4.   What is the significance of the lengths of the periods of restoration offered by the two contractors' alternatives? How would their significance change if it were a Gross Profit (European) policy?

A possible answer: Under the Gross Earnings policy, the period of restoration determines the period of indemnity. Therefore, the alternative with the shorter lead time decreases a potential business interruption loss by reducing the period of indemnity. Under the Gross Profit policy, on the other hand, the period of restoration *does not* determine the period of indemnity, which runs until "business returns to normal."

5.   What arguments could be made to refute the use of the preloss data (the average production rates, prices, etc.) for the loss calculation? Could you find any inconsistencies within his intended approach? How would your finding change if it were a sales-based calculation?

A possible answer: One of the clues that that case provides to answer this question is the seasonal nature of the business. Therefore, it may not be appropriate to apply preloss averages to the loss period because the market conditions before and after the loss may have markedly changed. Another inconsistency in Stan Ledger's intended approach is his erroneous consideration of inventories while calculating the loss on a production basis; inventories must be considered while using a sales-based approach.

Endnotes

[1] The answers we present in the following pages are not really "answers" in a traditional sense. Rather, they represent some of the due diligence issues that a claims adviser may explore in quantifying this loss. The goal is twofold: to introduce some of the likely complexity of this and similar cases and to engage you in working through some of these questions to come up with your own conclusions—albeit based on the limited information presented in this scenario.

Tulla Mulla Distillers

At the foot of the hill there abides a still
That mixes peat steam and rye.
And barley too with water through
For the sweetest poteen nearby.
Now fill the air with the sweetest fair
Of the whisky that's near and true—
And you will know the drink that goes
By the real ole mountain dew.

Anonymous, *"The Real Ole Mountain Dew"*

Peat is a mixture of organic matter, including grasses and other decomposing plant matter, typically dug from peatmires or bogs and then dried. Dried peat burns like a log in the fireplace, and—in those areas of the Northern hemisphere where agriculture has over the millennia denuded the land of trees or local conditions do not promote speedy regrowth—peat is cheaper and more widely available than wood. Peat, then, was once used predominantly in Ireland, Scotland, and England as fuel to heat the home. In some remote areas, it is still.

Ironically, a different kind of fire lies at the heart of our current claims scenario. Tulla Mulla Distillers, Inc., makes and sells some of the world's most popular brands of Scotch and other spirits. The Tulla Mulla brand also identifies the company's most successful Scotch malt whiskey, "The real ole mountain dew."[1] In its past few years, Tulla Mulla's sales and financial performance soared, mostly as a result of the cigar-and-Scotch comeback. Also during this time, the company implemented its "Ghost Tour of the Master Blender's Shop"—a Scotch-tasting event designed to promote the sale of its products.

Even discounting the recent surge in sales, Tulla Mulla's tried-and-true secret of success is the peat from O'Cohan's Mills used in the production of its Scotch. During the production of malt whiskey, the malt is sent to a kiln to be dried on a mesh over a peat fire, which imparts the unique earthly, charcoal flavor to the prized spirit. Tulla Mulla's relationship with O'Cohan's Mills goes back as far as 1847, when the mill supplied water, power, and peat to Tulla Mulla under a Contract of Utility. That same year, reviewers raved about Tulla Mulla, the whiskey. Ultimately, Tulla Mulla supplied its own power but continued to purchase water and peat from O'Cohan's Mills.

The Situation

One fateful evening, fire broke out at the finished goods warehouse of O'Cohan's Mills, igniting mounds of dried peat and destroying the entire finished-goods peat inventory. Then the fire burned through the acres of work-in-process peat inventory maturing in the fields. Tulla Mulla's new facility in Trahanoch, Scotland, now faces a potential interruption since it was designed solely to make efficient use of O'Cohan's Mills peat. Only six months old, the plant was ramping up to full production in the coming few weeks.

As the risk manager for Tulla Mulla, you receive a call from the CFO—who remembers your presentation, "The Importance of Contingent Business Interruption Insurance." He tells you that Tulla Mulla may lose sales from not having peat available for the next blend cycle. While O'Cohan's Mills may be able to supply alternative peat from a neighboring facility, the amount would be minimal. Since whiskey is a blend of various years' production, Tulla Mulla Distillers actually has enough inventory to continue to produce for the next twenty-four months. But the company will be continually short one year's worth of the particular (and popular) whiskey made with O'Cohan's Mills peat.

To make matters worse, though Tulla Mulla can certainly buy other manufacturer's peat from different districts inside or even outside of Scotland, it is unclear how this choice will impact the taste and marketability of its flagship product, Tulla Mulla. Different departments in the company have different points of view about whether Tulla Mulla can or should use other peat. Would it negatively impact the trusted taste of Tulla Mulla, thus undermining the brand? Will the crisis close down operations? O'Cohan's Mills expects it to take at least one year to grow and age new peat turfs.

As a result of the loss, the cost of Scottish and Irish peat has skyrocketed to an equivalent cost of $2 per caseload. Alternative suppliers of peat have been contacting Tulla Mulla ever since the fire, while the media has made the "whiskey crisis" an ongoing story. In an attempt to take market share from Tulla Mulla, a competitor, GlenMeltonmulla, begins running advertisements claiming the purist and longest running mills in Scotland.

What Is Contingent Business Interruption (CBI) Insurance?
Contingent business interruption and contingent extra expense insurance reimburse lost profits and extra costs resulting from the interruption of the business of a customer or supplier. Specifically:

In the event of physical damage to property of a supplier or customer's property, caused by a peril covered under the insured's policy, which in turn causes an interruption to the insured's business operation ... then, the contingent business interruption insurance covers the business interruption loss under the provisions of the policy for the defined indemnity period.

Contingent business interruption insurance is also known as contingent business income insurance or dependent properties insurance. Sometimes the term "contingent time element" is used when discussing both contingent business interruption and contingent extra expense. Time element simply refers to either business interruption or extra expense coverage.

Companies purchase this type of insurance as an extension to their standard property insurance. Coverage is usually triggered by physical damage to customers' or suppliers' property or to property upon which the insured company depends to attract customers. The type of physical damage must be the same as insured under the controlling policy.

Contingent business interruption insurance is widely used when the insured depends on (a) a single supplier or a few suppliers for materials, or (b) one or a few manufacturers or suppliers for most of its merchandise, or (c) one or a few recipient businesses to purchase the bulk of the insured's products, or (d) a neighboring business to help attract customers, known as a leader property.

Contingent business interruption insurance can reimburse the policyholder in each of these situations, covering the interruption in the insured's business caused by a peril specified in the policy.

Contingent business interruption insurance does not cover the following situations:

- Utility service interruption or an off-premises power interruption

- Civil or military authority interruption

- Lack of ingress or egress interruption

- Interdependency or downstream business interruption, when damage at an owned location causes a loss of revenue to another owned location

- Loss from a change in temperature due to damage to heating or cooling equipment

The Challenge

Tulla Mulla has a comprehensive property and business interruption policy, which includes endorsements for "contingent time element for business interruption" and "contingent extra expenses" (see sidebar for definitions). The loss period is defined as "when repairs are complete and the additional length of time for business to resume normal operations, but no longer than 36 months from the date of loss."

As the risk manager, you need to meet with department heads and others to get a better understanding of the loss and to prepare for the meeting with the adjuster. Your goal? Find out: (1) What happened? (2) How was the fire caused? (3) Are any parties at fault? Here are the tasks that should be part of that fact-gathering effort:

- Call the risk manager at O'Cohan's Mills to get that company's perspective; then, contact the purchasing manager and production manager at Tulla Mulla to investigate available supply and alternative options for buying other peat.

- Read the policy. Determine which endorsements apply to your situation(s).

- Call your broker. Put your carrier on notice.

- Identify what departments will be impacted. Meet with the department heads.

- Identify ways to mitigate the loss. Develop different loss scenarios.

- Consider outside help to assist you with your claim.

And here are issues your insurance company will be considering and will want to discuss. (So be prepared to address them!)

- Was the incident a fire or explosion? How did it happen? Is this an insured peril?

- How long does O'Cohan's Mills expect to be impaired?

- Who are Tulla Mulla's alternative suppliers?

- Is peat a utility? Can Tulla Mulla operate without a utility? Do you have a copy of the contract with O'Cohan's Mills?

- In the policy under "contingent business interruption," the word supplier or utility does not appear. But the policy does say "we will insure against damage to companies that have a commercial interest in your business." What does that mean?

- What was your budget for sales this year? Can we receive a copy of Tulla Mulla's financial statements to estimate the contingent business interruption loss?

- Do you mind if our associate stays behind? He is a CPA that works for Wee Lower Claims. He will help you with the claim, and the insurance company will pay for his fees. The first thing we need to focus on is an initial loss estimate.

- Is production estimated to change this year as a result of the incident?

- Does the policy's "growing crops" exclusion impact the loss recovery?

Facts Discovered and Questions Answered

The first question that must be asked is the obvious one: Is this a business interruption? Is there a claim? The next questions quickly follow: If yes, is the business interruption an economic loss, or is it simply a claim for expenses to reduce a loss? If Tulla Mulla can continue operating without any interruption to its current-year production, then does the company even experience a business interruption loss? And if the production loss is outside the indemnity period, is the amount payable reduced under the terms of the policy?

The next large issue to decide hinges on the relationship between Tulla Mulla and O'Cohan's Mills. If the supplier was a utility at one time but is currently a vendor, does that impact coverage? If the contingent business interruption coverage excludes utilities and the supplier contract is a Contract of Utility, does this automatically exclude the claim? Does the liberal policy wording of commercial interest reinstate coverage?

Working with the Insurance Company

The insurance company's two immediate objectives are (1) to mitigate the loss and (2) to provide an immediate estimate for a loss reserve. Any policyholder should understand that setting a reserve and managing the loss to that reserve are very important to insurers and reinsurers. Accordingly, a rush to estimate a reserve simply for the sake of having a number is something of a fool's journey; it may be prudent to refrain from setting a reserve until more information is available and properly prepared for the carrier. This could take several weeks, or a month, or even more. It is certainly sensible to develop and share several loss scenarios based on how much supply was available.

Another risk is that the policyholder and the carrier could come up with loss estimates at opposite ends of the spectrum, with the policyholder claiming one year's worth of lost sales and the carrier acknowledging nothing except extra expense. This claim scenario clearly shows the importance of wording in the policy, as well as tailoring a policy to fit the company's exact situation, including the potential for different large loss scenarios.

Complexity of Claims

At least two variables make this claim even more complex than usual. First is the ready availability of a raw material that is both common (that is, peat is easy to get from alternative suppliers) and unique (the peat from O'Cohan's Mills is of a particular quality). Is it fair to expect Tulla Mulla to replace the raw material, even though the substitute might be inferior in some hard-to-define way? Second is the question raised by the marketing campaign of the GlenMeltonmulla Company, that is, would or should insurance cover any increased marketing expense to counteract GlenMeltonMulla's claims? Would Tulla Mulla have to demonstrate how more marketing mitigated its loss? Or would the additional spending be covered under "extra expense?" (See Chapters 2 and 3 for discussions on extra expenses.)

A good framework for determining whether CBI coverage applies is the following set of conditions:

Figure T.1: Fulfilling the Conditions of Contingent Business Interruption Insurance

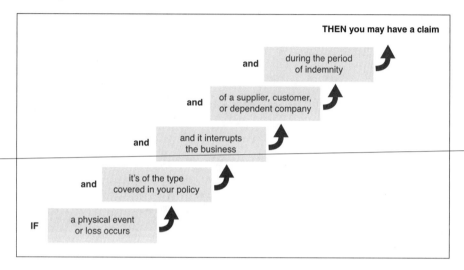

[1] Derived from the Gaelic word for "water of life," whiskey is a spirit distilled from fermented grain, such as barley, rye, or wheat; malt whiskey is made from barley malt, fermented with yeast and distilled in a pot. Scotch is simply whiskey blended in Scotland.

CHAPTER NINE

Business Interruption and the Law

Policies, Procedures, and Strategies for Resolution

In an ideal world, after an insured event impairs the policyholder's business, the insurer and policyholder work together to measure the loss. They agree on the amount covered, and the insurer pays the claim. Of course, in the real world, it does not always work out that way. There are many reasons why an insurer might deny all or part of a claim, and in that circumstance the parties might resort to various mechanisms to resolve their differences, including traditional court litigation, appraisal, arbitration, mediation, and/or negotiation. This chapter reviews some of the basic steps that policyholders and insurers may consider in anticipation of a dispute arising from an arguably insured event and describes what the parties might expect once a determination has been made to adopt some form of dispute resolution process.

The Policyholder's Predispute Checklist

Depending on policy language, an almost infinite variety of perils might result in a covered business interruption loss. Such perils can range from natural disasters, such as earthquakes, floods and hurricanes, to myriad man-made disasters, such as oil or chemical spills, underground gas leaks, and the unanticipated groundings of airliners. A business interruption can be fairly confined and uncomplicated in scope, as in the case of a brief, localized shutdown due to a utility outage; on the other hand, it can be catastrophic and immensely complex, such as in the case of a large-scale industrial explosion involving property damage, bodily injury, business interruption losses, on- and off-site contamination, and residential evacuations. In extreme cases, catastrophic events trigger state and federal OSHA investigations, criminal investigations, and the involvement of other local, state, and federal authorities. They also often lead to third-party tort and contract litigation, including subrogation actions, in addition to the policyholder's own property-related and business interruption losses. They may also create adverse publicity for the organizations involved. Such events may require a well-conceived comprehensive crisis management plan, in which the policyholder's insurance recovery effort is but one part of multi-faceted response strategy. (Crisis Management is discussed in Chapter 6.)

Of course, a property and business interruption loss does not always translate into coverage litigation—let alone collateral civil, regulatory, and criminal proceedings. But after an event that, among other things, impairs the policyholder's operations and thereby leads to a loss of profits or gross earnings and extra expense losses, a policyholder should consider a basic series of actions to maximize and expedite its insurance claim. A nonexhaustive checklist of these predispute steps and considerations follows.

Don't Write or Say Anything That Could Be Used Against You

After a loss, even the smartest, most experienced persons (including risk managers or others involved in responding to a loss) will sometimes make premature, ill-considered, and incorrect proclamations about the coverage that later could be used as a basis for denying the coverage. Substantive evaluations of the coverage (such as "I never thought that was covered" or "We can't get coverage for that," etc.) generally should not be documented or otherwise communicated after a loss. Oftentimes, it is important to get in-house or outside counsel involved in any communications regarding the substantive issues, to establish and use the attorney-client privilege in order to protect such communications from compelled disclosure down the road. This issue is discussed further in this chapter in the subsequent extended discussion on *Privilege and Confidentiality Concerns.*

Review the Coverage

Not all policies cover the same categories of losses. A careful inspection of the policy—which can easily dictate multiple readings—is necessary to confirm that no coverages are being overlooked. The policyholder should obtain complete copies of its current first-party property policies from the broker or insurer if it does not already have them on hand. The policyholder then should carefully review the policies, any certificates or attached endorsements, and any and all correspondence about those policies between the policyholder, broker, and the insurer. In so doing, the policyholder should note the various categories of losses and expenses that may be covered and the key conditions to coverage that will require some sort of action, such as notice or mitigation, from the policyholder.

Notice

Virtually every policy contains one or more provisions that describe the policyholder's duties in the event of a potentially covered loss. One of the most important is the *notice* provision, requiring that notice be provided to the insurer "as soon as practicable," "immediately," "within a reasonable time," or within some other time period specified under the policy. Frequently, all that is required is sending a description of the covered event to the broker with directions to forward the information to the potentially affected insurers. In such cases, the policyholder should be sure to confirm that notice was in fact sent to each insurer by requesting a copy of the broker's transmittal letters. Often, but not always, the policy will provide directions on to who notice should be sent and the manner in which it can be provided (*e.g.*, facsimile, electronic mail, via an Internet claims site, certified mail, or standard mail). Many brokers provide a claim-submission service.

A failure to timely notify the insurer can create difficulties. It may in some circumstances provide the insurer with a basis for denying coverage. In most states, however, a failure to provide timely notice will not bar coverage unless the insurer was "prejudiced" or "substantially prejudiced" by the late notice. In some jurisdictions, the insurer may avoid providing coverage by showing that the timing of the notice was unreasonable under the circumstances. Of course, the best way to eliminate untimely notice as an issue is to provide notice promptly after the loss, even if all details are not immediately known; additional details of the loss can be provided as they are learned.

Proof of Loss

Most property policies require the insured to prepare and submit a proof of loss, sometimes under oath. This document will outline the types of covered losses claimed and the amount claimed by category; it will also confirm the insured's ownership interest in the property at the time of loss and include other information that the organization must attest is true and accurate. Additionally, the policy may provide a time deadline for submission of a proof of loss, and the submission of a proof of loss often will initiate a time limit within which the insurer is obligated to pay the claim. There is typically no prescribed format for a proof of loss, and the broker or insurer usually will provide a format.

In the property and business interruption claim context, it is common practice to submit a proof of loss only after agreement by the insurer and policyholder on the total loss or to document agreement on the amount of an advance payment requested by the policyholder (whereby the policyholder would submit a partial proof of loss). This practice contrasts with other types of first-party claims, such as fidelity claims, in which the policyholder generally submits a proof of loss prior to any agreement on the amount of loss.

A proof of loss submitted before the loss has been fully adjusted by the insurer, or before agreement on the amount of property damage or business interruption loss, is often described as a *hostile* proof of loss. Insurers often view such a proof of loss as hostile because (1) policyholders may submit proofs for tactical reasons, such as a desire to trigger action on behalf of the insurer (*i.e.*, under the policy the insurer might have as few as thirty days to pay adjusted claims after a proof of loss is submitted), and (2) such a proof of loss may signal a lack of interest in working with the insurer to come to a mutually agreeable valuation for the loss. The result of such a proof of loss may be a claims adjustment that is more adversarial than cooperative, less likely to yield a mutually satisfactory resolution to the claim, and more likely to lead to alternative dispute resolution (ranging from appraisal to litigation). Insurers often view a premature proof of loss as hostile regardless of the policyholder's intent. Thus, the policyholder should carefully consider the ramifications of filing a proof of loss prior to agreement on the amount of loss. In cases where the policyholder determines that a hostile proof of loss is in its best interests, a common issue is whether the policyholder has submitted something that constitutes a proof of loss, as opposed to some other document. An insurer may dispute whether the policyholder has filed a true proof of loss in order to avoid obligations triggered upon the filing. In such cases, insurance experts and/or legal counsel should be consulted.

Generally, the best way for the policyholder to deal with the proof of loss question (in a complex claim) is to raise the question with the insurer and get a written understanding of when and how to submit. This will avoid timing issues.

Cooperation

Most policies expressly require that the policyholder cooperate in specific respects with the insurer after a loss; cooperation may also be required under the common law of some states. This duty often extends to making facilities, witnesses, and relevant, nonprivileged documents available to the insurer. It also may require the insured to submit to an examination under oath by the insurer or its representative. Examinations under oath are rare but are becoming increasingly prevalent in cases involving large or questionable losses. Failing to cooperate sometimes can provide an insurer with a basis for denying coverage, although, as in the case of untimely notice, an insurer may be required to show that a lack of cooperation was prejudicial to the insurer to avoid its coverage obligations on that basis.

After an event resulting in property damage, insurers with potential exposure for losses arising from the event typically will undertake some investigation (or will retain an independent adjuster to perform that function) to quantify the loss and to determine whether and to what extent the loss is covered. The duty to cooperate may require that the policyholder share information collected as part of any investigation of a covered event. It may further require that the insured provide proprietary or otherwise sensitive information to the insurer if that information is relevant to the adjustment of the loss. The policyholder may have concerns about relinquishing control—to anyone—of any information that could be used by other entities to the policyholder's detriment. Such outside parties conceivably could include third parties who have an interest in establishing the policyholder's tort liability or the policyholder's competitors. Before providing any information in connection with the insurer's investigation and adjustment, therefore, policyholders who have such concerns are well advised to request from their insurers an agreement that formalizes the latter's obligation to maintain such information as strictly confidential. Even if the insurance policy does not expressly require the insurer to execute such an agreement, insurers often are willing to do so. Outside the litigation context, this generally can be accomplished through a confidentiality agreement that details the scope of such obligation, including the extremely limited circumstances under which such information may be released to third parties. In the litigation context, confidentiality agreements also can be effected through a judge's protective order, after agreement by the parties on its terms.

After a loss, the focus of the insurer is usually twofold. **First,** the company will take the steps appropriate to assist its customer—the policyholder—in evaluating and responding to the loss. **Second,** the insurer will take the steps appropriate to ensure that it is protecting its own interests, for example, by providing coverage only to the extent that such coverage is provided under the policy form and by taking steps to perfect its subrogation rights, if any. Insurers often correctly conclude that executing a confidentiality agreement will not detract from either objective but instead will facilitate the loss investigation and adjustment process by providing the policyholder with some comfort regarding the confidentiality of its documents and internal information. Some policies affirmatively require that the insurer execute a confidentiality agreement in connection with any postloss investigation by the insurer.

While sometimes broad, the duty of cooperation is not unlimited. The insurance contract and applicable law should be consulted to ascertain the scope of such an obligation, but in general policyholders should not be expected to provide assistance beyond what is reasonable and practicable under the circumstances. Neither should they be expected to incur substantial expenses in response to an insurer's requests for information. Arguably, such expenses should be borne by the insurer, and, indeed, many policies contain express provisions entitling the insured to be reimbursed for claim preparation expenses. Moreover, policyholders are sometimes asked to provide substantial assistance to counsel and experts retained by the insurer in connection with actual or potential insurer subrogation actions (see the discussion on subrogation that begins on page 291). The insurance contract generally will specify the policyholder's duties to cooperate in connection with subrogation matters arising from the loss. However, there will be cases in which the insurer has asked for such cooperation even though it has yet to actually reimburse the policyholder for its losses or even agree to provide coverage. In such cases, it is at least questionable whether the policyholder should be required to provide any additional assistance relating specifically to subrogation matters, since the insurer has technically not been subrogated to the rights of the policyholder in pursuing third-party claims. Again, the terms of the policy and the applicable law should be consulted with regard to such requests for cooperation.

Mitigation

Many policies cover only those losses that could not be avoided through reasonable postloss mitigation efforts. With respect to business interruption coverage in particular, a policyholder is often required to exercise due diligence to repair covered property damage and resume operations. Thus, after a loss, the policyholder should evaluate whether there are reasonable steps it can take to avoid additional losses. Also, to the extent feasible and appropriate, the policyholder may want to involve or at least notify its insurer regarding mitigation efforts to provide an opportunity for input and to avoid complaints after the fact.

Cost-Tracking

In general, a policyholder bears the burden of measuring, documenting, and establishing its claim. To facilitate that claim's handling, or to document proof of the loss should disputes arise with the insurer, the policyholder should systematically track all potentially covered losses. This includes establishing an internal accounting cost code, developing a system for collecting hard copies of invoices, and organizing and maintaining the data in a user-friendly format. This should be done as soon as possible following a loss—especially for complicated claims involving large and diverse sets of costs. Otherwise, the policyholder could be faced with the daunting task of reconstructing costs from scratch months later. Collecting loss information is helpful in pursuing not only covered losses but also possible claims against third parties.

Retention of Counsel

Companies make different decisions about retaining outside counsel, depending on the size and severity of the event and the relevant experience of that counsel. At minimum, insurance coverage lawyers may add value by evaluating coverage and advising on its potential scope. Put differently, outside coverage counsel can help to identify possibilities for ensuring coverage in the policy terms for categories of costs that policyholders might not otherwise have included in their claims. Often, courts have interpreted insurance policy language in a way that may not be immediately obvious—which may in some circumstances favor the policyholder and, in other cases, the insurer. In the extreme case, an insured event raises the vast array of third-party liability and regulatory concerns noted previously, in addition to first-party property and business interruption losses. In such a case, it is advisable to retain outside counsel who can handle and coordinate a comprehensive postcatastrophe response. This can include responding to civil and criminal inquiries and actions by state or federal authorities, defending against third-party liability actions, handling jury trials or other adjudicative processes, and managing the policyholder's public relations strategy. At the same time, counsel will shepherd the policyholder's first and third-party insurance claims to negotiated or adjudicated resolutions. In the latter scenario, the outside counsel (and retained experts, such as are discussed later) generally must function as a highly coordinated team, to ensure that the company's review of facts and development of theories remains consistent as they pull together the various pieces of the postloss puzzle. At the same time, outside counsel will strive to ensure that the team is working to minimize the policyholder's potential liability and losses while simultaneously maximizing the policyholder's insurance assets. (See the discussion on Crisis Management in Chapter 6.) Finally, and perhaps most importantly, it is often critical to involve counsel early in order to ensure that important discussions and documents are privileged and protected from forced disclosure. Part of this calculus is determining which individuals are part of the privilege and which are not and proceeding accordingly. Questions concerning privilege are addressed in detail later in this chapter.

Retention of Experts

Depending on the complexity of an insured event, one of the policyholder's most important first steps is hiring the right experts. Some specialists focus on determining the causes of a loss; others can help counsel and/or the policyholder to prepare claims and calculate damages. With respect to property damage and business interruption losses, the policyholder can retain independent loss adjusters, accountants, economists, forensic accountants, and engineers who can assist with tracking costs, developing and negotiating claim(s), and mitigating losses. It is important to select a group that is independent of the applicable insurance company and its agents. If the event implicates third-party liability concerns, the insured may turn to experts on cause and origin issues and/or to those who can address the potential multitude of third-party liability issues. An insured must consider the possibility of future litigation, both between the insured and insurer and between the insured and third parties. In most circumstances, the policyholder should consider retaining experts who are experienced and can present fact or expert testimony in connection with a formal adjudication of disputes arising from the event (*see* discussion on Testifying and Nontestifying Experts).

TESTIFYING AND NONTESTIFYING EXPERTS

A testifying expert is an individual who will provide testimony during a trial or hearing. Such an expert is subject to very expansive discovery rules. (See the discussion about Discovery on page. 294). In general, they must reveal all of the bases for their opinions, including all of the calculations, assumptions, and factual data underlying those opinions as well as other information as required by the governing state or federal law. Because of this, any party to litigation must be very careful in disclosing to a testifying expert any information that is privileged or protected by the work-product doctrine. (See discussion regarding Privileged Communications on page 286).

It is a regular and highly advisable practice of litigants involved in large-scale, expert-dependent litigation to retain separate testifying and nontestifying experts. Nontestifying experts assist in investigation, claim development, etc., but, because they will not testify in court, they typically are not subject to the same broad discovery as testifying experts. Consequently, absent a waiver or some other legal principle overriding the privilege or work-product protection, a party to litigation often may share with the nontestifying expert information that is privileged or protected by the work-product doctrine without fear of discovery. So long as it is conducted at the direction of counsel and in anticipation of litigation, the work of the nontestifying experts is generally protected from disclosure, because the nontestifying expert will be considered an agent of the attorney. In that regard, the nontestifying expert is often retained by the outside counsel, even with the understanding that the consultant's fees will be paid by the client.

Public Relations

Often a large insured event will lead to adverse publicity. At a minimum, it may dictate some communication to the public regarding the nature and efficacy of the policyholder's response. Policyholders that do not have the requisite expertise in-house may want to retain a professional public relations consultant who, in concert with in-house or outside counsel and policyholder representatives, can craft a message both appropriate for public consumption and consistent with the policyholder's overall postloss strategy.

Understanding Policy Provisions Bearing on Dispute Resolution

Insurance policies frequently contain provisions relating to dispute resolution. Some contain time limitations on bringing suit, which purport to preclude any action against the insurer after a specified period of time has elapsed. Contractual suit deadlines are often dramatically shorter than statutory limitations periods (*e.g.*, such contractual provisions often purport to require that suits against the insurer be filed within a period as short as one year from the date of loss). If such provisions were applied literally, however, they would often be impossible to meet, since other policy provisions often require time-consuming activities as a condition precedent to coverage. Such other activities could include provisions for mandatory appraisal, which would require a joint appraisal process that often can absorb a period of time that runs beyond the policy's time limitation for bringing suit. They could also include policy provisions purporting to prohibit any legal action until the policyholder has fully complied with every condition in the policy (including the appraisal condition) or until the loss is fully liquidated—which, again, can use up much of the suit-limitation clock. Such built-in suit limitations periods, however, may be automatically tolled under state law until the insurer formally denies the claim or for other equitable reasons and may even be unenforceable in some states. After a loss, a policyholder should always evaluate the potential effect of such provisions and should consider seeking a mutual tolling agreement in writing from its insurers to ensure that potentially applicable suit deadlines do not elapse while the parties endeavor to resolve the claim outside of litigation.

Some policies also contain mandatory arbitration and/or mediation provisions, forum selection clauses (which designate the location for adjudication of disputes in court or through arbitration), and choice of law provisions (which designate the substantive law that is applicable to any coverage dispute). These provisions—or their absence—often bear on a policyholder's insurance recovery strategy in the event of a disagreement with its insurers over the amount or existence of coverage.

Calendar Key Dates/Events

As a matter of organization, and to ensure that key deadlines that could result in loss of important rights are not overlooked, the policyholder should with the assistance of counsel carefully note applicable deadlines. These can include statutory suit deadlines, contractual suit deadlines (if any), the date for submitting a proof of loss, and other key dates bearing on the resolution of the insurance claim and any collateral matters arising from the insured event.

Exhaustion of Informal Dispute Resolution Alternatives

Coverage litigation is rarely the appropriate first step after a loss. Even when it appears that the parties may disagree on material aspects of the insurance claim, it often is advisable to engage in reasonable informal efforts to resolve the claim with expensive insurance coverage litigation a strategy of last resort. Such efforts may involve: (1) meetings between the policyholder and insurer representatives to discuss the claim; (2) using the broker to help resolve disagreements; (3) using experienced insurance consultants who specialize in negotiated resolutions; (4) relying on in-house and/or outside counsel to negotiate a resolution; (5) nonbinding mediation; (6) working with a specialized team consisting of the two or more of the above experts; and (7) use of a tolling agreement to extend the time in which suit may be filed.

Privilege and Confidentiality Concerns

After a loss, insurers and other third parties may request information relating to the event. If litigation is filed, the policyholder's adversaries will have a right to demand relevant documents and information, and the policyholder may have an obligation to comply with such requests, subject to some limitations. This process is called *discovery*, and is described beginning on page 294. Therefore, after an insured event, policyholders should take immediate steps to protect the confidentiality of proprietary business information. Moreover, they should anticipate the need to navigate the insurance claims process (and any collateral third-party liability and/or governmental processes) with a heightened sensitivity to the content of communications made and documents generated regarding the event. Put differently, the policyholder should not unnecessarily make its internal proprietary information available for the world to see. Neither should the policyholder make statements that it would not want repeated, nor should it create documents that it would not want read out loud and out of context in a courtroom at some later date.

Of course, there are measures a policyholder can adopt to protect itself when the insurer and/or other third parties start making demands for information. With respect to internal proprietary information such as trade secrets, other intellectual property, discussions of corporate strategy, and anything else that the policyholder deems confidential, the policyholder can be vigilant about what it makes available and the conditions under which it is made available. For example, the policyholder obviously should not carelessly provide to the insurer (or to any other third party) information that is not possibly relevant or information that is subject to some privilege and thus immune from discovery in a litigation context so long as it is maintained as confidential.

Moreover, the policyholder can insist that any information provided to its insurers is encompassed by a confidentiality agreement that places broad limitations on the insurers' ability to use such information or to communicate it to third parties. Should litigation be involved, the policyholder also can request that the court impose limitations on the use of such information. This is normally accomplished with a protective order that delineates conditions under which the information may be used and generally restricts the parties' ability to divulge the information to third parties.

With respect to postloss statements and documents generally, the policyholder should at a minimum be aware that nonprivileged communications eventually might be subject to discovery. Privileged communications are those that—in light of a specific public policy rationale—are generally immune from discovery by third parties. An example would be an overriding public interest in fostering open communications between certain groups of individuals. Well-known privileges include the attorney-client privilege, which protects communications between attorneys and clients; the work-product doctrine; the physician-patient privilege; and the spousal privilege. (Further discussion is included in the subsequent highlighted discussion of *Privileged Communications.*)

In the postloss context, the attorney-client privilege generally is the most relevant to the policyholder and insurer. But a policyholder cannot presume that communications with anyone other than counsel (or those designated by counsel as litigation consultants) are privileged and therefore immune from discovery by third parties. In other words, a policyholder's internal communications outside of the presence of counsel, internal documents not created at the direction of counsel, and communications with third parties—including insurers, brokers, and consultants—may be nonprivileged and therefore subject to discovery and use by adversaries in litigation. This issue has taken on added significance with the increased use of electronic mail, which has resulted in a culture of documented informal communications that were once reserved for oral discourse. It is not surprising that electronic mail is now viewed as one of the most fertile sources of useful information in litigation.

If litigation either against its insurers or against other third parties is a realistic possibility for the policyholder, the policyholder can take measures to protect the confidentiality of its statements and documents and limit the number of nonprivileged communications. These so-called prophylactic measures include instructing key individuals to limit their communications about the issues and taking extreme care with oral and written statements. They also would include ensuring that all key individuals are educated about the universe of issues and how the various pieces fit together (e.g., property insurance, liability insurance, third-party liability actions) to reduce the likelihood of inadvertent or careless statements or writings about one aspect of the loss (*e.g.*, property insurance) that could be used to undermine other aspects of the loss (*e.g.*, liability insurance and/or third-party suits). Further, such measures will include in-house or outside counsel on all communications regarding the claim to the extent practicable.

Finally, in some contexts it may be possible for the policyholder to establish a privilege (sometimes referred to as a privilege based on joint defense interests or a common interest) with insurers and their counsel. Doing so can be tricky and—depending on the applicable law and the circumstances—not without risk of some court ruling that the privilege did not attach. But such a step can be important in protecting against third-party claims and the like. It is a balancing act both to have a privilege with the insurers, while having other communications that are privileged as against the insurers, but in some cases it can and should be done.

PRIVILEGED COMMUNICATIONS

The term privilege is a shorthand legal term of art used to describe communications, documents, or other materials or information that are protected from forced disclosure by legal process. In the United States, federal courts employ civil rules of practice that allow broad discovery into any matters that may lead to evidence admissible in a litigation. Most state court systems have similarly broad discovery policies. (The distinction between federal and state courts is briefly summarized on pages 292-296; the concept of discovery is discussed on page 294.) Discovery requests under these broad rules may even be extended to third parties who are not plaintiffs or defendants in a litigation.

But privileges protect from this discovery process certain documents and oral and written communications that the law recognizes as highly important to a soundly functioning society and judicial system. Thus, for example, it is deemed beneficial to society to foster open and candid communications between clients and their attorneys. Therefore, the law privileges those communications with protection from discovery. Generally speaking, communications between a client and attorney in the course of a representation and for the purpose of representation are not subject to discovery or forced disclosure even if they are deemed potentially relevant to a particular matter. Other important relationships that are accorded privileged status include the spousal relationship, where one spouse cannot be forced to reveal the substance of communications with the other spouse; the doctor-patient relationship, in which a doctor cannot be compelled to reveal information given to that doctor in the course of a patient's treatment; the psychotherapist-patient relationship; and others.

Special considerations come into play when discussing the attorney-client privilege as it attaches to attorney representation of a corporation or other legal entity. In general, an attorney (including both in-house and outside counsel) represents the organization itself and not its directors, officers, or employees. Therefore, any privilege that attaches to communications between the attorney and employees of the entity belongs to the entity and not to the individual employees. This is an important distinction because it is possible to waive a privilege, either inadvertently or intentionally. This distinction also means that not every conversation between an attorney and an employee may be subject to a claim of privilege.

It is important to understand that privileges can be waived by the holder of the privilege—in some cases, even unintentionally. In an attorney-client relationship, the privilege belongs to the client. This means that the attorney generally may not waive the privilege; only the client may. Typically, a privilege will be waived when the confidential nature of the communication is violated by its holder. If a lawyer and client discuss issues in the presence of a third party who is not a party to the litigation in question, privilege may not attach to that conversation. After all, why should the law extend a special privilege to protect the confidentiality of a communication if the parties to that communication do not themselves protect it? Many jurisdictions will find a waiver of the privilege even where the disclosure of the confidential information or communication is inadvertent. So it is vitally important for employees of a corporation or other legal entity to be clearly instructed to maintain the confidential nature of communications with attorneys.

Closely related to the concept of privilege (specifically the attorney-client privilege) is a doctrine known as the work-product doctrine. Not technically a privilege, the work-product doctrine is driven by many of the same public policy concerns underlying the law of privileges. The work-product doctrine protects the thought processes, strategies, and legal work produced by an attorney or the attorney's agents or produced at or under the direction of an attorney. This doctrine does not protect all work performed by an attorney, only that performed in anticipation of litigation. The protection provided by the work-product doctrine is not as broad as that provided by the law of privilege and may be overridden in certain circumstances.

Obviously, much that an insured does after an insured event occurs will be covered by either the attorney-client privilege, the work-product doctrine, or both. Internal investigations, witness interviews, scientific analyses, and other matters performed by or at the direction of counsel and in anticipation of litigation are generally protected. Insurers often attempt to obtain access to their policyholder's attorney-client communications and work-product generated during these postevent investigations; courts vary as to whether insurers are entitled to them. Although it is presumed that an insured and insurer have a common interest in investigating the event and that the insured has an obligation to cooperate (usually a term in the policy), insurers often seek these materials not to assist the insured but to defeat coverage. It depends on the particular circumstances of the case, but courts have generally refused such insurer efforts, especially when it is clear that insurers seek the materials not for the legitimate purpose of investigating the claim but instead to defeat coverage or defend against a coverage action brought by the insured.

The Insurer's Predispute Checklist

On receiving an insured's notice of loss, insurers must take some basic steps as well, long before any potential dispute with the policyholder emerges. These include some of the same steps outlined previously: that is, to retain counsel, experts, and/or independent adjusters, to monitor communications to ensure that careless but substantively important nonprivileged communications are not being made, to calendar key dates, and to exhaust informal dispute resolution alternatives. In addition, insurers generally should consider the following issues.

Evaluate Coverage Obligations

Like the policyholder, the insurer should evaluate its coverage obligations after a loss to understand its potential obligations. What are the limits? What are the deductibles, retentions, and/or underlying limits? Does the policy also obligate the insurer to provide third-party liability coverage in any circumstances? If so, does the insurer have a duty to provide a defense against third-party claims? Does the policy contain nonstandard provisions that make this coverage broader than normal? Or more restrictive? In short, the claims person with lead responsibility for the claim should not make assumptions about what the policy provides. Neither should she completely delegate that task to a third party like an independent adjuster or outside counsel. Instead, she should take the time to understand the specific policy terms. Even policies issued by the same insurer can contain material variations by virtue of manuscripted terms, use of endorsements, and the use of different policy forms. Policies can also vary due to other reasons, such as inclusion of follow-form provisions that subject one insurer to terms contained in another insurer's policy. It is often advisable to request a copy of the policy from the insured to make sure that both the insurer and policyholder are evaluating the claim under an agreed policy form.

Reserve Rights

When a claim is tendered to the insurer, that insurer generally has a legal obligation to make a coverage determination (*i.e.*, to accept or deny coverage) within a reasonable period of time. In some jurisdictions, an insurer who merely reserves its rights will be deemed to have waived any coverage defenses that are not expressly reserved in writing after a loss. Thus, an insurer should ensure that its postloss response does not result in an inadvertent waiver of coverage defenses.

Be Responsive to the Policyholder

When a loss occurs, one of the insurer's primary concerns should be the welfare of the policyholder. This is not only a rational business approach (after all, the policyholder is the customer); it is required under the law. Specifically, insurers generally have duties to conduct their loss investigation in good faith and to elevate their policyholder's interests above their own. In some jurisdictions, insurers are even considered to be fiduciaries of their policyholders, meaning they owe duties of *utmost loyalty* to their policyholders. A breach of such duties—for instance, by taking some action that is harmful to their policyholder—can in some circumstances expose the insurer to compensatory and punitive damages. An insurer therefore should never conduct its investigation in a manner designed to minimize a claim, harm the policyholder's interests, or otherwise subordinate the interests of the policyholder beneath the insurers' self-interest. A fair, objective review of the facts, policy terms, and applicable law is not only required but is in everyone's best interest. Moreover, responsiveness to the needs of the policyholder often will reduce the prospects for disputes and litigation by increasing the likelihood that the claim can be resolved amicably. This does not mean, of course, that an insurer cannot take reasonable and appropriate steps to protect its own interests, including litigation of disputes over the existence or amount of coverage with a policyholder. However, such actions must be taken with good-faith obligations in mind.

Evaluate Subrogation

Once an insurer pays a loss on behalf of its insured, it might have a right to proceed against the party that the policyholder (or the insurer) believes is legally responsible for the loss. This is called subrogation. A subrogating insurer steps into the shoes of the policyholder and may assert its legal rights with respect to any claims the policyholder might have against parties who may have contributed to the loss. Most property policies contain subrogation provisions detailing the parties' rights and obligations in the subrogation context. Many policies, however, permit the policyholder to waive the insurer's right to subrogation before loss. Often, if a third party is deemed to be at fault, the insurer will subrogate—and that action will provide the policyholder with the opportunity to collect additional funds, such as the deductible and other uninsured losses, splitting any recovery with the insurer.

When the Parties Cannot Amicably Resolve the Claim

Policyholders and insurers will at times disagree about the existence and scope of coverage and/or the calculation of the loss. Frequently disputed issues include whether the policyholder is an insured under the policy, whether certain aspects of the loss fall within the insuring agreements of the policy, whether specific exclusions apply to some or all of the loss, whether the insured has complied with policy conditions, and whether the claimed losses have been properly quantified.

When the parties cannot agree on the policyholder's insurance claim, one or more mechanisms may be required to help resolve the dispute. Typical options of dispute resolution are state or federal court litigation, appraisal, arbitration, mediation, and negotiation (the latter three often referred to as alternative dispute resolution or ADR). Often, policy language will mandate an approach to resolving disputes, including appraisal, litigation in a specific court, binding arbitration after nonbinding mediation, and/or litigation in a court after nonbinding mediation. Unless these requirements are waived or postponed by mutual agreement, the policy may constrain the parties' options. Moreover, some of these options are not necessarily mutually exclusive. It is not unusual for parties for enter into nonbinding mediation during the course of formal litigation; neither is it unusual for parties to submit a matter to arbitration after litigating in state or federal court for some time. Often, too, in the first-party insurance context, the parties continue to negotiate certain aspects of the insurance claim—in effect, continuing to adjust the loss—while specific issues are being litigated.

A brief summary of the four primary dispute resolution approaches follows.

Traditional Litigation

The traditional forum for dispute resolution is a court of law. Roughly speaking, a judge presides over court proceedings; the parties are permitted to obtain information from each other according to specific rules, as part of the discovery process; and parties may attempt to win the case prior to trial based on technical or legal arguments. If the matter proceeds to trial, lawyers present evidence and make arguments, a judge or jury reaches a decision on the merits of the dispute, and the losing party may appeal to a higher court if they so choose. In the United States, when policyholders and insurers take their disputes to court, they end up in either state court, which is part of a particular state's judicial system, or a federal court, which is part of the United States' federal judiciary. Some important aspects of federal and state court litigation include the following:

Federal Court Versus State Court

United States federal courts may have jurisdiction over the subject matter of a dispute if the legal issues presented involve a federal question or if there is diversity of citizenship between the parties in the suit. Federal question jurisdiction refers to actions arising under the constitution, laws, or treaties of the United States and involving a minimum dollar amount. Diversity of citizenship jurisdiction refers to cases involving citizens of different states; in broad terms, this requires that each party on one side of the case be a citizen of a state different from each party on the opposing side. Most insurance disputes are of the latter variety; they usually do not raise federal questions.

State courts determine jurisdiction based on the type of proceeding involved and the amount in controversy. To bring a claim in a particular state court, the plaintiff must satisfy the statutory requirements, which differ from state to state. Therefore, it is important to consult the local rules and statutes before deciding where to file a complaint. In addition to having jurisdiction over the subject matter of a suit, a plaintiff must satisfy the courts' requirements of personal jurisdiction and venue. Personal jurisdiction refers to the power of the court to decide a case with respect to a particular individual. Whether a court has properly obtained personal jurisdiction over a defendant is governed by the federal constitution and statutes, state constitution and statutes, and court rules. Although it is not practicable to explain the principles of personal jurisdiction completely here, in general a defendant must have a sufficiently close nexus to the forum in which the court sits to be subject to the jurisdiction of that court. What constitutes a sufficient nexus depends on the facts and circumstances of each case and is informed by a large body of federal and state case law. Venue refers to the specific location of the courthouse. Generally, even where jurisdiction is proper, a plaintiff must still choose a court that has some relationship to the events that happened in the case or where a defendant is located or may be found. Again, venue is controlled by both statute and court rule.

Applicable Law

Given the dual federal and state governmental systems in the United States, it is not always immediately apparent precisely which law will apply in a given case. For cases governed by state law, as most insurance coverage cases are, a question of which state's law applies often arises. In the event of disputes involving non-U.S. entities and losses, the question can even arise about which country's law applies. Deciding which law applies in a given situation is not a merely academic exercise; it is often dispositive of the matter, since the law that determines the outcome on an important issue might differ from state to state or country to country.

For example, suppose a policyholder is headquartered in Michigan and has seven insurers variously headquartered in Maryland, Connecticut, New York, Florida, London, Bermuda, and Switzerland. What state's law will apply to business interruption claims if a catastrophic event damages a supplier's facility in California—and the damage to the supplier's property adversely affects the policyholder's operations in Oregon, Arizona, Maine, and Hawaii? To resolve questions like these, courts have evolved a doctrine known as the law of conflicts of laws, which involves an often-complex analysis of the facts and circumstances of the case. Moreover, in the United States, each state has its own rules for determining which law to apply to a given dispute brought in one of its courts. Therefore, it may be very difficult to determine precisely which law will apply until the matter ends up in a court and the judge decides the choice of law issue. For just this reason, parties often include choice of law provisions in their insurance contracts, specifying that when a dispute arises out of the contract, the parties agree that the law of a specific jurisdiction governs the dispute.

Discovery

As noted previously, discovery is the mechanism by which parties to a litigation exchange information in their possession, custody, or control that is relevant to the issues to be decided. In discovery, parties can demand from one another documents, written answers to written questions (called interrogatories), depositions of employees as well as the organization itself (called a corporate designee deposition or "30(b)(6)" deposition, referring to the federal rule that authorizes such depositions), and other information. Under certain circumstances, discovery can be extended to third parties. Federal court rules, and most state court systems, provide for very broad discovery, to allow both sides to a dispute to marshal the evidence they believe they need to litigate the matter. While this broad policy is beneficial to parties in that it reduces surprise in litigation, it can also be expensive. In a large insurance coverage dispute, gathering documents and data, answering interrogatories, and preparing for and attending depositions can run into the hundreds of thousands (or even millions) of dollars and place significant strain on employees' time.

While discovery rules can be broad, they are not unlimited. In some cases, a party may seek to take discovery beyond permissible limits. For example, parties generally are not allowed to obtain from their adversary information that is protected by some privilege or information that is not relevant or even reasonably calculated to lead to the discovery of admissible evidence. Moreover, when discovery becomes burdensome, harassing, or overbearing, the party to whom the discovery is directed may seek relief from the court in the form of a protective order. Discovery in a large, complex case can last for months, even years.

Motions

Motions practice, which may begin as soon as a complaint is filed and served, is an important part of any large-scale, complex litigation including insurance coverage disputes. Motions are the mechanism by which a party asks a court to take some action by issuing an order. In the early stages of a litigation, parties may bring motions to dismiss the complaint on various grounds. These can include lack of jurisdiction, a failure to properly serve the complaint, or a failure to state a legally cognizable claim in the complaint. Further motions can ask to strike portions of the complaint or answer or for temporary restraining orders and preliminary injunctions that either prevent the other side from taking some action or compel them to take some action during the lawsuit. During discovery, parties may bring motions to compel responses to discovery requests or motions to quash discovery demands or limit their scope. After discovery ends, parties often bring motions for summary judgment, which ask the judge to resolve the matter before trial on the grounds that no material facts are in dispute and that the material facts are such that judgment can be granted by the court as a matter of law. Prior to and during trial, parties may bring motions *in limine*, which seek to limit the types or amount of evidence that the other side may introduce during trial. During trial, parties may also file motions for directed verdict, which ask the court to resolve the matter prior to sending it to the jury for decision. After trial, parties may file motions for new trial or judgment notwithstanding the verdict.

Trial

Both federal and state courts use the trial system to determine contested facts and apply the appropriate law to those facts to reach a final judgment. Parties can choose either a jury or a judge trial. In the former, the parties can interview potential jurors, in the process called *voir dire*, and strike certain of them from the jury panel if they determine bias or other reasons for disqualification. During trial, the parties each present their evidence, typically as testimony from witnesses and by introducing documents and other evidence. Complex rules govern the introduction of both testamentary and tangible evidence in a trial, although those rules may be somewhat relaxed in a trial by a judge as opposed to a trial by jury. Each party also has the opportunity to object to the evidence offered by the other side and may file motions *in limine*. The plaintiff bears the burden of proving its claims; failure to do so results in a judgment for the defendant. Under most circumstances in a civil matter, the plaintiff must prove its claims only by a preponderance of the evidence, which usually is interpreted to mean that it is more likely than not that the allegations are true. More stringent burdens of proof may apply in certain unique circumstances.

Trials in large insurance coverage matters may be very complex, involving the testimony of multiple witnesses—including witnesses called to testify to facts of the case as well as expert witnesses called to render professional opinions. Such trials can last for many weeks or even months. If a complex insurance case involves multiple losses or multiple sites, the court may order an initial trial on test sites, so that results of the test case can hopefully be applied to the balance of the coverage dispute.

Appeals

Once all posttrial motions are resolved and the court enters a judgment, either side may appeal all or part of the judgment. There are specific (and typically short) time limits within which an appeal must be sought after entry of judgment. On appeal, parties often have only a limited ability to dispute a jury's (or judge's) factual findings. Appeals, however, generally are available to remedy errors of law that either tainted the trial process or simply resulted in an incorrect outcome—that is, had the law been properly interpreted and applied, the result would have been different. A litigant generally may appeal once as of right (in the federal court system to a Circuit Court of Appeals and in state systems to intermediate appellate courts). Appeals beyond that are usually only discretionary. For example, very few appeals are allowed to the Supreme Court of the United States as of right. Rather, parties must petition the Supreme Court to hear an appeal. The vast majority of such petitions are denied, so that—in the federal system—the Circuit Court of Appeals is effectively the parties' last chance to change a result determined in a lower court. With few exceptions, the U.S. Supreme Court only hears cases involving federal questions, and therefore such an appellate step is rarely available for most insurance law disputes.

Arbitration

Arbitration is the most traditional form of alternative dispute resolution, where the parties present their case to one or more persons designated to resolve the dispute. Many arbitrations follow rules prescribed by the American Arbitration Association (AAA). Federal and state statutes also govern specific aspects of an arbitration, such as the method for choosing arbitrators and the appropriate way to have the courts confirm or vacate an arbitration award. For example, the Federal Arbitration Act, 9 U.S.C. §§ 1 *et seq.*, provides for the enforceability of arbitration clauses in contracts involving interstate commerce. It includes procedures for the appointment of arbitrators by the court in those cases where the underlying contract fails to provide such a procedure or where the contract's specified procedure for choosing an arbitrator fails to work. Similarly, various state arbitration acts vest the state courts with the power to confirm and enforce arbitration awards arising from arbitration and specify procedures that parties must follow to have these awards enforced. Some of the key characteristics of arbitration include the following:

Trial before One or More Arbitrators/No Jury

Arbitrations are akin to bench trials in a traditional court of law, in which the judge—without a jury—serves as the sole arbiter of the dispute. In an arbitration, one or more persons acting as judges fulfill that same function: they make factual findings, rule on motions, and ultimately deliver rulings and an award. In an arbitration, the litigants generally can select their arbitrator and often agree on a person (or persons) with expertise in the particular field concerning the dispute. A typical approach is for each side to the dispute to select one arbitrator (often referred to as party arbitrators), and then the party arbitrators select a third arbitrator (often called the neutral arbitrator) as the chairperson. Arbitrators often charge the parties an hourly or daily fee for their services.

Flexible and Limited Discovery, Evidentiary and Motion Rules

Arbitrations generally are conducted similarly to court litigation, although pretrial and trial procedures (including discovery, motion practice, and rules of evidence) may be relaxed or modified in some respects. Under the complex rules of the American Arbitration Association for commercial arbitration, for example, parties may introduce any evidence that is "relevant and material to the dispute," and arbitrators are expressly *not* required to conform their evidentiary rulings to legal rules of evidence. Similarly, under the AAA rules, arbitrators have wide discretion in how they choose to conduct the proceedings, as long as the parties are treated with equality, have the right to be heard, and have a fair opportunity to present their case. Under the Uniform Arbitration Act, adopted in one form or another by the majority of states, the scope of discovery may be limited by the Act's express goal of making the proceedings expeditious and cost-effective. Thus, extensive discovery and depositions may be discouraged, depending on what rules apply in a given arbitration.

Limited Grounds for Appeal

Arbitrations may be nonbinding—in which case any party not satisfied with the result may opt out of the arbitration process and seek a trial *de novo*. This means they start all over again in the court system without regard to what happened in the arbitration hearing. Arbitrations can also be binding—in which case their rulings are generally final and enforceable in a court of law. Under the laws of many states, and under federal law, a binding arbitration decision may be reversed only on specific and limited grounds, such as a showing of arbitrator bias, corruption, or fraud, or a showing that the arbitrators completely failed to follow the substantive law applicable to the dispute.

Confidentiality

Arbitrations are often conducted in a manner that avoids the publicity inherent in a civil action. Indeed, under the rules of the AAA, arbitrators are required to maintain the privacy of arbitration hearings unless applicable law prevents them from doing so. The AAA's Code of Ethics for arbitrators further requires arbitrators to keep confidential all matters relating to the proceedings and to the arbitrator's decision. Under the Uniform Arbitration Act, an arbitrator may issue a protective order preventing disclosure of confidential or privileged information by any party.

Resolutions Are Often Reached More Quickly

For several reasons, decisions are often reached more quickly than in a traditional court. First, arbitrators are not often burdened with the same overwhelming caseload with which many trial court judges must contend. Second, arbitrators often are amenable to general case streamlining, including restrictions on the amount of discovery, accelerated pretrial motion schedules, and limitations on the time allotted for trial. Third, arbitrators often are required by the applicable rules to issue a decision within a specified time (such as thirty days after trial). Lastly, the parties in arbitration may have only limited grounds for an appeal, whereas in the traditional court system, appeal and postappeal activity can add years to a dispute.

Appraisal

Most property policies allow either the insurer or the policyholder to demand an appraisal if they cannot agree on the cash value of the amount of loss. The appraisal process generally is not intended to encompass disputed issues other than the *amount* of loss. In other words, an insurer's defenses to coverage (such as the application of an exclusion) are not subject to appraisal. Many policies contain detailed terms regarding the appraisal process.

For example, under most policies, each party has the right to appoint a competent and disinterested appraiser. Questions sometimes arise regarding whether an individual nominated by a party is truly "disinterested," such as an appraiser who has had previous business relations with the nominating party; an insurer-nominated appraiser who has previously held similar positions for many insurers, including the nominating insurer, but no policyholders; or even an appraiser previously retained by one of the parties to make computations on the very claim at issue. Courts faced with such issues often affirm the appointment of such an appraiser absent evidence of prejudicial misconduct or some indication that the appraiser is under the direction and control of the nominating party.

The two appraisers then may jointly select a disinterested umpire to resolve dis-agreements between them; many policies provide that a judge may select the umpire if the appraisers cannot agree on one. The appraisers may then make an award in writing that determines the amount of loss. Such an award often follows an evidentiary hearing, perhaps following a request for such a hearing by one or both parties. The policy generally will not specify the nature and applicable proce-dures for such hearings, and they are often rather informal. A court generally will not set an award aside unless it is tainted by fraud, collusion, or impartiality. Policies also often provide that each appraiser shall be paid by the party selecting her, and the expense of the appraisal and umpire are paid by the parties equally.

Whether to demand appraisal often raises strategic considerations that turn on the circumstances and applicable law. In many instances, both parties may agree that an appraisal is the quickest and most cost-effective way to resolve a dispute concerning the amount of covered loss. A party that believes it has relatively weak arguments on valuation may conclude that appraisal will provide an opportunity to obtain a better outcome than it could achieve through litigation or negotiation, on the (not always correct) assumption that an appraisal is likely to result in a split-the-baby outcome. A more difficult question is whether appraisal is appropriate when the parties' dispute extends beyond the amount of loss or when the insurer has yet to agree to provide coverage subject to final valuation of the loss. At a min-imum, an appraisal in such a context raises the possibility that nonvaluation issues could be inserted into the valuation process; that the insurer could use the apprais-al proceeding as a means of developing evidence for use in connection with a later dispute on coverage issues; or that the insurer is simply interested in wearing down the policyholder, in the hope of securing a favorable settlement by utilizing multi-ple dispute resolution tools. Such a strategy could raise questions concerning the insurer's good faith. Moreover, the applicable law could have a bearing on whether the parties can be compelled to appraise on demand of the other and the conse-quences, if any, of withdrawing from an appraisal once it is initiated (including potential loss of the right to maintain a suit on the policy).

Although often compared to arbitration, appraisal differs in many respects. Appraisal is often less formal, and it is far less like traditional litigation than is arbi-tration. Also, it is by definition limited in scope because it encompasses only the amount of loss, while arbitration is not subject to any such limitation of the breadth of issues that may be raised and resolved. As one court noted, in distinguishing the two:

> Appraisement, in particular, is perhaps most often confused with arbitration. While some of the rules of law that apply to arbitration apply in the same manner to appraisement, and the

terms have at times been used interchangeably, there is a plain distinction between them. In the proper sense of the term, arbitration presupposes the existence of a dispute or controversy to be tried and determined in a quasi judicial manner, whereas appraisement is an agreed method of ascertaining value or amount of damage, stipulated in advance, generally as a mere auxiliary or incident feature of a contract, with the object of preventing future disputes, rather than of settling present ones. (*Hartford Fire Ins. Co. v. Jones,* 108 So. 2d 571, 572 (Miss. 1959) (internal quotations omitted)).

Mediation

Mediation differs from other forms of dispute resolution in that the parties, with the help of the mediator, generally have the freedom to explore a broad range of possible solutions. In mediation, a neutral third party—often jointly selected by the parties—generally facilitates candid discussion between the parties to help them settle their dispute. The mediator may be someone with relevant substantive expertise or simply someone with dispute resolution skills. In some jurisdictions, litigants must submit to mandatory, nonbinding mediation before trial. Frequently, however, parties who can resolve their disputes themselves resort to mediation voluntarily.

Though more formal than a settlement discussion, mediation is typically far less formal than traditional court litigation or arbitration and generally is not subject to formal procedural or evidentiary rules. Indeed, in a mediation, the parties are often allowed to make their own rules, and mediators themselves may impose their own unique rules. Moreover, unless the mediation proceeds pursuant to a court order, the parties generally may withdraw at any time.

Mediation also usually remains confidential to the parties involved. Communications between the parties (and with the mediator) are often protected settlement discussions, meaning that statements made and documents created for purposes of such settlement discussions typically are considered inadmissible in a formal litigation pursuant to evidentiary rules. Parties often enter into written agreements that make the confidential nature of the process explicit.

Mediation can be utilized at any point in the dispute resolution process, including after litigation has been instituted. A mediator may hear presentations, review written submissions, and tell each party what she thinks about the merits of their respective cases. However, as a general rule, the mediator's views are not binding in any way. Parties are generally free to structure a mediation in any way they want, including giving the mediator some power to issue a binding ruling, but that would be the exception rather than the norm.

Negotiation

Parties to a coverage dispute are always free to engage in settlement discussions, either face-to-face or through their representatives. Such discussions may encompass an entire insurance claim or only parts of a claim and can occur before or during litigation. Indeed, one of the unique aspects of disputes in the first-party insurance context is that insurers and policyholders can and often do adjust the claim with respect to issues on which there may ultimately be no disagreement or which may not readily lend themselves to formal adjudication. Such issues may include the measurement of the loss, which may be extremely complicated and expensive to litigate even if there are disagreements. Such adjustments can proceed even where the parties have disputes in litigation, such as an insurer's assertion that an exclusion applies to some part of the loss. It is not entirely uncommon for the first-party insurer and policyholder to work together on certain issues, while at the same time facing off as adversaries in litigation. Settlement negotiations are understood to be confidential, whereby the parties' settlement-related statements may not be used in any litigation, and this understanding is often documented in a written agreement.

Conclusion

The purchase of insurance should not be tantamount to the purchase of a lawsuit. When the policyholder claims what it is entitled to claim, and the insurer does not have a good-faith basis for disputing the claim, there is no reason why the insurer should not pay the claim promptly and without disagreement. Unfortunately, disputes—both large and small—often play a material role in the claims process, and policyholders and insurers must be ready for them by taking the right steps after a loss and ultimately by utilizing the dispute-resolution tools best suited to the circumstances. In all events, after a loss both policyholder and insurer should have in place the right team to ensure that their interests are fully protected, including the individuals who can guide them through the complexities of dispute resolution.

A Conversation with Dan Sobczynski

FORMER DIRECTOR OF CORPORATE INSURANCE

Ford Motor Company

This interview records a conversation between Dan Sobczynski, the retired Director of Corporate Insurance for Ford Motor Company, and David Barrett, an attorney at Latham & Watkins and a coauthor of this book. Dan is presently a risk management and insurance consultant and an adjunct instructor in risk management and insurance at Lawrence Technological University.

Sobczynski: Businesses own or lease property to produce a revenue stream. When the property is damaged or destroyed, that revenue stream is disrupted or additional expenses must be incurred to maintain that revenue. Using risk management techniques to maintain business income is equally important as protecting the physical assets—perhaps even more so. The ability of a business to survive a disastrous loss is contingent on restoring the physical assets and resuming and protecting the resultant revenue.

Question: What different factors might come into play, depending on the size or type of company?

Sobczynski: The issue a company faces is not whether it should protect its ability to generate revenue. That's a given. All businesses, from a single-location operation to a global enterprise, must be concerned about preserving their ability to maintain market presence and continue in operation. The core issue is to determine the best risk management techniques; and business interruption and extra expense insurance, in their many and various forms, are generally the best such techniques for protecting a company's ability to operate.

The essential difference between a small and large company's business interruption and extra expense loss exposure is the size of the absolute loss potential. The larger and more vertically integrated a company is, the greater the loss potential. Multitier supplier dependence, just-in-time inventory techniques, infrastructure dependence, and synchronized manufacturing processes increase the complexity and size of business interruption exposures. There are no "one-size-fits-all" answers with respect to business interruption and extra expense risk management, other than that these exposures must be professionally and thoughtfully addressed.

Question: Can you describe generally the role of an in-house risk management department on a large business interruption claim?

Sobczynski: If a large business interruption loss occurs, the risk manager—regardless of his or her education, experience, or training—is at an automatic disadvantage when dealing with the insurer's loss adjuster. Insurance adjusters handle business interruption losses for a living, whereas the risk manager may see one or two such losses during a career. The risk manager's role, then, is to level the playing field by assembling a team that has knowledge comparable to that of the insurer's team of loss adjusters, accountants, and lawyers. The risk manager essentially becomes the project coordinator. Also, she or he must keep senior management apprised of the loss status and anticipated recoveries. Coordination and communication is as important internally as externally.

Question: Can you describe the different outside experts that a risk manager might turn to in the event of a large property or business interruption claim?

Sobczynski: Again, there are no simple or cookie-cutter answers. The risk manager must carefully analyze the loss to determine what outside assistance is necessary. An insurance broker will help communicate with insurers and manage those relationships. Accountants assist in expense tracking and claim preparation. The adjuster should welcome the presence of the insured's outside accounting experts precisely because of their additional expertise. All insurance policies are legal contracts that require competent and experienced insurance counsel. Loss causation experts may be necessary because of regulatory issues or state inquiries. Insurance consultants familiar with insurance policy wordings and industry practices can also add value.

Question: How about the role of in-house counsel in connection with significant insurance claims?

Sobczynski: A large loss will typically interest senior management, including the Board of Directors. In-house counsel is an excellent resource for legal guidance and also helps maintain the attorney-client privilege for intracompany communications. In-house counsel can also assess the need for outside legal assistance.

Question: Should a company assume the insurer will understand its business? Or should company personnel spend time educating insurers about its business?

Sobczynski: Because businesses are frequently unique, the insured should not assume that their insurer's adjuster fully understands its business. The insurer's underwriter may understand the business, but the risk manager cannot assume that the loss adjuster has the same knowledge. After a loss, then, the insured has the obligation to prove its loss, educating and informing the insurer so the latter understands those aspects of the business that affect how the insurer will measure the loss.

Question: How important is it to establish a timetable during a claims adjustment process, and what obstacles may arise in trying to achieve your goals and deadlines?

Sobczynski: Most insurance policies have strict time bars that must be observed to avoid potentially prejudicing a claim under the policy. Policies differ, but typical time bars include notice of loss, filing proof of loss, and the filing of any lawsuit. Timetables and milestones are critical from both a legal and business perspective. Depending on circumstances, the insured may not receive any compensation for interest between the time of loss and the claim payment. The insured's goal is to expedite the claim payment while the insurer's goal may be the opposite.

Question: What other advice would you give to risk managers at small or large companies following a significant business interruption loss?

Sobczynski: Adjusting a complex business interruption or extra expense loss is a team sport—and you have to build a team with experienced, high-skill players. A risk manager who plays alone is frequently overmatched when compared to the insurance company adjuster and other insurer resources. Insurers recognize that significant money is at stake; so should the risk manager.

Question: What advice would you give to risk managers regarding how best to handle or manage the expectations of upper management after a large loss?

Sobczynski: I'm an advocate of telling the truth—and that goes for approaching senior management. Because the dollar amounts are large, the process can quickly become adversarial and expensive. The risk manager must inform senior management that the process is not easy and frequently not quick.

Question: What unanticipated surprises can arise in dealing with a large claim?

Sobczynski: Large losses frequently arise when several events with a low probability of occurring do occur simultaneously. Similarly, unexpected events can occur during the loss process. The methods to reduce these unexpected events are organization, planning, control, and execution. Again, there are no easy, quick answers. Large, complex losses result in difficult loss adjustments.

A P P E N D I X

MUTUAL CORPORATION
NON-ASSESSABLE POLICY

Factory Mutual Insurance Company
P.O. Box 7500
Johnston, Rhode Island 02919
1-800-343-7722

DECLARATIONS

Policy No.	Previous Policy No.	DATE OF ISSUE
Account No.	Replaces Binder No.	

In consideration of this Policy's Provisions, Conditions, Stipulations, Exclusions and Limits of Liability, and of premium charged, Factory Mutual Insurance Company, hereafter referred to as the Company, does insure:

INSURED:

[Type Insured's Name]

(For Complete Title See Policy)

The term of this Policy is from the　　　day of [month and year] to the　　　day of [month and year] at 12:01 a.m., Standard Time, at the Locations of property involved as provided in this Policy.

This Policy covers property, as described in this Policy, against ALL RISKS OF PHYSICAL LOSS OR DAMAGE, except as hereinafter excluded, while located as described in this Policy.

By virtue of this Policy and any other policies purchased from the Company being in force, the Insured becomes a member of the Company, subject to the provisions of its charter and by-laws, and is entitled to one vote either in person or by proxy at any and all meetings of said Company.

Assignment of this Policy will not be valid except with the written consent of the Company.

This Policy is made and accepted subject to the above provisions and those hereinafter stated, which are made a part of this Policy, together with such other provisions and agreements as may be added to this Policy.

In Witness, this Company has issued this Policy at its office in the city of Johnston, R. I.
this　　　day of [month and year]

_____
Authorized Signature

Countersigned (if required) this　　　day of　　　　_____
　　　Agent

Printed in U.S.A.

TABLE OF CONTENTS
(Order In Which They Appear)   Page No.

Account No.
Policy No.

TABLE OF CONTENTS
(Order In Which They Appear)

Page No.

TABLE OF CONTENTS
(Order In Which They Appear)

Page No.

DECLARATIONS - SECTION A

1. **NAMED INSURED AND MAILING ADDRESS**

   <Fill-In Insured's full name>
   <Fill-In Corporate Address>
   <Fill-In City, State>

2. **POLICY DATES**

FROM:	<Fill-In>
TO:	<Fill-In>
TERM:	<Fill-In>

3. **TERRITORY**

   This Policy covers Insured Locations worldwide except for loss or damage in the following countries:

   <Fill-In appropriate countries>,

   or any other country where trade relations are unlawful as determined by the Government of the United States of America or its agencies.

4. **INSURED LOCATION**

   A. The coverages under this Policy apply to an Insured Location unless otherwise provided.

      Insured Location is a location:

      <Fill-In - select what applies per the following list

      1) scheduled on this Policy.

      1) listed on a Schedule of Locations attached to this Policy.

      1) listed on a Schedule of Locations on file with the Company.

      2) covered as a Miscellaneous Unnamed Location.

      3) covered under the terms and conditions of the Automatic Coverage or Errors and Omissions provisions.>

   B. References and Application. The following term(s) wherever used in this Policy means:

      1) Location:

a) as specified in the schedule of locations, except for Miscellaneous Unnamed Locations; or

b) if not so specified or if a Miscellaneous Unnamed Location, a building, yard, dock, wharf, pier or bulkhead (or any group of the foregoing) bounded on all sides by public streets, clear land space or open waterways, each not less than fifty feet wide. Any bridge or tunnel crossing such street, space or waterway will render such separation inoperative for the purpose of this References and Application.

<C. Schedule of Locations are:<to be used only with A.1 scheduled on this Policy>

5.   CURRENCY

All amounts, including deductibles and limits of liability, indicated in this Policy are in the currency of the United States of America, except for Insured Locations in Canada where such amounts will be in Canadian currency. Losses will be adjusted and paid as provided in the CURRENCY FOR LOSS PAYMENT clause of the LOSS ADJUSTMENT AND SETTLEMENT section.

Premium for this Policy is in the currency of the United States of America except for the premium applying for Insured Locations in Canada where such amounts will be in Canadian currency.

6.   LIMITS OF LIABILITY

The Company's maximum limit of liability in a single occurrence regardless of the number of Locations or coverages involved will not exceed the Policy limit of liability of $<Fill-In>, except as follows. When a limit of liability for a Location or other specified property is shown, such limit will be the maximum amount payable for any loss or damage arising from physical loss or damage at such Location or involving such other specified property.

If a lesser limit of liability is stated below or elsewhere in this Policy, the lesser limit will apply. The limits of liability stated below or elsewhere in this Policy are part of and not in addition to the Policy limit of liability.

Limits of liability stated below apply in the aggregate per occurrence for all Locations and coverages involved.

When a limit of liability is shown as applying in the Aggregate During Any Policy Year, the Company's maximum limit of liability will not exceed such limit during any policy year regardless of the number of locations, coverages or occurrences involved.

In the event an occurrence results in liability payable under more than one policy issued to the Named Insured by the Company, or its representative companies, the maximum amount payable in the aggregate under all such policies will be the applicable limit(s) of liability indicated in this Policy regardless of the number of coverages, locations or perils involved.

Limits of Liability

$<Fill-In>:   <Fill-In>

Time Limits

In addition to the time limits shown elsewhere in this Policy, the following apply:

<Fill-In> day period but not to exceed a $$<Fill-In> limit:	AUTOMATIC COVERAGE
<Fill-In> day period but not to exceed a $$<Fill-In> limit:	INGRESS/EGRESS
<Fill-In> day period:	EXTENDED PERIOD OF LIABILITY
12 month period:	GROSS PROFIT
12 month period:	TIME ELEMENT loss as respects TERRORISM and NON CERTIFIED ACT OF TERRORISM combined

This Time Limit for TERRORISM coverage and NON CERTIFIED ACT OF TERRORISM shall not be considered additive to any other Time Limits or to any PERIOD OF LIABILITY applying to any coverage provided in the TIME ELEMENT section, and shall be subject to the limit of liability for TERRORISM and NON CERTIFIED ACT OF TERRORISM.

7. **PREMIUM**

This Policy is issued in consideration of an initial premium. If the term of this Policy is longer than one year, for each subsequent year of coverage, premium will be due at the anniversary and will be subject to rules and rates in effect at that time.

8. **PREMIUM PAYABLE**

<Fill-In Name of party paying the premium> pays the premium under this Policy, and any return of the paid premium accruing under this Policy will be paid to the account of <Fill-In same name as above>.

9. **VALUE REPORTING PROVISIONS**

The Insured will provide the Company 100% values by location.

These statement(s) of values are due on the date(s) shown below.

Values as Of	Due Date	Type of Values
<Fill-In date>	<Fill-In date>	Property values in accordance with the VALUATION clause of the LOSS ADJUSTMENT AND SETTLEMENT section.

<Fill-In date>	<Fill-In date>	In addition, Stock and Supplies on the average and maximum values based on the previous 12 month period.
<Fill-In date>	<Fill-In date>	Time Element values anticipated for the 12 months following the "Value as Of" date, and the actual Time Element values for the previous 12 month period.

10. WAITING PERIOD

For the purposes of applying SERVICE INTERRUPTION Coverage, the Waiting Period is <Fill-In>.

For the purposes of applying DATA, PROGRAMS OR SOFTWARE Coverage when the loss or damage is caused by the malicious introduction of a machine code or instruction, the Waiting Period is 48 hours.

11. DEDUCTIBLES

In each case of loss covered by this Policy, the Company will be liable only if the Insured sustains a loss in a single occurrence greater than the applicable deductible specified below, and only for its share of that greater amount.

Unless otherwise stated below:

A.   When this Policy insures more than one location, the deductible will apply against the total loss covered by this Policy in any one occurrence.

B.   If two or more deductibles provided in this Policy apply to a single occurrence, the total to be deducted will not exceed the largest deductible applicable, unless otherwise provided.

Policy Deductible(s)

$<Fill-In> combined all coverages, except as follows.

Exceptions to Policy Deductible(s)

<Fill-In>

References and Application. The following term(s) means:

◇   Day Equivalent:

An amount equivalent to the number of days stated times the 100% daily Time Element value that would have been earned following the occurrence at the Location where the physical damage occurred and all other Locations where TIME ELEMENT loss ensues.

Account No.
Policy No.

PROPERTY DAMAGE - SECTION B

1. PROPERTY INSURED

This Policy insures the following property, unless otherwise excluded elsewhere in this Policy, located at an Insured Location or within 1,000 feet thereof, to the extent of the interest of the Insured in such property.

A. Real Property, including new buildings and additions under construction at an Insured Location, in which the Insured has an insurable interest.

B. Personal Property:

1) owned by the Insured, including the Insured's interest as a tenant in improvements and betterments. In the event of physical loss or damage, the Company agrees to accept and consider the Insured as sole and unconditional owner of improvements and betterments, notwithstanding any contract or lease to the contrary.

2) of officers and employees of the Insured.

3) of others in the Insured's custody to the extent the Insured is under obligation to keep insured for physical loss or damage insured by this Policy.

4) of others in the Insured's custody to the extent of the Insured's legal liability for physical loss or damage to Personal Property. The Company will defend that portion of any suit against the Insured that alleges such liability and seeks damages for such insured physical loss or damage. The Company may, without prejudice, investigate, negotiate and settle any claim or suit as the Company deems expedient.

This Policy also insures the interest of contractors and subcontractors in insured property during construction at an Insured Location or within 1,000 feet thereof, to the extent of the Insured's legal liability for insured physical loss or damage to such property. Such interest of contractors and subcontractors is limited to the property for which they have been hired to perform work and such interest will not extend to any TIME ELEMENT coverage provided under this Policy.

2. PROPERTY EXCLUDED

This Policy excludes:

A. currency, money, precious metal in bullion form, notes, or securities.

B. land, water or any other substance in or on land; except this exclusion does not apply to:

1) land improvements consisting of landscape gardening, roadways and pavements, but not including any fill or land beneath such property.

2) water that is contained within any enclosed tank, piping system or any other processing equipment.

C.   animals, standing timber, growing crops.

D.   watercraft or aircraft, except when unfueled and manufactured by the Insured.

E.   vehicles of officers and employees of the Insured or vehicles otherwise insured for physical loss or damage.

F.   underground mines or mine shafts or any property within such mine or shaft.

G.   dams and dikes.

H.   property in transit, except as otherwise provided by this Policy.

I.   property sold by the Insured under conditional sale, trust agreement, installment plan or other deferred payment plan after delivery to customers, except as provided by the DEFERRED PAYMENTS coverage of this Policy.

J.   electronic data, programs and software, except when they are stock in process, finished goods manufactured by the Insured, raw materials, supplies or other merchandise not manufactured by the Insured or as otherwise provided by the DATA, PROGRAMS OR SOFTWARE coverage of this Policy.

3.   ADDITIONAL COVERAGES

This Policy includes the following Additional Coverages for physical loss or damage insured by this Policy.

These Additional Coverages:

1)   are subject to the applicable limit of liability;

2)   will not increase the Policy limit of liability; and

3)   are subject to the Policy provisions, including applicable exclusions and deductibles,

all as shown in this section and elsewhere in this Policy.

A.   ACCOUNTS RECEIVABLE

This Policy covers any shortage in the collection of accounts receivable, resulting from insured physical loss or damage to accounts receivable records, including accounts receivable records stored as electronic data, while anywhere within this Policy's TERRITORY, including while in transit. The Company will be liable for the interest charges on any loan to offset impaired collections pending repayment of such sum uncollectible as the result of such loss or damage. Unearned interest and service charges on deferred payment accounts and normal credit losses on bad debts will be deducted in determining the recovery.

Account No.
Policy No.

1) In the event of loss to accounts receivable records, the Insured will use all reasonable efforts, including legal action, if necessary, to effect collection of outstanding accounts receivable.

2) The Insured agrees to use any suitable property or service:

   a) owned or controlled by the Insured; or

   b) obtainable from other sources,

   in reducing the loss under this Additional Coverage.

3) This Policy covers any other necessary and reasonable costs incurred to reduce the loss, to the extent the losses are reduced.

4) If it is possible to reconstruct accounts receivable records so that no shortage is sustained, the Company will be liable only for the reasonable and necessary cost incurred for material and time required to re-establish or reconstruct such records, and not for any costs covered by any other insurance.

5) ACCOUNTS RECEIVABLE Exclusions: The following exclusions are in addition to the EXCLUSIONS clause of this section:

   This Additional Coverage does not insure against shortage resulting from:

   a) bookkeeping, accounting or billing errors or omissions; or

   b) (i) alteration, falsification, manipulation; or

      (ii) concealment, destruction or disposal,

      of accounts receivable records committed to conceal the wrongful giving, taking, obtaining or withholding of money, securities or other property; but only to the extent of such wrongful giving, taking, obtaining or withholding.

6) The settlement of loss will be made within 90 days from the date of physical loss or damage. All amounts recovered by the Insured on outstanding accounts receivable on the date of loss will belong and be paid to the Company up to the amount of loss paid by the Company. All recoveries exceeding the amount paid will belong to the Insured.

B.   AUTOMATIC COVERAGE

This Policy covers insured property at any Location rented, leased or purchased by the Insured after the inception date of this Policy. This coverage applies from the date of rental, lease or purchase.

This Additional Coverage does not apply to property insured in whole or in part by any other insurance policy.

This coverage will apply until whichever of the following occurs first:

1) The Location is bound by the Company.

2) Agreement is reached that the Location will not be insured under this Policy.

3) The Time Limit shown in the LIMITS OF LIABILITY clause in the DECLARATIONS section has been reached. The Time Limit begins on the date of rental, lease or purchase.

C. BRANDS AND LABELS

If branded or labeled property insured by this Policy is physically damaged and the Company elects to take all or any part of that property, the Insured may at the Company's expense:

1) stamp "salvage" on the property or its containers; or

2) remove or obliterate the brands or labels,

if doing so will not damage the property. In either event, the Insured must relabel such property or its containers to be in compliance with any applicable law.

D. COINSURANCE DEFICIENCY AND CURRENCY DEVALUATION

This Policy covers the deficiency in the amount of loss payable under the Insured's locally written admitted primary and/or underlying policy(ies), if any, and its renewals, issued by the Company or its representatives, solely as the result of:

1) the application of a coinsurance (or average) clause; or

2) official government devaluation of the currency in which the local policy is written,

for physical loss or damage of the type insured under such local policy(ies) to property of the type insured under this Policy and not otherwise excluded by this Policy.

The Insured agrees to adjust the Policy values as a result of such devaluation within 30 days after the date of the currency's devaluation.

There is no liability under the terms of this coverage if the Insured is unable to recover any loss under such local policy(ies), and its renewals, if such inability is the result of intentional under insurance by the Insured.

E. CONSEQUENTIAL REDUCTION IN VALUE

This Policy covers the reduction in value of insured merchandise that is a part of pairs, sets, or components, directly resulting from physical loss or damage insured by this Policy to other insured parts of pairs, sets or components of such merchandise. If settlement is based on a constructive total loss, the Insured will surrender the undamaged parts of such merchandise to the Company.

F. CONTROL OF DAMAGED PROPERTY

This Policy gives control of physically damaged property consisting of <Fill-In> as follows:

1) The Insured will have full rights to the possession and control of damaged property in the event of insured physical damage to such property provided proper testing is done to show which property is physically damaged.

2) The Insured using reasonable judgment will decide if the physically damaged property can be reprocessed or sold.

3) Property so judged by the Insured to be unfit for reprocessing or selling will not be sold or disposed of except by the Insured, or with the Insured's consent.

4) Any salvage proceeds received will go to the:

   a) Company at the time of loss settlement; or

   b) Insured if received prior to loss settlement and such proceeds will reduce the amount of loss payable accordingly.

G. DATA, PROGRAMS OR SOFTWARE

This Policy covers insured Physical Loss Or Damage To Electronic Data, Programs Or Software, including physical loss or damage caused by the malicious introduction of a machine code or instruction, while anywhere within this Policy's TERRITORY, including while in transit.

1) With respect to Physical Loss Or Damage caused by the malicious introduction of machine code or instruction, this Additional Coverage will apply when the Period of Liability is in excess of the time shown as Waiting Period in the WAITING PERIOD clause of the DECLARATIONS section.

2) This Additional Coverage also covers the cost of the following reasonable and necessary actions taken by the Insured:

   a) Actions to temporarily protect and preserve insured electronic data, programs or software;

   b) Actions taken for the temporary repair of insured Physical Loss Or Damage To Electronic Data, Programs Or Software and to expedite the permanent repair or replacement of such damaged property,

provided such actions are taken due to actual insured Physical Loss Or Damage To Electronic Data, Programs Or Software.

3) This Additional Coverage also covers the reasonable and necessary costs incurred by the Insured to temporarily protect or preserve insured electronic data, programs or software against immediately impending insured Physical Loss Or Damage To Electronic Data, Programs Or Software. In the event that the physical loss or damage does not occur, the costs covered under this item 3 will be subject to the deductible that would have applied if the physical loss or damage had occurred.

4) Costs recoverable under this Additional Coverage are excluded from coverage elsewhere in this Policy.

5) This Additional Coverage excludes loss or damage to data, programs or software when they are stock in process, finished goods manufactured by the Insured, raw materials, supplies or other merchandise not manufactured by the Insured.

6) DATA, PROGRAMS OR SOFTWARE Exclusions: The exclusions in the EXCLUSIONS clause of this section do not apply to DATA, PROGRAMS OR SOFTWARE except for A1, A2, A6, B1, B2, B3a, B4 and B5. In addition as respects DATA, PROGRAMS OR SOFTWARE the following exclusions apply:

    This Policy does not insure:

    a) errors or omissions in processing, or copying; all unless physical damage not excluded by this Policy results, in which event, only that resulting damage is insured.

    b) loss or damage to data, programs or software from errors or omissions in programming or machine instructions; all unless physical damage not excluded by this Policy results, in which event, only that resulting damage is insured.

    c) deterioration, inherent vice, vermin or wear and tear; all unless physical damage not excluded by this Policy results, in which event, only that resulting damage is insured.

7) References and Application. The following term(s) means:

    a) Physical Loss Or Damage To Electronic Data, Programs Or Software:

        The destruction, distortion or corruption of electronic data, programs or software.

H.   DEBRIS REMOVAL

This Policy covers the reasonable and necessary costs incurred to remove debris from an Insured Location that remains as a direct result of physical loss or damage insured by this Policy.

This Additional Coverage does not cover the costs of removal of:

1) contaminated uninsured property; or

2) the contaminant in or on uninsured property,

whether or not the contamination results from insured physical loss or damage. Contamination includes, but is not limited to, the presence of pollution or hazardous material.

I.   DECONTAMINATION COSTS

If insured property is contaminated as a direct result of physical damage insured by this Policy and there is in force at the time of the loss any law or ordinance regulating contamination, including but not limited to the presence of pollution or hazardous material, then this Policy covers, as a direct result of enforcement of such law or ordinance, the increased cost of decontamination and/or removal of such contaminated insured property in a manner to satisfy such law or ordinance. This Additional Coverage applies only to that part of insured property so contaminated as a direct result of insured physical damage.

The Company is not liable for the costs required for removing contaminated uninsured property nor the contaminant therein or thereon, whether or not the contamination results from an insured event.

J.   DEFERRED PAYMENTS

This Policy covers insured physical loss or damage to Personal Property of the type insured sold by the Insured under a conditional sale or trust agreement or any installment or deferred payment plan and after such property has been delivered to the buyer. Coverage is limited to the unpaid balance for such property.

In the event of loss to property sold under deferred payment plans, the Insured will use all reasonable efforts, including legal action, if necessary, to effect collection of outstanding amounts due or to regain possession of the property.

There is no liability under this Policy for loss:

1) pertaining to products recalled including, but not limited to, the costs to recall, test or to advertise such recall by the Insured.

2) from theft or conversion by the buyer of the property after the buyer has taken possession of such property.

3) to the extent the buyer continues payments.

4) not within the TERRITORY of this Policy.

K.   DEMOLITION AND INCREASED COST OF CONSTRUCTION

1) This Policy covers the reasonable and necessary costs incurred, described in item 3 below, to satisfy the minimum requirements of the enforcement of any law or ordinance regulating the demolition, construction, repair, replacement or use of buildings or structures at an Insured Location, provided:

a) such law or ordinance is in force on the date of insured physical loss or damage; and

    b) its enforcement is a direct result of such insured physical loss or damage.

2) This Additional Coverage does not cover loss due to any law or ordinance with which the Insured was required to comply had the loss not occurred.

3) This Additional Coverage, as respects the property insured in item 1 above, covers:

    a) the cost to repair or rebuild the physically damaged portion of such property with materials and in a manner to satisfy such law or ordinance; and

    b) the cost:

        (i) to demolish the physically undamaged portion of such property insured; and

        (ii) to rebuild it with materials and in a manner to satisfy such law or ordinance,

    to the extent that such costs result when the demolition of the physically damaged insured property is required to satisfy such law or ordinance.

4) This Additional Coverage excludes any costs incurred as a direct or indirect result of enforcement of any laws or ordinances regulating any form of contamination including but not limited to the presence of pollution or hazardous material.

5) The Company's maximum liability for this Additional Coverage at each Insured Location in any occurrence will not exceed the actual cost incurred in demolishing the physically undamaged portion of the property insured in item 1 above plus the lesser of:

    a) the reasonable and necessary actual cost incurred, excluding the cost of land, in rebuilding on another site; or

    b) the cost of rebuilding on the same site.

L. DIFFERENCE IN CONDITIONS

This Policy is designated the Master Global Insuring Policy for Insured Locations under this Policy and which are insured under an underlying policy(ies) issued by the Company or its representative companies.

As respects such Insured Locations, this Policy covers:

1) the difference in definitions, perils, conditions or coverages between any underlying policy and this Policy.

2) the difference between the limit(s) of liability stated in any underlying policy and this Policy provided that:

a) the coverage is provided under this Policy;

b) the limit(s) of liability has been exhausted under the underlying policy, and

c) the deductible(s) applicable to such claim for loss or damage in the underlying policy has been applied.

Any coverage provided by the underlying policy that is not provided in this Policy does not extend to this Policy.

M.   EARTH MOVEMENT

This Policy covers physical loss or damage caused by or resulting from Earth Movement.

This Additional Coverage does not apply to loss or damage caused by or resulting from flood; surface waters; rising waters; waves; tide or tidal water; the release of water; the rising, overflowing or breaking of boundaries of natural or man-made bodies of water; or the spray therefrom; or sewer back-up resulting from any of the foregoing; all regardless of any other cause or event contributing concurrently or in any other sequence to the loss.

1) References and Application. The following term(s) wherever used in this Policy means:

a) Earth Movement:

Any natural or man-made earth movement including, but not limited to earthquake or landslide, regardless of any other cause or event contributing concurrently or in any other sequence of loss. However, physical damage by fire, explosion or sprinkler leakage resulting from Earth Movement will not be considered to be loss by Earth Movement within the terms and conditions of this Policy. All earth movements within a continuous 72 hour period will be considered a single Earth Movement.

b) High Hazard Zones for Earth Movement:

Property located in California, Hawaii, Alaska, the Commonwealth of Puerto Rico, Mexico, Japan <Fill-In – specifically describe any other high hazard areas>.

N.   ERRORS AND OMISSIONS

If physical loss or damage is not payable under this Policy solely due to an error or unintentional omission:

1) in the description of where insured property is physically located;

2) to include any Location:

a) owned, rented or leased by the Insured on the effective date of this Policy; or

b) purchased, rented or leased by the Insured during the term of this Policy; or

3) that results in cancellation of the property insured under this Policy;

this Policy covers such physical loss or damage, to the extent it would have provided coverage had such error or unintentional omission not been made.

It is a condition of this Additional Coverage that any error or unintentional omission be reported by the Insured to the Company when discovered and corrected.

O. EXPEDITING COSTS

This Policy covers the reasonable and necessary costs incurred to pay for the temporary repair of insured damage to insured property and to expedite the permanent repair or replacement of such damaged property.

This Additional Coverage does not cover costs:

1) recoverable elsewhere in this Policy; or

2) of permanent repair or replacement of damaged property.

P. FINE ARTS

This Policy covers insured physical loss or damage to Fine Arts articles while anywhere within this Policy's TERRITORY, including while in transit.

1) This Additional Coverage excludes loss or damage if the Fine Arts cannot be replaced with other of like kind and quality, unless it is specifically declared to the Company.

2) FINE ARTS Exclusion: The exclusions in the EXCLUSIONS clause of this section do not apply to FINE ARTS coverage except for A1, A2, A6, A7, B1, B2, B3a, B4, B5 and D4. In addition, as respects FINE ARTS, the following exclusions apply:

This Policy does not insure against:

a) deterioration, wear and tear or inherent vice.

b) loss or damage from any repairing, restoration or retouching process.

3) References and Application. The following term(s) wherever used in this Policy means:

a) Fine Arts:

Paintings; etchings; pictures; tapestries; rare or art glass; art glass windows; valuable rugs; statuary; sculptures; antique furniture; antique jewelry; bric-a-brac; porcelains; and similar property of rarity, historical value, or artistic merit excluding automobiles, coins, stamps, furs, jewelry, precious stones, precious metals, watercraft, aircraft, money, securities.

Account No.
Policy No.

Q. FLOOD

This Policy covers physical loss or damage caused by or resulting from Flood.

1) References and Application. The following term(s) wherever used in this Policy means:

   a) Flood:

   Flood; surface waters; rising waters; waves; tide or tidal water; the release of water, the rising, overflowing or breaking of boundaries of natural or man-made bodies of water; or the spray therefrom; or sewer back-up resulting from any of the foregoing; regardless of any other cause or event contributing concurrently or in any other sequence of loss. However, physical damage by fire, explosion or sprinkler leakage resulting from Flood is not considered to be loss by Flood within the terms and conditions of this Policy.

R. LAND AND WATER CONTAMINANT OR POLLUTANT CLEANUP, REMOVAL AND DISPOSAL

This Policy covers the reasonable and necessary cost for the cleanup, removal and disposal of contaminants or pollutants from uninsured property consisting of land, water or any other substance in or on land at the Insured Location if the release, discharge or dispersal of contaminants or pollutants is a direct result of insured physical loss or damage to insured property.

This Policy does not cover the cost to cleanup, remove and dispose of contaminants or pollutants from such property:

1) at any location insured for Personal Property only.

2) at any property insured under AUTOMATIC COVERAGE, ERRORS AND OMISSIONS or Miscellaneous Unnamed Location coverage provided by this Policy.

3) when the Insured fails to give written notice of loss to the Company within 180 days after inception of the loss.

S. NEIGHBOUR'S RECOURSE AND TENANT'S LIABILITY

Coverage under this provision is limited to Insured Locations within the following countries: France, the French Territories, Spain, Italy, Belgium, Greece, Portugal and Luxembourg.

This Policy covers the Insured's liability:

1) as a tenant or occupant under the articles of any civil or commercial code toward the owner for direct physical damage of the type insured to Real or Personal Property of the owner of the premises.

2) under articles of any civil or commercial code toward neighbours, co-tenants and other third parties for direct physical damage of the type insured to the Real or Personal Property of neighbours, co-tenants and other third parties.

3) as landlord under articles of any civil or commercial code for direct physical damage of the type insured to the Personal Property of tenants as a result of construction defects or lack of maintenance.

4) as tenant or occupant under the articles of any civil or commercial code for total or partial loss of use by the owner of the premises resulting from direct physical damage of the type insured.

T.   NON-ADMITTED INCREASED TAX LIABILITY

This Policy covers the Non-Admitted Increased Tax Liability as described herein of the Insured for a loss covered under this Policy.

1) If a loss recovery under this Policy cannot be paid in the country of its occurrence because of local law or otherwise, such loss is to be paid in the currency of this Policy in a country designated by the Insured where such payment is legally permissible. In the event of such a payment, the Company will pay in addition to the loss, the net amount required to offset local taxes on income with due consideration to any tax relief/credit that accrues because of such payment. The amount of such additional payment is to be calculated as follows:

Additional Payment = $[a\,(1+c)\,/\,(1\text{-}b)]$ -a

Where:
a =Loss otherwise payable under this Policy except for operation of this coverage, after due consideration for any applicable deductible(s).
b =The net effective rate of the sum of: any taxation (a positive number) plus any tax relief/credit (a negative number) that accrues in the country where loss payments are received.
c =The net effective rate of the sum of: any taxation (a positive number) plus any tax relief/credit (a negative number) that accrues in the country where the loss occurred.

2) The formula herein will not apply if the calculation of additional payment results in an amount less than zero. The rates referred to herein will be the respective corporate income tax rates in effect on the date of the loss.

3) The Insured will cooperate with the Company in making every reasonable effort to pay the loss or portion thereof locally in the country in which the loss occurred.

4) Any payment under this coverage will be made only after completion and acceptance by the Company of audited tax returns for the period in question for both the country where a payment hereunder is made and the country where the loss occurred. The actual payment under this coverage will be adjusted and reduced by all appropriate tax credits and/or tax relief entitled and/or received by the Insured and/or the local entity where the loss occurred provided that an income tax liability is incurred.

U. PROFESSIONAL FEES

This Policy covers the actual costs incurred by the Insured, of reasonable fees payable to the Insured's accountants, architects, auditors, engineers, or other professionals and the cost of using the Insured's employees, for producing and certifying any particulars or details contained in the Insured's books or documents, or such other proofs, information or evidence required by the Company resulting from insured loss payable under this Policy for which the Company has accepted liability.

1) This Additional Coverage will not include the fees and costs of attorneys, public adjusters, and loss appraisers, all including any of their subsidiary, related or associated entities either partially or wholly owned by them or retained by them for the purpose of assisting them nor the fees and costs of loss consultants who provide consultation on coverage or negotiate claims.

2) This Additional Coverage is subject to the deductible that applies to the loss.

V. PROTECTION AND PRESERVATION OF PROPERTY

This Policy covers:

1) reasonable and necessary costs incurred for actions to temporarily protect or preserve insured property; provided such actions are necessary due to actual, or to prevent immediately impending, insured physical loss or damage to such insured property.

2) reasonable and necessary:

   a) fire department fire fighting charges imposed as a result of responding to a fire in, on or exposing the insured property.

   b) costs incurred of restoring and recharging fire protection systems following an insured loss.

   c) costs incurred for the water used for fighting a fire in, on or exposing the insured property.

This Additional Coverage does not cover costs incurred for actions to temporarily protect or preserve insured property from actual, or to prevent immediately impending, physical loss or damage covered by TERRORISM coverage as provided in this section of the Policy.

This Additional Coverage is subject to the deductible provisions that would have applied had the physical loss or damage occurred.

W. SERVICE INTERRUPTION PROPERTY DAMAGE

1) This Policy covers insured physical loss or damage to insured property at an Insured Location when such physical loss or damage results from the interruption of the specified incoming services consisting of electricity, gas, fuel, steam, water,

refrigeration or from the lack of outgoing sewerage service by reason of any accidental occurrence to the facilities of the supplier of such service located within this Policy's TERRITORY, that immediately prevents in whole or in part the delivery of such usable service.

2) This Additional Coverage will apply when the Period of Service Interruption is in excess of the time shown as Waiting Period in the WAITING PERIOD clause of the DECLARATIONS section.

3) The exclusions in the EXCLUSIONS clause of this section do not apply to SERVICE INTERRUPTION PROPERTY DAMAGE coverage except for:

    a) A1, A2, A3, A6, B1, B2, D1, and

    b) B4 with respect to incoming or outgoing voice, data, or video.

    In addition, as respects SERVICE INTERRUPTION PROPERTY DAMAGE coverage the following exclusion applies:

    This Policy excludes loss or damage directly or indirectly caused by or resulting from the following regardless of any other cause or event, whether or not insured under this Policy, contributing concurrently or in any other sequence to the loss:

    a) Earth Movement for property located in California, in the New Madrid Seismic Zone as described in Appendix <Fill-In> and in the Pacific Northwest Seismic Zone as described in Appendix <Fill-In>.

    b) Terrorism.

4) Additional General Provisions:

    a) The Insured will immediately notify the suppliers of services of any interruption of such services.

    b) The Company will not be liable if the interruption of such services is caused directly or indirectly by the failure of the Insured to comply with the terms and conditions of any contracts the Insured has for the supply of such specified services.

5) References and Application. The following term(s) means:

    a) Period of Service Interruption:

        The period starting with the time when an interruption of specified services occurs; and ending when with due diligence and dispatch the service could be wholly restored.

X.   TAX TREATMENT OF PROFITS

Account No.
Policy No.

This Policy is extended to cover the increased tax liability from an insured loss at an Insured Location if the tax treatment of:

1) the profit portion of a loss payment under this Policy involving finished stock manufactured by the Insured; and/or

2) the profit portion of a TIME ELEMENT loss payment under this Policy;

is greater than the tax treatment of profits that would have been incurred had no loss occurred.

Y.   TEMPORARY REMOVAL OF PROPERTY

1) When insured property is removed from an Insured Location for the purpose of being repaired or serviced or in order to avoid threatened physical loss or damage of the type insured by this Policy, this Policy covers such property:

   a) while at the location to which such property has been moved; and

   b) for physical loss or damage as provided at the Insured Location from which such property was removed.

2) This Additional Coverage does not apply to property:

   a) insured, in whole or in part, elsewhere in this Policy.

   b) insured, in whole or in part, by any other insurance policy.

   c) removed for normal storage, processing or preparation for sale or delivery.

Z.   TRANSPORTATION

1) This Policy covers the following Personal Property, except as excluded by this Policy, while in transit within the TERRITORY of this Policy:

   a) owned by the Insured.

   b) shipped to customers under F.O.B., C & F or similar terms. The Insured's contingent interest in such shipments is admitted.

   c) of others in the actual or constructive custody of the Insured to the extent of the Insured's interest or legal liability.

   d) of others sold by the Insured, that the Insured has agreed prior to the loss to insure during course of delivery.

2) This Additional Coverage excludes:

   a) samples in the custody of salespeople or selling agents.

b) property insured under import or export ocean marine insurance.

    c) waterborne shipments, unless:

        (i) by inland water; or

        (ii) by roll-on/roll-off ferries operating between European ports; or

        (iii) by coastal shipments.

    d) airborne shipments unless by regularly scheduled passenger airlines or air freight carriers.

    e) property of others, including the Insured's legal liability for it, hauled on vehicles owned, leased or operated by the Insured when acting as a common or contract carrier.

    f) any transporting vehicle.

    g) property shipped between continents, except by land or air between Europe and Asia.

3) Coverage Attachment and Duration:

    a) This Additional Coverage covers from the time the property leaves the original point of shipment for transit. It then covers continuously in the due course of transit:

        (i) within the continent in which the shipment commences until the property arrives at the destination within such continent; or

        (ii) between Europe and Asia, for land or air shipments only, from when the shipment commences until the property arrives at the destination.

    b) However, coverage on export shipments not insured under ocean cargo policies ends when the property is loaded on board overseas vessels or aircraft. Coverage on import shipments not insured under ocean cargo polic ies begins after discharge from overseas vessels or aircraft.

4) This Additional Coverage:

    a) covers general average and salvage charges on shipments covered while waterborne.

    b) insures physical loss or damage caused by or resulting from:

        (i) unintentional acceptance of fraudulent bills of lading, shipping or messenger receipts.

        (ii) improper parties having gained possession of property through fraud or deceit.

Account No.
Policy No.

5) The exclusions in the EXCLUSIONS clause of this section do not apply to TRANSPORTATION coverage except for A1 through A4, B1 through B4, C1, C3, C5, C6, D1 through D4.

6) Additional General Provisions:

   a) This Additional Coverage will not inure directly or indirectly to the benefit of any carrier or bailee.

   b) The Insured has permission, without prejudicing this insurance, to accept:

      (i) ordinary bills of lading used by carriers;

      (ii) released bills of lading;

      (iii) undervalued bills of lading; and

      (iv) shipping or messenger receipts.

   c) The Insured may waive subrogation against railroads under side track agreements.

   Except as otherwise stated, the Insured will not enter into any special agreement with carriers releasing them from their common law or statutory liability.

AA. VALUABLE PAPERS AND RECORDS

This Policy covers insured physical loss or damage to Valuable Papers and Records while anywhere within this Policy's TERRITORY, including while in transit.

1) This Additional Coverage excludes loss or damage to:

   a) property described below, if such property cannot be replaced with other of like kind and quality, unless specifically declared to the Company.

   b) currency, money or securities.

   c) property held as samples or for sale or for delivery after sale.

2) VALUABLE PAPERS AND RECORDS Exclusions: The exclusions in the EXCLUSIONS clause of this section do not apply to VALUABLE PAPERS AND RECORDS coverage except for A1, A2, A6, A7, B1, B2, B3a, B4, B5 and D4. In addition, as respects VALUABLE PAPERS AND RECORDS the following exclusions apply:

   This Policy does not insure:

a) errors or omissions in processing, or copying; all unless physical damage not excluded by this Policy results, in which event, only that resulting damage is insured.

b) deterioration, inherent vice, vermin or wear and tear; all unless physical damage not excluded by this Policy results, in which event, only that resulting damage is insured.

3) References and Application. The following term(s) wherever used in this Policy means:

a) Valuable Papers and Records:

Written, printed or otherwise inscribed documents and records, including books, maps, films, drawings, abstracts, deeds, mortgages and manuscripts, all of which must be of value to the Insured.

BB. TERRORISM

This Policy covers physical loss or damage caused by or resulting from Terrorism only at locations as specifically described on the Schedule of Locations and Miscellaneous Unnamed Locations.

Any act which satisfies the definition of Terrorism in item B2f of the EXCLUSIONS clause in this section of the Policy shall not be considered to be vandalism, malicious mischief, riot, civil commotion, or any other risk of physical loss or damage covered elsewhere in this Policy.

Amounts recoverable under this Additional Coverage are excluded from coverage elsewhere in this Policy.

This Additional Coverage does not cover loss or damage which also comes within the terms of item B2a of the EXCLUSIONS clause in this section of the Policy.

This Additional Coverage does not in any event cover loss or damage directly or indirectly caused by or resulting from any of the following, regardless of any other cause or event, whether or not insured under this Policy contributing concurrently or in any other sequence to the loss:

1) that involves the use, release or escape of nuclear materials, or that directly or indirectly results in nuclear reaction or radiation or radioactive contamination; or

2) that is carried out by means of the dispersal or application of pathogenic or poisonous biological or chemical materials; or

3) in which pathogenic or poisonous biological or chemical materials are released, and it appears that one purpose of the terrorism was to release such materials; or

4) that involves action taken to prevent, defend against, respond to or retaliate against Terrorism or suspected Terrorism.

As respects this Additional Coverage, this Policy does not insure any TIME ELEMENT loss as provided in the TIME ELEMENT section of this Policy for more than the number of months shown in the LIMITS OF LIABILITY clause of the DECLARATIONS section.

4. **APPLICATION OF POLICY TO DATE OR TIME RECOGNITION**

    A.   With respect to situations caused by the so-called "Year 2000" problem or any other Date or Time Recognition problem by Electronic Data Processing Equipment or Media, this Policy applies as follows.

        1) This Policy does not pay for remediation, change, correction, repair or assessment of any Year 2000 or any other Date or Time Recognition problem in any Electronic Data Processing Equipment or Media, whether preventative or remedial, and whether before or after a loss, including temporary protection and preservation of property. This Policy does not pay for any TIME ELEMENT loss resulting from the foregoing remediation, change, correction, repair or assessment.

        2) Failure of Electronic Data Processing Equipment or Media to correctly recognize, interpret, calculate, compare, differentiate, sequence, access or process data involving one or more dates or times, including the Year 2000, is not physical loss or damage insured against by this Policy. This Policy does not pay for any such incident or for any TIME ELEMENT loss resulting from any such incident.

        Subject to all of its terms and conditions, this Policy does pay for physical loss or damage not excluded by this Policy that results from a failure of Electronic Data Processing Equipment or Media to correctly recognize, interpret, calculate, compare, differentiate, sequence, access or process data involving one or more dates or times, including the Year 2000. Such covered resulting physical loss or damage does not include any loss, cost or expense described in 1 or 2 above. If such covered resulting physical loss or damage occurs, and if this Policy provides TIME ELEMENT coverage, then, subject to all of its terms and conditions, this Policy also covers any insured Time Element loss directly resulting therefrom.

    B.   References and Application. The following term(s) wherever used in this Policy means:

        1) Date or Time Recognition:

        The recognition, interpretation, calculation, comparison, differentiation, sequencing, accessing or processing of data involving one or more dates or times, including the Year 2000.

        2) Electronic Data Processing Equipment or Media:

        Any computer, computer system or component, hardware, network, microprocessor, microchip, integrated circuit or similar devices or components in computer or non-computer equipment, operating systems, data, programs or other software stored on electronic, electro-mechanical, electro-magnetic data processing or production equipment, whether the property of the Insured or not.

5.   EXCLUSIONS

The following exclusions apply unless specifically stated elsewhere in this Policy:

A.   This Policy excludes:

1)   indirect or remote loss or damage.

2)   interruption of business, except to the extent provided by this Policy.

3)   loss of market or loss of use.

4)   loss or damage or deterioration arising from any delay.

5)   mysterious disappearance, loss or shortage disclosed on taking inventory, or any unexplained loss.

6)   loss from enforcement of any law or ordinance:

a)   regulating the construction, repair, replacement, use or removal, including debris removal, of any property; or

b)   requiring the demolition of any property, including the cost in removing its debris;

except as provided by the DECONTAMINATION COSTS and DEMOLITION AND INCREASED COST OF CONSTRUCTION coverages of this section of this Policy.

7)   loss resulting from the voluntary parting with title or possession of property if induced by any fraudulent act or by false pretense.

B.   This Policy excludes loss or damage directly or indirectly caused by or resulting from any of the following regardless of any other cause or event, whether or not insured under this Policy, contributing concurrently or in any other sequence to the loss:

1)   nuclear reaction or nuclear radiation or radioactive contamination. However:

a)   if physical damage by fire or sprinkler leakage results, then only that resulting damage is insured; but not including any loss or damage due to nuclear reaction, radiation or radioactive contamination.

b)   this Policy does insure physical damage directly caused by sudden and accidental radioactive contamination, including resultant radiation damage, from material used or stored or from processes conducted on the Insured Location, provided that on the date of loss, there is neither a nuclear reactor nor any new or used nuclear fuel on the Insured Location. This coverage does not apply to any act, loss or damage excluded in item B2f of this EXCLUSIONS clause.

2) a) hostile or warlike action in time of peace or war, including action in hindering, combating or defending against an actual, impending or expected attack by any:

   (i) government or sovereign power (de jure or de facto);

   (ii) military, naval or air force; or

   (iii) agent or authority of any party specified in i or ii above.

   b) discharge, explosion or use of any nuclear device, weapon or material employing or involving nuclear fission, fusion or radioactive force, whether in time of peace or war and regardless of who commits the act.

   c) insurrection, rebellion, revolution, civil war, usurped power, or action taken by governmental authority in hindering, combating or defending against such an event.

   d) seizure or destruction under quarantine or custom regulation, or confiscation by order of any governmental or public authority.

   e) risks of contraband, or illegal transportation or trade.

   f) Terrorism, including action taken to prevent, defend against, respond to or retaliate against Terrorism or suspected Terrorism, except to the extent provided in the TERRORISM coverage in this section of the Policy. However, if direct loss or damage by fire results from any of these acts (unless committed by or on behalf of the Insured), then this Policy covers only to the extent of the Actual Cash Value of the resulting direct loss or damage by fire to property insured. This coverage exception for such resulting fire loss or damage does not apply to any coverage provided in the TIME ELEMENT section of this Policy or to any other coverages provided by this Policy.

   Any act which satisfies the definition of Terrorism as provided herein shall not be considered to be vandalism, malicious mischief, riot, civil commotion, or any other risk of physical loss or damage covered elsewhere in this Policy.

   If any act which satisfies the definition of Terrorism as provided herein also comes within the terms of item B2a of this EXCLUSIONS clause then item B2a applies in place of this item B2f exclusion.

   If any act excluded herein involves nuclear reaction, nuclear radiation or radioactive contamination, this item B2f exclusion applies in place of item B1 of this EXCLUSIONS clause.

   References and Application. With the exception of PROVISIONS APPLICABLE TO SPECIFIC JURISDICTIONS clause in the GENERAL PROVISIONS section, the following term wherever used in this Policy means:

   Terrorism:

Any act, involving the use or threat of: force, violence, dangerous conduct, interference with the operations of any business, government or other organization or institution, or any similar act,

When the effect or apparent purpose is:

?   To influence or instill fear in any government (de jure or de facto) or the public, or any segment of either; or

?   To further or to express support for, or opposition to, any political, religious, social, ideological or similar type of objective or position.

3)   any dishonest act, including but not limited to theft, committed alone or in collusion with others, at any time:

a)   by an Insured or any proprietor, partner, director, trustee, officer, or employee of an Insured; or

b)   by any proprietor, partner, director, trustee, or officer of any business or entity (other than a common carrier) engaged by an Insured to do anything in connection with property insured under this Policy.

This Policy does insure acts of direct insured physical damage intentionally caused by an employee of an Insured or any individual specified in b above, and done without the knowledge of the Insured. This coverage does not apply to any act excluded in B2f of this EXCLUSIONS clause. In no event does this Policy cover loss by theft by any individual specified in a or b above.

4)   lack of the following services:

a)   incoming electricity, fuel, water, gas, steam, refrigerant;

b)   outgoing sewerage;

c)   incoming or outgoing voice, data or video,

all when caused by an occurrence off the Insured Location, except as provided in SERVICE INTERRUPTION in the PROPERTY DAMAGE or TIME ELEMENT section of this Policy. But, if the lack of such a service directly causes physical damage insured by this Policy on the Insured Location, then only that resulting damage is insured.

<5) Earth Movement for property located at Miscellaneous Unnamed Locations in California, in the New Madrid Seismic Zone as described in Appendix <Fill-In> and in the Pacific Northwest Seismic Zone as described in Appendix <Fill-In>.>

C.   This Policy excludes the following, but, if physical damage not excluded by this Policy results, then only that resulting damage is insured:

1) faulty workmanship, material, construction or design from any cause.

2) loss or damage to stock or material attributable to manufacturing or processing operations while such stock or material is being processed, manufactured, tested, or otherwise worked on.

3) deterioration, depletion, rust, corrosion or erosion, wear and tear, inherent vice or latent defect.

4) settling, cracking, shrinking, bulging, or expansion of:

    a) foundations (including any pedestal, pad, platform or other property supporting machinery).

    b) floors.

    c) pavements.

    d) walls.

    e) ceilings.

    f) roofs.

5) a) changes of temperature damage (except to machinery or equipment); or

    b) changes in relative humidity damage,

    all whether atmospheric or not.

6) insect, animal or vermin damage.

7) loss or damage to the interior portion of buildings under construction from rain, sleet or snow, whether or not driven by wind, when the installation of the roof, walls and windows of such buildings has not been completed.

D. This Policy excludes the following unless directly resulting from other physical damage not excluded by this Policy:

1) contamination including but not limited to the presence of pollution or hazardous material.

2) shrinkage.

3) changes in color, flavor, texture or finish.

4) fungus, mold or mildew.

TIME ELEMENT - SECTION C

1.   LOSS INSURED

A.   This Policy insures TIME ELEMENT loss, as provided in the TIME ELEMENT COVERAGES, directly resulting from physical loss or damage of the type insured by this Policy:

1)   to property described elsewhere in this Policy and not otherwise excluded by this Policy or otherwise limited in the TIME ELEMENT COVERAGES below;

2)   used by the Insured, or for which the Insured has contracted use;

3)   located at an Insured Location; or

4)   while in transit, as provided by this Policy, and

5)   during the Periods of Liability described in this section.

B.   This Policy insures TIME ELEMENT loss only to the extent it cannot be reduced through:

1)   the use of any property or service owned or controlled by the Insured;

2)   the use of any property or service obtainable from other sources;

3)   working extra time or overtime; or

4)   the use of inventory,

all whether at an Insured Location or at any other location. The Company reserves the right to take into consideration the combined operating results of all associated, affiliated or subsidiary companies of the Insured in determining the TIME ELEMENT loss.

C.   This Policy covers expenses reasonably and necessarily incurred by the Insured to reduce the loss otherwise payable under this section of this Policy. The amount of such recoverable expenses will not exceed the amount by which the loss has been reduced.

D.   Except as respects LEASEHOLD INTEREST, in determining the amount of loss payable, the Company will consider the experience of the business before and after and the probable experience during the PERIOD OF LIABILITY.

2.   TIME ELEMENT COVERAGES

A.   GROSS EARNINGS

As respects <Fill-In which locations this applies to>

1)   Measurement of Loss:

a) The recoverable GROSS EARNINGS loss is the Actual Loss Sustained by the Insured of the following during the PERIOD OF LIABILITY:

  (i) Gross Earnings;

  (ii) less all charges and expenses that do not necessarily continue during the interruption of production or suspension of business operations or services;

  (iii) plus all other earnings derived from the operation of the business.

b) In determining the indemnity payable as the Actual Loss Sustained, the Company will consider the continuation of only those normal charges and expenses that would have been earned had no interruption of production or suspension of business operations or services occurred.

c) There is recovery hereunder but only to the extent that the Insured is:

  (i) wholly or partially prevented from producing goods or continuing business operations or services;

  (ii) unable to make up lost production within a reasonable period of time, not limited to the period during which production is interrupted;

  (iii) unable to continue such operations or services during the PERIOD OF LIABILITY; and

  (iv) able to demonstrate a loss of sales for the operations, services or production prevented.

2) References and Application. The following term(s) means:

Gross Earnings, as used in item 1ai:

a) for manufacturing operations: the net sales value of production less the cost of all raw stock, materials and supplies used in such production; or

b) for mercantile or non-manufacturing operations: the total net sales less cost of merchandise sold, materials and supplies consumed in the operations or services rendered by the Insured.

Any amount recovered under property damage coverage at selling price for loss or damage to merchandise will be considered to have been sold to the Insured's regular customers and will be credited against net sales.

B. GROSS PROFIT

As respects <Fill In which locations this applies to>

1) Measurement of Loss:

a) The recoverable GROSS PROFIT loss is the Actual Loss Sustained by the Insured of the following due to the necessary interruption of business during the PERIOD OF LIABILITY: (i) Reduction in Sales, and (ii) Increase in Cost of Doing Business. The amount payable as indemnity hereunder will be:

(i) with respect to Reduction in Sales: The sum produced by applying the Rate of Gross Profit to the amount by which the sales during the PERIOD OF LIABILITY will fall short of the Standard Sales. In determining the Reduction in Sales, any amount recovered under property damage coverage at selling price for loss or damage to or destruction of finished goods or merchandise will be credited against lost sales.

(ii) with respect to Increase in Cost of Doing Business:

(a) the additional expenditure necessarily and reasonably incurred for the sole purpose of avoiding or diminishing the reduction in sales which, but for that expenditure, would have taken place during the PERIOD OF LIABILITY; but

(b) not exceeding the sum produced by applying the Rate of Gross Profit to the amount of the reduction thereby avoided,

all less any sum saved during the PERIOD OF LIABILITY with respect to such of the Insured Fixed Charges as may cease or be reduced because of such interruption of business.

b) In determining the indemnity payable as the Actual Loss Sustained:

(i) if any fixed charges of the business are not insured hereunder, then, in computing the amount recoverable hereunder as Increase in Cost of Doing Business, that proportion only of the additional expenditure will be recoverable hereunder which the sum of the Net Profit and the Insured Fixed Charges bears to the sum of the Net Profit and all the fixed charges.

(ii) if during the PERIOD OF LIABILITY goods will be sold or services will be rendered elsewhere than at the Insured Locations for the benefit of the business, either by the Insured or by others on the Insured's behalf, the money paid or payable in respect of such sales or services will be included in arriving at the amount of sales during the PERIOD OF LIABILITY.

c) The Insured will act with due diligence and dispatch in repairing or replacing physically damaged buildings and equipment to the same or equivalent physical and operating conditions that existed prior to the damage; and take whatever actions are necessary and reasonable to minimize the loss payable hereunder.

2) GROSS PROFIT Exclusions: As respects GROSS PROFIT, the TIME ELEMENT EXCLUSIONS B and C of this section do not apply and the following applies instead:

This Policy does not insure against any increase in loss due to fines or damages for breach of contract or for late or noncompletion of orders, or penalties of any nature.

3) Additional Condition:

   a) As respects all Insured Locations where GROSS PROFIT applies, Item B under the VALUATION clause of the LOSS ADJUSTMENT AND SETTLEMENT section is replaced by the following:

      B. On finished goods manufactured by the Insured, the replacement cost.

   b) Coverage under GROSS PROFIT for the reduction in sales due to contract cancellation will include only those sales that would have been earned under the contract during the PERIOD OF LIABILITY.

4) References and Application. The following term(s) mean:

   a) Gross Profit:

      The amount produced by adding to the Net Profit the amount of the Insured Fixed Charges, or if there be no Net Profit the amount of the Insured Fixed Charges less that proportion of any loss from business operations as the amount of the Insured Fixed Charges bears to all Fixed Charges.

   b) Net Profit:

      The net operating profit (exclusive of all capital receipts and accruals and all outlay properly chargeable to capital) resulting from the business of the Insured at the Insured Locations after due provision has been made for all fixed charges and other expenses including depreciation but before the deduction of any taxes on profits.

   c) Insured Fixed Charges:

      All fixed charges unless specifically excluded herein.

   d) Sales:

      The money paid or payable to the Insured for goods sold and delivered and for services rendered in the conduct of the business at an Insured Location.

   e) Rate of Gross Profit:

      The rate of Gross Profit earned on the sales during the twelve full calendar months immediately before the date of the physical loss or damage to the described property.

   f) Standard Sales:

The sales during that period in the twelve months immediately before the date of the physical loss or damage to the described property which corresponds with the PERIOD OF LIABILITY.

C.   EXTRA EXPENSE

1) Measurement of Loss:

The recoverable EXTRA EXPENSE loss will be the reasonable and necessary extra costs incurred by the Insured of the following during the PERIOD OF LIABILITY:

a) Extra expenses to temporarily continue as nearly normal as practicable the conduct of the Insured's business; and

b) Extra costs of temporarily using property or facilities of the Insured or others,

less any value remaining at the end of the PERIOD OF LIABILITY for property obtained in connection with the above.

2) EXTRA EXPENSE Exclusions: As respects EXTRA EXPENSE, the following are also excluded:

a) Any loss of income.

b) Costs that normally would have been incurred in conducting the business during the same period had no physical loss or damage occurred.

c) Cost of permanent repair or replacement of property that has been damaged or destroyed.

d) Any expense recoverable elsewhere in this Policy.

3) References and Application. The following term(s) means:

a) Normal

The condition that would have existed had no physical loss or damage occurred.

D.   LEASEHOLD INTEREST

1) Measurement of Loss:

The recoverable LEASEHOLD INTEREST incurred by the Insured of the following:

a) If the lease agreement requires continuation of rent; and if the property is wholly untenantable or unusable, the actual rent payable for the unexpired term of the lease; or if the property is partially untenantable or unusable, the proportion of the rent payable for the unexpired term of the lease.

b) If the lease is canceled by the lessor pursuant to the lease agreement or by the operation of law; the Lease Interest for the first three months following the loss; and the Net Lease Interest for the remaining unexpired term of the lease.

2) References and Application. The following term(s) means:

a) Lease Interest:

The excess rent paid for the same or similar replacement property over actual rent payable plus cash bonuses or advance rent paid (including maintenance or operating charges) for each month during the unexpired term of the Insured's lease.

b) Net Lease Interest:

That sum which placed at 6% interest rate compounded annually would equal the Lease Interest (less any amounts otherwise payable hereunder).

3) LEASEHOLD INTEREST Exclusions: As respects LEASEHOLD INTEREST, TIME ELEMENT EXCLUSIONS A, B, and C do not apply and the following applies instead:

This Policy does not insure any increase in loss resulting from the suspension, lapse or cancellation of any license, or from the Insured exercising an option to cancel the lease; or from any act or omission of the Insured that constitutes a default under the lease.

In addition, there is no coverage for the Insured's loss of LEASEHOLD INTEREST directly resulting from physical loss or damage to Personal Property.

E.   RENTAL INSURANCE

1) Measurement of Loss:

The recoverable RENTAL INSURANCE loss is the Actual Loss Sustained by the Insured of the following during the PERIOD OF LIABILITY:

a) The fair rental value of any portion of the property occupied by the Insured;

b) The income reasonably expected from rentals of unoccupied or unrented portions of such property; and

c) The rental income from the rented portions of such property according to bona fide leases, contracts or agreements in force at the time of loss,

all not to include noncontinuing charges and expenses.

2) RENTAL INSURANCE Exclusions: As respects RENTAL INSURANCE, TIME ELEMENT EXCLUSIONS A does not apply and the following applies instead:

A. This Policy does not insure any loss of rental income during any period in which the insured property would not have been tenantable for any reason other than an insured loss.

F. COMMISSIONS, PROFITS AND ROYALTIES

1) Measurement of Loss:

   a) The recoverable COMMISSIONS, PROFITS AND ROYALTIES loss is the Actual Loss Sustained by the Insured of the following during the PERIOD OF LIABILITY:

      (i) Commissions, Profits and Royalties;

      (ii) Less noncontinuing expenses and charges during the PERIOD OF LIABILITY.

   b) The Commissions, Profits And Royalties payable hereunder will be the Actual Loss Sustained of income to the Insured during the PERIOD OF LIABILITY under any royalty, licensing fee or commission agreement between the Insured and another party which is not realizable due to physical loss or damage insured by this Policy to property of the other party of the type insured by this Policy located within the Policy's TERRITORY.

   c) The Insured will influence, to the extent possible, said party(ies) with whom the agreements described above have been made to use any other machinery, supplies or locations in order to resume business so as to reduce the amount of loss hereunder, and the Insured will cooperate with that party in every way to effect this. This Policy does not cover any cost to effect the above unless authorized in advance by the Company.

   d) In determining the indemnity payable hereunder, the Company will consider the amount of income derived from such agreements before and the probable amount of income after the date of loss or damage.

   e) There is recovery hereunder but only if such loss or damage interrupts the delivery of goods in whole or in part to the Insured or for their account.

2) COMMISSIONS, PROFITS AND ROYALTIES Exclusions: As respects COMMISSIONS, PROFITS AND ROYALTIES, TIME ELEMENT EXCLUSIONS C does not apply. In addition the following additional exclusion applies:

   This Policy does not insure against:

   Any loss resulting from physical loss or damage caused by or resulting from Terrorism, regardless of any other cause or event, whether or not insured under this Policy, contributing concurrently or in any other sequence to the loss.

3) References and Application. The following term(s) means:

   a) Commissions:

The income that would have been received by the Insured from the sale of goods not owned by the Insured.

b) Profits:

The amount that would have been received by the Insured from the sale of goods belonging to the Insured, in excess of the cost to the Insured of such goods.

c) Royalties:

The income the Insured is not able to collect under royalty or licensing agreements.

3. TIME ELEMENT COVERAGE EXTENSIONS

A. CONTINGENT TIME ELEMENT

This Policy covers the Actual Loss Sustained and EXTRA EXPENSE incurred by the Insured during the PERIOD OF LIABILITY:

1) directly resulting from physical loss or damage of the type insured; and

2) to property of the type insured,

at any locations of direct suppliers or customers located within the TERRITORY of this Policy.

The term "supplier or customer" does not include any company supplying to or receiving from the Insured Location, as described elsewhere in this Policy, electricity, fuel, gas, water, steam, refrigeration, or sewage.

CONTINGENT TIME ELEMENT Exclusion: As respects CONTINGENT TIME ELEMENT, the following exclusions apply:

This Policy does not insure loss resulting from:

1) lack of incoming or outgoing transmission of voice, data or video.

2) Earth Movement for property located in California, in the New Madrid Seismic Zone as described in Appendix <Fill-In> and in the Pacific Northwest Seismic Zone as described in Appendix <Fill-In>.

3) physical loss or damage caused by or resulting from Terrorism, regardless of any other cause or event, whether or not insured under this Policy, contributing concurrently or in any other sequence of loss.

B. EXTENDED PERIOD OF LIABILITY

The GROSS EARNINGS coverage is extended to cover the reduction in sales resulting from:

1) the interruption of business as covered by GROSS EARNINGS;

2) for such additional length of time as would be required with the exercise of due diligence and dispatch to restore the Insured's business to the condition that would have existed had no loss occurred; and

3) commencing with the date on which the liability of the Company for loss resulting from interruption of business would terminate if this Extension had not been included herein.

However, this Extension does not apply to GROSS EARNINGS loss resulting from physical loss or damage caused by or resulting from Terrorism.

EXTENDED PERIOD OF LIABILITY Exclusions: As respects EXTENDED PERIOD OF LIABILITY, the TIME ELEMENT EXCLUSIONS B of this section does not apply and the following applies instead:

This Policy does not insure against any increase in loss due to fines or damages for breach of contract or for late or noncompletion of orders, or penalties of any nature.

Coverage under this Extension for the reduction in sales due to contract cancellation will include only those sales that would have been earned under the contract during the extended period of liability.

Coverage under this Extension does not apply for more than the number of consecutive days shown in the LIMITS OF LIABILITY clause of the DECLARATIONS section.

C.   **INGRESS/EGRESS**

This Policy covers the Actual Loss Sustained and EXTRA EXPENSE incurred by the Insured due to the necessary interruption of the Insured's business due to prevention of ingress to or egress from an Insured Location, whether or not the premises or property of the Insured is damaged, provided that such prevention is a direct result of physical damage of the type insured by this Policy, to the kind of property not excluded by this Policy.

INGRESS/EGRESS Exclusions: As respects INGRESS/EGRESS, the following exclusions are applicable:

This Policy does not insure loss resulting from:

1) lack of incoming or outgoing service consisting of electric, fuel, gas, water, steam, refrigerant, sewerage and voice, data or video.

2) picketing or other action by strikers except for physical damage not excluded by this Policy.

3) physical loss or damage caused by or resulting from Terrorism, regardless of any other cause or event, whether or not insured under this Policy, contributing concurrently or in any other sequence to the loss.

This Policy does not provide coverage under this Extension for more than the number of consecutive days shown in the LIMITS OF LIABILITY clause of the DECLARATIONS section.

D.   ON PREMISES SERVICES

This Policy covers the Actual Loss Sustained and EXTRA EXPENSE incurred by the Insured during the PERIOD OF LIABILITY directly resulting from physical loss or damage of the type insured to the following property located within 1,000 feet of the Insured Location:

1) Electrical equipment and equipment used for the transmission of voice, data or video.

2) Electrical, fuel, gas, water, steam, refrigeration, sewerage, voice, data or video transmission lines.

E.   PROTECTION AND PRESERVATION OF PROPERTY – TIME ELEMENT

This Policy covers the Actual Loss Sustained by the Insured for a period of time not to exceed 48 hours prior to and 48 hours after the Insured first taking reasonable action for the temporary protection and preservation of property insured by this Policy provided such action is necessary to prevent immediately impending physical loss or damage insured by this Policy at such insured property.

This Extension does not cover the Actual Loss Sustained by the Insured to temporarily protect or preserve insured property from actual, or to prevent immediately impending, physical loss or damage covered by TERRORISM coverage as provided in the PROPERTY DAMAGE section.

This Extension is subject to the deductible provisions that would have applied had the physical loss or damage occurred.

F.   RELATED REPORTED VALUES

If reported TIME ELEMENT values include:

1) locations used by the Insured (such as branch stores, sales outlets and other plants) but not listed on a schedule under this Policy; and

2) a TIME ELEMENT loss would result at such locations,

3) from insured physical loss or damage at an Insured Location,

then this Policy provides coverage for such resulting TIME ELEMENT loss in accordance with the coverage applicable at such Insured Location.

G.   RESEARCH AND DEVELOPMENT

The GROSS EARNINGS and GROSS PROFIT coverages are extended to insure the Actual Loss Sustained by the Insured of continuing fixed charges and ordinary payroll directly attributable to the interruption of research and development activities, that in themselves would not have produced income during the PERIOD OF LIABILITY.

The PERIOD OF LIABILITY for this TIME ELEMENT COVERAGE EXTENSION will be the period from the time of direct physical loss or damage of the type insured by this Policy to the time when the property could be repaired or replaced and made ready for operations, but not to be limited by the date of expiration of this Policy.

H.   SERVICE INTERRUPTION TIME ELEMENT

1) This Policy covers the Actual Loss Sustained and EXTRA EXPENSE incurred by the Insured during the Period of Service Interruption at Insured Locations when the loss is caused by the interruption of incoming services consisting of electricity, gas, fuel, steam, water, refrigeration or from the lack of outgoing sewerage service by reason of any accidental occurrence to the facilities of the supplier of such service located within this Policy's TERRITORY, that immediately prevents in whole or in part the delivery of such usable services.

2) This Extension will apply when the Period of Service Interruption is in excess of the time shown as Waiting Period in the WAITING PERIOD clause of the DECLARATIONS section.

3) The exclusions in the EXCLUSIONS clause of the PROPERTY DAMAGE section do not apply to SERVICE INTERRUPTION TIME ELEMENT coverage except for:

    a) A1, A2, A3, A6, B1, B2, D1, and

    b) B4 with respect to incoming or outgoing voice, data or video.

    In addition, as respects SERVICE INTERRUPTION TIME ELEMENT coverage the following exclusion applies:

    This Policy excludes loss or damage directly or indirectly caused by or resulting from the following regardless of any other cause or event, whether or not insured under this Policy, contributing concurrently or in any other sequence to the loss:

    a) Earth Movement for property located in California, in the New Madrid Seismic Zone as described in Appendix <Fill-In> and in the Pacific Northwest Seismic Zone as described in Appendix <Fill-In>.

    b) Terrorism.

4) Additional General Provisions:

a) The Insured will immediately notify the suppliers of services of any interruption of such services.

    b) The Company will not be liable if the interruption of such services is caused directly or indirectly by the failure of the Insured to comply with the terms and conditions of any contracts the Insured has for the supply of such specified services.

5) References and Application. The following term(s) means:

    a) Period of Service Interruption:

       (i) The period starting with the time when an interruption of specified services occurs; and ending when with due diligence and dispatch the service could be wholly restored and the Location receiving the service could or would have resumed normal operations following the restorations of service under the same or equivalent physical and operating conditions as provided by the PERIOD OF LIABILITY clause in this section.

       (ii) The Period of Service Interruption is limited to only those hours during which the Insured would or could have used service(s) if it had been available.

       (iii) The Period of Service Interruption does not extend to include the interruption of operations caused by any reason other than interruption of the specified service(s).

4.   PERIOD OF LIABILITY

A.   The PERIOD OF LIABILITY applying to all TIME ELEMENT COVERAGES, except GROSS PROFIT and LEASEHOLD INTEREST and as shown below or if otherwise provided under the TIME ELEMENT COVERAGE EXTENSIONS, and subject to any Time Limit provided in the LIMITS OF LIABILITY clause in the DECLARATIONS section, is as follows:

1) For building and equipment, the period:

    a) starting from the time of physical loss or damage of the type insured against; and

    b) ending when with due diligence and dispatch the building and equipment could be:

       (i) repaired or replaced; and

       (ii) made ready for operations,

    under the same or equivalent physical and operating conditions that existed prior to the damage.

    c) not to be limited by the expiration of this Policy.

2) For building and equipment under construction:

a) the equivalent of the above period of time will be applied to the level of business that would have been reasonably achieved after construction and startup would have been completed had no physical damage happened; and

b) due consideration will be given to the actual experience of the business compiled after completion of the construction and startup.

This item does not apply to COMMISSIONS, PROFITS AND ROYALTIES.

3) For stock-in-process and mercantile stock, including finished goods not manufactured by the Insured, the time required with the exercise of due diligence and dispatch:

a) to restore stock in process to the same state of manufacture in which it stood at the inception of the interruption of production or suspension of business operations or services; and

b) to replace physically damaged mercantile stock.

This item does not apply to RENTAL INSURANCE.

4) For raw materials and supplies, the period of time:

a) of actual interruption of production or suspension of operations or services resulting from the inability to get suitable raw materials and supplies to replace similar ones damaged; but

b) limited to that period for which the damaged raw materials and supplies would have supplied operating needs.

5) If water:

a) used for any manufacturing purpose, including but not limited to as a raw material or for power;

b) stored behind dams or in reservoirs; and

c) on any Insured Location,

is released as the result of physical damage of the type insured against under this Policy to such dam, reservoir or connected equipment, the Company's liability for the actual interruption of production or suspension of operations or services due to inadequate water supply will not extend beyond 30 consecutive days after the damaged dam, reservoir or connected equipment has been repaired or replaced.

This item does not apply to RENTAL INSURANCE.

6) For physically damaged exposed films, records, manuscripts and drawings, the time required to copy from backups or from originals of a previous generation. This time

Account No.
Policy No.

does not include research, engineering or any other time necessary to restore or recreate lost information.

This item does not apply to RENTAL INSURANCE.

7) For physically damaged or destroyed property covered under DATA, PROGRAMS OR SOFTWARE, the time to recreate or restore including the time for researching or engineering lost information.

This item does not apply to RENTAL INSURANCE.

8) If an order of civil authority prohibits access to the Insured Location and provided such order is the direct result of physical damage of the type insured against under this Policy at the Insured Location or within 1,000 feet of it, the period of time:

    a) starting at the time of such physical damage; but

    b) not to exceed 30 consecutive days.

B.   The PERIOD OF LIABILITY applying to GROSS PROFIT is as follows:

1) The period:

    a) starting from the time of physical loss or damage of the type insured against; and

    b) ending not later than the period of time shown in the LIMITS OF LIABILITY clause of the DECLARATIONS section,

during which period the results of the business shall be directly affected by such damage.

    c) not to be limited by the expiration of this Policy.

2) For property under construction, the period:

    a) starting on the date that production, business operation or service would have commenced if physical damage of the type insured against had not happened; and

    b) ending not later than the period of time shown in the LIMITS OF LIABILITY clause of the DECLARATIONS section,

during which period the results of the business shall be directly affected by such damage.

    c) not to be limited by the expiration of this Policy.

The Rate of Gross Profit and Standard Sales will be based on the experience of the business after construction is completed and the probable experience during the PERIOD OF LIABILITY.

3) If an order of civil authority prohibits access to the Insured Location and provided such order is the direct result of physical damage of the type insured against under this Policy at the Insured Location or within 1,000 feet of it, the period of time:

    a) starting at the time of such physical damage; but

    b) not to exceed 30 consecutive days.

C.   The PERIOD OF LIABILITY does not include any additional time due to the Insured's inability to resume operations for any reason, including but not limited to:

    1) making changes to equipment.

    2) making changes to the buildings or structures except as provided in the DEMOLITION AND INCREASED COST OF CONSTRUCTION clause in the PROPERTY DAMAGE section.

    3) restaffing or retraining employees.

    If two or more Periods of Liability apply such periods will not be cumulative.

5.   TIME ELEMENT EXCLUSIONS

In addition to the exclusions elsewhere in this Policy, the following exclusions apply to TIME ELEMENT loss:

This Policy does not insure against:

A.   Any loss during any idle period, including but not limited to when production, operation, service or delivery or receipt of goods would cease, or would not have taken place or would have been prevented due to:

    1) physical loss or damage not insured by this Policy on or off of the Insured Location.

    2) planned or rescheduled shutdown.

    3) strikes or other work stoppage.

    4) any other reason other than physical loss or damage insured by this Policy.

B.   Any increase in loss due to:

    1) suspension, cancellation or lapse of any lease, contract, license or orders.

    2) fines or damages for breach of contract or for late or noncompletion of orders.

    3) for penalties of any nature.

4) any other consequential or remote loss.

C. Any loss resulting from loss or damage to finished goods manufactured by the Insured, nor the time required for their reproduction.

D. Any loss resulting from the Actual Cash Value portion of direct physical loss or damage by fire caused by or resulting from Terrorism.

\<E. Any loss resulting from physical loss or damage as provided in the TERRORISM coverage in the PROPERTY DAMAGE section of this Policy for property located in Spain.\>
\<USE when Time Element from Consorcio is offered but not purchased\>

6.   TIME ELEMENT INTERDEPENDENCY

If there is a loss at an Insured Location that involves interdependency at one or more other Insured Locations, the loss, including any resulting interdependency loss, will be adjusted based on the TIME ELEMENT coverage that applies at the Insured Location where the physical loss or damage insured by this Policy occurred.

LOSS ADJUSTMENT AND SETTLEMENT - SECTION D

1.   LOSS ADJUSTMENT/PAYABLE

Loss, if any, will be adjusted with and payable to <Fill-In>, or as may be directed by <Fill-In>. Additional insured interests will also be included in loss payment as their interests may appear when named as additional named insured, lender, mortgagee and/or loss payee in the Certificates of Insurance on file with the Company or named below.

2.   CURRENCY FOR LOSS PAYMENT

Losses will be adjusted and paid in the currency of the United States of America, except in Canada where losses will be paid in Canadian currency, unless directed otherwise by the Insured.

In the event of a loss adjustment involving currency conversion, the exchange selling rate will be calculated as follows:

A.   As respects the calculation of deductibles and limits of liability, the rate of exchange published in The Wall Street Journal on the date of loss.

B.   As respects loss or damage to Real and Personal Property:

1) the cost to repair or replace Real and Personal Property will be converted at the time the cost of repair or replacement is incurred based on the rate of exchange published in The Wall Street Journal.

2) if such property is not replaced or repaired, the conversion will be based on the rate of exchange published in The Wall Street Journal as of the date of loss.

C.   As respects TIME ELEMENT loss the conversion will be based on the average of the rate of exchange published in The Wall Street Journal on the date of loss and the rate of exchange published in The Wall Street Journal on the last day of the Period of Liability.

If The Wall Street Journal was not published on the stipulated date, the rate of exchange will be as published on the next business day.

3.   VALUATION

Adjustment of the physical loss amount under this Policy will be computed as of the date of loss at the location of the loss, and for no more than the interest of the Insured, subject to the following:

A.   On stock in process, the value of raw materials and labor expended plus the proper proportion of overhead charges.

B.   On finished goods manufactured by the Insured, the regular cash selling price at the Location where the loss happens, less all discounts and charges to which the finished goods would have been subject had no loss happened.

C.   On raw materials, supplies and other merchandise not manufactured by the Insured:

1)   if repaired or replaced, the actual expenditure incurred in repairing or replacing the damaged or destroyed property; or

    2)   if not repaired or replaced, the Actual Cash Value.

D.   On exposed films, records, manuscripts and drawings, that are not Valuable Papers and Records, the value blank plus the cost of copying information from back-up or from originals of a previous generation. These costs will not include research, engineering or any costs of restoring or recreating lost information.

E.   On property covered under DEFERRED PAYMENTS, the lesser of the:

    1)   total amount of unpaid installments less finance charges.

    2)   Actual Cash Value of the property at the time of loss.

    3)   cost to repair or replace with material of like size, kind and quality.

F.   On FINE ARTS articles, the lesser of:

    1)   the reasonable and necessary cost to repair or restore such property to the physical condition that existed on the date of loss.

    2)   cost to replace the article.

    3)   the value, if any, stated on a schedule on file with the Company.

In the event a Fine Arts article is part of a pair or set, and a physically damaged article cannot be replaced, or repaired or restored to the condition that existed immediately prior to the loss, the Company will be liable for the lesser of the full value of such pair or set or the amount designated on the schedule. The Insured agrees to surrender the pair or set to the Company.

G.   On property covered under DATA, PROGRAMS OR SOFTWARE:

    1)   The cost to repair, replace or restore data, programs or software including the costs to recreate, research and engineer;

    2)   If not repaired, replaced or restored within two years from the date of loss, the blank value of the media.

H.   On VALUABLE PAPERS AND RECORDS, the lesser of the following:

    1)   The cost to repair or restore the item to the condition that existed immediately prior to the loss.

    2)   The cost to replace the item.

3) The amount designated for the item on the schedule on file with the Company.

I. On property in transit:

1) Property shipped to or for the account of the Insured will be valued at actual invoice to the Insured. Included in the value are accrued costs and charges legally due. Charges may include the Insured's commission as selling agent.

2) Property sold by the Insured and shipped to or for the purchaser's account will be valued at the Insured's selling invoice amount. Prepaid or advanced freight costs are included.

3) Property not under invoice will be valued:

   a) for property of the Insured, at the valuation provisions of this Policy applying at the location from which the property is being transported; or

   b) for other property, at the actual cash market value at the destination point on the date of occurrence,

   less any charges saved which would have become due and payable upon arrival at destination.

J. On property that is damaged by fire and such fire is the result of Terrorism, the Actual Cash Value of the fire damage loss. Any remaining fire damage loss shall be adjusted according to the terms and conditions of the VALUATION clause in this section of the Policy and shall be subject to the limit(s) of liability for TERRORISM and NON CERTIFIED ACT OF TERRORISM as shown in the LIMITS OF LIABILITY clause in the DECLARATIONS section.

K. On all other property, the loss amount will not exceed the lesser of the following:

1) The cost to repair.

2) The cost to rebuild or replace on the same site with new materials of like size, kind and quality.

3) The cost in rebuilding, repairing or replacing on the same or another site, but not to exceed the size and operating capacity that existed on the date of loss.

4) The selling price of real property or machinery and equipment, other than stock, offered for sale on the date of loss.

5) The cost to replace unrepairable electrical or mechanical equipment, including computer equipment, with equipment that is the most functionally equivalent to that damaged or destroyed, even if such equipment has technological advantages and/or represents an improvement in function and/or forms part of a program of system enhancement.

6) The increased cost of demolition, if any, resulting from loss covered by this Policy, if such property is scheduled for demolition.

7) The unamortized value of improvements and betterments, if such property is not repaired or replaced at the Insured's expense.

8) The Actual Cash Value if such property is:

   a) useless to the Insured; or

   b) not repaired, replaced or rebuilt on the same or another site within two years from the date of loss.

The Insured may elect not to repair or replace the insured real and/or personal property lost, damaged or destroyed. Loss settlement may be elected on the lesser of repair or replacement cost basis if the proceeds of such loss settlement are expended on other capital expenditures related to the Insured's operations within two years from the date of loss. As a condition of collecting under this item, such expenditure must be unplanned as of the date of loss and be made at an Insured Location under this Policy. This item does not extend to DEMOLITION AND INCREASED COST OF CONSTRUCTION.

References and Application. The following term(s) wherever used in this Policy means:

   a) Actual Cash Value:

      The amount it would cost to repair or replace insured property, on the date of loss, with material of like kind and quality, with proper deduction for obsolescence and physical depreciation.

4. LOSS CONDITIONS

A. REQUIREMENTS IN CASE OF LOSS

The Insured will:

1) give immediate written notice to the Company of any loss.

2) protect the property from further loss or damage.

3) promptly separate the damaged and undamaged property; put it in the best possible order; and furnish a complete inventory of the lost, destroyed, damaged and undamaged property showing in detail the quantities, costs, Actual Cash Value, replacement value and amount of loss claimed.

4) give a signed and sworn proof of loss to the Company within 90 days after the loss, unless that time is extended in writing by the Company. The proof of loss must state the knowledge and belief of the Insured as to:

   a) the time and origin of the loss.

   b) the Insured's interest and that of all others in the property.

c) the Actual Cash Value and replacement value of each item and the amount of loss to each item; all encumbrances; and all other contracts of insurance, whether valid or not, covering any of the property.

    d) any changes in the title, use, occupation, location, possession or exposures of the property since the effective date of this Policy.

    e) by whom and for what purpose any location insured by this Policy was occupied on the date of loss, and whether or not it then stood on leased ground.

5) include a copy of all the descriptions and schedules in all policies and, if required, provide verified plans and specifications of any buildings, fixtures, machinery or equipment destroyed or damaged.

6) further, the Insured, will as often as may be reasonably required:

    a) exhibit to any person designated by the Company all that remains of any property;

    b) submit to examination under oath by any person designated by the Company and sign the written records of examinations; and

    c) produce for examination at the request of the Company:

        (i) all books of accounts, business records, bills, invoices and other vouchers; or

        (ii) certified copies if originals are lost,

at such reasonable times and places that may be designated by the Company or its representative and permit extracts and machine copies to be made.

B.   COMPANY OPTION

The Company has the option to take all or any part of damaged property at the agreed or appraised value. The Company must give notice to the Insured of its intention to do so within 30 days after receipt of proof of loss.

C.   ABANDONMENT

There may be no abandonment of any property to the Company.

D.   SUBROGATION

The Insured is required to cooperate in any subrogation proceedings. The Company may require from the Insured an assignment or other transfer of all rights of recovery against any party for loss to the extent of the Company's payment.

The Company will not acquire any rights of recovery that the Insured has expressly waived prior to a loss, nor will such waiver affect the Insured's rights under this Policy.

Any recovery from subrogation proceedings, less costs incurred by the Company in such proceedings, will be payable to the Insured in the proportion that the amount of:

1) any applicable deductible; and/or

2) any provable uninsured loss,

bears to the entire provable loss amount.

E. APPRAISAL

If the Insured and the Company fail to agree on the amount of loss, each will, on the written demand of either, select a competent and disinterested appraiser after:

1) the Insured has fully complied with all provisions of this Policy, including REQUIREMENTS IN CASE OF LOSS; and

2) the Company has received a signed and sworn proof of loss from the Insured.

Each will notify the other of the appraiser selected within 20 days of such demand.

The appraisers will first select a competent and disinterested umpire. If the appraisers fail to agree upon an umpire within 30 days then, on the request of the Insured or the Company, the umpire will be selected by a judge of a court of record in the jurisdiction in which the appraisal is pending. The appraisers will then appraise the amount of loss, stating separately the Actual Cash Value and replacement cost value as of the date of loss and the amount of loss, for each item of physical loss or damage or if, for TIME ELEMENT loss, the amount of loss for each TIME ELEMENT coverage of this Policy.

If the appraisers fail to agree, they will submit their differences to the umpire. An award agreed to in writing by any two will determine the amount of loss.

The Insured and the Company will each:

1) pay its chosen appraiser; and

2) bear equally the other expenses of the appraisal and umpire.

A demand for APPRAISAL shall not relieve the Insured of its continuing obligation to comply with the terms and conditions of this Policy, including as provided under REQUIREMENTS IN CASE OF LOSS.

The Company will not be held to have waived any of its rights by any act relating to appraisal.

F. SUIT AGAINST THE COMPANY

Account No.
Policy No.

No suit, action or proceeding for the recovery of any claim will be sustained in any court of law or equity unless:

1)   the Insured has fully complied with all the provisions of this Policy; and

2)   legal action is started within twelve months after inception of the loss.

If under the insurance laws of the jurisdiction in which the property is located, such twelve months' limitation is invalid, then any such legal action needs to be started within the shortest limit of time permitted by such laws.

5.   SETTLEMENT OF CLAIMS

The amount of loss, except for ACCOUNTS RECEIVABLE coverage, for which the Company may be liable will be paid within 30 days after:

A.   proof of loss as described in this Policy is received by the Company; and

B.   when a resolution of the amount of loss is made either by:

   1)   written agreement between the Insured and the Company; or

   2)   the filing with the Company of an award as provided in the APPRAISAL clause of this section.

6.   COLLECTION FROM OTHERS

The Company will not be liable for any loss to the extent that the Insured has collected for such loss from others.

7.   PARTIAL PAYMENT OF LOSS SETTLEMENT

In the event of a loss occurring which has been ascertained to be insured loss or damage under this Policy and determined by the Company's representatives to be in excess of the applicable Policy deductible, the Company will advance mutually agreed upon partial payment(s) on the insured loss or damage, subject to the Policy's provisions. To obtain said partial payments, the Insured will submit a signed and sworn Proof of Loss as described in this Policy, with adequate supporting documentation.

8.   JURISDICTION

This Policy will be governed by <United States of America or Canadian> Law. Any disputes arising hereunder will be exclusively subject to <United States of America or Canadian> jurisdiction.

GENERAL PROVISIONS - SECTION E

1. ADDITIONAL INSURABLE INTERESTS/CERTIFICATES OF INSURANCE

Additional insured interests are automatically added to this Policy as their interest may appear when named as additional named insured, lender, mortgagee and/or loss payee in the Certificates of Insurance on a schedule on file with the Company. Such interests become effective on the date shown in the Certificate of Insurance and will not amend, extend or alter the terms, conditions, provisions and limits of this Policy.

2. CANCELLATION/NON-RENEWAL

This Policy may be:

A. cancelled at any time at the request of the Insured by surrendering this Policy to the Company or by giving written notice to the Company stating when such cancellation will take effect; or

B. cancelled by the Company by giving the Insured not less than:

   1) 60 days' written notice of cancellation; or

   2) 10 days' written notice of cancellation if the Insured fails to remit, when due, payment of premium for this Policy; or

C. non-renewed by the Company by giving the Insured not less than 60 days' written notice of non-renewal.

Return of any unearned premium will be calculated on the customary short rate basis if the Insured cancels and on a pro-rata basis if the Company cancels this Policy. Return of any unearned premium will be made by the Company as soon as practicable.

3. INSPECTIONS

The Company, at all reasonable times, will be permitted, but will not have the duty, to inspect insured property.

The Company's:

A. right to make inspections;

B. making of inspections; or

C. analysis, advice or inspection report,

will not constitute an undertaking, on behalf of or for the benefit of the Insured or others, to determine or warrant that the insured property is safe or healthful. This Company will have no liability to the Insured or any other person because of any inspection or failure to inspect.

When the Company is not providing jurisdictional inspections, the Owner/Operator has the responsibility to assure that jurisdictional inspections are performed as required, and to assure that required jurisdictional Operating Certificates are current for their pressure equipment.

4.   PROVISIONS APPLICABLE TO SPECIFIC JURISDICTIONS

A.   If the provisions of this Policy conflict with the laws of any jurisdictions in which this Policy applies, and if certain provisions are required by law to be stated in this Policy, this Policy will be read so as to eliminate such conflict or deemed to include such provisions for Insured Locations within such jurisdictions.

B.   The Company will provide to the Insured copies of endorsements mandated for use by the laws of provinces in Canada. The endorsements may modify this Policy with respect to any insured property located in the province in which the endorsement applies.

C.   For any insured property located in Greece, in the event of any loss payable, Stamp Duty will be deducted from any loss settlement.

D.   Coverage is provided for physical loss or damage and any resulting TIME ELEMENT loss as provided in the TIME ELEMENT section of this Policy to insured property in Northern Ireland occasioned by or happening through or in consequence directly or indirectly of:

   1)   riot, civil commotion and (except in respect of loss or damage and resulting TIME ELEMENT loss by fire or explosion) strikers, locked-out workers or persons taking part in labor disturbances or malicious persons; and

   2)   Terrorism as described in item B2f of EXCLUSIONS in the PROPERTY DAMAGE section,

   subject to liability of the Company only to be for the extent of the loss not recoverable by the Insured under the "Criminal Damage (Compensation) (Northern Ireland) Order 1977" or subsequent legislation; and to all other terms, conditions and limits of this Policy.

E.   For any insured property located in Norway, this Policy insures against loss or damage to insured property resulting from Natural Catastrophe perils as designated in the Act of Natural Perils of June 16th, 1989.

F.   With respect to any insured property in South Africa, the following conditions additionally apply:

   Notwithstanding anything contained herein to the contrary:

   1)   This Policy does not cover loss of or damage directly or indirectly to property related to or caused by:

      a)   civil commotion, labor disturbances, riot, strike, lockout or public disorder or any act or activity which is calculated or directed to bring about any of the above;

b) war, invasion, act of foreign enemy, hostilities or warlike operations (whether war be declared or not) or civil war;

c) (i) mutiny, military rising, military or usurped power, martial law or state of siege, or any other event or cause which determines the proclamation or maintenance of martial law or siege;

(ii) insurrection, rebellion or revolution.

d) any act (whether on behalf of any organization, body or person, or group of persons) calculated or directed to overthrow or influence any state or government, or any provincial, local or tribal authority with force, or by means of fear, terrorism or violence;

e) any act which is calculated or directed to bring about loss or damage in order to further any political aim, objective or cause or to bring about any social or economic change, or in protest against any state or government, or any provincial, local or tribal authority, or for the purpose of inspiring fear in the public, or any section thereof;

f) any attempt to perform any act referred to in clause d or e above;

g) The act of any lawfully established authority in controlling, preventing, suppressing or in any other way dealing with any occurrence referred to in clause a, b, c, d, e or f above.

If the Insurers allege that by reason of clauses a, b, c, d, e, f, or g of this exclusion, loss or damage is not covered by this Policy, the burden of proving the contrary will rest on the Insured.

2) This policy does not cover loss or damage caused directly or indirectly by or through or in consequence of any occurrence for which a fund has been established in terms of the War Damage Insurance and Compensation Act 1976 (No. 85 of 1976) or any similar Act operative in any of the territories to which this Policy applies.

G. In respect of any insured property in Spain and as applies to Physical Damage coverage only, this Policy does not insure against physical loss or damage caused by:

1) events separately insured by the Consorcio de Compensacion de Seguros, or events classified by the Public Authorities in Spain as an "extraordinary circumstance."

2) all losses where, despite being of an extraordinary and catastrophic nature, the Consorcio de Compensacion de Seguros does not acknowledge the rights of the Insured on account of the Insured's failure to comply with any of the conditions and stipulations contained in the Reglamento y Disposiciones Complementaras in force at the time of the occurrence as well as those occurring within the payment free period specified by the aforementioned authority. The Consorcio de Compensacion de Seguros will indemnify claims of an extraordinary nature, within the terms of the various laws and/or Royal Decrees and/or Regulations of Spain which govern Consorcio de Seguros.

<In respect of any insured property in Spain, this Policy does not insure against any TIME ELEMENT loss as provided in the TIME ELEMENT section of this Policy resulting from terrorism as defined by Consorcio de Compensacion de Seguros.>
<USE when TIME ELEMENT is purchased from Consorcio>

H.   Great Britain Terrorism Exclusion: Notwithstanding anything contained in this Policy to the contrary, for property located in Great Britain there is no coverage under this Policy for loss or damage and any resulting TIME ELEMENT loss, as provided in the TIME ELEMENT section of this Policy, caused by events separately insured by Pool Reinsurance Company Limited under the European policy issued by FM Insurance Company Ltd.

References and Application: The following term wherever used in this Policy means:

Great Britain:

England and Wales and Scotland but not the territorial seas adjacent thereto as defined by the Territorial Sea Act 1987 nor the Isle of Man nor the Channel Islands.

I.   As respects property in France or in French territories, the Insured is required to carry coverage for terrorism under the European/local policy issued by FM Insurance Company Ltd. Coverage provided under this Policy shall not extend the coverage for terrorism provided under such European/local policy.

J.   Terrorism Risk Insurance Act of 2002: As respects the United States, its territories and possessions and the Commonwealth of Puerto Rico any recovery under this Policy for any insured loss or damage from acts of terrorism, as covered under this Policy, may be partially reimbursed by the United States Government in accordance with the Terrorism Risk Insurance Act of 2002. Reimbursement by the United States Government will be under a formula established by Federal Law.

K.   Australia Terrorism Exclusion: Notwithstanding anything contained in this Policy to the contrary, there is no coverage for loss or damage and any resulting TIME ELEMENT loss, as provided in the TIME ELEMENT section of this Policy, caused by or resulting from the following regardless of any other cause or event contributing concurrently or in any other sequence to the loss:

     1)   Terrorism as defined in item B2f of the EXCLUSIONS clause in the PROPERTY DAMAGE section of this Policy for property located in Australia.

L.   The Company will provide to the Insured copies of endorsements mandated for use by the laws of states in the United States of America. The endorsements may modify this Policy with respect to any insured property located in the state in which the endorsement applies.

5.   LIBERALIZATION

If during the period that insurance is in force under this Policy, any filed rules or regulations affecting the same are revised by statute so as to broaden the insurance without additional premium charge, such extended or broadened insurance will inure to the benefit of the Insured within such jurisdiction, effective the date of the change specified in such statute.

6.   **MISREPRESENTATION AND FRAUD**

This entire Policy will be void if, whether before or after a loss, an Insured has:

A.   willfully concealed or misrepresented any material fact or circumstance concerning this insurance, the subject thereof, any insurance claim, or the interest of an Insured.

B.   made any attempt to defraud the Company.

C.   made any false swearing.

7.   **LENDERS LOSS PAYEE AND MORTGAGEE INTERESTS AND OBLIGATIONS**

A.   The Company will pay for loss to specified property insured under this Policy to each specified Lender Loss Payee (hereinafter referred to as Lender) as its interest may appear, and to each specified Mortgagee as its interest may appear, under all present or future mortgages upon such property, in order of precedence of the mortgages.

B.   The interest of the Lender or Mortgagee (as the case may be) in property insured under this Policy will not be invalidated by:

1)   any act or neglect of the debtor, mortgagor, or owner (as the case may be) of the property.

2)   foreclosure, notice of sale, or similar proceedings with respect to the property.

3)   change in the title or ownership of the property.

4)   change to a more hazardous occupancy.

The Lender or Mortgagee will notify the Company of any known change in ownership, occupancy, or hazard and, within 10 days of written request by the Company, may pay the increased premium associated with such known change. If the Lender or Mortgagee fails to pay the increased premium, all coverage under this Policy will cease.

C.   If this Policy is cancelled at the request of the Insured or its agent, the coverage for the interest of the Lender or Mortgagee will terminate 10 days after the Company sends to the Lender or Mortgagee written notice of cancellation, unless:

1)   sooner terminated by authorization, consent, approval, acceptance, or ratification of the Insured's action by the Lender or Mortgagee, or its agent.

2)   this Policy is replaced by the Insured, with a policy providing coverage for the interest of the Lender or Mortgagee, in which event coverage under this Policy with respect to such interest will terminate as of the effective date of the replacement policy, notwithstanding any other provision of this Policy.

D.   The Company may cancel this Policy and/or the interest of the Lender or Mortgagee under this Policy, by giving the Lender or Mortgagee written notice 60 days prior to the effective date of cancellation, if cancellation is for any reason other than non-payment. If the debtor, mortgagor, or owner has failed to pay any premium due under this Policy, the Company may cancel this Policy for such non-payment, but will give the Lender or Mortgagee written notice 10 days prior to the effective date of cancellation. If the Lender or Mortgagee fails to pay the premium due by the specified cancellation date, all coverage under this Policy will cease.

E.   The Company has the right to invoke this Policy's SUSPENSION clause. The suspension of insurance will apply to the interest of the Lender or Mortgagee in any machine, vessel, or part of any machine or vessel, subject to the suspension. The Company will provide the Lender or Mortgagee at the last known address a copy of the suspension notice.

F.   If the Company pays the Lender or Mortgagee for any loss, and denies payment to the debtor, mortgagor or owner, the Company will, to the extent of the payment made to the Lender or Mortgagee be subrogated to the rights of the Lender or Mortgagee under all securities held as collateral to the debt or mortgage. No subrogation will impair the right of the Lender or Mortgagee to sue or recover the full amount of its claim. At its option, the Company may pay to the Lender or Mortgagee the whole principal due on the debt or mortgage plus any accrued interest. In this event, all rights and securities will be assigned and transferred from the Lender or Mortgagee to the Company, and the remaining debt or mortgage will be paid to the Company.

G.   If the Insured fails to render proof of loss, the Lender or Mortgagee, upon notice of the Insured's failure to do so, will render proof of loss within 60 days of notice and will be subject to the provisions of this Policy relating to APPRAISAL, SETTLEMENT OF CLAIMS, and SUIT AGAINST THE COMPANY.

H.   Other provisions relating to the interests and obligations of the Lender or Mortgagee may be added to this Policy by agreement in writing.

8.   OTHER INSURANCE

A.   If there is any other insurance that would apply in the absence of this Policy, this Policy will apply only after such insurance whether collectible or not.

B.   In no event will this Policy apply as contributing insurance.

C.   The Insured is permitted to have other insurance over any limits or sublimits of liability specified elsewhere in this Policy without prejudice to this Policy. The existence of any such insurance will not reduce any limit or sublimit of liability in this Policy. Any other insurance that would have provided primary coverage in the absence of this Policy will not be considered excess.

D.   The Insured is permitted to have other insurance for all, or any part, of any deductible in this Policy. The existence of such other insurance will not prejudice recovery under this Policy. If the limits of liability of such other insurance are greater than this Policy's applicable deductible, this Policy's insurance will apply only after such other insurance has been exhausted.

E.   In the event this Policy is deemed to contribute with other insurance, the limit of liability applicable at each Location, for purposes of such contribution with other insurers, will be the latest amount described in this Policy or the latest Location value on file with the Company.

F.   When this Policy includes property in more than one jurisdiction, separate policies underlying this Policy may be issued by the Company in compliance with jurisdictional requirements. Such underlying policies will not be considered as additional insurance, but as duplicate insurance only.

9.   POLICY MODIFICATION

This Policy contains all of the agreements between the Insured and the Company concerning this insurance. The Insured and the Company may request changes to this Policy. This Policy can be changed only by endorsements issued by the Company and made a part of this Policy.

Notice to any agent or knowledge possessed by any agent or by any other person will not:

A.   create a waiver, or change any part of this Policy; or

B.   prevent the Company from asserting any rights under the provisions of this Policy.

10.   REDUCTION BY LOSS

Claims paid under this Policy will not reduce its' limit of liability, except claims paid will reduce any Policy Year Aggregate Limit of Liability.

11.   SUSPENSION

On discovery of a dangerous condition, the Company may immediately suspend this insurance on any machine, vessel or part thereof by giving written notice to the Insured. The suspended insurance may be reinstated by the Company. Any unearned premium resulting from such suspension will be returned by the Company.

12.   TITLES

The titles in this Policy are only for reference. The titles do not in any way affect the provisions of this Policy.

Index